A Lullaby to Awaken the Heart

The Aspiration Prayer of Samantabhadra and Its Tibetan Commentaries

Translated and Introduced by
Karl Brunnhölzl

Wisdom

Wisdom Publications
199 Elm Street
Somerville, MA 02144 USA
wisdompubs.org

Library of Congress Cataloging-in-Publication Data
Names: Brunnhölzl, Karl, translator.
Title: A lullaby to awaken the heart: the aspiration prayer of Samantabhadra and its Tibetan commentaries / translated and introduced by Karl Brunnhölzl.
Other titles: Kun bzang smon lam. English.
Description: Somerville, MA, USA: Wisdom Publications, 2018. | Includes a translation of the Tibetan prayer "Kun bzang smon lam" and related commentaries. | Includes bibliographical references.
Identifiers: LCCN 2018004201 (print) | LCCN 2018031141 (ebook) | ISBN 9781614295174 (e-book) | ISBN 9781614294979 (hard cover: alk. paper)
Subjects: LCSH: Rdzogs-chen. | Samantabhadra (Buddhist deity) | Prayer—Buddism.
Classification: LCC BQ7662.4 (ebook) | LCC BQ7662.4 .L85 2018 (print) | DDC 294.3/443—dc23
LC record available at https://lccn.loc.gov/2018004201

ISBN 978-1-61429-497-9 ebook ISBN 978-1-61429-517-4

22 21 20 19 18 5 4 3 2 1

Cover painting by Sunlal Ratna Tamang, www.tibetanart.com. Cover design by Gopa Campbell. Interior design by Tim Holtz. Set in DGP 12/15.

Wisdom Publications' books are printed on acid-free paper and meet the guidelines for permanence and durability of the Production Guidelines for Book Longevity of the Council on Library Resources.

Printed in the United States of America.

Contents

Publisher's Acknowledgment

The publisher gratefully acknowledges the generous help of the Hershey Family Foundation in sponsoring the production of this book.

Acknowledgments

My sincere thanks go to Khenpo Tsültrim Gyamtso Rinpoche and Dzogchen Ponlop Rinpoche for their wealth of Dzogchen teachings transmitted through body, speech, mind, qualities, and activities. I am also grateful to the many Western scholars and practitioners who have contributed to our knowledge of the Great Perfection and whose work has supported the writing of this book.

If there is anything in this volume that sounds good, makes sense, and serves as an antidote to ignorance, confusion, and suffering, may it be relished as originating from realized masters and vastly learned scholars. Everything else, including all mistakes, can safely be said to be mine.

Sarva maṅgalam.

Abbreviations

The Aspiration Prayer	*The Aspiration Prayer of Samantabhadra*
BDRC	Buddhist Digital Resource Center (www.tbrc.org)
CV	Common version of *The Aspiration Prayer* extracted from the *Tantra of Samantabhadra's Unobstructed Awakened Mind*
Ketaka	The Fifteenth Karmapa's commentary on *The Aspiration Prayer*: *A Commentary on the Meaning of* The Aspiration Prayer of Samantabhadra *Found in the* Great Tantra of the Unobstructed Awakened Mind *from the Northern Treasures, an Explanation Called* Ketaka *Lucidly Arranged in the Form of a Few Glosses*
Lamp	Tsültrim Sangpo's commentary on *The Aspiration Prayer*: *An Exposition of* The Aspiration Prayer of Samantabhadra *Found in the* Great Tantra of the Unobstructed Awakened Mind *from the Northern Treasures, Called* The Lamp That Clearly Illuminates the Short Path of Samantabhadra
Lancet	Jigmé Lingpa's commentary on *The Aspiration Prayer*: *Clearing the Guide to* The Aspiration Prayer of Samantabhadra *with the Lancet of a Ṭīkā*
RTV	The version of *The Aspiration Prayer* in the *Treasury of Precious Treasures* (Rgod kyi ldem 'phru can dngos grub rgyal mtshan 199?)
TOK	Jamgön Kongtrul Lodrö Tayé's *Treasury of Knowledge* (Kong sprul blo gros mtha' yas 1982)

TV1 The version of *The Aspiration Prayer* contained in the *Tantra of Samantabhadra's Unobstructed Awakened Mind* (Rgod kyi ldem 'phru can dngos grub rgyal mtshan 1973b)

TV2 The version of *The Aspiration Prayer* contained in the *Tantra of Samantabhadra's Unobstructed Awakened Mind* (Rgod kyi ldem 'phru can dngos grub rgyal mtshan 2015)

Preface

The Aspiration Prayer of Samantabhadra, one of the most famous and often-recited Dzogchen texts, is a uniquely profound prayer with two distinct levels of meaning, and it also serves as an on-the-spot practice instruction. On its surface, this is a prayer offered by the primordial buddha, Samantabhadra, who aspires that all sentient beings may recognize the true nature of their minds as self-arising awareness, thereby becoming buddhas. Actually, however, this aspiration is made by this very same nature of the mind—primordial basic awareness, or *rigpa*,[1] which is referred to as "Samantabhadra"—in order to recognize itself, which is nothing other than the ultimate awakening of buddhahood. Thus, it is a wake-up call by our own buddha nature to be revealed as it is, by way of seeing through its adventitious, fleeting obscurations. The prayer not only outlines the profound view of Dzogchen in a nutshell but also provides clear instructions on how to discover the five wisdoms of a buddha in the very midst of the five main mental afflictions.

To give a brief overview of the structure and contents of this book, the first part begins by addressing the question of who or what Samantabhadra in the tradition of the Great Perfection is, what he teaches, and what his instantaneous freedom consists of. This is followed by an elucidation of five aspects or meanings of Samantabhadra in different contexts by Longchen Rabjampa Trimé Öser[2] (1308–64), as well as of the iconography and symbolism of both Samantabhadra and Samantabhadrī.

The second part of the book conducts a detailed examination of the background, context, and nature of *The Aspiration Prayer of Samantabhadra*, beginning with its source, the scriptural collection called the Northern Treasures. After a general presentation of the nature and functions of aspiration prayers in Buddhism, we explore the unique character of *The Aspiration Prayer of Samantabhadra*, its nonreferential and nondual language, its structure, and the textual versions available to us. This part concludes with an explanation of *The Aspiration Prayer* as a meditative practice and an overview of the three extant Tibetan commentaries.

The third part consists of three translations of *The Aspiration Prayer* based on different versions of the text, as well as translations of its three Tibetan commentaries by Jigmé Lingpa, the Fifteenth Karmapa, and Tsültrim Sangpo.[3]

Among the appendices, the first one presents the outlines of the three Tibetan commentaries. The following appendices unpack the crucial elements of the view of the Great Perfection in terms of ground, path, and fruition, and serve as guides to the context and meanings of the technical terms and concepts in *The Aspiration Prayer* and its commentaries. These appendices include excerpts from Longchenpa's *Precious Treasury of Words and Their Meanings* (appendices 2–6) and *Precious Treasury of the Supreme Yāna* (appendix 7), with support drawn from two commentaries on Jigmé Lingpa's *Treasury of Precious Qualities* by Yönten Gyatso (nineteenth century) and Kangyur Rinpoche (1897–1975) (appendices 2, 3, 6, and 7). Appendices 2 to 7 respectively explore the ground of the Great Perfection, its manifestations, and Samantabhadra's freedom; the arising of delusion and the unchanging inherent purity of all saṃsāric manifestations; how buddha nature and its pure qualities pervade all sentient beings; the distinctions between the all-ground and the dharmakāya as well as between mind and wisdom; the five kāyas and the five wisdoms; and the various notions of freedom in the Dzogchen teachings. Appendix 8 is a translation of Jigmé Lingpa's *Aspiration Prayer for Ground, Path, and Fruition*, and appendices 9 and 10 render two short texts by Patrul Rinpoche[4] (1808–87) on the essential point of practice—all thoughts and afflictions being free in themselves—and on recognizing the five afflictions as the five wisdoms, respectively.

Finally, a concluding chart details the relationships between the ground, its manifestations, the resulting delusion or freedom, the five main afflictions, and the five corresponding wisdoms.

Part I

Samantabhadra and His Legacy

1

Who or What Is Samantabhadra?

As its title states, *The Aspiration Prayer of Samantabhadra* is a verbal expression of the wish to benefit ourselves and others uttered by Buddha Samantabhadra.[5] So let's begin by looking at who this buddha is and what he teaches.

In the Tibetan Buddhist tradition, particularly in the Nyingma School, Samantabhadra is considered to be the first or original buddha (Skt. *ādibuddha*), comparable in status to Vajradhara in the schools of the new translations. Samantabhadra appears in a number of Dzogchen[6] tantras and many rediscovered treasure texts (Tib. *gter ma*) as the principle of primordial buddhahood or the dharmakāya, usually portrayed as speaking and teaching in the first person.[7] In that way, this original buddha is the originless origin of the timeless teachings of the Great Perfection. The transmission of these teachings is usually explained as comprising three lineages: (1) the lineage of the awakened mind of the victors, (2) the symbolic lineage of awareness holders, and (3) the ear-whispered lineage of persons.

(1) The lineage of the awakened mind of the victors begins with Samantabhadra, who is nothing other than the instantaneous self-recognition and complete awakening of primordial awareness within the primordial expanse of the *dharmadhātu*, free from any notion of bondage and liberation. The awakened mind of Samantabhadra has never strayed from the inseparable kāyas and wisdoms of perfect buddhahood. Within this dimension of the dharmakāya of inner luminosity, the realm called the Vajra Heart of Luminosity,[8] the three aspects of omniscient wisdom—essence, nature, and

compassionate responsiveness[9]—are the naturally present three kāyas of the original, nondual expanse. It is within this excellent realm—the inconceivable dharmadhātu, or the timeless, formless, and immutably pure dharmakāya realm of Akaniṣṭha[10]—that the excellent teacher Samantabhadra (the lord of the sixth buddha family) provides a mind transmission without words to his excellent disciples—the vast assembly of the five kinds of primordial wisdom, whose nature is not at all different from Samantabhadra's own wisdom mind. This excellent, ocean-like assembly of wisdom consists of the natural manifestations of the five families of sambhogakāya buddhas, led by Vajrasattva, along with their infinite retinues. The excellent time when this happens is the duration of dharmatā,[11] which is without change or transition.[12] The excellent teaching consists of the natural Great Perfection—the alpha-pure awakened mind of utter lucidity within the sphere of innate presence.[13] Though all of this is entirely beyond any ordinary notions of teacher, teaching, disciples, place, and time, conventionally, it is referred to as "the self-arising unborn speech of ultimate reality of the dharmakāya" or "the *yāna* of the Vajra Heart of Luminosity."[14]

(2) The symbolic lineage of awareness holders refers primarily to the sambhogakāya Vajrasattva's teaching the god named "Endowed with the Superior Intention"[15] in the divine realm of Trāyastriṃśa.[16] This god is said to have been an emanation of Vajrasattva, as well as Garab Dorjé's[17] immediately preceding incarnation. He received a transmission from Vajrasattva by way of symbols with very few words, called "the empowerment of the anointing vase with the means of the victors." There was also a transmission by Vajrapāṇi to a number of other human and nonhuman awareness holders.

(3) Finally, the ear-whispered lineage of persons consists of masters in the human sphere who teach other humans primarily through words, such as Garab Dorjé's instructing Mañjuśrīmitra, who in turn taught Śrī Siṃha and Buddhajñānapāda. Śrī Siṃha then transmitted the teachings of the Great Perfection on various occasions to Jñānasūtra, Padmasambhava, Vimalamitra, and the Tibetan translator Vairocana (all eighth century). Through the

latter three, the three main cycles of Dzogchen (later classified as the Mind Series, Expanse Series, and Pith Instructions Series) eventually reached Tibet.[18]

It is said that the Mind Series and Expanse Series were primarily transmitted by Vairocana, though Vimalamitra also translated and taught a significant number of Mind Series texts. The lineage of the Pith Instructions Series is twofold: the oral (Tib. *bka' ma*) or "long" lineage that is transmitted from one lineage holder to another (beginning with Garab Dorjé), which entered Tibet through Vimalamitra; and the treasure lineage or "short" lineage that originated with Padmasambhava. He concealed many teachings and other artifacts that were later discovered by treasure revealers throughout the following centuries up to this day.[19] With great emphasis on the Pith Instructions Series, all these transmissions were later revived and systematized primarily by Longchenpa and Jigmé Lingpa[20] (1729/30–1798), as well as others.[21]

2

The Shortest Biography of Any Buddha Ever

Samantabhadra's Instantaneous Freedom

As the state of original primordial awakening, Samantabhadra is bound neither by any dimensions or limits of time, space, location, or physical conditions; nor by any gradual path of progressing from delusion to eventual freedom or liberation; nor by any evolving from an ordinary deluded sentient being to a perfectly awakened buddha. Rather, Samantabhadra was awakened before there were even the notions of buddhas, sentient beings, saṃsāra, nirvāṇa, delusion, and freedom. Longchenpa's autocommentary on his *Precious Treasury of the Dharmadhātu*, called *A Treasure Trove of Scriptures*, says this:

> The primal expanse—the sugata heart—is expressed as the buddhahood that is innately present by nature. There is no saṃsāra or nirvāṇa other than, respectively, not realizing or realizing this very expanse. Prior to it, not even the conventional expressions "buddha" or "sentient being" could be established. For if awareness did not exist, there would not be anyone or anything to ascertain saṃsāra or nirvāṇa, nor would there be any basis for evaluating delusion or freedom. As the explanatory tantra *Self-Arising Awareness* [says]:
>
> > Previously, when I did not exist,
> > there were neither buddhas nor sentient beings,
> > so how could there be any path or accomplishment?

There is nothing that did not arise from me.
I am the great emptiness.
From me, the five elements developed.
I am the great sovereign of the elements.

I am the ancestor of all buddhas.
Previously, when I did not exist,
there was not even the name "buddha."

I am the pāramitā of means.
Since I have no characteristic attributes,
my mind is without movement.
I am the charnel ground of all buddhas—
they are buried in me, the changeless burial ground.
I am the abode of all sentient beings:
latent tendencies appear as if they were bodies.
I am the inseparable prajñā:
outer, inner, and secret are perfect in me.
I am the kāya of the vajra heart:
buddhas spring forth from me.
I am the actuality of unborn awareness:
I am free from phenomena that are entities.

Since I have no characteristics,
I raise sentient beings from their graves.
Since compassionate responsiveness arises from me,
I am beyond empty words.
Since the lucidity dimension arises from me,
I will illuminate the darkness.[22]

Thus, although Samantabhadra often appears to be described as a person or a realized being, usually speaking in the first person in Dzogchen tantras, it is important to understand that the name Samantabhadra refers to nothing other than the nature of our own mind's instantaneous and irreversible recognition of itself, its own face, or its own essence,[23] before there is even a stirring of nonrecognition or delusion about it. In the cycle of texts that form the

Heart Essence of the Great Expanse (*Longchen Nyingtig*),[24] the *Subsequent Tantra of Pith Instructions on the Great Perfection* declares this:

> I, Samantabhadra, the primal protector,
> the ancestor of all buddhas,
> have become a buddha through overcoming within the expanse
> all the unawareness[25] of appropriating
> the lucid luminosity that is nothing whatsoever.
> Thus, I have not experienced any wandering in saṃsāra
> and hence am known as the primal protector.
>
> Then, when out of the expanse the dynamic energy of awareness
> is arrayed as the clouds of innately present compassionate
> responsiveness,[26]
> through that compassion, saṃsāric sentient beings
> are established in my own overwhelming state.
>
> In order to do this, I explain innately present, self-arising
> dynamic energy as the continuum of ground, path, and fruition:[27]
> the ground is the unconditionedness of saṃsāra and nirvāṇa,
> the path is the arising of clear luminosity in its differentiations,
> and the fruition is the sphere of innate presence without
> searching—
> this is buddhahood without bondage or freedom.
>
> . . . .
>
> Neither contrived by good buddhas
> nor altered by bad sentient beings,
> this unfabricated awareness of the present
> that is naked, stainless, and self-luminous
> is me, the primal protector.
>
> Sentient beings who are unaware of this
> may think[28] of me as form—
> even if they do so for eons, they will not see me.
> They may think of me as sound
> or may gauge awareness, but will not accomplish me.

> They may think of me as compassionate wisdom,
> but this too is just a thought that clings to duality.[29]

The *Tantra of the Wisdom Expanse of Samantabhadra*, also from the *Heart Essence of the Great Expanse*, says that Samantabhadra immediately recognized the fundamental problem of the initial dim cognizance that begins to stir from the primordial, undifferentiated ground of awareness and promptly devolves into the dichotomy of subject and object. Therefore, Samantabhadra never committed even the kind of dualistic virtue of following a path from first being a deluded sentient being to eventually becoming a perfect buddha. Thus, he says:

> Knowing this huge flaw of cognizance's stirring from the ground, transforming into the mental consciousness, and thus serving as the support of karma and latent tendencies through associating with the great demons of apprehender and apprehended—I, Samantabhadra, did not commit even the minutest particle of contaminated virtue but was awakened as the ancestor of all buddhas.[30]

Thus, Samantabhadra's buddhahood comes about through rigpa's true nature simply recognizing itself, by itself, without any further conditions or fabrications: it does not arise through any causes or conditions that are extrinsic or external to it, such as teachers, accumulations of conditioned merit, study, reflection, or contrived forms of meditation beyond the sheer recognition of rigpa by itself.

The same tantra explicitly states that Samantabhadra is not a person, mind stream, or buddha emanation separate from rigpa, but the timeless self-recognition of basic awareness—prior to saṃsāra or nirvāṇa—which is innate in the very heart of all sentient beings and instantaneously manifests as natural freedom:

> "Is it suitable or unsuitable to present an argument about time or any 'before' and 'after' with regard to the split of saṃsāra and nirvāṇa? Also, Teacher Samantabhadra, are you

an illusion-like creation within the perspective of virtuous appearances for others or a truly established appearance of an entity consisting of some other mind stream? Please, Teacher, state how it is."

Samantabhadra said, "The appearance dimension of nirmāṇakāyas is presented in terms of the three times (past, future, and present). However, I, Samantabhadra, am the inexpressible dharmatā of phenomena. Therefore, the words "primal protector," which suggest a beginning for inconceivable time—Samantabhadra—represent merely an alias with which I am labeled. For that reason, it is only following the arising of the prajñā that examines and analyzes saṃsāra and nirvāṇa that one speaks of the diverging of saṃsāra and nirvāṇa, because the single ground has arisen as two paths.[31]

"Oh Vajra of Realization, if you think that the one who is called 'the primal protector who possesses the heart of all buddhas, the glorious Bhagavān Samantabhadra' consists of a mind stream apart from the ocean-like realm of sentient beings, this is the view of extinction in which saṃsāra and nirvāṇa remain disconnected, while they are [actually] connected. Also, since sentient beings would lack the seed of buddhahood, the teachings of the ocean-like path of the two accumulations would become depleted.

"For that reason, become an expert in the mode of being of the ground, because in my nature—the Great Perfection—there are both [the path of] freedom and the path of delusion within the ground. Thus, understand the Dharma that the [ground's] self-arising as buddha [realms] or the realms of sentient beings occurs by virtue of two factors: being free from all stains of [the ground's] own face, or being ensnared by karma and afflictions, respectively. Do not search with any hope for me, Samantabhadra, as a buddha who consists of some other mind stream, or as a buddha who is an illusion-like fabricated creation within the appearance dimension [of a buddha for others]."[32]

In brief, Samantabhadra is the instantaneous, full recognition of mind's intrinsic and primordial unity of basic awareness and emptiness, which is the very ground of everything that can possibly appear and be experienced, whether in saṃsāra or nirvāṇa. This ground is also called buddha nature, the nature of the mind, original basic awareness, and the fundamental dharmakāya. It is furthermore said that the empty essence of this primordial and self-arising awareness is alpha-purity, its luminous nature is innate presence, and its unceasing compassionate responsiveness is all-pervasive. Thus, it is in the sense of this instantaneous and all-encompassing recognition or realization of that which is most excellent—the intrinsic nature of the mind of all beings, which is the dharmakāya—that the name Samantabhadra is to be understood.

As the conclusion of the first chapter of Longchenpa's *Precious Treasury of Words and Their Meanings* explains, Buddha Samantabhadra bears his name not only because the awakened state he represents is utterly pure and devoid of any distortions in terms of ego, dualistic perception, and corporeality, but also because he represents the direct awakening and freedom that occurs immediately within the initial seeming exteriorization of the primordial ground as its own ground manifestations. Thus, unlike in the case of other (historical) buddhas, Samantabhadra's hallmark is that there is absolutely no straying into saṃsāra at first and thus no gradual return with great difficulty to the very source—the natural expanse of primordial awareness—from which such straying would have occurred. In other words, Samantabhadra stands for the instantaneous awakening through the immediate recognition of the ground manifestations for what they are—nondual basic awareness—devoid of even a brief experience of nonrecognition, delusion, ignorance, or impurity. Here is Longchenpa's explanation:

> At the very moment of their rising from the ground, the ground manifestations—the eight gateways of innate presence[33]—dawn as [the ground's] self-appearance. An impartial state of mind without grasping [at these ground

> manifestations] as something other will recognize them as [the ground's] natural self-radiance. Through that, this stirring [of the ground manifestations] is [immediately] cut through, directly within itself: through what dawns as self-appearance recognizing its own face in the first instant, realization arises, and thus the ground manifestations are differentiated [as what they actually are]. In the second instant, through delusion having been purified (Tib. *sangs*) and wisdom having expanded (Tib. *rgyas*),[34] the ground is matured as the fruition. Thus, the essence—primordial awakening [purity and expansion]—is said to be re-awakened [re-purified and re-expanded] through realization. The teacher who has thus awakened prior to everything, right within the ground, through the dissolution of its self-appearances within alpha-purity, is called "Samantabhadra." ...
>
> The seed-like awareness that rises from the ground [as the ground manifestations] is indeterminate in terms of whether it causes freedom or delusion. Therefore, it is called "nonmatured awareness." Its maturation into awakening is caused by the prajñā of realization. ... When [this awareness] is realized as itself by virtue of not straying outward into discernment, through joining the dissolution process [of the ground manifestations] with an impartial state of mind, it remains within inner luminosity.[35]

In brief, everything that appears as the ground manifestations arises from the ground of rigpa, while not being different from it. Recognizing these manifestations as nothing other than this basic ground means being free. Thus, both delusion and freedom—and therefore everything in saṃsāra and nirvāṇa—occurs within this basic awareness and never goes beyond it. In looser parlance, this could be phrased by adapting the famous dictum about Las Vegas: "Whatever happens in rigpa stays in rigpa."

Moreover, since Samantabhadra is nothing but a name for instantaneously becoming a buddha through directly recognizing the ground manifestations as primordial awareness, the freedom of Samantabhadra can and does occur in the mind streams of all kinds of beings, all the time. It does not just refer to some individual's attainment of such a freedom in the past. Pema Ledreltsal[36] says this:

> One shouldn't think that the mode of freedom of Universal Goodness [Samantabhadra] ... is a matter of a liberation that was attained in an ancient time. Because at the very time of our speaking now, there are many beings who are being deluded from the basis [ground], who are liberated, and who are confused on the border between freedom and delusion.[37]

Tsültrim Sangpo's *Lamp* discusses at which time Samantabhadra is free, through what he is free, how he is free, what is freedom, and in what location he is free:

> At which time is [Samantabhadra] free? Master Vimala[mitra] declares this:
>
> > As for the natural ground of primal alpha-purity,
> > its essence is that it is not established as anything
> > whatsoever,
> > while its nature is that it appears as anything whatsoever.
> > Its compassionate responsiveness is to be free in dawning
> > as anything whatsoever.
>
> Accordingly, [Samantabhadra] is free at the time when the seal of the inner expanse's sphere of innate presence is rent open, [this sphere of innate presence] rises from the ground, and is seen as the ground manifestations.[38]
>
> Through what is [Samantabhadra] free? ... [Samantabhadra] is free through the prajñā of self-appearances' being realized and appearing as the play of wisdom and their being differentiated from the characteristics of entities, which are other-appearances.[39]

How is [Samantabhadra] free? He is free by way of realizing [self-appearances] to be self-appearances, through differentiating them from other-appearances.[40]

What is freedom? Through the power of being without adventitious stains, freedom does not arise from anything other, but merely consists of revealing primordially free wisdom as complete freedom. ...

In which location is [Samantabhadra] free? ... The primal alpha-purity that rests in its very own place is free as the original inner expanse. ... Thus, at the time of the unceasing wisdom that is like eternity, the changeless dharmakāya—the kāya that is like a vajra—is endowed with the water of uninterrupted samādhi that is like nectar and the light of the unobscured awakened mind that is like the sun and the moon. Therefore, this is called "having seized awareness's very own place."

Accordingly, the dharmakāya of having come face to face with realization abides as the completely perfect primal buddha—Samantabhadra, whose character consists of the three dharmas[41] and who is self-arising as the sphere of innate presence, which is the consummate fruition.[42]

3

The Five Aspects of Samantabhadra

Longchenpa's *Treasure Trove of Scriptures* first elucidates the text's opening homage through five distinct meanings of Samantabhadra and then explains that Samantabhadra—one of the most common Dzogchen names for the state of original buddhahood—is nothing other than the primordial, innate awareness that is naturally free, even before any notions of "buddhas" or "sentient beings" have emerged:

> *I pay homage to glorious Samantabhadra.*
>
> *Glorious* refers to having found the genuine dharmakāya (one's own welfare) and, while never departing from this expanse, benefiting sentient beings through genuine rūpakāyas, for as long as saṃsāra lasts (the welfare of others). Thus, [*glorious*] has the meaning of the consummate qualities of relinquishment and realization.
>
> Who has such [glory]? It is "*Samantabhadra*." This primal protector, who has arrived as the guru of all of saṃsāra and nirvāṇa, is the excellent teacher who has primordially perfected the powerful mastery over innately present enlightened activity, as the genuine guide who demonstrates the path. It is *to* this [teacher] that the author *pays homage* with fervent faith; that is, he pays homage with great, supreme devotion of the three gates [of body, speech, and mind].
>
> Is this homage only paid to this [Samantabhadra]? Homage is not only paid to him but to all that is present as the five aspects of Samantabhadra in terms of representing the

branches [that are the aids] for realizing the subject matter [of this text]: that is, all buddhas (because they have become buddhas as the essence of Samantabhadra) and all phenomena of the ground, path, and fruition.

(1) Samantabhadra as teacher means that all buddhas, while residing in the forms of the sambhogakāya and the dharmakāya in Akaniṣṭha, promote the welfare [of all sentient beings] through sending forth [countless] emanations to all the distinct realms of those to be guided. The [opening verse of Dharmakīrti's] *Pramāṇavārttika* says this:

I pay homage to Samantabhadra
with his profound and vast kāyas
that dispel the web of thoughts
and his pervasively radiating brilliance.[43]

(2) Samantabhadra as ground is the dharmatā of all phenomena—suchness. This is [also] called "Samantabhadra as nature."

(3) Samantabhadra as adornment refers to the appearances of all phenomena, which are self-arising as the play of the bearers of the nature [of phenomena]. This consists of [all] that is completely pure, in that its nature is illusory.

(4) Samantabhadra as awareness is self-arising wisdom,[44] the sugata heart. It refers to exactly what the *Uttaratantra* describes:

Since the perfect buddhakāya radiates,
since suchness is undifferentiable,
and because of the disposition,
all beings always possess the buddha heart.[45]

(5) Samantabhadra as realization is the fundamental basic nature. Through realizing it well, the eyes of freedom are found. This is [also] called "Samantabhadra as the path." These [five aspects] are also mentioned in the *Mirror of Samantabhadra's Mind*:

All phenomena are to be understood as having the nature of the five [aspects of] Samantabhadra. What are these? They are as follows: (1) Samantabhadra as nature, (2) Samantabhadra as adornment, (3) Samantabhadra as teacher, (4) Samantabhadra as awareness, and (5) Samantabhadra as realization.[46]

The detailed explanation of the meaning of this homage consists of a praise of bodhicitta, which is equal to space:

The originally and innately present Dharma that is so marvelous and amazing
is the luminosity of self-arising wisdom, which is bodhicitta,[47]
the treasury from which all that appears and is possible—container, contents,[48] saṃsāra, and nirvāṇa—arises.
I pay homage to this unwavering freedom from reference points.

This teaches the topic of the treatise in a general manner. It says that naturally pure mind as such[49] has not been produced by anyone but is *originally* self-arising. Therefore, it is *innately present* as the buddhahood [at the time] of the ground—the suchness that is the dharmakāya without any change or transition. Since the qualities of this expanse—the kāyas and wisdoms—are primordially present [in it] in an inseparable manner, it is present as *the Dharma that is so marvelous and amazing*. It abides as *the luminosity of* ever-unchanging *self-arising wisdom, which is bodhicitta*. Though it may *arise* as *saṃsāra* or *nirvāṇa* by virtue of the condition of its either being realized or not realized, this essence [always] abides as the natural Great Perfection—the dharmatā that does not change or transition into anything whatsoever. It is to this genuine character [of mind as such] that *I pay homage*, as an aspect of understanding this basic nature. *Self-Arising* [*Awareness*] says this:

In the essence of actual reality,
there is neither a buddha nor a sentient being.
Since awareness is without clinging, it is empty.
Given that it does not dwell in emptiness,
it dwells in its own state of great bliss.

The powerful sovereign of all buddhas
should be understood to be our own awareness.
This king of self-appearing awareness
exists in all but is not realized by all.[50]

4

Samantabhadra's Appearance

Iconographically, as a completely naked and unadorned blue figure, Samantabhadra symbolizes the original buddha—the utterly formless and ungraspable dimension of the dharmakāya, which is like a completely cloud-free, deep-blue sky.[51] Samantabhadra's one face represents the single ultimate reality of the face, or essence, of basic awareness, which defies identification as one or many. His two hands are in the mudrā of meditation, which symbolizes the realization that awakened and unawakened beings are equal. Being seated in the cross-legged position stands for the union of nonconceptual *prajñā* and nonreferential compassion (or skill in means). Remember that Samantabhadra is not an ordinary being, or a buddha with certain characteristics, such as a blue body, one face, two eyes, two hands, and so on; he stands for the ultimate dimension of the awakened mind, the realization of which is as deep and vast as the spaciousness of the deep-blue sky, while completely transcending any identifiable characteristics, such as form, color, physicality, or concepts.

Samantabhadra is often depicted in sexual union with the female buddha Samantabhadrī, who is equally naked but white in color. White here stands for the complete purity, transparency, nonsolidity, and lack of characteristics of the primordial state, or emptiness. Just as white is not actually a color at all, the stainless crystal of the dharmadhātu is completely colorless in itself.

The embrace between Samantabhadra and Samantabhadrī represents the inseparable union of the pure awareness of self-arising, luminous wisdom, and the vast open expanse of the dharmadhātu, or emptiness.[52] The vibrantly clear insight and awareness of this wisdom arises naturally within the open spaciousness of the expanse of emptiness, radiating throughout it and pervading it. Their inseparable union is not just a nonconceptual cognitive dimension; its affective dimension or tone is the experience of the inexhaustible great bliss that is completely unconditional and free from all mundane emotions, such as desire, attachment, clinging, and pride. Their lotus seat symbolizes their freedom from all stains of conditioned phenomena and characteristics. Just as a mother gives birth to children, all phenomena arise from and within the open yet fertile and luminous space of emptiness.[53]

Thus, the symbolism of the feminine principle makes it clear that emptiness is not a blank voidness, an utter nonexistence, a negative, or some static state, but the indeterminate yet dynamic dimension of infinite potentiality. The masculine principle refers to the awareness of nonconceptual wisdom that is accompanied by the warm heart of compassion; this is what moves within, permeates, and is aware of the spaciousness of this boundless realm, manifestly expressing all its enlightened and enlightening possibilities and qualities.

In their function as the "parents" of awakening, Samantabhadra and Samantabhadrī are the ultimate source of bodhicitta, as well as of all levels of realization of the noble ones in the Śrāvakayāna, Pratyekabuddhayāna, Mahāyāna, and Vajrayana; Samantabhadra and Samantabhadrī are also the central figures in the maṇḍala of the one hundred peaceful and wrathful deities.[54]

Part II

The Aspiration Prayer of Samantabhadra

5

The Northern Treasures

The source of *The Aspiration Prayer* is the collection of treasure texts called the Northern Treasures, which was discovered by Rigdzin Gökyi Demtruchen Ngödrub Gyaltsen[55] (1337–1408) in the cave of Sangsang Lhatra.[56]

Ngödrub Gyaltsen was born to the northeast of Mount Trasang[57] and is considered a reincarnation of Nanam Dorjé Düjom,[58] one of the twenty-five main disciples of Padmasambhava. In accordance with a prophecy, when he was in his twelfth year, three feathery growths appeared on the crown of his head, and two more appeared by the time he was twenty-four. Since these growths looked like vulture feathers, he became generally known as Rigdzin Gökyi Demtruchen (in short Rigdzin Gödemchen)—"the Vulture-Feathered Awareness Holder."

Though Rigdzin Gödemchen was the primary revealer of the Northern Treasures, this collection originated with the hermit Sangpo Tragpa from Manglam,[59] who was a Kagyü Mahāmudrā practitioner. In 1364 he found a number of scrolls at Gyang Yönpolung,[60] including the key to the treasures to be found later by Rigdzin Gödemchen, a prophetic guide on how to identify this destined revealer, and specific instructions for him. The scrolls also contained the famous collection of prayers to Padmasambhava commonly referred to as the *Supplications in Seven Chapters*.[61] Thus, in 1365, Sangpo Tragpa entrusted these scrolls to a *vinaya* master named Tönpa Sönam Wangchug[62] and his two companions, instructing them to pass them on to a yogin carrying a statue and a rosary in his hands, whom they would meet to the east of Sangsang and who would mention the king of Kungtang[63] in an appreciative manner. Shortly thereafter, they indeed met a yogin who matched that description—none other than Rigdzin Gödemchen—and they handed all the texts over to him.

On April 19, 1366, Rigdzin Gödemchen first found the key to three major treasures and one hundred minor treasures in the form of seven paper scrolls in a cavity near the summit of Mount Trasang, which had been indicated to him by a beam of white light.[64] About two months later, on June 14, he revealed the actual collection of the Northern Treasures in the cave of Sangsang Lhatra, which is located on the eastern slope of Rock Mountain Resembling a Cluster of Poisonous Snakes,[65] in the vicinity of Mount Trasang in Northern Latö.[66]

The original treasure consisted of a square blue treasure chest containing five separate chambers arranged in the form of a maṇḍala, each of which contained one hundred topics and various sacred objects. In the central chamber, made of deep red leather, Rigdzin Gödemchen found three ritual daggers,[67] a number of relics of Padmasambhava and his disciples, and the Northern Treasures' central cycle of Dzogchen instructions, called *Samantabhadra's Unobstructed Awakened Mind*.[68]

Rigdzin Gödemchen spent the rest of his life transmitting the wealth of instructions in the Northern Treasures and upholding the teachings of the Nyingma lineage in general. The first three main recipients of the Northern Treasures were his wife, Lama Pema,[69] his short-lived son and direct lineage heir, Namgyal Gönpo (1399–1424),[70] and his disciple Dorjé Gönpo.[71] These transmissions resulted in three distinct lineages: the secret consort (Tib. *gsang yum*) lineage, the son lineage, and the disciple lineage, which became reunited by the seventeenth century. Furthermore, Rigdzin Gödemchen's many other disciples also passed on the Northern Treasures, including to the famous siddha Tangdong Gyalpo.[72]

Rigdzin Gödemchen also found the keys to and opened a number of "hidden lands,"[73] such as Sikkim.[74] In 1389 he was appointed as the personal spiritual teacher of the then king of Kungtang in

Central Tibet. He then founded the monastery of Sé Trasang[75] near Mount Trasang, which later became the seat of his son, Namgyal Gönpo, as well as the seat of a line of incarnations known as the Setön Lamas.[76]

Later, a lineage holder of the Northern Treasures named Legden Dorjé (1512–80?)[77] claimed to be the reincarnation of Rigdzin Gödemchen and was recognized as such at a mature age. In 1632, the rebirth of Legden Dorjé, Ngagi Wangpo[78] (1580–1639), founded the monastery Tubten Dorjé Tra Ewam Chogar[79] and assumed the title of the Third Dorjé Tra Rigdzin. Thus, Rigdzin Gödemchen and Legden Dorjé were retrospectively considered to be the First and Second Dorjé Tra Rigdzin, respectively. In addition to propagating the Northern Treasures, several of Rigdzin Gödemchen's reincarnations were also treasure revealers in their own rights. Led by these successive reincarnations as the throneholders of Dorjé Tra Monastery, it became one of the six main seats of the Nyingma School in Tibet[80] and remained the primary seat of the Northern Treasures lineage until the Chinese invasion.[81]

In 1984, in Indian exile, Taglung Tsétrul Rinpoche[82] (1926–2015) founded a new monastery modeled after the original Dorjé Tra Monastery, called Tubten Dorjé Tra Ewam Chogar Chökor Namgyal Ling,[83] in Shimla, Himachal Pradesh. Until his passing, Taglung Tsétrul Rinpoche served as the throneholder of this monastery and thus the head of the Northern Treasure lineage. In 2012, he was also elected as the supreme head of the Nyingma School.

6

The Source of *The Aspiration Prayer*

Samantabhadra's Unobstructed Awakened Mind

The Aspiration Prayer of Samantabhadra is no doubt the most popular text of the Northern Treasures revealed by Rigdzin Gödemchen; it is still recited daily by many thousands of Tibetan Buddhists. Its general textual source is the central cycle of the Northern Treasures, the four volumes of *Samantabhadra's Unobstructed Awakened Mind*, which is often praised for its profundity and clarity. This cycle represents a complete system of Dzogchen teachings, covering all aspects of the Great Perfection from its introductory levels to the highest instructions of Cutting through Solidity and Direct Leap.[84]

Samantabhadra's aspiration prayer is by no means an ad hoc, random, or isolated utterance. To understand and practice the instructions in this prayer, it is crucial to acknowledge and appreciate its general and specific sources, context, and timing. Buddha Samantabhadra presents his prayer as the culmination of his teaching, in the penultimate chapter of the explanatory tantra called the *Tantra That Teaches the Great Perfection as Samantabhadra's Unobstructed Awakened Mind*,[85] in the fourth and last volume of the cycle *Samantabhadra's Unobstructed Awakened Mind*. The tantra comments in detail on this cycle's root tantra, the *Tantra That Teaches Sentient Beings to Be Buddha Samantabhadra's Unobstructed Awakened Mind*,[86] as well as the other tantras contained in the third volume. This means that Samantabhadra offers his aspiration prayer after having already taught all the essentials of the ground, path, and fruition of the Great Perfection. Thus, his prayer not only represents a pithy concluding summary of both the root tantra and its explanatory tantra but also presents the crowning instructions for revealing the nature of the five main mental afflictions as the five primordial wisdoms. These instructions are squarely based on all the teachings concerning the primordial ground of innately present awareness and its qualities, the path of the self-recognition of this ground without meditation, and the fruition of its being fully revealed without attaining anything new, all of which Samantabhadra previously discussed in the root tantra and its explanatory tantra.

To outline the wider thematic context—or the inner mental landscape—of this aspiration prayer, let's begin with the tantra that represents its root. The *Tantra That Teaches Sentient Beings to Be Buddha Samantabhadra's Unobstructed Awakened Mind* is a short text of fifteen pages in which Samantabhadra answers a number of questions posed by the bodhisattva Vajrapāṇi, who is referred to by his epithet "Lord of Secrets." The tantra's eight chapters teach (1) the manner in which the seed of the dharmakāya abides in sentient beings, (2) the dharmakāya and the kāya of unobstructed wisdom, (3) uncontrived awareness as the essence of buddhahood, (4) the dharmakāya as the nature and the view, (5) the qualities of the dharmakāya, (6) the pith instructions for awakening, (7) the time when sentient beings become free, and (8) the awakened mind of Samantabhadra.

The first chapter of the tantra, concerning the seed of the dharmakāya, begins with questions that sound like a brief summary of the key themes of *The Aspiration Prayer of Samantabhadra*: from the single ground, the two paths of delusion and self-recognition diverge, leading to the two results of saṃsāric sentient beings with their afflictions and Samantabhadra's freedom with its wisdoms, respectively:

> The Lord of Secrets asked: "Kye! Primal buddha, Samantabhadra, how do the [two] distinct paths diverge in all sentient beings of the six realms, who are one as self-arising

> innate presence? Of what kind are the inconceivable karmas and afflictions in all sentient beings of the six realms and the inconceivable appearances of wisdom in Samantabhadra?"[87]

Samantabhadra answers these questions in a way that closely resembles the more detailed discussion of these themes in his aspiration prayer:

> The primal buddha, Samantabhadra, responded: "Lord of Secrets, listen well. I and all sentient beings of the six realms originated in a self-arising manner within the ground, the locus of innate presence. Therefore, all of saṃsāra and nirvāṇa is self-arising. At the time when the dynamic energy of the five elements stirs within what is self-arising, conceit about self-appearances begins to flare up[88] and leads to delusion in the form of [many] thoughts of dualistic appearances. Through proliferating as all kinds of thoughts, the sentient beings of the six realms experience inconceivable karmic appearances.
>
> "When the [ground's] dynamic energy stirs from the ground, this occurs in a self-arising manner. The path consists of being aware that this dynamic energy is [nothing but the ground's] self-appearances. Since there is no mental state of conceit or doubt, this is the buddhahood that occurs in the manner of [both] saṃsāra and nirvāṇa being severed through a single strike. Why is that? Buddhas have the wisdom of being aware of self-appearances. Sentient beings have the karma of the delusion of dualistic appearances."[89]

Finally, Samantabhadra affirms the general existence of the seed of the dharmakāya in all sentient beings and its specific way of being in humans, which serves as the foundation of the path of the Great Perfection:

> The Lord of Secrets asked: "Kye! Primal buddha, Samantabhadra, does the seed of the dharmakāya abide in sentient beings or not? If it abides [in them], how does it abide?"

> Samantabhadra replied: "The seed of the dharmakāya abides in all sentient beings. In the sentient beings of the three miserable realms, there is the seed of the dharmakāya that resembles [a reflection of] the moon in water being stirred by a strong wind. In the three [kinds of] abodes of the higher realms, there is the seed of the dharmakāya that resembles the sun or moon when clouded over. Lord of Secrets, listen: In the center of the heart of those sentient beings who are humans, there abides the seed of the dharmakāya of the buddhas, which resembles the sun surrounded by the five lights. Its lucidity dwells in the center of the eyes."[90]

In the sixth chapter, which teaches the pith instructions for awakening, Samantabhadra explains the meanings of Samantabhadra, Samantabhadrī, their union, and Samantabhadra's unobstructed awakened mind as follows:

> Realizing that the essence of awareness is empty, it is Samantabhadrī. Not being an emptiness that is an utter voidness, the luminosity of awareness is Samantabhadra. Since awareness consists of lucid radiance within emptiness, it is present as inseparable emptiness and lucidity. Precisely this is the sole completely perfect buddhahood. Through mind's relaxing at ease, awareness dawns in a self-arising and lucid manner. This represents the samādhi of Mahāmudrā. As a sign of this, one's upper torso exists as being empty. Through directing the eyes into space, the dharmakāya of the buddhas that abides in the center of one's heart appears directly. This is called "the buddhahood of the nature that is innate presence." Allowing just this unceasing and unobstructed vision to settle in the center of one's eyes in a vividly clear manner—unobscured by any thoughts of dualistic appearances and without clinging—is the unobstructed awakened mind of Samantabhadra.[91]

Finally, in the eighth chapter of the tantra, Buddha Samantabhadra describes his own awakened mind in more detail as follows:

> My awakened mind is unconditioned; there is no awakening through conditioned phenomena. Since my body abides as the kāya of prajñā, it lacks any form with characteristics. My body is the kāya of wisdom. It is buddhahood beyond Dharma. My awakened mind is not arrived at by meditating and practicing. Since it is free from efforts, recognition of its own face is sufficient. I do not have a material body. I am not tainted by virtuous or evil karma. My body exists as the kāya of wisdom. Awareness exists as a sphere of light. Free from any becoming more lucid or fading, the appearances of wisdom exist in a resplendent manner. If persons with pure karma dispel the thoughts of mind and awareness seizes its own place, the body of flesh and blood is discarded and the body of luminosity dawns. Once the thoughts of mind have been severed, nonconceptual wisdom dawns. Once the appearances of delusion have ceased, pure appearances dawn. Through the dawning of the appearances of wisdom, my appearances are without meeting and parting.[92]

Thus, Samantabhadra's unobstructed awakened mind is the state of freedom of our own awareness: the boundless primordial realization of the stainless, all-pervasive, open, and unobstructed awakened mind of the original buddha, Samantabhadra, is nothing other than the natural state of primordial awareness, without its ever having strayed into any state of delusion.

As for the specific scriptural source of *The Aspiration Prayer of Samantabhadra*, this prayer constitutes the nineteenth chapter of one of several tantras that explain the root *Tantra That Teaches Sentient Beings to Be Buddha Samantabhadra's Unobstructed Awakened Mind.* This explanatory tantra refers to itself using three different but related titles: The cover title is the *Great Dzogchen Tantra of Samantabhadra's Unobstructed Awakened Mind, the Tantra of Becoming a Buddha Merely Through Seeing, Hearing, Wearing, and Making Aspiration Prayers* (which I will mostly refer to as *Tantra of Samantabhadra's Unobstructed Awakened Mind*).[93] At its beginning, the tantra is also called the *Tantra That Teaches the Awakened Mind of All Victors—the Intrinsic Wisdom That Is the Blazing Light of Awareness*.[94] Each chapter ends with reference to the text as the *Tantra That Teaches the Great Perfection as Samantabhadra's Unobstructed Awakened Mind*.[95] As the following will show, each of these three titles focuses on the specific contents of certain chapters among the twenty in this tantra.

A brief overview of their contents: (1) the first chapter describes the setting as the dharmadhātu realm of Akaniṣṭha, in which Samantabhadra resides with his retinue of the five buddha families and their billions of retinues. It is here that Vajradhara—the foremost among all sambhogakāyas who emanate from the dharmakāya—supplicates the dharmakāya buddha Samantabhadra to explain each of the following as Samantabhadra's unobstructed awakened mind: the sambhogakāyas (the forty-two peaceful buddhas and bodhisattvas as well as the ocean of wrathful buddhas and deities) who appear from within the natural state of the dharmadhātu free from reference points, their pure realms and abodes, their arising and dwelling therein, their visions, their emanations of compassionate responsiveness, and the beings to be guided by them. In sum, Vajradhara requests that Samantabhadra describe the beginning, middle, and end of his unobstructed awakened mind, with the beginning being the innately present ground, the middle being innately present self-arising awareness, and the end being the innately present three kāyas.

(2) In response, the second chapter explains that all the many forms of the sambhogakāya and nirmāṇakāya are emanations of the dharmakāya, Samantabhadra. These kāyas present all the teachings of all yānas, which are divided into the three categories of teachings of expedient meaning, teachings with an indirect intention, and teachings of definitive meaning. The latter—the teachings of the Great Perfection—lead to buddhahood in a single lifetime.

The remaining chapters discuss the following topics: (3) the general ground of both saṃsāra and nirvāṇa, (4) how saṃsāra and nirvāṇa diverge from this ground, (5) the dharmadhātu wisdom of Akaniṣṭha as the palace of self-appearances, (6) the inseparability of the three kāyas, (7) the awakening of unaware sentient beings through instructing them on the ground, path, and fruition, (8) the manner in which the dharmakāya abides within the bodies of unaware sentient beings, (9) the example for that—a wish-fulfilling jewel in a jeweled casket, (10) the means for becoming a buddha in the nirvāṇa without remainder through being shown dharmatā directly, (11) the manner in which persons who encounter this Dharma become buddhas, (12) how persons with lesser intelligence are introduced to this, (13) the four kāyas and five wisdoms, (14) the essential points of the intermediate state, (15) that through the three eminent ways of extracting the quintessence of Samantabhadra's mind, sentient beings are powerless not to awaken, (16) that through engaging in special practices, sentient beings are powerless not to awaken, (17) awakening through seeing, hearing, and touching self-arising letters, (18) the methods of drawing and handling that which frees through wearing, (19) that through making the aspiration prayer of great power, sentient beings are powerless not to awaken, and (20) the qualities of this tantra and to whom it should be entrusted.

Thus, our *Aspiration Prayer*, along with two introductory and concluding sentences, constitutes the nineteenth of the twenty chapters in this tantra. Nevertheless, neither this chapter nor the aspiration prayer itself are actually titled *The Aspiration Prayer of Samantabhadra*. The opening sentence of the chapter refers to what follows as the "special aspiration prayer of saṃsāric sentient beings' powerlessness not to awaken" and its concluding sentence similarly says that this chapter "teaches that through making this aspiration prayer of great power, sentient beings are powerless not to awaken." Thus, this aspiration prayer is also known as the Aspiration of Great Power.[96]

In brief, the ultimate scriptural source of *The Aspiration Prayer of Samantabhadra* is the revealed *Tantra of Samantabhadra's Unobstructed Awakened Mind*, while its inner spiritual source is the actual unobstructed awakened mind of Samantabhadra—the unobscured and all-pervasive realization of primordial buddhahood—from which this aspiration prayer reverberates on its own as a natural expression of the dynamic energy of this awakened mind.

7

The Nature of *The Aspiration Prayer*

What Is a Buddhist Aspiration Prayer?

Bhante Shravasti Dhammika's website "Guide to Buddhism from A to Z" explains the notion of "aspiration" in a general Buddhist context and distinguishes it from ambition as follows:

> Ambition (*chanda* or *icchā*) is an eagerness to acquire personal advantage—wealth, power, status or fame—while aspiration (*patthāna*) is a gentle but firm determination to achieve something. The English word ambition comes from the Latin *ambitionem* meaning "going around" while aspiration is related to the Latin *spiritus*, breath, and comes from the French *aspirare* meaning "to breathe out."[97] Ambition is not necessarily negative, but it does have a tendency to override integrity in its drive to get what it wants. And when it does get what it wants, it sometimes misuses it. ... As the Buddha said: "Because of his craving for riches, the fool undermines himself" (Dhp.355). All too often, ambition just keeps us "going round," i.e. it further entangles us in saṃsāra. ...
>
> Aspiration is a form of desire tempered by thoughtfulness, integrity and a self-interest that takes into account the interests of others too. While ambition is focused totally on the goal, aspiration never loses sight of either the goal or the means used to attain it. Aspiration allows us to "breathe freely" (*assāsa*, M.I,64) after we have achieved our goal,

> because we know we have done it without compromising our values or disadvantaging others. Aspiration also understands that, while mundane goals may be useful in this life, spiritual goals benefit us in both this and the next life and will eventually lead to the state of complete fulfilment where we no longer strive for any goal, i.e. nirvana. The Buddha said one should, "put forth his whole desire, exert himself, make a strong effort, apply his mind and resolve" to attain such goals (A.IV,364). And when he said that one practising Dhamma should be "moderate in his desires," he meant we should aspire towards worthwhile goals without allowing our aspiration to degenerate into ambition.[98]

In the Tibetan tradition, a general distinction is made between "aspiration" (Skt. *prārthanā* or *āśaṃsā*, Tib. *smon pa*) and "aspiration prayer" (Skt. *praṇidhāna*, Tib. *smon lam*).[99] "Aspiration" is explained to be "the mindset of wishing to attain something," while an "aspiration prayer" is "the expression of a mental aspiration on the path of words."[100] Simply put, an aspiration prayer is an expression of good wishes in order to benefit ourselves and others.

More specifically, the *Mahāyānasūtrālaṃkāra* presents three verses on aspiration prayers as they are understood in the Mahāyāna:

> Intention associated with striving
> and impelled by wisdom—
> the aspiration prayers of the intelligent
> are unequaled on all bhūmis.
>
> They are to be understood as being causes
> and results accomplished through the mind.
> Their functionality is to bring about future goals,
> because they are successful merely through the mind.
>
> Diverse, great, and pure
> on the higher and higher bhūmis
> until awakening, they are what accomplish
> the bodhisattvas' own welfare and that of others.[101]

According to Sthiramati's commentary,[102] these verses describe (1) the nature, (2) the cause, (3) the levels, (4) the classification, and (5) the function of aspiration prayers.

(1) In general, "intention" is defined as the mind's stirring and moving, and "striving" arises for desirable entities. Here, the nature of aspiration prayers is the articulation of a bodhisattva's thinking about, and striving for, the ways to attain the fruition of unsurpassable awakening after having given rise to bodhicitta.

(2) Since the aspiration prayers of bodhisattvas arise from the cause that is nonconceptual wisdom, they are said to be "impelled by wisdom." Alternatively, "impelled by wisdom" refers to their being dedicated in order to attain such wisdom.[103]

(3) Worldly people make aspiration prayers in order to attain certain pleasant fruitions within the realms of gods and humans, while śrāvakas and *pratyekabuddha*s make aspiration prayers in order to attain their individual supramundane fruitions. However, since the aspiration prayers of the intelligent bodhisattvas on the ten *bhūmi*s are far superior to all aspiration prayers by ordinary beings, śrāvakas, and pratyekabuddhas, they are said to be "unequaled."

(4) As for the classification of the aspiration prayers of bodhisattvas, they are to be understood as being the causes for accomplishing all goals: that is, a bodhisattva's own welfare and that of others, in both this and other lifetimes. "Results accomplished through the mind" refers to results that come about merely through the aspiration prayers made in the mind of a bodhisattva. There are immediate results of such prayers in this life: given that ultimately neither the body nor speech perform any function, even in this life, a bodhisattva's own welfare and that of others will be accomplished merely through making aspiration prayers.[104] "Their functionality is to bring about future goals, because they are successful merely through the mind." The same goes for subsequent lives: ultimately, nothing can be accomplished through the body or speech—it is merely through the intention or the aspiring mind of bodhisattvas that the entire welfare of themselves and others will be fulfilled.

Furthermore, during the time of the two paths of accumulation and preparation, the aspiration prayers of bodhisattvas are called "diverse." At that time, since they have not yet realized the characteristic of the dharmadhātu's omnipresence (which is only realized on the first bhūmi), their many different aspiration prayers are made in a great number of dissimilar ways. The aspiration prayers of bodhisattvas on the first bhūmi are called "great," because they accomplish the ten great aspiration prayers of bodhisattvas.[105] "Pure on the higher and higher bhūmis until awakening" refers to the aspiration prayers from the second bhūmi up to reaching buddhahood. Compared to the purity of aspiration prayers on lower bhūmis, those on higher bhūmis are more noble and distinguished.

(5) The function of the aspiration prayers of bodhisattvas is to fully accomplish both their own welfare and that of others.

The Eighth Karmapa's commentary on the *Abhisamayālaṃkāra* explains the difference between "aspiration prayer" and "dedication" as follows:

> As for the difference between dedication and aspiration prayer, [the former means the following]. Through specifically selecting any conditioned or unconditioned roots of virtue and then making them into the common roots of virtue of all sentient beings, these virtues are dedicated as the causes for oneself and [all] others attaining great awakening. In the case of aspiration prayers, without specifically selecting any particular roots of virtue, one aspires from the depth of one's heart that all sentient beings will become buddhas and also expresses the power of this truth verbally, making prayers accordingly.[106]

Thus, in its specific Mahāyāna sense, an aspiration prayer is actually much more than a simple wish or aspiration, because its ultimate goal is always the greatest imaginable good for all sentient beings—every being's completely perfect buddhahood, which in turn is the source of further boundless benefits for all other beings. In addition, many Mahāyāna aspiration prayers are very eloquent and profound formulations, of more or less distinct aspirations, which often include essential instructions concerning view, meditation, conduct, and fruition.

In the sense of wishing for the ultimate goal that all sentient beings will attain perfect buddhahood, the most basic aspiration prayer in the Mahāyāna, which includes all others, is the bodhicitta of aspiration (a.k.a. bodhisattva vow). It consists of the mere aspiration of generating the resolve to lead all beings to awakening, while the bodhicitta of application means to actively engage in the methods—the practice of the pāramitās—to achieve this goal. The classical definition of the bodhicitta of aspiration is found in the *Abhisamayālaṃkāra*:

> The generation of bodhicitta is, for the welfare of others,
> the desire for completely perfect awakening.[107]

Thus, the two goals of this aspiration are perfect awakening or buddhahood (what is to be attained by bodhisattvas for themselves) and the ensuing welfare of all sentient beings (the objective to benefit and liberate all others). Thus, bodhisattvas do not simply vow to become buddhas for the sake of their own liberation from saṃsāra; their primary vow is to benefit and awaken all sentient beings, no matter how long it may take and how difficult it may be. Among these two goals of buddhahood and the welfare of others, the latter is the main objective of bodhisattvas, whereas complete buddhahood is simply the most efficient state for accomplishing such welfare. In other words, for bodhisattvas, buddhahood is the best means to the end of benefiting and liberating others—but never an end in itself.

There is also a difference between an "aspiration prayer" and a "supplication."[108] A supplication is always directed toward a certain person or persons (such as buddhas, bodhisattvas, or gurus), in order to be granted certain wishes (be they related to the Buddhist path or not), and/or to generate devotion. An aspiration prayer is usually not directed toward a certain person; it represents a strong, heartfelt wish that beneficial things—temporarily and ultimately, in accordance with the Buddhist path—will happen for oneself and others.

More specifically, mastery of aspiration prayers, defined as the ability to display awakening in any buddha realm and at any time, makes up the seventh of the ten masteries of bodhisattvas.[109]

Aspiration prayers also constitute the eighth among the ten *pāramitās*.[110] This pāramitā consists of the aspiration that we, in all lifetimes, may never be separated from bodhicitta, and that our engagement in the pāramitās for the welfare of all sentient beings may be uninterrupted. It also includes dedicating all positive actions of body, speech, and mind, by ourselves and others within the framework of the ten pāramitās, to the perfect buddhahood of all sentient beings. In this way, bodhisattvas make aspiration prayers by not disregarding even the smallest virtues but bringing them all together in their mind and directing them to the ultimate goal of the awakening of all beings. Thus, aspiration prayers represent the pāramitā that utilizes speech in order to accomplish the skill in means for all qualities of the path and the fruition to arise and increase so that they become inexhaustible.

In brief, in accordance with the bodhicitta of aspiration, the pāramitā of aspiration prayers is twofold: aspirations for a bodhisattva's own awakening and aspirations for the welfare of beings. The many different functions of these aspiration prayers for our own welfare and that of others include consistently securing rebirths (including those in pure buddha realms) that are conducive to practicing the bodhisattva path until the attainment of buddhahood, avoiding the eight states without freedom,[111] and meeting the Dharma, authentic teachers, and conducive companions, again and again throughout all lifetimes. Such aspiration prayers also serve as means to rule out inferior forms of awakening (such as arhathood, which lacks enlightened activity for the benefit of beings); to sustain, expand, and enhance bodhicitta; to accomplish all kinds of physical and mental benefits for others on the path; to assemble the conducive conditions for uninterruptedly practicing all ten pāramitās; and to be born in certain places or as certain beings to benefit beings in innumerable ways (such as taking rebirths as gods, animals, and so on for the welfare of others). In addition, aspiration prayers are the basis for knowing all knowable objects that are required to skillfully and individually lead all beings to buddhahood (omniscience); for manifesting certain physical appearances, objects, realms, and necessities; for engaging in virtue in an uninterrupted manner, and thus accumulating vast merit and wisdom; for attaining all kinds of *samādhis* that benefit oneself (through inner calm abiding and superior insight) and others (through outward displays of miraculous powers and so on); for attaining all the fruitions of the dharmakāya and the many forms of *rūpakāyas*, causing the resultant enlightened activity for the welfare of all sentient beings to be uninterrupted; and for always engaging in what pleases all buddhas and bodhisattvas.

In brief, the pāramitā of aspiration prayers means to constantly cultivate and enhance all facets of the heartfelt wish that we, in all lifetimes, may never be separated from bodhicitta, and that our engagement in all ten pāramitās for the welfare of all sentient beings may always be uninterrupted, both on the path and at buddhahood.

The characteristics that signify the purity of the aspiration prayers of bodhisattvas are that they lack any appearance of any characteristics of a self, what is mine, or the duality of subject and object, nor do they cling to any of these things.

The cause of the mastery over the pāramitā of aspiration prayers in accordance with how these prayers were made by bodhisattvas in the past is the perfection of the pāramitā of vigor. Through the buddhas' past cultivation of vigor, their every conceivable action was brought to perfection. By cultivating vigor without any idleness, as did the bodhisattvas of the past, they were able to complete all tasks. With such vigor as the cause, buddhas are able to accomplish all their aspiration prayers as they wish. In other words, the full accomplishment of the pāramitā of aspiration prayers means that the buddhas' effortless enlightened activity cannot be affected by any obstacles or negative forces (Skt. *māra*).

The opposite causal relationship between the pāramitā of aspiration prayers and the pāramitā of vigor also applies. For example, bodhisattvas may be unable to meditate constantly due to their many afflictions, unable to settle their minds within due to their weak altruistic intentions based on their inferior constitutions and aspirations, and unable to accomplish supramundane prajñā due to not having fully cultivated *dhyāna* based on the focal object of the bodhisattva scriptures. When they then garner even a small accumulation of merit and make aspirations to have few afflictions and obstacles in subsequent lives, this constitutes their pāramitā of aspiration prayers at that time. Through this, they will be able to lessen their afflictions and hindrances, while enthusiastically engaging with untiring vigor. Therefore, the pāramitā of aspiration prayers also serves to aid the pāramitā of vigor.

The pāramitā of aspiration prayers is perfected on the eighth bhūmi of the bodhisattva path. This also represents the mastery over aspiration prayers mentioned before. At this point, all aspirations that a bodhisattva has ever made come to maturation and are fulfilled, just as they were expressed, such as displaying awakening in any buddha realm and at any time the bodhisattva pleases, or filling the whole universe with buddhas. The cause for everything becoming natural and effortless for bodhisattvas at this stage consists of the power of the altruistic efforts embraced by prajñā, skill in means, and the aspiration prayers that they made previously on the path.

The value of prior aspirations is important to understand because it is sometimes said in Dzogchen or Mahāmudrā that any effort is unnecessary, and that we can simply rest and click into the natural state of awakening. We might think that this is a great meditation, because we do not have to do anything. However, such thinking only feeds our ego and laziness, and when we try to meditate in that way, we find that there is no way of getting to an effortless state of realization merely through doing nothing at all. It is only because bodhisattvas have put tremendous effort into their practice at the beginning that it becomes effortless on the eighth bhūmi. Similarly, many aspects of the Dzogchen path require significant effort before an experience of effortless resting at ease can dawn.

On the tenth bhūmi, when bodhisattvas are not in formal meditation, it is again by virtue of their previous aspiration prayers that they appear to be equal to buddhas, in that they are able to display the rūpakāyas and perform enlightened activity, in the same way that buddhas do. Thus, the tenth bhūmi is sometimes called the "buddhabhūmi."[112] For example, bodhisattvas are able to emanate a continuous stream of innumerable buddhas and bodhisattvas. They are also capable of appearing as all kinds of gods, kings, queens, śrāvakas, pratyekabuddhas, and perfect buddhas, always managing to teach the Dharma in any way that is necessary and beneficial for all sentient beings to be guided.

Finally, once buddhahood is attained, one of the many unique qualities of a buddha is "the knowledge through aspiration." This means that the buddhas' wisdom knows all knowable objects, by virtue of their previous aspiration prayers to be able to do so. By virtue of the buddhas' having accomplished their prior aspirations to eliminate attachment, doubt, and so forth of those who entertain reference points and characteristics, despite all phenomena being free from any reference points and characteristics, those buddhas' wisdom engages in the welfare of all sentient beings for as long as saṃsāra lasts, until all beings are completely awakened and liberated. This also means that such buddha wisdom engages not only with ordinary beings in saṃsāra but also with arhats and bodhisattvas on the bhūmis, who are already liberated from saṃsāra but have not yet attained buddhahood.

A buddha's knowledge through aspiration always operates naturally from within a state of meditative equipoise, for the welfare of others, and without any effort. It is free from any attachment to form and so on, by virtue of not clinging to any inner or outer entities. It is unobstructed with regard to all knowable objects, by virtue of having relinquished all afflictive and cognitive obscurations including their latent tendencies. It persists forever because it remains for the welfare of sentient beings for as long as saṃsāra lasts and resolves all their questions and doubts by virtue of having attained fourfold discriminating awareness.[113]

In general, the occurrence of a buddha's enlightened activity is said to depend on three factors: the power or blessings of that buddha's dharmakāya, that buddha's aspiration prayers, when still a bodhisattva, to be able to promote the welfare of all beings, and the (at least somewhat) purified karmas and minds of sentient beings as the recipients of such enlightened activity. When the enlightened wisdom of a buddha displays its activity, it manifests in a natural and unceasing way that is completely effortless and nonconceptual. However, it is through the power and momentum of a buddha-to-be's previous aspiration prayers and great compassion that the dharmakāya's enlightened activity appears uninterruptedly as the two rūpakāyas and teaches the Dharma. Thus, we might liken a bodhisattva's progress—through aspiration prayers and the resultant accumulations of merit and wisdom, on the path that eventually results in such buddha activity within the expanse of the nonreferential dharmadhātu—to the flight path of a rocket. Initially, a lot of energy is required to launch a rocket off the ground, but the higher it ascends, the easier and faster it moves, and the less energy it needs. Finally, once it enters the vacuum of outer space, it can travel forever without needing any further fuel or energy, simply due to the energy of the fuel previously spent.

Similarly, the often-discussed triad of completion, maturation, and purification[114] at the time of buddhahood refers to the following: (1) The full extent of the completion of aspiration prayers is the complete perfection of the power of the virtues that are the causes for the ability to effortlessly and naturally promote the welfare of others while one-pointedly resting in meditative equipoise within dharmatā. (2) The full extent of the maturation of sentient beings is the complete perfection of the power of the virtues that are the causes for the ability to display millions of physical manifestations in millions of buddha realms, and to establish the countless retinues surrounding each such manifestation on the path of the noble ones, by virtue of teaching them just a single verse of Dharma. (3) The full extent of the purification of buddha realms that a bodhisattva must accomplish in order to display the infinite enlightened activity of a perfect buddha (as opposed to the state of the individual nirvāṇa of arhats, in which no activity for others occurs) is the complete perfection of the power of the virtues that are the causes for accomplishing the particular buddha realm in which this bodhisattva is to become enlightened (just as the full extent of the ripening of fruits is their readiness to be enjoyed).[115]

In a verse from the tradition of the Fivefold Mahāmudrā of the Drikung Kagyü, the purpose of aspiration prayers is illustrated through the example of cleansing a wish-fulfilling jewel:

> If the wish-fulfilling jewel of mind as such
> is not polished with aspiration prayers,
> the results that are needed and desired will not arise.
> Hence, earnestly apply yourself to concluding dedications.

The wish-fulfilling jewel of mind as such refers to mind's basic nature, with its empty essence, its luminous nature, and the inseparable dynamics of those two aspects. This nature of the mind is the same in buddhas and sentient beings: it is not improved by buddhas or worsened by ordinary beings but exists such that it pervades all equally. However, if it is not joined with excellent aspiration prayers and thus polished by them, its qualities will not be revealed. For example, it is said that if one polishes a wish-fulfilling gem that has been obscured by contaminations, and then presents it in its fully cleansed state as an object of veneration, it will grant whatever is needed and desired through praying to it. However, without cleaning it, no such thing will happen. The purpose of joining the nature of the mind with aspiration prayers is just like that. Therefore, bodhisattvas should earnestly apply themselves to dedications and aspiration prayers as a conclusion of their main practices, because all results and qualities needed and desired by themselves and others will arise accordingly.

In brief, the significance of aspiration prayers—their scope, power, functions, and results for ourselves and others, both during the path of bodhisattvas and at the fruition of buddhahood—cannot be overestimated.

The Uniqueness of *The Aspiration Prayer*

As outlined in the previous chapter, Buddha Samantabhadra utters his particular aspiration prayer as the culmination of the *Tantra That Teaches the Great Perfection as Samantabhadra's Unobstructed Awakened Mind*. Thus, it is first of all crucial to be aware of the context and timing of this aspiration prayer, because it represents not only a pithy summary of the entire tantra but also its key instructions on how to reveal the nature of the five main mental afflictions as the five primordial wisdoms, which are squarely based on all the teachings on the ground, path, fruition, and meditation practice of the Great Perfection that Samantabhadra already gave earlier in this tantra.

Thus, this aspiration prayer can be interpreted on two distinct levels. Conventionally speaking, it appears to be an aspiration prayer by the primordial buddha, Samantabhadra, that all sentient beings may recognize their minds' true nature and become buddhas, such as when it says:

> Since I am the primal buddha,
> through making my aspiration prayer,
> may the sentient beings who cycle through the three realms
> recognize the face of self-arising awareness
> and fully unfold great wisdom.

Actually, however, it is an aspiration prayer of mind's own nature—primordial rigpa—itself (referred to as Samantabhadra) to recognize itself, its own face, or its own essence, which is nothing other than perfect buddhahood, or the dharmakāya. It is rigpa itself that aspires, "may what obscures me be seen through or become translucent." Indications of this thrust include passages such as the following:

> Through this aspiration prayer of myself, the buddha,
> may all saṃsāric sentient beings'
> darkness of dull mindlessness be dispelled,
> their cognizance of clinging to duality be translucent,
> and their awareness recognize its own face.

Thus, the recurring phrase "I, Samantabhadra" in *The Aspiration Prayer* can be understood in two ways: In a literal sense, it refers to the primordially awakened buddha, Samantabhadra, who makes this aspiration prayer for the sake of all sentient beings. Ultimately, however, it refers to the mind's basic nature—our own buddha nature, or basic awareness—whose essence has never been obscured or deluded and thus is primordially free and aware.

As *Lamp* says, the speaker of *The Aspiration Prayer* is the awakened mind of Samantabhadra, which is to be realized as the genuine treasury of the qualities of the three secrets of the primal buddha, the path of Dzogchen Atiyoga, and the goal or destination of all of Samantabhadra's aspirations. Thus, this aspiration prayer represents in fact the very unity of the ground, path, and fruition of Dzogchen. It is in itself an expression of rigpa itself, attempting to shine through our momentary adventitious stains that seem to obscure it.

According to *Webster's Third New International Dictionary*, the most common use of the word *prayer* in ordinary English is in the theistic sense of "a solemn and humble approach to Divinity in word or thought usu. involving beseeching, petition, confession, praise or thanksgiving." Etymologically, *prayer* comes from the Latin word *precarius*, which means "obtained by entreaty or prayer." Thus, *Webster's* also says that *prayers* can simply mean "earnest good wishes." Hence, a prayer does not have to be theistic in the sense of being addressed to some higher being or force, or for that matter, to anyone at all. It is in this sense that *The Aspiration Prayer* clearly represents the most nontheistic prayer possible: what prays and what is prayed to are in fact identical, and neither of them is a person, higher being, or god. Rather, mind's true nature prays for its own nature to be revealed in the midst of the obscurations that appear as sentient beings. To be sure, *The Aspiration Prayer* is not about some generic nature of the mind or the nature of someone else's mind (such as Samantabhadra's) but about the nature of our very own mind. Consequently, the cause and the result of this prayer are identical. Thus, it is not a typical aspiration prayer uttered by a sentient being, bodhisattva, or buddha to benefit other sentient beings; it's an aspiration prayer for every sentient being's innate nature to recognize itself, dispel what obscures it, and free itself—and also an attempt to achieve that. Dowman offers this explanation:

> The unique difference here is that the words emerge from the mouth of the Ādibuddha—it is as if God the Absolute were uttering the prayer. Thus, not only is the prayer bound to be answered, but there is no error in it. It is the perfect prayer, and if only for this reason it will be fulfilled. It is mantra, and mantra in the mouth of the guru manifests its true meaning. In the dimension of Dzogchen there is no subject/object dichotomy, and true to this verity, the prayer is addressed to its author: the supplicant, disposer, and vision are one. In the very act of expression lies the *immediate naked clarity* of Kuntu Zangpo's dynamic.[116]

In this sense, this aspiration prayer can be considered a nice double-entendre of the definition of *aspiration* in *Webster's*: "a strong desire for realization"; here, "realization" is both awareness's self-recognition and the fulfillment of the aspiration. Obviously, the primary meaning of "realization" in *The Aspiration Prayer* is not the realization of some dream or of something that was not there before: it refers to rigpa's irreversible realization of its own true nature, which entails freedom from all suffering and its causes.

All of this also means that sentient beings are a bit secondary here. Indeed, not only are sentient beings not the ultimate beneficiaries of this prayer, but they are precisely what obscures innate timeless awareness. It is not that sentient beings *have* obscurations but they *are* the obscurations. The *Garland of Pearls* says this:

> The sky-like dharmakāya
> is obscured by the clouds of adventitious sentient beings.[117]

Longchenpa's *Precious Treasury of Words and Their Meanings* states this:

> Within the natural state of awareness, phenomena such as the *skandhas* resemble clouds in the sky: though they appear within awareness, they are just floating [there] as empty forms without [ever] tainting awareness.[118]

Similarly, in the context of distinguishing mind (Tib. *sems*) from wisdom (Tib. *ye shes*), Longchenpa's text explains:

> *Mind* refers to saṃsāric phenomena, that is, the flaws that arise as stains, whose nature consists of karma and latent tendencies. At the time when awareness is associated with it, awareness is labeled a *sentient being* (Tib. *sems can*; lit. "having mind"). It is this mind that causes delusion in the form of the individual six forms of existence. At the time when awareness has become free from mind, it is called "buddhahood free from adventitious stains." *Wisdom* refers to nirvāṇic phenomena: since it burns up karma and latent tendencies, it resembles a fire, and it has the nature of empty, lucid space, free from all imagination.[119]

Thus, mind (*sems*) is exactly what distinguishes an ordinary sentient being (*sems can*) from a buddha, who is characterized by primordial wisdom. Consequently, it is only primordial wisdom, or rigpa itself, that can become a buddha—not a sentient being or any being's state of mind.

Given that, it also makes no sense that deluded and disturbed states of mind (such as the afflictions) could be transformed into awakened states of mind (such as wisdom). All the more so since the former are illusory, deceiving, adventitious, and obscuring, while the latter are ultimately reliable, completely unfabricated, and only to be revealed. This is made clear in Longchenpa's *Precious Treasury of the Supreme Yāna* when he discusses the principle that primordial awareness, along with everything that appears in it, is primordially free, in and of itself:

> In this king of paths that delivers from the afflictions, the vajra heart of Ati, the afflictions are not relinquished but are

pure in their ground. Therefore, this is unlike their becoming pure through relinquishing them as śrāvakas and pratyekabuddhas do, relinquishing them as bodhisattvas do, transforming[120] them as in the creation stage and making them subside on their own as in the completion stage of the lower mantra[yāna], taming them through remedies as in the general common yāna, settling them within their own natural way as in the Mind Series, or taking the [afflictions] themselves to be dharmatā as in the Expanse Series.

You may wonder why that is. If it is not understood how the afflictions primordially never existed, they [can]not be relinquished through [any form of] relinquishment. If the afflictions were relinquished through mind, since what is to be relinquished and what relinquishes it are of the same substance, it is not feasible for [the afflictions] to become pure. If they were relinquished by wisdom, since mind does not see wisdom and wisdom does not see mind, these two are directly opposed in that they cannot exist simultaneously; and in that case, the conventional notions of what is to be relinquished and what relinquishes it are not feasible. Nor is there any relinquishment of a former [affliction] through a later [remedy]: since what is past and what is future are of opposing substance, at the time when the one exists, the other one has [already] ceased. But if they were simultaneous, they would tamper with each other, and thus it would follow that what is to be relinquished is the remedy and the remedy is what is to be relinquished, because they [exist] at the same time in a single mind stream. Moreover, given that afflictions arise from the mind itself, which resembles a body and its shadow [that accompanies it], there is no time for their relinquishment through [any form of] relinquishment. The same applies to [the notion of] purification and so on ... Therefore, this is to be understood as the essential point of being free in itself by itself, just like a drawing on water.[121]

Thus, realization or awakening is not just some altered state of consciousness or a mental upgrade, because it is what is revealed and remains after the *entirety* of the dualistic mind and its associated mental factors has dissolved. In other words, as the *Mirror of Samantabhadra's Mind* says, buddhahood or the dharmakāya is not any sort of mind:

> If you assert the all-ground as the dharmakāya, you stray from me.
> If you assert mind as buddhahood, you stray from me.[122]

Longchenpa's *Precious Treasury of the Supreme Yāna* elaborates on the reasons why buddhahood is neither mind nor derived from mind:

> If one posits the triad of buddhahood, the path, and the ground to be mind, since the basis of this position—this very mind—involves apprehender and apprehended, it would follow that its ground, path, and fruition in their entirety [likewise] involve apprehender and apprehended. If this is accepted, it would follow that buddhahood is not accomplished [at all] or, even if it is accomplished, is delusion because it is not free from apprehender and apprehended. Also, just as mind gathers all kinds of latent tendencies and karmas, the same would follow for ground, path, and fruition. If that is accepted, there would be the flaw of it following that [ground, path, and fruition] are delusions.
>
> An opponent may say, "If there were no mind, buddhahood would thereby not be reasonable because you also assert that buddhahood is distinguished by a mind that is to be purified." In answer, we state that it is not the case that buddhahood [occurs] by virtue of the existence or nonexistence of mind. Rather, it occurs by virtue of the existence or nonexistence of the wisdom of the dharmakāya. Though it is true that buddhahood (Tib. *sangs rgyas*) is distinguished by mind's delusion having been cleared away (Tib. *sangs*), it is due to [the existence of] the buddhahood that consists of the innately present ground that it is still far from certain

> that [merely having cleared away delusion is what constitutes buddhahood]. Therefore, this is not actual, real [buddhahood]. Though what is to be purified has been cleared away, that which is to be purified and has been cleared away is not [in itself] buddhahood. Hence, buddhahood does not arise from mind ... If buddhahood were accomplished in the actual mind, [notions such as] what is to be purified and fundamental change would be meaningless.[123]

In brief, from the Dzogchen point of view, to claim that mind is a necessary condition for buddhahood, or even is the substrate of buddhahood, is as meaningless as saying that dark clouds are a necessary condition for a cloud-free, luminous sky, or even are the substrate of a cloud-free, luminous sky.

This very same stance is also found in *The Aspiration Prayer* when it speaks about the dissolution of the five main afflictions and the dawning of the corresponding five wisdoms:

> May sentient beings with the clinging of desirous attachment
> neither cast out the torment of desire
> nor welcome the clinging of desirous attachment within,
> but may awareness take its very own seat
> through letting cognizance relax in its own state,
> and may discriminating wisdom thus be attained.

The same approach is suggested for anger, pride, envy, and ignorance: let the afflictions be, without trying to get rid of them, indulging in them, or feeding them; thus, relax the grip of the dualistic mind and allow primordial awareness to reveal itself in its five facets of wisdom. Thus, there is no transformation of desire into discriminating wisdom and so on. Rather, the afflictions vanish on their own when we allow them to, and awareness dawns on its own when we let it. In both cases, this comes down to "we" or our dualistic mind simply getting out of awareness's way.

As a result of all this, the colophon of *The Aspiration Prayer* states that "through making this aspiration prayer of great power, sentient beings are powerless not to awaken." Since the true nature of all sentient beings is primordial awareness, sooner or later it will recognize its own face, by virtue of being invoked through the view and the meditation techniques of the Great Perfection, as outlined in this prayer. When engaging in this process, sentient beings are powerless to prevent the attainment of buddhahood, which is nothing other than the revelation of alpha-pure, innately present awareness, as it always has been. Again, all that sentient beings as the obscurations can do is to get out of the way of this awareness and not interfere with the process of its becoming revealed. Kapstein explains:

> Throughout the prayer, qualities that arise owing to the very nature of the ground are referred to as "self-emergent," "self-manifest," and the like. That is to say, they arise from the ground in and of itself, naturally, without depending on other, extraneous causes and conditions. Because the unsullied, pristine awareness of the buddha's enlightenment may arise in this way, we need only learn to recognize it: there is nothing we can do to cause it to come into being. Because this enlightenment is grounded in our essential nature, when it is indicated to us we become, in a sense, powerless not to become buddhas.[124]

The situation of sentient beings who fail to recognize basic awareness may be compared to a starving person who is in complete darkness but surrounded by delicious food. The irony is that this person is sleeping atop and thus completely covering a brilliant lamp with the power to illuminate everything. Despite the lamp's brilliance, everything remains in utter darkness, and despite an abundance of tasty food, the person suffers from hunger. In this case *The Aspiration Prayer* is like the lamp itself requesting, "Please, get up and let me illuminate all this richness!"

Similarly, this prayer is a wake-up call from rigpa to all sentient beings with their afflictions. In fact, it includes several such wake-up calls: a general one in terms of the basic Dzogchen view of self-recognition in the beginning, and five more specific wake-up calls related to recognizing the five main afflictions as the five buddha wisdoms.

In sum, *The Aspiration Prayer* combines aspirations that are expressions of both relative and ultimate bodhicitta (buddha nature or the nature of mind), with the extraordinary view and practice of the Great Perfection. More conventionally, Samantabhadra aspires that all sentient beings may leave the six realms of saṃsāra behind and awaken in the dharmadhātu. He also aspires that beings may recognize the inexpressible ground, awareness, or self-arising wisdom. Finally, there are the typical Dzogchen aspirations, mainly in connection with the five primary afflictions, that sentient beings with their dualistic mindset may simply get out of the way of basic awareness, by allowing their afflictions to relax in themselves so that basic awareness can recognize its own face, on its own accord.

Kapstein summarizes the distinctive features of *The Aspiration Prayer* as follows:

> The *Prayer of Great Power* is of interest in part because it recasts several of the fundamental elements commonly attributed to prayer, while at the same time conforming to normative conventions in important respects. How this is so may be made clear with reference to the brief phenomenology of prayer suggested by Gerardus van der Leeuw,[125] who begins his account by considering the relationship between prayer and magical formulas, the efficacious recitation of which always demands that they be repeated with perfect accuracy. Their power may be enhanced by additional factors, too, especially the introduction of what van der Leeuw terms the *magical antecedent*, often a mythical narrative invoking the past efficacy of the formula concerned. Again, we find incorporated in prayer exclamations that originally served to summon the deity, or "to remind the god of the pact that had been concluded," and even to "compel the presence of divine Power."
>
> Prayer, properly speaking, emerges "[w]hen man recognizes first of all Form, and later Will, within Power." These

are among the key terms of van der Leeuw's phenomenology of religion, and elsewhere he explains that "in the three terms *Power, Will,* and *Form,* there lies practically the entire concept of the Object of Religion"; that is, whatever object is deemed "sacred."[126] The recognition of Form and Will here gives rises to the characteristically dialogic aspect of prayer: "it is an address from man to the Will which he knows to be above him, and the reply of this Will." Finally, in mystical faith, prayer may lose its dialogic character and become "a monologue saturated with religious energy," a "merging in God." "[P]rayer attains its highest form in *submersion,* while the dialogue type of supplication, on the other hand, always remains word and entreaty, practical demonstration of Will to will, even when it prays in *its* highest form: 'not my will, but thine, be done.'"

It will be seen at once that the phenomena of prayer are thoroughly bound up with mnemonics: perfect accuracy of recitation necessitates perfect recall; the "magical antecedent" involves the recollection of past events; the exclamatory summoning of the deity requires both summoner and summoned to remember their compact; dialogic prayer presupposes the petitioner's recollection of the object of faith; and mystical prayer, the exercise of mindful self-collection. In the *Prayer of Great Power* all of these elements, with interesting variations, are in evidence. Moreover, the prayer traces a path through the cosmogony and soteriology of amnesis and mnemic engagement.[127]

The relationship of the prayer we are considering to magical power is made explicit even in its title, and is further asserted in its concluding passage, in which the most propitious times for recital are described. The "magical antecedent," a remembrance of mythical events, is incorporated into the main body of the text itself, which details the manner in which the awakening of the primordial buddha and the amnesis of sentient beings have originated in a common ground. The exclamations *ho!* and *aho!* used throughout Tibetan religious poetry and prayer, are always intended to recall a sense of awe and wonderment, and the ejaculation *tsitta ā!* with which this prayer is introduced, uniquely recalls the primordial purity (*ka-dag*) of the Great Perfection.

Where the *Prayer of Great Power* curiously departs from the examples examined by van der Leeuw, however, is in its remarkable simultaneous instantiation of both dialogic and mystical paradigms: the petitioner reestablishes a primordial relationship with the buddha Samantabhadra by *becoming* Samantabhadra. The mnemonics of prayer are thus called upon to reawaken one's original affinity with the dharmakāya; that is to say, to arouse the reflexive mnemic engagement of the dharmakāya, to introduce a convergence of will and Will. According to its own logic, then, all beings are indeed powerless not to become buddhas on reciting this prayer; and *that* is its magic and power.[128]

8

A Language of Self-Recognition without a Self, an Agent, or Duality

The use of Asian languages in Buddhist texts that discuss mind's ultimate nature and its realization, such as in the dohās of the Indian siddhas, Milarepa's songs of realization, and many Ch'an, Zen, Mahāmudrā, and Dzogchen works (I will focus on the latter here) differs greatly from the everyday use of these languages and even more so from the use of language in modern Western idioms. Western languages ordinarily require a grammatical subject (or agent); a direct or indirect object; personal, demonstrative, or possessive pronouns or adjectives; declensions of all these words; verb conjugations in the first, second, or third person; and indications of singular or plural for nouns, verbs, adjectives, and pronouns. By contrast, Mahāmudrā and Dzogchen works (as well as dohās) typically and frequently lack some or all of those elements. They are often further distinguished by a very nuanced and content-relevant way of using intransitive verbs versus transitive verbs,[129] as well as active versus passive ones. Thus, I argue that the above and other features of English grammar and syntax—which are naturally reflections of the underlying thinking—greatly influence and often distort the meaning of sentences found in texts that deliberately speak about mind's nature from a nondual perspective: that is, without a self, without a person, without a subject, without a direct object (or any object at all), without an agent, and without action. Such passages are indeed attempts to convey the inexpressible and nondual through language, which is by nature dualistic.

One could thus speak of "the art of the syntax of nonself, nonduality, and nondoing"—a language without a speaker—that conveys being rather than doing, recognizing rather than attaining, revealing rather than creating, and seeing through rather than relinquishing. In addition, such being is without a be-er, recognizing occurs without a recognizer, revealing happens without a revealer, nondoing does not involve a nondoer, occurring is without an occurer, and even if some action happens, it is without an agent. Thus, the distinction between rigpa's recognizing itself, or simply being itself, and thus being free, and its not recognizing itself, or not being itself, and thus being deluded in saṃsāra, resonates in Shakespeare's famous statement: "To be or not to be—that is the question."

Dzogchen texts make it very clear that it is not some "I," a person, a sentient being, or any form of dualistic consciousness, that recognizes or meets rigpa's true nature, because by definition, a self, person, sentient being, and the eight consciousnesses involve unawareness, duality, and delusion—whereas the true nature of the mind completely transcends being an object of any ordinary consciousness, let alone an object of a self, "me," or a person. Instead, Dzogchen describes primordial awareness recognizing itself for what it is, rather than being obscured by dualistic, deluded sense perceptions, thoughts, emotions, and ego-clinging. To reiterate, all we as persons or sentient beings can do is step back and allow the nondual, innate awareness that abides within us to fully manifest, or simply be what it always was. So the question is "What is my mind without me?" In other words, can I let "my" mind be what it is on its own, with "me" completely out of the picture and never coming back?

Thus, from a Dzogchen point of view, statements such as "may I realize the nature of my mind," "I recognize my own nature," "I rest in natural awareness," "we meditate on rigpa," "I relax in mind's nature," "they settle in the nature of thoughts," "she looks at her rigpa," "you recognize your own essence," and "we become buddhas" are complete and utter oxymorons and quite misleading.[130] By contrast, statements appearing in Mahāmudrā and Dzogchen texts often lack an explicit grammatical subject, as well as personal, demonstrative, and possessive pronouns and adjectives. For example: "May mind's nature be realized," "the own nature is recognized," "recognition of the own nature happens," "natural awareness is resting (in itself)," "becoming or being familiar with rigpa," "familiarity with rigpa happens," "relaxing in mind's nature occurs," or "being buddha or buddhahood takes place."

In the same vein, imperatives such as "rest your awareness," "rest in mind's nature," "settle within awareness," and "relax in mind's nature" are problematic because they imply someone or something different from mind's nature or basic awareness that rests, settles, or relaxes in it. Even worse is "rest or place your mind in its own nature," sounding as if mind is something separate from its nature, and as if "I" or our ordinary dualistic mind is somehow plopped into something else that is its nature. Of course, conventionally speaking, the mind can be placed or settled on an object other than the mind, such as a pebble or a visualization. In that context, "placing" is fine, but not when describing the mind settling or resting in itself without any object. Even when the mind is placed or focused on an object, the main point in Mahāmudrā and Dzogchen is always that the mind rests, settles, and relaxes in itself, or is simply let be; any placement on an object merely serves as an initial aid to its own natural self-settling without any reference point. In such a settling, there is no settler, nothing that is settled, and nothing that it is settled upon.

In brief, statements such as those above that imply subject and object and so on maybe work as a manner of speech in adaptation to common English, but they greatly and consistently miss the essential point. Thus, it seems more conducive to say something like "allow rigpa to settle," "let mind's nature rest in itself," or simply "let be," although even these statements are ultimately dualistic, because the English implies a "you" that is being addressed. The only way this can be expressed through language is by saying things such as "settling occurs," "resting takes place," "relaxing happens," "seeing occurs," or "recognizing happens."

Again, none of the eight consciousnesses, let alone a self or a person, are capable of resting, settling, or relaxing in rigpa. Similarly, there is nothing extrinsic to basic awareness that is able to *make* it rest, settle, or relax. Instead, it is a matter of allowing awareness to rest in itself, by itself. Simply letting it be allows it to clearly manifest its very own nature of already being free primordially. This is like letting muddy water settle on its own instead of stirring it up, thus allowing it to become clear and transparent all by itself. We take a "hands-off approach" to rigpa, just as when someone says to us, "Just let me be," which means for us to step back and avoid interfering with or manipulating basic awareness at all, leaving it to its own devices. In other words, only rigpa itself can recognize, realize, relax, and settle itself—all "we" as sentient beings can and must do is to refrain from preventing this from happening.

Likewise, phrases such as "meditating on rigpa" and "cultivating the nature of the mind" make no sense at all—it is impossible to meditate on or cultivate primordial awareness, nor is there any need for such. Rigpa is not an object of meditation, cannot be perceived by a meditator or a meditating mind, and cannot be enhanced or improved in any way by anything. The only thing to do is to let familiarity with rigpa's natural state develop, or rather to simply let it be what it is in the first place. This cannot really be called "meditating" because this word usually requires a direct or indirect object and also implies a subject. By contrast, Milarepa is often said to have declared that "familiarization is not familiarizing; it is to be(come) familiar" (Tib. *sgom pa sgom min goms pa yin*).[131] That is, in the final picture, familiarization or "meditation" means not to deliberately meditate or focus on anything; instead, it means to allow the mind's nature to become completely familiar with itself, just as it is, without straying into any kind of unawareness, nonrecognition, or delusion about its own state.

Similarly, the *Supplication to the Dagpo Kagyü* by Pengar Jampel Sangpo[132] (fifteenth century) says this:

> Just as it is taught that nondistraction is the actual meditation,
> to great meditators who allow the fresh essence
> of whatever thought that arises rest as (or in) just this being
> uncontrived,

> grant your blessings to be free from a mind with anything to
> meditate on.

By contrast, some common renderings of this verse read:

> Undistracted attention is the main body of meditation, it is said.
> Whatever arises, is the fresh nature of realisation,
> For the meditator who naturally rests just so.
> Grant your blessing that meditation is free from
> conceptualization.[133]

Or:

> Awareness is the body of meditation, as is taught.
> Whatever arises is fresh—the essence of realization.
> To this meditator who rests simply without altering it
> Grant your blessings so that my meditation is free from
> conception.[134]

Putting aside the replacing of "thoughts" with "realization" (Tib. *rtog* versus *rtogs* in some manuscripts), "meditation free from conception" is a too narrow rendering of Tib. *bsgom bya blo dang bral ba*. It does not mean simply having no concepts or thoughts, but also not having, not finding, and not entertaining anything at all to meditate upon, which implies that there is no meditator either. As the commentary on this verse by Khenchen Thrangu Rinpoche makes clear, it refers to letting be, or resting directly and evenly in the fresh, uncontrived, and unaltered nature of whatever thought may arise—just this ordinary, uncontrived mind—without pursuing the past, anticipating the future, or assessing the present mind. Thus, the request of the supplicant is to grant the blessing to be free from a mind that involves clinging to any hope for meditation to be good; any fear of it being flawed; any thoughts of "being in meditation" or "not being in meditation"; anything to meditate on; any notion of a meditator; any meditation flaws such as being scattered, agitated, dull, or drowsy; and so on.[135]

Another term that is often used in Mahāmudrā and Dzogchen texts in relation to mind's nature or rigpa is Tib. *skyong ba* (lit. "to protect," "to guard"). The usual renderings, such as "sustaining" basic awareness, seem somewhat problematic because awareness cannot and need not be sustained by anything extrinsic to it, least of all an "I" or a dualistic consciousness. Only rigpa is able to sustain itself—if it can be sustained at all—but not in a deliberate, effortful, or active manner. It simply sustains itself by virtue of its own natural flow. Thus, we may say "allowing awareness to sustain itself" rather than suggesting that "I" can somehow sustain awareness. We may also understand this term in a more literal sense to mean protecting or guarding the natural flow of awareness from any intrusions, interferences, manipulations, or contrivances attempted by our dualistic mind and our afflictions, thus allowing it to manifest on its own, in a completely unaltered way.

Moreover, given what was said before about it being impossible for sentient beings—as the stains or obscurations—to become buddhas, even such common statements as "May all sentient beings become buddhas!" or "May sentient beings realize the nature of their minds!" are actually also oxymorons. Just as a dark cloud itself cannot transform into a cloudless, luminous sky, a sentient being, as the sum total of what obscures buddhahood, cannot transform into a buddha.

As a consequence of all this, many instructions in Mahāmudrā and Dzogchen (as well as in Zen) use language in a deconstructive rather than a constructive manner. Here is Forman's explanation of the nature of deconstructive language in Buddhism:

> Like most instructions, words like "place your right foot on your left thigh, and your left foot on your right thigh" function as a *description* of the act of getting into the lotus position, and as an *instruction* to do so. Similarly, words like "do not think" also seem simultaneously to *describe* and *instruct*. Hence, it would appear from surface grammar that these two statements function similarly.

Having heard the instructions "place your right foot ...," someone may perceive or imagine such an act in just these terms. Having done so, she/he may employ these words or notions in part to construct his/her perception. To perceive something as a foot, as over or under, or as a religious act (an act in a religious context) already introduces interpretive and discriminative categories. It acts, *mutatis mutandis*, like "look at the door" or "paint those Gothic archways!"

"Do not think" seems to be similar. It appears at first glance to be another constructive perceptual description or instruction which sets up a category by means of which one will see or perceive something. Here, however, is where the mistake is. The advocate of this position [the constructivist] is mistaking a *deconstructive* instruction for a *constructive* perceptual description or instruction.

Not every instructive utterance serves to set up experiential categories. If you say to Monet, "forget about your Gothic expectations and look again,"[136] you will not be providing him with new categories for his experience. Perhaps some other of his previously acquired expectations or beliefs about buildings may start playing a role .... But in giving your instruction, you, the instructor in this case, *have not introduced that expectation or any other* to him. You have only told him that his old one had misled him. You have spoken in the *via negativa*, if you will. You have simply deconstructed, in more modern parlance, his constructive expectation on the basis of which he had painted. If he obeys you, your statement will have played a role in stopping him from constructing his experience in terms of his habits and expectation.

Many instructions serve to deconstruct: "Forget it," "Put aside your expectations," "Just listen!" and so forth ... Such instructions do not attempt to provide a new set of expectations; all counsel someone to stop perceiving or behaving on the basis of old perceptual or behavioral patterns. ...

The fact that there are deconstructive instructions may go largely unnoticed. That is because had Monet been told that he had imposed his expectations onto his perception, he might have dropped "Gothic" but he would not have been able to drop every expectation and belief. There are many complex and interconnecting levels of construction in ordinary experience, and no one, relatively simple deconstructive process could possibly address all of these.

However, Buddhist instructions and meditation practices are not as simple as a single deconstructive remark. The Buddhist procedures are, as I see them, complex and polyvalent systems of physiological, psychological, and intellectual practices and performances which together, it is hoped, will bring about a progressively less discriminated form of experience until an entirely nondiscriminated event occurs. ... [T]aken together and practiced for years, [such procedures] are designed to reduce systematically the number and significance of perceptual and behavioral discriminations. Such interactive deconstructive techniques together may serve to do what the system claims for itself, that is, to allow one to cease discriminating and seeing in terms of subject and object. ...

Since the constructivist lays such stress on the formative role of the tradition itself, it is especially revealing that Buddhist texts ... overtly attempt to dissuade the practitioner from employing expectations about Buddha, *Nirvāṇa*, Bodhisattvaship, and so forth. When Dōgen instructs, "having stopped the various functions of your mind, give up even the idea of becoming a Buddha," he singles out the key concept which may lead one to expect and construct in Buddhist terms. He encourages his reader or disciple to cease employing such a loaded idea. As any piece of language must, this utterance does stand as part of the language of the tradition; yet his intention is clearly *de*constructive. His instruction is not designed to function like a constructive

> perceptual description. To confuse the two forms of instruction would be a mistake.[137]

If someone says to us, "Don't think!" or "Forget it!" or "AH!" we are not really being instructed to *do* anything. We are being told, "Stop doing whatever you are doing," but we are not advised what to do instead—there is a sense of open-endedness. Usually we are fixated on wanting to hear what we will be doing or what we are supposed to do. If we do not receive instructions on what to do, we get antsy and wonder, "What is all of this about, anyway? I just want to hear how I am supposed to meditate. I just want to know what I should do." However, Dzogchen teachings are often very elusive in this regard. They do make statements, but many of them serve only as means to undermine and cut off our ideas about what to do or what to hang on to. In this process of deconstruction, the mind continuously observes itself and its reactions as all its toys are taken away, one by one. So what is a toyless mind? What is a mind that does not seek to entertain itself in any way whatsoever? What is a mind that does not grasp at anything, including itself? Eventually, the mind is left in a state where there is nothing to hold on to—which is the whole point. In a sense, the instructions push us to the edge of the cliff of our dualistic, conceptual mind—and then our only recourse is to leap into the groundlessness of "no-mind."

In this vein, Dzogchen texts like Longchenpa's *Precious Treasury of the Dharmadhātu* emphasize the need to refrain from all effort, from looking, meditation, analysis, adopting, and rejecting in order to become free. Instead, we simply need to get out of the way of rigpa's primordial, natural freedom. Longchenpa's autocommentary *A Treasure Trove of Scriptures* describes mind's primordial freedom:

> In brief, all phenomena of saṃsāra and nirvāṇa are primordially empty, beyond thought and expression, and already free in the original expanse. They lack any nature of their own, and thus there is no need for them to become free again through any effort—they are primordially free ...

To present the justification of these [points], it is pointless to make any effort or exert yourself:

Even if you made any effort in this, since it is pointless:
Don't engage! Don't engage! Don't engage in effort or accomplishing!
Don't look! Don't look! Don't look at the phenomena of mentation!
Don't meditate! Don't meditate! Don't meditate on the phenomena of mental states!
Don't analyze! Don't analyze! Don't analyze the traces of objects and mind!
Don't accomplish! Don't accomplish! Don't accomplish results of hope and fear!
Don't relinquish! Don't relinquish! Don't relinquish afflictions and karma!
Don't adopt! Don't adopt! Don't adopt the perfect Dharma!
Don't bind! Don't bind! Don't bind your own mind stream!

Since the essence of awareness is unobstructed, it is with regard to this essence, which is not established as anything whatsoever, that these negations are repeated twice, which serves to stop the twofold mode of apprehender and apprehended. In the essence of awareness, there is nothing apprehended (a phenomenon to act upon) nor an apprehender (a phenomenon that acts). Therefore, I emphasize, "Don't engage! Don't engage in either something for which to make effort or any action of accomplishing!" ... In the essence of awareness, there is neither anything to look at nor anything that looks. Therefore, don't look with mind as the looker at awareness as the object! In the essence of awareness, there is neither anything to meditate upon nor anything that meditates. Therefore, don't meditate! Likewise, I instruct, "Don't analyze,[138] accomplish, relinquish, adopt, bind, or cling!" For [awareness] is beyond existence, nonexistence, apprehender, and apprehended.[139]

Therefore, it is very clear that the approach of the Great Perfection is not about doing anything but about constantly undoing all the things that our dualistic mind usually does. Instead of learning some new tricks, the point is to undo all our old ones; instead of doing, it is a matter of simply "don'ting,"[140] which is quite daunting from the perspective of the "doing" mind. Thus, the *Precious Treasury of the Dharmadhātu* adds:

> There is no reference point [such as] "What is it?" "How is it?" or "This is it."
> What can any of you do? Where is the "I"?
> What could anyone do about what was relevant before but now is gone?
> Ha! Ha! Just a burst of laughter at such a great marvel as this![141]

A Treasure Trove of Scriptures explains this as follows:

> Any previously existing [notion of] some amazing dharmakāya of naked self-lucidity has been left behind in such a way that there is not [even] any certainty where it may have gone. Therefore, with any [notions such as] "This is it" or "This is not it" and any clinging to the basic nature having been cast off, what was relevant before is now gone within dharmatā's own domain. What is there to do in this about freedom, delusion, or a fruition that is the dharmakāya? Looking at outer appearances, they are unobstructed, vibrantly clear, fleeting, and evanescent. They do not exist in this as any limited dimensions or any biased items of being or not being something. Looking at inner self-aware cognizance in its own domain, it cannot be pinned down, vanishes in its emptiness, is undifferentiated, clear of thoughts, insubstantial, and has the nature of the empty space of openness that is without a trace.[142] Having fused with this, I do not exist as anything whatsoever right now, so where does that leave all of you? Ha! Ha![143]

The experience and realization of this ungraspable lucid awareness without any discursiveness or reference points leads us to the important Dzogchen notion of "freedom" or "being free." In general, the intransitive Tibetan verb *grol ba* can mean "to dissolve," "to come or become undone," "to become unraveled," and "to be free" or "to become free." Its transitive forms *'grol ba* and *sgrol ba* mean "to untie," "to unravel," "to liberate," and "to free." In its specific Dzogchen use, *grol ba* means to be naturally free on its own accord, without anyone or anything making it free or liberating it. The quotes immediately below, as well as the explanations in *Ketaka*, *Lamp*, and appendix 7, make clear that "being free" refers to the state of rigpa's intrinsic primordial freedom (as well as the natural freedom of everything that manifests within rigpa), as opposed to being free from something or being free to do something.[144] Even "to become free" is inappropriate here because strictly speaking, rigpa cannot and need not *become* or *be made* free—it always has been, is, and will be free, all by itself, which is its natural condition. Thus, to use the transitive English verb "to liberate" here is inappropriate, because rigpa is not liberated by anyone or anything—not even by itself.

Nevertheless, the Tibetan verb or verbal noun *grol ba*, as well as a number of Dzogchen technical terms that include it, are frequently and misleadingly translated using the English words "liberate(d)" or "liberation," such as "to self-liberate," "primordial liberation," "nakedly liberated," and so on. However, speaking about liberation or being liberated necessarily implies prior bondage, whereas the whole point of *grol ba* in Dzogchen is the utter lack of any bondage, in the past, present, or future. In particular, even conventionally, "primordial liberation" is an oxymoron, because if liberation existed primordially, from what could one be liberated? And if there is nothing to be liberated from, how can one even speak of liberation?[145] Thus, I prefer to use expressions such as "being free in itself" (*rang grol*),[146] "being primordially free" (*ye grol*), and "being nakedly free" (*gcer grol*) or their corresponding nouns.[147]

The *Tantra of the Universes and Transformations of Sound*[148] explains that mind—here meaning mind's nature—is naturally free in itself, without having to be freed or liberated by anything:

> What is called "one's own mind being free"
> is without any succession from one to another.
> As for this mind that is not to be freed (Tib. *bkrol*) through anything,
> since it is perfect in the ground, it lacks any coming and going.
> It is not found through examination and thus lacks any reason.
> Since it is without base and root, it is present as being empty.
> It is the mind that is present as self-lucidity.
> Since it is free through the essential point, it is unbiased.
> Since it is free of time, it lacks any basis to depend on.
> Since it is free without toil, there is no exerting or accomplishing.
> Since it is free through confidence, there is no effort.
> Here, its being free through confidence is explained:
> Since it is primordially free, there is no ground to be delivered to.
> Since it is free by itself, there is no remedy.
> Since it is nakedly free, all vanishes in the place of its being seen.
> Since it is completely free, there is no effort.[149]

Later, the tantra describes the dharmatā of being free as follows:

> Furthermore, the dharmatā of being free is explained:
> Since it is free through the essential point, any effort is exhausted.
> Since it is primordially free, there is no need for repetition.
> Since it is free in itself, there is no remedy.
> Since it is nakedly free, all vanishes in the place of its being seen.
> Since it is completely free, its nature is pure.
> Since it is free of time, there is no need for becoming familiar with it.
> Since it is naturally free, it is uncontrived.
> "Being free" is nothing but a conventional expression:
> Whose attributes are realization and nonrealization?
> In whom is "being free in it" observed?

> For whom is engaging in the three realms possible?
> This is the dharmatā of being free from the extreme of [saṃsāric] existence.[150]

Longchenpa's *Precious Treasury of the Supreme Yāna* explains this primordial freedom as follows:

> Based on the essential point that primordial freedom lacks any basis for repetition, being free is taught to not be contingent on any effort in terms of view or meditation. This means that it is unproduced and uncontrived, due to the general pervasiveness of wisdom. It is ever unchanging in not arising from anywhere, not going anywhere, and not abiding anywhere. Since being free (Tib. *grol*) is not like freeing (or liberating; Tib. *bkrol*), there is no need for any effort through view or meditation. "Being free" means [simply] being present in its own natural condition, while lacking any modification or contrivance. Since that is the case, "being free" refers to body, speech, and mind being relaxed in their own natural condition, and mind as such resting in its genuine state. Since being primordially free always remains this way, it is more distinguished than the common yānas. ...
>
> As for the understanding of being primordially free, the essential point is that since it refers to already being free from the very beginning, and not suddenly at some point, there is nothing to become free again right now.[151] Awareness arises from never having experienced delusion. ...
>
> As for the mode of being free, since mind is empty, it cannot even be designated by the merely conventional terms "being free" or "not being free." Therefore, as a sign that it is already free primordially, there is no need for it to become free again right now, because mind is primordially awakened. Thus, it is understood that there is nothing to become free in what is already free primordially.[152]

Thus, Higgins emphasizes that "freedom" is the primary mode of being of mind, and not some distant goal to be achieved at some point. It is not freedom of something or freedom to do something; it simply means being naturally free from the beginning, without any cause for such freedom. Thus, it is different from the more classical Buddhist notion of a newly attained freedom that is the liberation from obscurations through the methods of the path:

> Freedom is here construed as a primary mode of being rather than a teleocratic goal, whether the latter is defined negatively (freedom from) or positively (freedom to). In the same way that health is best understood not simply as the absence or opposite of illness but as a basic condition of well-being, freedom is best understood not simply as the absence of bondage but as the most fundamental way of being of the subject. Freedom reframed in this way has nothing to do with capacities and properties of agents. It has more to do with *how we are* than *what we can or cannot do*. Understood as a mode of being rather than the capacity of an agent—as it is conceived, for example, in the Western theophilosophical problem of "free will"—ontological freedom is both prior to and a condition of possibility of all choice and deliberation. This understanding is implicit in the term *grol ba* ... that is construed grammatically as an intransitive verbal noun (perhaps best translated as "being free") and radically distinguished from earlier Buddhist conceptions of liberation (*mokṣa* : *thar pa*) which carry the sense of "becoming free *of* or *from*". ...
>
> [F]reedom is to be understood neither as an absence of constraint (negative freedom), as in the goal of "freedom from saṃsāra", nor as a disposition of the will (positive freedom), as in deliberative striving toward the pre-established goal of awakening (*bodhi*), but rather as the ontological precondition of both these ...

> This letting be in freedom is less quietistic than the passage may suggest. For, it will be recalled that letting be (noninterference) is interpreted not as an end in itself, but as a way of letting the ground of being manifest in all its fecundity without (mis)taking its outward shining forth for something it is not, namely, as an "inner" subject apprehending "outer" objects. It is important here as in all other dimensions of rDzogs chen thought to bear in mind this dialectical intertwining between emptiness and luminosity, primordial purity and innate presence ...
>
> In short, the classical rDzogs chen tradition reconceptualizes freedom in such a way that it no longer implies the mere absence of error and conditioning but the disclosive ground of its possibility; it is the originary mode of being to which one remains attuned through recognition or from which one errs through nonrecognition but which, in either case, abides as it is. That freedom is a precondition of errancy means not only that it makes the range of phenomena subsumed under the category of errancy intelligible (both logically and phenomenologically) but also that the recognition of errancy *as* errancy is a necessary condition of the consciousness of freedom ... reinterpretation of freedom as an ontological precondition of errancy is integral to its understanding of the ground as ontologically prior to the all-ground.[153]

And he adds this:

> The problem of "finding freedom," the goal of all lesser Buddhist paths, is resolved in the recognition that human beings do not *have* freedom but fundamentally *are* free; freedom is not an attribute of a subject, not something we *have*, but the ontological precondition of human existence.[154]

All of this also has profound consequences for the whole idea of a "path." All notions of a path—as something that starts somewhere and on which one progresses further and further, until a hitherto unattained goal or fruition is ultimately reached—are rooted in ordinary dualistic mind (Tib. *sems*) as opposed to naturally present primordial awareness (Tib. *rigpa*). Thus, the path in the Great Perfection is neither a causal progression nor a process of going from anywhere to anywhere else. Rather, it means being able to recognize and remain in the original, innate freedom that has always been the true nature of the minds of all sentient beings, as the early Nyingma master Rongsom Chökyi Sangpo[155] (1042–1136) points out in his *Entering the Approach of the Mahāyāna*:

> [The great path] is not as in the lower yānas where a distinct fruition is attained through having trained in a path that is other [than that fruition]. That all sentient beings [always] remain naturally free as having the nature of this [primordially free awareness] is what is called "the great path." Through a yogic person's realizing exactly this and having confidence in it, they are equal to glorious Vajrasattva or Samantabhadra. This is called "being free" and also "being buddha once again."[156]

He also says this:

> Through wishing to traverse the stages of the path, one strays from the path of nothing to be traversed.[157]

Higgins summarizes the characteristics of the Great Perfection's self-unfolding "path without progression" on which no one travels or reaches a destination under the following five points:

> (1) The path is *endogenous*: since it is found nowhere apart from existence and is only *dis*covered to the extent that all that obscured it has cleared, it does not depend on extraneous means or ends as in the cause-determined vehicles. (2) It is *self-emergent*: since it is not already there for us to follow but emerges in our going along, it is different from linear representations of the path which abstract from lived

space and time, relocating the path in an idealized representational space. (3) It is *spontaneous* and *effortless*: since it arises effortlessly, it does not require deliberative action, viz. the accumulation of virtues and knowledge advocated by Mahāyāna. (4) It is *nondiscursive*: since it discloses one's natural condition in its unmodified simplicity only when mentalistic-linguistic proliferations have subsided, it supersedes the mind-forged path-models adhered to by the lower vehicles. (5) It is *endotelic*: since the path is the self-disclosure of an ever-present goal, it is in no sense predetermined, having no pre-established point of departure, no trajectory and no destination. In short, the rDzogs chen path as a process of existential disclosure is neither instrumental (pursued as a means toward an end) nor teleocratic (channeled toward a pre-established end); it is a path that is forged in the going, without one knowing precisely where or even why one is going. It is in this sense "a path without progression."

This brief overview of rDzogs chen nonprogressivist path conceptions casts light on how the presentational path of primordial knowing becomes the animating principle of all rNying ma path hermeneutics. The problem of reconciling *Lakṣaṇayāna[158] and Mantrayāna here gives way to the problem of accommodating a path espousing purposive progression to an effortless rDzogs chen path that spontaneously unfolds precisely when the willful deliberations of dualistic mind have ceased. How is this accommodation possible? The key to addressing this question lies in Klong chen pa's definition of the path ... as the progressive familiarization with ever-present primordial knowing that reveals itself to the extent that the turbulence of mind and its mental operations has come to rest. This familiarization is understood as the disclosure of an unconditioned mode of being and awareness that is nonetheless a precondition for all the conceptual representations that flow and follow from it. This path as a

> disclosive clearing process is not to be confused with the linear schemes used to represent it. To do so is to confuse the map with the territory.[159]

Of course, it is impossible or at least very hard to be completely free of all such biased expressions, because thinking and language are by nature dualistic and, at least in regular parlance, bound to a subject, object, pronouns, and so on. But this is not just an issue of grammar, syntax, or linguistics. What we say and how we say it reveal our habitual dualistic and ego-oriented approach, which underlies all we think, say, and do: everything centers on the "I" who does something, achieves something, improves something, purifies something, or relinquishes something. Our language reflects the deeply ingrained ways in which we perceive, think, feel, and try to own or take credit for everything. From a Dzogchen point of view, our regular language patterns are clear indications that we are thinking and operating in the realm of ordinary dualistic ego-mind (Tib. *sems*), as opposed to being in the sphere of bare primordial awareness (Tib. *rigpa*). Thus, by using such dualistic language, we constantly obscure and go against the Great Perfection's most central distinction between "mind" and "awareness." In other words, we mistakenly speak and think about rigpa from the perspective of "mind," instead of letting rigpa speak for itself.

Therefore, it seems to be worthwhile to at least make an attempt (as I have done in this volume) to break through these patterns. To unquestioningly follow them, especially since they further support, solidify, and enhance our habitual patterns of duality and ego-clinging—especially in the context of the very instructions and practices that are designed to dissolve these patterns and their consequences—is clearly counterproductive. Such an attempt at a "nondual" language of nonself and nonaction may sound awkward at first, but this is mostly because we are not used to it, and also because language has inherent limits of being usable in nondual, ego-free, and action-free ways. But if we use language to unravel language itself, as well as its underlying mental patterns, we may open up a deeper understanding and "blow our minds" in the best way possible—by breaking free of the superficial confines of the dualistic mind to reveal its boundless true nature.

9

The Structure of *The Aspiration Prayer* and Its Different Versions

Generally speaking, *The Aspiration Prayer* has two main parts: The first explains the ground, which is Samantabhadra's primordially free awakened mind, and how it is obscured by unawareness. The second describes how the five main afflictions are to be recognized as the five wisdoms, which are their intrinsic nature.

Following is a more specific outline of *The Aspiration Prayer*, based in part on the topical outlines of its commentaries *Ketaka* and *Lamp*:

(A) The introductory section of the text begins with a brief instruction on the single ground, the two paths of delusion and recognition, and the two corresponding fruitions of saṃsāra and freedom (lines 1–7). This is followed by a more detailed explanation of the basic nature or essence of the ground, which clarifies that the primordial ground itself is free from both saṃsāra and nirvāṇa; it also links the ground with the fruition by asserting that buddhahood is nothing other than the recognition or full awareness of the ground itself (8–14).

(B) The main part of the prayer is a detailed presentation of how saṃsāra and nirvāṇa diverge from the ground and then unfold in their own ways:

  (1) This begins with an explanation of Samantabhadra's instantaneous mode of freedom through taking the recognition of the ground as the path: that is, through recognizing the ground manifestations as self-appearances

of the ground. The actual manner of Samantabhadra's freedom is described through (a) the six distinctive features of his freedom (15–25) and (b) his perfect awakening through the self-appearances of the kāyas and wisdoms of innate presence, which manifest as the maṇḍala of the forty-two peaceful and sixty wrathful deities (26–39). (c) This freedom results in promoting the welfare of all sentient beings through Samantabhadra's countless emanations ("other-appearances") (40–45). Thus, Samantabhadra's instantaneous freedom, at the very moment when the ground manifestations first appear, represents the ideal scenario (or "plan A"): what appears—rigpa—recognizes itself for what it really is and thus is free, all by itself, before any trace of delusion has even stirred.

(2) However, once delusion has begun to arise instead of self-recognition, the ground manifestations are misperceived and reified as saṃsāra. Thus, the prayer next describes how sentient beings become progressively more deluded in saṃsāra, due to not recognizing the actuality of the ground through the three kinds of unawareness. The most basic kind of unawareness or nonrecognition is "the unawareness that has the same identity as the cause"—the nonrecognition that the ground manifestations are nothing but the primordial ground's own appearances. This basic lack of awareness further devolves into the two subsequent kinds of unawareness—"connate unawareness" (the simultaneously arising failure to recognize this basic unawareness for what it is) and "imaginative unawareness" (the ensuing clinging to the duality of self and other)—as well as all afflictions, karmas, and sufferings that make up the six realms of saṃsāra (46–71).[160]

(3) The instructions on the path of this threefold unawareness and its results being free in themselves consist of

first teaching the manner of cycling through the realms of saṃsāra under the sway of the five mental afflictions (which constitute the dependent origination of delusion as it arises from this unawareness) and then showing how to become free from these afflictions through recognizing their dharmatā as being nothing but the five wisdoms (this is "plan B"). In other words, the path of delusion, as illustrated by the five afflictions, comes to its end once the ground has been revealed, just as it is.

Thus, the prayer explains how desire, which usually results in being reborn as a hungry ghost, can be free as primordial awareness or wisdom. By neither rejecting desire nor indulging in it, but letting it relax and settle in its very own state, its dharmatā—primordial awareness—is allowed to dawn in the form of discriminating wisdom (72–89).[161]

Similarly, hatred, which normally leads to rebirth as a hell being, can also be free as primordial wisdom. By letting it be in its own natural state without adopting or rejecting, its dharmatā is revealed as mirror-like wisdom (90–101).

Likewise, pride—which typically matures as a lofty existence in the god realm with its concluding suffering of plunging down from such a paradise into the miserable realms of animals, hungry ghosts, or hell beings—is recognized as being nothing other than the wisdom of equality (102–12).

Envy, or jealousy, with its competitive mindset, generally results in becoming an asura or demigod, who constantly is at war with the gods of the desire realm. When this mental affliction is not let run wild but allowed to relax in its own nature, it shines as the unobstructed wisdom that is able to accomplish everything (113–22).

Finally, our many layers of ignorance, which usually result in being reborn as an animal, may radiate as lucid mindfulness and awareness, thus turning the dark night of unawareness into the bright sky of dharmadhātu wisdom (123–30).[162]

(4) This revelation of the five afflictions as the five wisdoms is followed by a concluding summary that also shows how the qualities of the fruition—the dharmadhātu free from stains—manifest just as they are (131–40).

(C) Finally, the text explains the benefits of reading and hearing this aspiration prayer, including the two ways of reciting it. Ideally, the aspiration prayer is read as it is truly intended by yogic practitioners of the highest caliber: they will have already attained stability in the path of the Great Perfection while resting within the state of self-luminous awareness free of delusion, which represents the timeless, continuous yoga of supreme persons who are free from reference points. In such a case, the benefit is that all those who hear this aspiration prayer will become buddhas within three lifetimes (141–46). When the prayer is read by other practitioners while visualizing themselves as Buddha Samantabhadra, which represents the yoga of persons with reference points, which is performed at certain crucial points in time (such as eclipses or solstices), those who hear it will attain buddhahood in a more gradual fashion (147–55).

There are four main versions of this aspiration prayer available to us, and they exhibit a number of significant variant readings: (1)–(2) the two versions in two editions of the *Tantra of Samantabhadra's Unobstructed Awakened Mind* (which I will refer to as TV1 and TV2, respectively),[163] (3) the version in the *Treasury of Precious Treasures* (RTV), and (4) the commonly used version that is available in a number of printed and digital editions (CV).[164]

TV1 differs the most from all other versions. TV2 shares some significant readings with TV1 but also has much in common with CV and, to a lesser degree, RTV. At the same time, TV2 exhibits a number of readings that are not shared with any other version.[165]

RTV sometimes agrees with TV1, sometimes with TV2, sometimes with CV, and sometimes differs from all three other versions.

CV is the version that is used by virtually everyone today, as evidenced by the currently available Tibetan hard copies and digital inputs as well as the available translations into other languages, which are virtually all based on CV.[166]

As their colophons state, both RTV and CV were originally extracted from some unspecified versions of the tantra. However, it is impossible to tell whether their variant readings are based on TV1, TV2, or some other version of the tantra that is no longer available. The variants in RTV and CV may also have evolved later in the process of multiple copying: the tantra itself was revealed in the mid-fourteenth century, while the earliest available commentary that embeds the text of *The Aspiration Prayer* is from the mid-eighteenth century.[167]

In this volume, I offer rather literal translations of both TV1 and CV that take the details of the commentarial explanations into account. In addition, I present a more diplomatic and free-flowing—and hopefully more poetic—translation for recitation purposes that attempts to follow the most common readings among the four versions. All variants between TV1, TV2, CV, and RTV are documented in the notes to the translation of TV1.

10

The Aspiration Prayer as a Practice

The Aspiration Prayer of Samantabhadra is not only a prayer but also a meditation instruction for recognizing all mental events as being nothing other than the dynamic energy and play of basic awareness. Thus, before beginning to recite the text, we are encouraged to allow our awareness to rest in its own natural state of open, spacious, and relaxed presence. Out of this state then unfold—in an effortless and nonconceptual manner—all the appearances and activities of our body, our speech, and our mind, as we aspire that all beings who do not recognize this basic awareness will recognize it.

In terms of our body, we do not recite this prayer in our ordinary form or with ordinary dualistic perception and clinging. Instead, we visualize ourselves as Buddha Samantabhadra, with or without Samantabhadrī (as they were described in chapter 4 above, "Samantabhadra's Appearance"), in the midst of a pure realm or simply the dharmadhātu—the dharmakāya realm of Akaniṣṭha, free from directions and abodes but filled with rainbow light. Thus, we assume the ultimate rainbow body of wisdom and compassion within the sphere of the inseparability of alpha-purity and innate presence. From ourselves as Samantabhadra and Samantabhadrī, rainbow-colored light rays of loving-kindness, compassion, and wisdom radiate in all directions to all sentient beings. Alternatively, we can visualize Samantabhadra and Samantabhadrī in front of us. In addition, we can imagine that a multitude of other buddhas, bodhisattvas, and lineage masters are present in front of us and around us.

In term of speech, our voice is the natural, self-resounding speech that continuously arises from and within the dharmadhātu, or Samantabhadra's compassionate responsiveness. This sound pervades all phenomena without bias and resonates with all beings' primordial awareness, teaching each one in accordance with her or his capacities.

In terms of mind, we attempt to let basic awareness settle and simply be, in its own naturally free and perfect manner, just as *The Aspiration Prayer* suggests. At the same time, we let our compassion radiate throughout the universe and aspire that all sentient beings may hear this prayer and realize its meaning.

We begin by taking refuge in the Three Jewels as well as Samantabhadra and Samantabhadrī. This is followed by the above-described visualization and the recitation of the aspiration prayer, while letting our minds be open, spacious, and relaxed. At the end, we gradually dissolve the visualization into light, which vanishes within the dharmadhātu from which it arose. Then we let our awareness rest in its natural state without any reference points. Finally, we conclude by dedicating the merit from having recited and meditated in this way to the fulfillment of this aspiration prayer for the benefit of all beings.

In terms of our own welfare, we make this prayer as a wake-up call or reminder to recognize or return to our original true nature, which is primordial awareness and wakefulness, free from any delusion or suffering. The prayer's text is a Dzogchen teaching and practice explaining how to discover our innate awareness and allow it to sustain itself. It is an introduction to the nature of our own mind, commonly called a "pointing-out instruction."[168] However, this aspiration is definitely more of a "pointing-in instruction": our inner buddha nature points to itself so that it can recognize itself—and so that we will let it be what it always has been. Thus, in answer to the crucial question "What is my mind without me?" we try to give our mind the space to be a mind: we let it be itself without any interference or manipulation by "us."

In terms of the welfare of others, while reciting the aspiration prayer we imagine that all sentient beings of the six realms and three times can hear it (irrespective of language or distance) and focus on dispelling their many sufferings in this very instant, by way of restoring all beings to their original, innate nature. We also recognize that other beings' primordial awareness is not in any way different from our own. Thus, we recite this prayer without any limitations of space, time, inside, outside, self, or others.

When we recite the passages related to the five primary afflictions of desire, hatred, pride, envy, and ignorance, with their resultant rebirths as hungry ghosts, hell beings, gods, asuras, and animals, we specifically focus on the beings in whom these causal afflictions arise, as well as on the corresponding resultant sufferings of these beings. We can also deliberately give rise to these afflictions in ourselves and then practice with them, as the prayer explains.

Thus, we recite *The Aspiration Prayer* in order to get in sync with primordial awareness, allow it to take over, and thereby let any notions of the one who aspires, the recipients, and the activity of aspiring fall away. In this way, reciting becomes the resounding of awareness itself, aspiring represents the self-appearing play of awareness, being single-minded or "one-pointed" means awareness is naturally settled in its own native state, and recognition is the inseparability of all this as the unobstructed dynamic energy of the primordial unity of alpha-purity and innate presence. In this way, there is a gradual process of relaxation and letting be, progressing from the busy scatteredness or "multi-pointedness" of ordinary distraction to the "one-pointedness" of meditation and finally to the "zero-pointedness" of the natural state of awareness, just as is, on its own.

In this way, *The Aspiration Prayer* teaches how to recognize basic awareness and allow it to sustain itself, both during formal meditation sessions and when engaging in our daily activities. Instead of welcoming or trying to eliminate our afflictions and thoughts, we directly face them and allow them to relax and settle into the natural state of primordial awareness.

Therefore, *The Aspiration Prayer* is not just an aspiration prayer for certain occasions (such as earthquakes or solstices) but a daily—or even moment-to-moment—meditation practice, though out-of-the-ordinary situations can certainly enhance its effect, as Dowman says:

> If the prayer is recited during times of great danger or radical change, such as during an eclipse, an earthquake, a solstice, or at the end of the year, its efficacy is exponentially increased. At such times the mind's propensities become more fluid, and attachments to one's fixed mental dispensation are loosened. The Nyingma School recognizes a lineage of initiation through prayer. Thus the recitation of these verses can be as potent a skillful means of attaining buddhahood as the practice of difficult yogas, prolonged service to the lama, or maintaining *samaya* with the ḍākinī.[169]

On the qualities of Samantabhadra's awakened mind or "dynamic" that are evoked through *The Aspiration Prayer*, Dowman states this:

> He is the Ādibuddha, the Primal, First, Original Buddha. He represents primal awareness of total presence, and that is the universe. His name means All-Good, where his goodness is transcendent and supramoral. He also represents Dzogchen itself in its resultant phase. Kuntu Zangpo's *dynamic* is the power of his mind, or active presence. The word *mind* is rejected because of the danger of conceiving it as a substantial entity. It consists of no more than its motive power or intentionality, and its modes can be defined as primal awareness, communicative vibration, responsiveness, transforming activity, and magical quality. These modes are induced by the prayer.[170]

Among the above-mentioned five aspects of Samantabhadra, *The Aspiration Prayer* represents an expression of Samantabhadra as realization or the path. Thus, it is a "path of aspiration" (the literal meaning of Tib. *smon lam*) in the true sense of the word—awareness takes its power of aspiring for self-recognition as the path, which reveals awareness to itself.

Further to the earlier discussion of "don'ting" rather than doing, Dowman explains the Dzogchen "hands-off" approach of dealing with our conflicting emotions as follows:

> The deceptive simplicity of language and concept in the second part of the prayer need not induce the belief that a specious technique of mind manipulation is involved. This eminently practicable meditation is essentially contemplation upon the emptiness of the events of daily life. As the Buddha guides us through the various types of mental events, each dominated by a different passion, at each stage he exhorts the yogin to relax and relieve the stress. Thus the Dzogchen precept repeatedly emphasized in this yoga is "Do nothing! Indulge and cultivate nothing! Reject and abandon nothing! Simply be aware and let it be!" To say "Identify the emptiness inherent in simple sensory perception of every situation" would be to cultivate the seeking and striving that precludes attainment. ... [W]hen the yogin stands back, as it were, from the violent or at least highly intense circumstances, detaching himself from the emotionally charged structures that conceptual ignorance has woven around him, Kuntu Zangpo expresses the result of this in terms of spontaneously arising total presence. ... Pure sensory awareness, free of emotional taint and with the full intensity of mindfulness generated by the high-voltage situation, gives access to emptiness, suchness, the here-and-now-ness, of the event, and total presence is the cognitive aspect of emptiness. Thus the Buddha is urging us to "do" one thing: to relax and allow total presence to assume its rightful primacy. Another way to say it is, "Retrieve the part of the mind that has been stolen away by the fascinating or offensive object, and severing all attachment to the object, and bringing it back, stuff it into the heart center—then, no-mind!"
>
> In each case, the villain of the piece is dualizing mind, the unconscious process of differentiating subject and object that arises after the loss of total awareness.[171]

As its colophon states, *The Aspiration Prayer* stems from the *Great Dzogchen Tantra of Samantabhadra's Unobstructed Awakened Mind, the Tantra of Becoming a Buddha Merely Through Seeing, Hearing, Wearing, and Making Aspiration Prayers*. Accordingly, this prayer combines the practice approaches of becoming a buddha through hearing (the audience) and making aspiration prayers (the yogic practitioners who recite it).[172] Turpeinen says this:

> The prayer of Samantabhadra is the most open method to distribute the liberatory power of the sacred letters. Unlike the amulets that should only be given to worthy recipients, the text encourages the yogi to generate himself as Samantabhadra and recite the prayer of Samantabhadra so that everyone can hear it during the auspicious days, such as the time of solar and lunar eclipses, earth quakes and equinox. This is said to have a liberatory effect on the entire three realms. Thus, we see how the practices of the liberation through wearing highlight the social position of the master as the source of the amulets and their power, strengthening the ties of the yogis and their devotees through the practice of making and giving out the amulets. The prayer of Samantabhadra, on the other hand, reaches beyond the relationships of masters and devotees to all the people present in the prayers, and ultimately to all sentient beings. In this way, it crystallizes the compassionate vision of Samantabhadra ... in the vision of universal liberation of the three realms.[173]

11

The Three Tibetan Commentaries

Jigmé Lingpa's *Lancet*

Jigmé Lingpa Rangjung Dorjé Kyentsé Öser[174] (1729/30–98) was born in the southern part of central Tibet in a family with strong ties to the Drukpa Kagyü lineage. His family's clan was the same as that of Longchenpa, to whom he always felt connected. At the age of six, Jigmé Lingpa joined Palri[175] Monastery, a neighboring monastery of Mindröl Ling. As he was not a recognized tulku, he received no special treatment there, and his autobiography says that he received no formal course of education under the guidance of a teacher but studied extensively on his own, suggesting that he was mostly an autodidact.

His account of the teachings he received is a representative selection from the Nyingma corpus at the beginning of the eighteenth century, as transmitted to him through his affiliation with the lineages of Mindröl Ling and also Dorjé Tra (the Northern Treasures). There is no evidence of his having studied the classical scholastic topics, such as vinaya, *abhidharma*, and Madhyamaka, while he lists an abundance of tantras and ritual texts for tantric practice. At the age of thirteen, Jigmé Lingpa met Tugchog Dorjé,[176] whom he took as his primary teacher.

From the age of twenty-five he pursued a course of strict meditation practice, and at twenty-eight he entered two consecutive retreats spanning more than five years, one at his monastery and one at the Nyang caves at Samyé Chimphu[177] (one of Longchenpa's retreat places). During these retreats, the works of Tselé Natsog

Rangdröl[178] (born 1608), Longchenpa, and Trengpo Terchen Sherab Öser[179] (1518–84) had a strong influence on Jigmé Lingpa's writing, especially his composition of the *Heart Essence of the Great Expanse* (*Longchen Nyingtig*), and he also had visions of the first two masters, as well as of Tangdong Gyalpo. In 1764, Jigmé Lingpa made the *Heart Essence of the Great Expanse* public, giving the first transmission of the cycle in Tseringjong Padma Ösal Tegchog Ling,[180] a small monastery he had founded in 1762, which remained his permanent residence until his death. Besides the *Heart Essence of the Great Expanse*, Jigmé Lingpa's major works include the *Treasury of Precious Qualities* and *Wisdom Guru.*[181]

Since Jigmé Lingpa's commentary does not mention many of the passages of *The Aspiration Prayer* that contain variant readings in the different versions, it is hard to tell which one he uses.[182] His commentary (six pages) is by far the shortest of the three and only explains selected passages of the prayer. It begins by saying that the two paths to buddhahood and saṃsāra, with their two fruitions of buddhas and sentient beings, arise from the ground, which is in itself indeterminate (lines 1–7). In terms of the ground as alpha-purity, its recognition is buddhahood, while unawareness of it characterizes a sentient being (8–14). This ground lacks any causes and conditions. It is free from any duality of an inner apprehender and outer apprehended objects. However, awareness is not an utterly blank emptiness: while being empty, its lucidity is unceasing, which is the cause for the arising of purified phenomena (15–25). The single ground matures as five wisdoms, one hundred kinds of deities, and countless emanations (26–45). Saṃsāric delusion evolves from basic unawareness, connate unawareness, and imaginative unawareness as the twelve links of dependent origination, which blossom into the afflictions and karma. The essential point of delusion and freedom is to cut through the nonrecognition of awareness and let it sustain its own steady flow (46–71). As for the five afflictions and the five corresponding wisdoms, Jigmé Lingpa advises us not to pursue, analyze, stop, deny, or affirm the afflictions, but to let them rest within the very place of their arising, without contrivance. If this "ordinary mind" is allowed to sustain itself—through mindfulness within its own inexpressible state of self-settled freshness—the causes of saṃsāra become exhausted and the fruition is realized. In brief, there is really nothing but the juncture of saṃsāra and nirvāṇa either recognizing or not recognizing its own face (72–140). The text offers no comments on the concluding part of *The Aspiration Prayer* (141–55).

The Fifteenth Karmapa's *Ketaka*

The Fifteenth Karmapa, Kakyab Dorjé[183] (1870/71–1921/22), was born in Tsang in Central Tibet and spent most of his life in meditation retreats at his main seat, Tsurphu Monastery. He also established a new monastic college there and had a number of works by important masters reprinted, such as Jamgön Kongtrul's *Treasury of Precious Treasures*. In addition, he was renowned for recognizing some one thousand tulkus, foremost among them the Eleventh Tai Situpa, Pema Wangchug Gyalpo[184] (1866–1952), and the Second Jamgön Kongtrul, Kyentsé Öser[185] (1904–53), who was one of the Karmapa's three sons. His two main teachers were Jamgön Kongtrul Lodrö Tayé[186] (1813–99) and Jamyang Kyentsé Wangpo.

The Fifteenth Karmapa was the only Karmapa who became a treasure revealer, and his revelations include both earth and mind treasures. Revealers of earth treasures typically have to travel to specific locations to unearth their treasures. But in the case of the Fifteenth Karmapa, the guardians to whom certain treasures had been entrusted approached him and offered their treasures freely, sometimes even placing them upon the table in his room. By the end of his life, the Karmapa had received about forty boxes of such earth treasures.

Kakyab Dorjé also had a strong connection with the Chogling Tersar[187] lineage of treasures through Lama Samten Gyatso[188] (1881–1945/46), a grandson of the treasure revealer Chogyur Lingpa[189] (1829–70), from whom he received the empowerments of this treasure collection. The Karmapa valued the Chogling Tersar so highly that he became one of its major lineage holders. At Lama Samten's request, he also composed liturgies and empowerment texts to supplement and complete those in the existing treasures. In return, Lama Samten received a number of empowerments from the Karmapa, whom he considered one of his main teachers.

It is generally held that treasure revealers need to take a consort in order to unlock their treasures and to prevent illness and premature death. However, since all Karmapas before (and after) the fifteenth were monks, taking a consort was considered highly inappropriate by both the Karmapa himself and his community. Nevertheless, when the Karmapa fell seriously ill, many great masters advised him to take a consort to avoid his untimely passing. He finally agreed, and his first consort was the daughter of a noble family from central Tibet, who was instrumental in the revealing of his treasures. Toward the end of his life, the Karmapa became gravely ill again. This event had been prophesied by Padmasambhava, in a treasure which indicated that the Karmapa would have to find a very special consort—a ḍākinī in human form—who alone would be able to prolong his life. Based on the descriptions in that treasure and his own dreams, the Karmapa was able to meet a young woman named Urgyen Tsomo, who was an emanation of Padmasambhava's consort, Yeshé Tsogyal. She became very renowned as "the Great Ḍākinī of Tsurphu," spending most of her life in hermitages above Tsurphu and attaining a high level of realization. Her current reincarnation is Khandro Tsering Paldrön Rinpoche[190] (born 1967), a daughter of the Eleventh Minling Trichen, Künsang Wangyal[191] (1930/31–2008).

The Fifteenth Karmapa's main disciples were the Eleventh Tai Situpa, the Second Jamgön Kongtrul, the Eleventh Gyaltsab Rinpoche, Tragpa Gyatso[192] (1902–52), Lama Samten Gyatso, and the Great Ḍākinī.[193]

The Fifteenth Karmapa's commentary on *The Aspiration Prayer* is the second-longest (twenty-nine pages). It is the only commentary that not only explains *The Aspiration Prayer* itself but also cites and comments on its introductory and concluding lines, as they are found in the nineteenth chapter of the *Tantra of Samantabhadra's Unobstructed Awakened Mind.* Interestingly, *Ketaka*'s comments on the actual prayer are based on a version that primarily follows TV2, but also contains many elements of CV and RTV, as well as some of TV1. The ground in which both saṃsāra and nirvāṇa are pure is explained through its essence (lines 1–7) and through linking the ground with the fruition (8–14). The manner in which saṃsāra and nirvāṇa diverge is discussed by way of wisdom's full unfolding based on Samantabhadra's mode of freedom (15–25), the array of the self-appearances of the kāyas and wisdoms of natural perfection (26–39), and the manner in which emanations unfold as appearances for others (40–45). By contrast, sentient beings' mode of delusion consists of the manner in which connate and imaginative unawareness evolve from the unawareness that has the same identity as the cause (46–60) and the details of this process (61–71). The path for this unawareness to become free in itself is taught through introducing the delusive five afflictions as actually being the five corresponding wisdoms (72–130). This is followed by a summary of the topic at hand (131–40). Finally, the text speaks about the performances and the benefits of both the timeless, continuous yoga of supreme persons free from reference points (141–46) and the yoga of persons with reference points that is practiced at certain times (147–55).[194]

Tsültrim Sangpo's *Lamp*

Tsültrim Sangpo (1884–1957?)[195] was a student of the treasure revealer Sogyal Lerab Lingpa[196] (1856–1926), the Third Dodrupchen Jigmé Tenpé Nyima[197] (1865–1926), and Anyé Khenpo Damchö Öser[198] (nineteenth century) of Dodrupchen Monastery. His main residence was Shugjung[199] Monastery, which is located about twenty miles from Dodrupchen Monastery and belongs to the Northern Treasures tradition. He also spent time at Khordong[200] Monastery, which was led by his younger brother, Gyurmé Dorjé.[201] Tsültrim Sangpo usually remained in meditation posture, hardly ever moving. When he was not in meditation, he often worked as a scribe for Dodrupchen Jigmé Tenpé Nyima, copying many texts for the latter's personal library and receiving teachings. He is reported to have passed away peacefully in meditation posture and remained in a meditative state for six weeks thereafter, without any decay of the body.

Tsültrim Sangpo was a monk as well as an accomplished tantric practitioner. His collected writings in sixteen volumes include commentaries on Ngari Paṇchen's *Ascertainment of the Three Vows*, Padmasambhava's *Garland of Views*, and Jigmé Lingpa's *Treasury of Precious Qualities*; several texts on the Great Perfection, including an instruction manual for the ṭreasure cycle *Samantabhadra's Unobstructed Awakened Mind*; and many works related to the tantras of the new translations. His primary students were Khordong Tertrul Chime Rigdzin[202] (1922–2002), Orgyen Tendzin, known as Tulku Gyenlo[203] (died 1972), and Shichen Ontrul Rinpoche.[204]

Tsültrim Sangpo's *Lamp* (fifty-four pages)[205] uses a version of *The Aspiration Prayer* that clearly corresponds in most cases to TV2, though there are also a few distinct elements of CV. The text begins with a brief presentation of the ground, path, and fruition (1–7). The detailed explanation of the ground opens with an explanation of its basic nature (8–14), which includes a detailed discussion of six mistaken assertions versus the correct one concerning the nature of the ground of the Great Perfection. This is followed by Samantabhadra's mode of freedom through taking the recognition of this ground as the path, and then promoting the welfare of others (15–45). The explanation of the ground concludes with the manner in which sentient beings are deluded in saṃsāra due to not recognizing the ground (46–71). The presentation of the path consists of delusion's coming to its end once the ground has been revealed, discussed in terms of the manner in which the five afflictions are free as the five corresponding wisdoms (72–130). Finally, the fruition is the revelation of all qualities free from stains, just as they are (131–40). The commentary concludes with the benefits of reading and hearing this aspiration prayer as it is intended by yogic practitioners who have attained stability in the path of the Great Perfection (141–46) and an instruction on the crucial points in time for reciting it (147–55).[206]

Similar to Longchenpa's Dzogchen texts, the literary style of *Ketaka* as well as *Lamp* can be considered sprawling, with long sentences—sometimes running a whole Tibetan page or more, and containing many appositions and secondary clauses—that seem to flow like a big meandering river. This makes such texts challenging to read, as it is often hard to keep in mind how a sentence or passage began when one has reached its end. However, this approach seems to be characteristic of Dzogchen writings, and perhaps a crucial element, as it creates a contemplative, spacious, sometimes even dreamlike atmosphere that transcends mere records of ordinary content or other kinds of literature. These texts point at our basic awareness from many different angles, repeating the same angles several times, so one could say that their style literally "talks us into rigpa." Unlike more mundane writings with a rambling style, these texts do not lull us into sleep but into basic awareness, its recognition, the sustaining of that recognition, and even glimpses of awakening (thus being "a lullaby of rigpa" in the most excellent sense). Though there are grammatical, syntactical, and stylistic limitations to rendering this approach using modern-day English, I have attempted to retain as much of it as possible in these translations. This may make them more difficult to read, sometimes seeming to involve redundancy, and requiring more attention than the average light bedtime reading (a daring suggestion in the age of rampant attention deficit disorder and 140-character limits). However, since it is such a crucial stylistic and pedagogical element of contemplative Dzogchen texts, I have tried to convey as much as possible of the spacious meditative ambience, transcending mere words, that is evoked when these texts are read in Tibetan.[207]

Part III

Translations

The Aspiration Prayer of Samantabhadra as the Nineteenth Chapter of the *Tantra of Samantabhadra's Unobstructed Awakened Mind*

CITTA A[208]

Then the primal buddha, Samantabhadra, spoke this special aspiration prayer of saṃsāric sentient beings' powerlessness not to awaken.

HO!
All that appears and is possible, saṃsāra as well as nirvāṇa,
has a single ground, yet two paths and two results—
the miraculous displays of awareness and unawareness.
Through the aspiration prayer of Samantabhadra,
may all awaken in a fully perfect manner
in the palace of the dharmadhātu.

The ground of all is unconditioned—
the self-arising, inexpressible, vast spaciousness
without the names of the dyad of saṃsāra and nirvāṇa.
If there is awareness of just this, it is buddhahood;
unaware, sentient beings wander in saṃsāra.
May all[209] sentient beings of the three realms
be aware of the actuality of the inexpressible ground.

I, Samantabhadra,
am aware that this very actuality of the ground
without causes and conditions is self-arising from[210] the ground,
unaffected by the flaws of outside and inside, or superimposition and denial,

and free from the stains of the darkness of mindlessness.[211]
Therefore, self-appearances are untainted by any flaws.

Within self-awareness's resting in its seat,
there is no fear or anxiety, even if the threefold existence is destroyed,
nor is there attachment to the five sense pleasures.
In nonconceptual, self-arising cognizance,
neither solid forms nor colors[212] exist.

The unceasing lucidity dimension of awareness
is of a single essence and yet has five wisdoms.
The five primal buddha families spring forth
from the maturation of these five wisdoms.
Through wisdom's fully unfolding from[213] that,
the forty-two buddhas originate.
Through the dawning of the dynamic energy of the five wisdoms,
the sixty blood-drinkers come to life.
Therefore, ground awareness was never deluded.
Since I am the primal buddha,
through making my[214] aspiration prayer,
may the sentient beings who cycle through the three realms
recognize the face of self-arising awareness
and fully unfold great wisdom.

My emanations are an uninterrupted flow,
unfolding as inconceivable billions
and displaying as a vast array of suitable guidance.
Through my compassionate aspiration prayer,
may all sentient beings who cycle through the three realms
leave the abodes[215] of the six families behind.

At first,[216] since deluded sentient beings
do not dawn as awareness in the ground,
they are absolutely mindless and oblivious.
Exactly that is unawareness, the cause of delusion.
From[217] being dazedly unconscious within that,
a fearful and anxious vague cognizance stirs.

From that, self and others as well as clinging to enemies arise.
Through the gradual blossoming of latent tendencies,
saṃsāra unfolds, taking its natural course.
By virtue of that,[218] the five poisons of the afflictions flourish
and the karmas of these five poisons become an incessant flow.
Thus, the ground of sentient beings' delusion
is mindless unawareness.
Hence, through this aspiration prayer of myself, the buddha,
may all know awareness itself.[219]

Connate unawareness
is mindless, oblivious[220] cognizance.
Imaginative unawareness
is the clinging to the duality of self and others.
This twofold connate and imaginative unawareness
is the ground of delusion of all sentient beings.
Through this aspiration prayer of myself, the buddha,
may all[221] saṃsāric sentient beings'
darkness of dull mindlessness be dispelled,
their cognizance of clinging to duality be translucent,
and awareness recognize its own face.

The mind of dualistic clinging is doubt—
due to the arising of subtle fixation,
dense latent tendencies gradually unfold.
Be it food, wealth, clothing, places, companions,
the five sense pleasures, or beloved relatives,
we are tormented by the desire attached to what is attractive.
These are mundane delusions—
the karmas of apprehender and apprehended are never exhausted.
When the results of clinging ripen,
we are born as hungry ghosts[222] tortured by craving[223]—
how pitiful is our hunger and thirst!
Through this aspiration prayer of myself, the buddha,
may sentient beings with the clinging of desirous attachment
neither cast out the torment of desire[224]

nor welcome the clinging of desirous attachment[225] within,
but may awareness take its very own seat
through letting cognizance relax in its own state,
and may discriminating wisdom thus be attained.

A subtle mind of fear stirs
around the appearance of outer objects,
and the unfolding of hatred's latent tendencies
leads to fixating on enemies and rough[226] beating and killing.
When the results of hatred ripen,
oh, how we suffer by being boiled and burned in hell!
Through this aspiration prayer of myself, the buddha,
when fierce hatred flares up
in all[227] sentient beings who migrate in six ways,
may it settle in its own state[228] without adopting or rejecting,
awareness take its very own seat,
and lucid wisdom thus be attained.

Due to[229] our own mind having become haughty,
our mind vies with others and our mentality dismisses them.
Through the arising of a mind of intense[230] pride,
we experience[231] the suffering of our fighting and struggling
with others.
When the results of those actions ripen,
we are born as gods experiencing transition and downfall.
Through this aspiration prayer of myself, the buddha,
when sentient beings give rise to a haughty mind,
may their cognizance relax in its own state,
awareness take its very own seat,
and the wisdom of equality thus be attained.[232]

Through the latent tendencies of rampant dualistic clinging,
the competitive mind of fighting and struggling blossoms
from the pain of praising ourselves and disparaging others.
Having thus been born in the asura realm of killing and slashing,
we take a deep plunge into the hell realms.

Through this aspiration prayer of myself, the buddha,
when a competitive mind, fighting, and struggling arise,[233]
may enmity not be entertained but relax in its own place,
cognizance take its very own seat,
and the wisdom of unobstructed enlightened activity[234] thus be.

Through[235] mindlessness, indifference, distraction,[236]
obtuseness, dullness, forgetfulness,
unconsciousness, laziness, and nescience,
we roam as animals, without shelter as a result.
Through this aspiration prayer of myself, the buddha,
may the radiance of lucid mindfulness shine
in the darkness of our nescience and dullness,
and may nonconceptual wisdom thus[237] be attained.

All[238] sentient beings of the three realms
are equal to myself, the buddha, the ground of all,
but it has become the ground of mindless delusion.
Right now, they engage in meaningless activities,
with the sixfold karmas being like the delusions in a dream.
I, however, am the original buddha.
In order to guide the six realms through emanations,
through this aspiration prayer of Samantabhadra,
may all sentient beings without exception
become awakened in the dharmadhātu.

A HO![239]

From now on, through yogic practitioners with great power
making this aspiration prayer of great power
within the state of[240] self-luminous awareness free of delusion,
all sentient beings who hear this
will fully awaken within three lives.

During the times of solar or lunar eclipses,
at the occurrence of loud noises or earthquakes,
at the solstices, or at the turn of the year,

if we let ourselves arise as Samantabhadra
and recite this within the hearing of all,
all sentient beings of the three realms,[241]
through the aspiration prayer of such yogic practitioners,
will gradually become free from suffering
and then swiftly[242] attain buddhahood.[243]

In the Tantra That Teaches the Great Perfection as Samantabhadra's Unobstructed Awakened Mind, *this is the nineteenth chapter,*[244] *which teaches that through making this aspiration prayer of great power, sentient beings*[245] *are powerless not to awaken.*

The Common Version of *The Aspiration Prayer of Samantabhadra*

HO!

All that appears and is possible, saṃsāra as well as nirvāṇa,
has a single ground, yet two paths and two results—
the miraculous displays of awareness and unawareness.
Through the aspiration prayer of Samantabhadra,
may all awaken in a fully perfect manner
in the palace of the dharmadhātu.

The ground of all is unconditioned—
the self-arising, inexpressible, vast spaciousness
without the names of the dyad of saṃsāra and nirvāṇa.
If there is awareness of just this, it is buddhahood;
unaware, sentient beings wander in saṃsāra.
May all sentient beings of the three realms
be aware of the actuality of the inexpressible ground.

I, Samantabhadra,
am aware that this very actuality of the ground,
without causes and conditions, is self-arising within the ground,
unaffected by the flaws of outside and inside, or superimposition and denial,
and untainted by the obscurations of the darkness of mindlessness.
Therefore, self-appearances are untainted by any flaws.
Within self-awareness's resting in its seat,
there is no fear or anxiety, even if the threefold existence is destroyed,
nor is there attachment to the five sense pleasures.

In nonconceptual, self-arising cognizance,
neither solid forms nor the five poisons exist.

The unceasing lucidity dimension of awareness
is of a single essence and yet has five wisdoms.
The five primal buddha families spring forth
from the maturation of these five wisdoms.
Through wisdom's fully unfolding from that,
the forty-two buddhas originate.
Through the dawning of the dynamic energy of the five wisdoms,
the sixty blood-drinkers come to life.
Therefore, ground awareness was never deluded.
Since I am the primal buddha,
through making my aspiration prayer,
may the sentient beings who cycle through the three realms
recognize the face of self-arising awareness
and fully unfold great wisdom.

My emanations are an uninterrupted flow,
unfolding as inconceivable billions
and displaying as a vast array of suitable guidance.
Through my compassionate aspiration prayer,
may all sentient beings who cycle through the three realms
leave the abodes of the six families behind.

At first, since deluded sentient beings
do not dawn as awareness in the ground,
they are absolutely mindless and oblivious.
Exactly that is unawareness, the cause of delusion.
From being dazedly unconscious within that,
a fearful and anxious vague cognizance stirs.
From that, self and others as well as clinging to enemies arise.
Through the gradual blossoming of latent tendencies,
saṃsāra unfolds, taking its natural course.
By virtue of that, the five poisons of the afflictions flourish
and the karmas of these five poisons become an incessant flow.

Thus, the ground of sentient beings' delusion
is mindless unawareness.
Hence, through this aspiration prayer of myself, the buddha,
may all[246] know awareness itself.

Connate unawareness
is mindless, distracted cognizance.
Imaginative unawareness
is the clinging to the duality of self and others.
This twofold connate and imaginative unawareness
is the ground of delusion of all sentient beings.
Through this aspiration prayer of myself, the buddha,
may all saṃsāric sentient beings'
darkness of dull mindlessness be dispelled,
their cognizance of clinging to duality be translucent,
and awareness recognize its own face.

The mind of dualistic clinging is doubt—
due to the arising of subtle fixation,
dense latent tendencies gradually unfold.
Be it food, wealth, clothing, places, companions,
the five sense pleasures, or beloved relatives,
we are tormented by the desire attached to what is attractive.
These are mundane delusions—
the karmas of apprehender and apprehended are never exhausted.
When the results of clinging ripen,
we are born as hungry ghosts tortured by craving—
how pitiful is our hunger and thirst!
Through this aspiration prayer of myself, the buddha,
may sentient beings with the clinging of desirous attachment
neither cast out the torment of desire
nor welcome the clinging of desirous attachment within,
but may awareness take its very own seat
through letting cognizance relax in its own state,
and may discriminating wisdom thus be attained.

A subtle mind of fear stirs
around the appearance of outer objects,
and the unfolding of hatred's latent tendencies
leads to fixating on enemies and powerful beating and killing.
When the results of hatred ripen,
oh, how we suffer by being boiled and burned in hell!
Through this aspiration prayer of myself, the buddha,
when fierce hatred flares up
in all sentient beings who migrate in six ways,
may it relax in its own state without adopting or rejecting,
awareness take its very own seat,
and lucid wisdom thus be attained.

With our own mind having become haughty,
our mind vies with others and our mentality dismisses them.
Through the arising of a mind of intense pride,
we experience the suffering of our fighting and struggling with others.
When the results of those actions ripen,
we are born as gods experiencing transition and downfall.
Through this aspiration prayer of myself, the buddha,
when sentient beings give rise to a haughty mind,
may their cognizance relax in its own state,
awareness take its very own seat,
and the actuality of equality thus be realized.

Through the latent tendencies of rampant dualistic clinging,
the competitive mind of fighting and struggling blossoms
from the pain of praising ourselves and disparaging others.
Having thus been born in the asura realm of killing and slashing,
we take a deep plunge into the hell realms.
Through this aspiration prayer of myself, the buddha,
for those in whom a competitive mind, fighting, and struggling arises,
may enmity not be entertained but relax in its own place,
cognizance take its very own seat,
and the wisdom of unobstructed enlightened activity thus be.

By virtue of mindlessness, indifference, and distraction,
there are obtuseness, dullness, forgetfulness,
unconsciousness, laziness, and nescience.
Through that, we roam as animals, without shelter as a result.
Through this aspiration prayer of myself, the buddha,
may the radiance of lucid mindfulness shine
in the darkness of our nescience and dullness
and may nonconceptual wisdom thus be attained.

All sentient beings of the three realms
are equal to myself, the buddha, the ground of all,
but it has become the ground of mindless delusion.
Right now, they engage in meaningless activities,
with the sixfold karmas being like the delusions in a dream.
I, however, am the original buddha.
In order to guide the six realms with emanations,
through this aspiration prayer of Samantabhadra,
may all sentient beings without exception
become awakened in the dharmadhātu.

A HO!

From now on, through yogic practitioners with great power
making this aspiration prayer of great power
from within self-luminous awareness free of delusion,
all sentient beings who hear this
will fully awaken within three lives.

During the times of solar or lunar eclipses,
at the occurrence of loud noises or earthquakes,
at the solstices, or at the turn of the year,
if we let ourselves arise as Samantabhadra
and recite this within the hearing of all,
through the aspiration prayer of such yogic practitioners
for all sentient beings of the three realms,
they will gradually become free from suffering
and then attain buddhahood in the end.

This is the ninth[247] *chapter excerpted from the* Tantra That Teaches the Great Perfection as Samantabhadra's Unobstructed Awakened Mind, *which teaches that through making this powerful aspiration prayer, all sentient beings are powerless not to awaken.*

The Aspiration Prayer of Samantabhadra for Recitation

HO!

Everything in saṃsāra and nirvāṇa that can possibly appear
has a single ground, two paths, and two results—
the miraculous displays of awareness and unawareness.
Through the aspiration prayer of Samantabhadra,
may all awaken in a fully perfect manner
in the palace of the dharmadhātu.

The ground of all is unconditioned—
the self-arising, inexpressible, vast spaciousness
without the names "saṃsāra" or "nirvāṇa."
The awareness of just this is buddhahood;
unaware, sentient beings wander in saṃsāra.
May all beings of the three realms
be aware of the reality of the inexpressible ground.

I, Samantabhadra,
am aware that this very reality of the ground
without causes and conditions, is self-arising within the
ground,
unaffected by the flaws of outer and inner, or superimposition
and denial,
and untainted by the stains of the darkness of mindlessness.
Therefore, self-appearances are not blemished by any flaws.
Within self-awareness resting in its seat,
there is no fear, even if the threefold existence is destroyed,
nor is there attachment to the five sense pleasures.

In nonconceptual self-arising mind,
neither solid forms nor the five poisons exist.

The unceasing dimension of awareness's lucidity
is of a single essence and yet displays as five wisdoms.
The five original buddha families spring forth
from the maturation of these five wisdoms.
Through wisdom's fully unfolding from that,
the forty-two buddhas originate.
Through the dawning of the dynamic energy of the five wisdoms,
the sixty blood-drinkers come to life.
Therefore, ground awareness was never deluded.
Since I am the original buddha,
through my aspiration prayer,
may all sentient beings cycling through the three realms
recognize the face of self-arising awareness
and fully unfold great wisdom.

My emanations form an unceasing stream,
unfurling as inconceivable billions
and displaying as a vast array of suitable guidance.
Through my compassionate aspiration prayer,
may all sentient beings cycling through the three realms
leave the six kinds of existence behind.

At first, since deluded sentient beings
do not dawn as awareness in the ground,
they are absolutely mindless and oblivious.
Exactly that is unawareness, the cause of delusion.
From within that vacuous swoon,
a fearful vague cognizance stirs.
From that, self and others as well as enmity arise.
Through the gradual blossoming of latent tendencies,
saṃsāra unfolds, taking its natural course.
Due to that, the five poisons of the afflictions flourish
and their karmas become an incessant flow.

Thus, the ground of sentient beings' delusion
is mindless unawareness.
Hence, through this aspiration prayer of myself, the buddha,
may all recognize awareness itself.

Connate unawareness
is mindless, oblivious cognizance.
Imaginative unawareness
is the clinging to the duality of self and other.
This twofold connate and imaginative unawareness
is the ground of delusion of all sentient beings.
Through this aspiration prayer of myself, the buddha,
may all saṃsāric sentient beings'
darkness of dull mindlessness be dispelled,
may their mind of dualistic clinging be translucent,
and may awareness recognize its own face.

The mind of dualistic clinging is doubt—
from the arising of subtle fixation,
dense latent tendencies gradually unfold.
Be it food, wealth, clothing, places, companions,
the five sense pleasures, or beloved relatives,
we are tormented by our attachment to what seems attractive.
These are mundane delusions—
the karmas of perceiver and perceived are never exhausted.
When the results of clinging ripen,
we are born as hungry ghosts tortured by craving—
how pitiful is our hunger and thirst!
Through this aspiration prayer of myself, the buddha,
may sentient beings full of attachment and clinging
neither cast out the torment of desire
nor welcome the craving of attachment,
but may awareness take its very seat
through letting mind relax in its own state,
and may discriminating wisdom be attained.

A subtle mind of fear stirs
around the appearance of external objects.
Thus, the unfolding of hatred's latent tendencies
leads to powerful enmity, beating, and killing.
When the results of hatred ripen,
oh, how we suffer by being boiled and burned in hell!
Through this aspiration prayer of myself, the buddha,
when fierce hatred flares up
in all sentient beings of the six realms,
may it relax in its own state without adopting or rejecting,
may awareness take its own seat,
and may lucid wisdom be attained.

Our own mind being haughty,
it vies with others and dismisses them.
Through the arising of intense pride,
we experience the suffering of our fighting and struggling with others.
When the results of those actions ripen,
we are born as gods experiencing transition and downfall.
Through this aspiration prayer of myself, the buddha,
when sentient beings give rise to such haughtiness,
may they let their mind relax in its own state,
may awareness take its very own seat,
and may the wisdom of equality be realized.

Triggered by the latent tendencies of rampant dualistic clinging,
the competitive mind of fighting and struggling blossoms
from the pain of praising ourselves and disparaging others.
Being thus reborn in the asura realm of killing and slashing,
we take a deep plunge into the realms of hell.
Through this aspiration prayer of myself, the buddha,
when a competitive mind, fighting, and struggling arise,
may we not entertain enmity but let it relax in its own place,
may mind take its very own seat,
and may the wisdom of unimpeded enlightened activity be.

Mindlessness, indifference, distraction,
obtuseness, dullness, forgetfulness,
unconsciousness, laziness, and bewilderment
result in our roaming as animals without any shelter.
Through this aspiration prayer of myself, the buddha,
may the radiance of lucid mindfulness shine
in the darkness of our bewildered dullness,
and may nonconceptual wisdom be attained.

All sentient beings of the three realms
are equal to myself, the buddha, the ground of all,
but for them it has become the ground of mindless delusion.
Right now, they engage in meaningless activities,
with the six kinds of karma being like delusions in a dream.
I, however, am the primordial buddha.
In order to guide the six kinds of beings through emanations,
through this aspiration prayer of Samantabhadra,
may all sentient beings without exception
become awakened in the dharmadhātu.

A HO!

From now on, whenever mighty yogic practitioners
make this powerful aspiration prayer
within self-luminous awareness free of delusion,
all sentient beings who hear it
will fully awaken within three lives.

During solar or lunar eclipses,
when clamor or earthquakes occur,
at the solstices, or at the turn of the year,
if we let ourselves arise as Samantabhadra
and recite this prayer within the hearing of all,
through the aspiration of us yogic practitioners,
all sentient beings of the three realms
will gradually become free from suffering
and then swiftly attain buddhahood.

This is from the nineteenth chapter in the Tantra That Teaches the Great Perfection as Samantabhadra's Unobstructed Awakened Mind, *which teaches that through making this powerful aspiration prayer, all sentient beings cannot help but awaken.*

Clearing the Guide to The Aspiration Prayer of Samantabhadra *with the Lancet of a Ṭīkā*[248]

Jigmé Lingpa

{592} Once there is absolutely universal freedom of being separated from or attaining
the basic element of the heart of having gone to absolutely universal bliss,
the spaciousness of the three doors to absolutely universal freedom,
this is the very nature of Absolutely Universal Goodness.[249]

Though the first [six] lines of verse, "**all that appears and is possible, saṃsāra as well as nirvāṇa, has a single ground ... palace of the dharmadhātu**," are easy to understand, the meaning of "**a single ground yet two paths ...**" is as follows. [To speak of] "a single ground" is a very rough presentation: in the tantras of the Great Perfection, after the ground is taught in seven ways, the primordial ground of alpha-purity is asserted to be the flawless position. Here, however, the position of asserting the indeterminate ground of all as the ground is taken.[250] If the dynamic energy of superior insight arises within this indeterminate cognizance and it thus becomes aware of its own face, this is the path to buddhahood; but if it is unaware [of its own face], this is the path to saṃsāra. From[251] these two [paths], the **two results** of buddhas and sentient beings, respectively, arise. Through this approach, the others [among these six lines] become easy to understand.

As for the meaning of "**the ground of all is unconditioned** ...," in terms of accepting the primordial **ground** of alpha-purity as the flawless position, the term "**self-arising vast spaciousness**" means that once this cognizance free from thinking, expression, and mind is **aware of** its own face, it **is buddhahood**; and when it is **unaware,** it is a **sentient being.** Thus, since it is [also] the nature of **saṃsāra,** Samantabhadra aspires that [all] **sentient beings be aware of the actuality** [of this unconditioned ground].[252] {593}

The meaning of "**I, Samantabhadra, am aware that this very actuality** ..." is as follows. The essential basic nature does not originate from a certain **cause and** does not arise from certain **conditions.** When there is the **awareness** that **this actuality** of **the ground is self-arising,** there is no **superimposition** that it exists as any actuality [or referent] on the **outside and** no **denial** in the sense that it does not exist as an actuality on the **inside. Untainted by the** flaws and **stains of mindlessness** that resemble gloomy **darkness,** fresh **awareness** is free from expression and without deliberate fixation.

If **resting within** the natural state of this [awareness], since this **threefold** [saṃsāric] **existence** is [merely] imputed by a mind that involves apprehender and apprehended, **even if it is destroyed** at [the end of] the eons [when the universe is annihilated] by fire, water, or wind,[253] **there is no** dread or **fear. Nor is there attachment to sense pleasures,** because the sense consciousnesses, such as the eye [consciousness], are pure. Why? For, fright, attachment, aversion, and so on arise from the apprehending mind's blending with its apprehended object. Therefore, "**in nonconceptual, self-arising cognizance, neither solid forms nor colors exist.**" Nonconceptual cognizance refers to the great self-lucidity that is beyond mind. Hence, there is no appropriation of the five skandhas or the eight collections [of consciousness] in that [cognizance]. Though this is the case, such awareness is not an utterly blank emptiness. Rather, while being empty, its lucidity dimension is unceasing, which is the cause of the arising of purified phenomena.

Hence, "**the unceasing lucidity dimension of awareness** ..." [means that] the genuine essence of **fivefold wisdom** (what is supported) along with {594} the three seats' completeness[254] (the support) **matures** as the one hundred **families. "Therefore, ground awareness was never deluded."**

Since it thus was never deluded, it is called "**the primal buddha**" or "the changeless *vajrakāya*." The eleven lines [beginning with "Since I am the primal buddha"] of the aspiration prayer made by this [buddha] are easy to understand.

"**At first, since deluded sentient beings**[255] ..." As for the meaning of "**ground**" and so on, in general, *ground* can have five meanings. However, [what it means] here is as follows. In the deep sleep of the fetters of [saṃsāric] existence or the neutral [state of a] mindless mind, **since** the glow or the lucidity dimension of **awareness does not dawn**, [there occurs a state of] **absolutely** not thinking (similar to the consciousnesses of the [sense] gates) as well as being **mindless and oblivious** (similar to having fainted). Since **that is** the root of **unawareness**, the mental consciousness rises **from** within that state. If the mode of saṃsāra is described in an easily understandable manner as the continuum of the twelve links of dependent origination, the **cognizance** of **clinging to** me and what is mine—which is **fearful and anxious** about the perishing of the objects that it apprehends as **self and others** and is [also] indifferent and **vague**—arises as anything whatsoever. By virtue of that, the **latent tendencies** of **clinging to enemies** and friends, attachment, hatred, and bias **blossom,**[256] and thereby **saṃsāra unfolds, taking its natural course.**[257] Thus, **the five poisons of the afflictions** (the desire of being attached to sense pleasures and friends, the hatred of feeling aversion toward enemies, the nescience of sleep and dullness, the pride of thinking, "This is me," and the envy of feeling aversion toward the riches of others) **flourish and become an incessant flow**. Since the continuum[258] of all that has arisen from the causes and conditions of [both] impaired **mindfulness** and [awareness's] own **unawareness** of its own face, [awareness's] **knowing its own** face is the nature of Samantabhadra. Hence, this is what is taught [here] through [using] the term "**aspiration prayer.**"

The meaning of "**connate unawareness is mindless, distracted cognizance** ..." is as follows. To slip into lacking alertness due to a presently existing mindfulness that boundlessly strays and becomes absent-minded is [called] "**connate unawareness.**" The subsequent examination, analysis, reflection, and scrutiny by thoughts is called "**imaginative unawareness.**" {595} If the face of **this twofold ground of delusion** is recognized, the **darkness of mindlessness is dispelled**, the appearances of **clinging to duality** subside, **and awareness recognizes its own face**. Therefore, just as hundreds of water drops come together under a bridge, the essential point of delusion and freedom is to cut through the root [of that nonrecognition]. Thus, it is simply within that state that awareness needs to [be allowed to] sustain its own steady flow. If it does not sustain [itself in that way], the mind of dualistic clinging links up with the objects on which it fixates, thinking, "Has what is over there arisen from me, or have I arisen from what is over there?"[259]

The manner of this [mind's linking up with its objects of fixation] is taught by [the lines] "**the mind of dualistic clinging is doubt** ..." Accordingly, the causes of cycling throughout the six classes [of sentient beings] consist of the conceptions **of apprehender and apprehended**, a **haughty mind**, a **competitive mind**, **pride**, **desire**, and **nescience**, as well as the minds and the fifty [-one] mental factors that are produced by them, whichever may arise. Since these are the causes of saṃsāra, do not pursue them, do not examine or analyze them, do not stop them with antidotes, and do not deny or affirm them, but let them rest directly within the place of their arising, and do not contrive the mind. This is called "ordinary mind."[260] If it is [allowed to] sustain [itself] through the sentry of mindfulness within the natural state of freshness, self-resting, and self-settling, free from expression, the causes of cycling throughout **the six realms** become exhausted and the fruition is realized, to which the conventional expression "[all beings] **are equal to myself, the buddha, the ground of all**" is applied. Sentient beings are **deluded** through their impaired **mindfulness** and the perceiving mind is attached to perceived objects. Thereby, they continuously cycle throughout the six classes [of sentient beings], **like in a dream.**

Hence, to sum it up, it needs to be understood that there is really nothing but the juncture of saṃsāra and nirvāṇa either recognizing or not recognizing its own face.

Though the conventions of ground, path, and fruition are well known
in all dharmas, in order to ascertain the basic nature of the Great Perfection's ground,
which is the crossroads where saṃsāra and nirvāṇa part from each other,
while not searching for it in texts that show redundancy or incompleteness,

the Seventeen Tantras[261] and the realization of their wisdom intention, {596}
just as it is, as well as the skill in instructing others [in it],
are not [attained] through [texts] other than the *Precious Treasury of the Supreme Yāna*,
a work that is elucidated by thousandfold stainless light rays.[262]

In accordance with the intention of Dortra Tulku,[263]
and in order to benefit those of inferior intellect,
this was [composed] by the Yogin of the Sky of the Great Expanse,[264]
through differentiating this text's words and their meanings in their own place.

A Commentary on the Meaning of The Aspiration Prayer of Samantabhadra *Found in the* Great Tantra of the Unobstructed Awakened Mind *from the Northern Treasures, an Explanation Called* Ketaka[265] *Lucidly Arranged in the Form of a Few Glosses*

The Fifteenth Karmapa

{488} Namo Guru Śrī Padmākara Uttārabhyoḥ[266]

The buddha of the undeluded ground is Samantabhadra.
His self-arising compassion appears as the teacher of the path.
The innately perfect fruition without seeking is the dharmakāya.
I bow with certainty to self-awareness, the original protector.

Lord Jamgön Pema Karwang,[267] who directly demonstrates
the excellent and supremely profound definitive secret of the nine
expanses in its three classes,[268]
the unobstructed awakened mind of Samantabhadra,
is inseparable from the lotus lake of my mind's devotion.

When I take to the location of the ravine of nescience in this
[mind],
even the chatter uttered by the demon of wrong understanding
you aptly transform into the lion's roar of the king of yānas—
seeing the fox of ignorance faint, I break into tears.

However, though the muddiness in the well of wrong paths
increases,
if the depths of the ocean of the profound and vast tantric
scriptures of the supreme yāna {489}
are not touched by the light rays of the Keta [jewel] of stainless
enlightened speech,
the work to be done by the minds of the intelligent remains
limited.

Therefore, based on the tantric text that is the primal protector's
speech,
this aspiration prayer with its vajra lines of definitive meaning,
I shall teach in a few words some clarifications
that purify all obscuration by the darkness of wrong ideas.

Here, after the original protector, glorious Samantabhadra, was awakened as the primordially pure nature within the primal ground, he saw that through not recognizing their own [true] faces, adventitiously deluded sentient beings meaninglessly experience [all kinds of] saṃsāric sufferings that appear while not existing, though [these beings in fact] never depart from primal buddhahood and dharmatā, without good or bad. [Having seen that,] great nonreferential compassion arose [in him] and he pronounced the special Dharma of this marvelous aspiration prayer of the powerful dharmatā that represents the definitive meaning. {490}

Its explanation has three parts:

1. The initial composition [of this aspiration prayer]
2. Explaining the actual meaning of the text
3. Summary of the topic at hand

1. The initial composition [of this aspiration prayer]

Through the inexpressible dharmatā's own unceasing reverberation, [Samantabhadra] previously taught eighteen chapters of the *Tantra of Samantabhadra's Unobstructed Awakened Mind*.[269]

Then the buddha Samantabhadra—the timeless and permanent wheel of the continuum of great nondual wisdom, which does not appear as the sphere of dualistic appearances with a beginning and an end distinguished by the moments of the three times, the awareness connate with dharmatā, without beginning or end, which is indicated by the conventional term "**primal**" and consists of the definite inseparability of ground and fruition—having in mind the great purity and equality of the basic nature of **being powerless not to awaken, spoke this special aspiration prayer** of revealing the enlightened activity of the uncontrived Great Perfection, beyond the extremes of hopes, fears, and mental aspirations, in which the clinging to causes and results as purifying and being free, respectively, and the characteristics of factors to be relinquished and their remedies being opposing and conducive, respectively, are free in their very own places. For within the state of alpha-pure dharmatā, in which so-called **saṃsāric sentient beings** primordially never existed, all phenomena that consist of the containers and the contents of the three realms are self-appearing as the maṇḍalas of the innately present kāyas and wisdoms, which have the nature of bodhicitta.

2. [Explaining] the actual meaning of the text

{491} This has two parts:

1. Making the special aspiration prayer of the purity of saṃsāra and nirvāṇa within the ground
2. Clearly teaching its benefits, including the performances

2.1. Making the special aspiration prayer of the purity of saṃsāra and nirvāṇa within the ground

This has two parts:

1. Brief introduction to the essence
2. Detailed differentiation of the nature

2.1.1. Brief introduction to the essence

The meaning [of this] is as follows. "**HO**" is an abbreviation of "E MA HO," just as it is said in the commentary on the *Guhya[garbhatantra* by] *Sūryaprabhāsasiṃha[270] and *Eliminating the Darkness*[271] to have the meaning of being delighted and satisfied due to being amazed.[272]

All phenomena are primordially awakened as the maṇḍala of great equality and perfection. However, emptiness unfolds[273] such that **saṃsāra** with its three realms—**what appears** in the form of the containers and supports that consist of the five elements **and** what **is possible** as their contents that consist of the five skandhas or the four names[274]—arises from the perspective of the delusion of apprehender and apprehended. The great, lesser, and middling [kinds of] **nirvāṇa** are [presented] in dependence on the manner in which the latent tendencies of adopting this saṃsāra rise.

Within the essence of the **single** primordial ultimate **ground** of all,[275] which is the great all-encompassing dharmatā, **all** phenomena that are indicated by [saṃsāra and nirvāṇa] are not established as any objects that can be distinguished as good or bad. Still, in terms of the factor of encountering or not encountering the wisdom of alpha-pure awareness, the dominant condition for linking with buddhahood if realized and with saṃsāra if not realized, it is in accordance with the eight ways of the arising of the appearances of innate presence that the ultimate all-ground of linking dawns as the crossroads from which **two paths** diverge. If the basic nature seizes its very own place through differentiating its self-appearances as what they actually are, the indeterminate [all-ground of linking] comes to be self-obliterated and thus {492} [these self-appearances mature as] the result of buddhahood, in which the dynamic energy of the two wisdoms has been perfected, and which has the character of the inseparability of the three kāyas. If these self-appearances' own face is not recognized, they mature as the **result** of saṃsāra with [all] its suffering, due to the all-ground of diverse latent tendencies being associated with the demons of unawareness and apprehender and apprehended.

Though these **two** [results of buddhahood and saṃsāra] arise, they only represent the mere names through which the conditions or **the miraculous displays of awareness and unawareness** are labeled as the two temporary dependent phenomena that are saṃsāra and nirvāṇa. The great alpha-pure depth-lucidity, whose own essence is primordially unconditioned, lacks any flaws or qualities, anything to be accomplished or to be dispelled, and any change or transition.[276] Therefore, **through the aspiration prayer** that the three realms may be completely free, which I, **Samantabhadra**, make[277] in the manner of [this aspiration prayer's] being primordially[278] accomplished without seeking, **may all** superimpositions of clinging to the biases of saṃsāra and nirvāṇa **awaken in a fully perfect**, self-arising, and innately present **manner in the palace of the** actual **dharmadhātu**—great, unbiased, all-encompassing equality—as all the qualities of the kāyas and wisdoms that are [the dharmadhātu's] own dynamic energy.

2.1.2. Detailed differentiation of the nature

This has two parts:

1. Brief introduction to linking the ground with the fruition
2. Detailed explanation of the way in which saṃsāra and nirvāṇa diverge

2.1.2.1. Brief introduction to linking the ground with the fruition

Buddhahood does not arise through realizing "the primordial ultimate ground of all" and saṃsāra does not arise through not realizing it. Rather, before being differentiated into either saṃsāra or nirvāṇa, the dharmadhātu, free from anything conceivable that is expressible, is empty and space-providing, as well as lucid and unimpeded. Though its essence is alpha-pure, its nature consists of the unimpeded gateways of innate presence. Though its compassionate responsiveness—the wisdom of awareness—{493} is unobscured, it does not arise as discernment. Therefore, **the ground**[279] **of all** of saṃsāra and nirvāṇa's own essence, which abides as the very heart of omniscience that is inner luminosity, **is** abiding as being **unconditioned** in terms of arising and perishing. Hence, though it is not suitable as the causes and conditions of saṃsāra or nirvāṇa, it is suitable as the ground of the differentiation of saṃsāra and nirvāṇa, in dependence on whether what is to be purified—the adventitious obscurations—exists or does not exist [within the ground]. Since it is primordially and innately **self-arising**, not confined in any way, and not biased in any way at all, it is **vast spaciousness**. Since it is not an object to which any terms or thoughts could apply, it is the **inexpressible** fundamental state of dharmatā. Since this way of its abiding lacks any points of going astray that consist of either flaws or qualities, it is **without** even **the** mere **names of the dyad of saṃsāra and nirvāṇa**.

If there is awareness of just this dharmatā, through the obscurations of not being aware of dharmatā's own face coming to an end, **it is** the **buddhahood** of its own qualities' having become revealed[280] because [omniscient] knowledge's own dynamic energy has become perfected. **Unaware** of [dharmatā's] own face though never separated from the dharmatā of omniscience, similar to a prince wandering among common people due to his being uncertain about his own pedigree, all **sentient beings**, who are deceived by their deluded thoughts of apprehender and apprehended, **wander** around **in** the [desolate] plain of the sufferings of **saṃsāra**, which do not [really] exist and yet appear.[281] Thus, the flourishing of the latent tendencies of the samādhis that are associated with [only] the ālaya[-consciousness] and the afflicted mind represents the formless [realm], the experiences of the dhyānas that are associated with the consciousnesses of the five [sense] gates and the afflicted mind constitute the form [realm], and {494} the experiences that are associated with [both] the afflictions of the desire [realm] that surge up as the manifest conceptual mental consciousness and the afflicted mind make up the desire **realm**.

May all beings who possess the latent and manifest minds and mental factors **of** the eight collections [of consciousness] that cycle through **the three** [realms] **be aware of the actuality of the inexpressible**, primordially pure **ground**—the reality of dharmatā—through the eye of wisdom, which is unobscured by the imagination that consists of the cognizance of dualistic clinging.

2.1.2.2. Detailed explanation of the way in which saṃsāra and nirvāṇa diverge

This has two parts:

1. The aspiration prayer for wisdom to fully unfold that is based on Samantabhadra's mode of freedom
2. The aspiration prayer for the pit of saṃsāra to be emptied [from its depths][282] that is based on the mode of delusion of unaware sentient beings

2.1.2.2.1. The aspiration prayer for wisdom to fully unfold that is based on Samantabhadra's mode of freedom

This has two parts:

1. The aspiration prayer in terms of the manner in which awakening is found as self-appearances
2. The aspiration prayer in terms of the manner in which emanations unfold as other-appearances

2.1.2.2.1.1. The aspiration prayer in terms of the manner in which awakening is found as self-appearances

This has two parts:

1. [The aspiration prayer in terms of] the manner of truly becoming a buddha in the form of being endowed with the six distinctive features of alpha-purity
2. The aspiration prayer in terms of the manner of fully and perfectly becoming a buddha through the array of the self-appearances of the kāyas and wisdoms of innate presence

2.1.2.2.1.1.1. [The aspiration prayer in terms of] the manner of truly becoming a buddha in the form of being endowed with the six distinctive features of alpha-purity[283]

(1) Ground Samantabhadra—the primordially completely pure nature—refers to all experiential objects' being perfect as the wheel of the kāyas and wisdoms, which are [the ground's] own dynamic energy. Through the pure vision of the wisdom of knowing this nature, without being contingent on any conditions of exerting effort, path Samantabhadra comes to be the single panacea that cuts [through every delusion]. Through that, the level of self-arising qualities is obtained in a manifest way, and thus the fruitional buddha **Samantabhadra**—the fully perfect buddhahood before [anything in] the entirety of saṃsāra and nirvāṇa [could possibly have arisen]—{495} has the character of pervading all of [saṃsāric] existence and peace.

(2) Therefore, apart from [the mere fact that] this original victor—"**I**"—may be labeled in the form of the merely symbolic, conventional term "I," great primordially free alpha-purity, as the result that does not arise from any **causes and conditions** of exerting effort, is superior to **this very actuality of the ground**—[the door to] liberation that consists of causes' being **without** any signs[284]—as follows.

(3) **From** within **the** ultimate all-**ground** of linking, which appears as the [ground's] own unceasing and unobstructed dynamic energy of the six modes of appearing and the two gateways [that dawn] as the ground manifestations within the sphere of secret, precious innate presence, it is through the pith instructions that do not originate from the scriptures that the entirety of the dynamic energy of the wisdom of **self-arising awareness** is differentiated as [the ground's] self-appearances.[285] Thereby, indeterminate connate unawareness becomes without a base and thus there are no objects of the [false] imagination of apprehending **outside and inside** as being two. Therefore, [the wisdom of self-arising awareness] dwells within the essence that is **unaffected by the flaws of superimposition and**

denial in terms of existence, nonexistence, being, nonbeing, permanence, extinction, and so on—[the door to] liberation that consists of emptiness.

(4) However, unlike during the state of the one-pointed abiding of the all-ground of neutral obscurations that are present as dormant latent tendencies, **untainted by the stains of the darkness of mindless** nescience, the buddhahood that does not arise from mind is the revelation of inner luminosity—the omniscient wisdom that is unceasingly luminous. **Therefore**, since the **self-appearances** [of the ground] are free right upon their being differentiated [as such self-appearances], they **are** primordially **untainted** or have never been tainted **by any flaws** that obscure them in an adventitious fashion. {496}

(5) [Samantabhadra's freedom] does not involve dependence on anything extraneous, that is, conditional thoughts in terms of apprehender and apprehended.

(6) Thus, **within** the **resting** (or through the resting) **of self-awareness**—the dharmakāya—**in its** [own] fresh way of being without departing from its very own domain, **there is no** shifting of mind into **fear or anxiety, even if the** [entirety of saṃsāra's] **threefold existence is destroyed** at the same time. **Nor is there attachment to the five sense pleasures**, such as forms, that is based on experiencing feelings conditioned by their contact with the eye [sense faculty] and so on, because the experiential sphere of dharmatā that does not possess any āyatanas has been found. Though there is **no** stirring of imaginative **conceptions**, including their basis, this is the **self-arising** wisdom with the unimpeded faculty of being endowed with the perfect **cognizance** whose [objective] aspect is the dharmadhātu.[286] **In** [this wisdom, the latent tendencies of] **forms** with the **solidity** of being obstructive and obscuring, as well as the latent tendencies of **the five poisons** (the formations of clinging to what is to be adopted and to be rejected [that come about] through the arising of the discriminations of apprehending good and bad characteristics, which are [in turn] conditioned by the appropriating feelings [that arise] from [perceiving] those [forms])

and so on, are [all] pure from their very ground up and remain factors whose characteristic it is to never arise again. This awakening within the [door to] liberation that consists of the wishlessness of results constitutes Samantabhadra's mode of freedom.

2.1.2.2.1.1.2. The aspiration prayer in terms of the manner of fully and perfectly becoming a buddha through the array of the self-appearances of the kāyas and wisdoms of innate presence

This wisdom of unconditioned alpha-pure depth-lucidity arises in an **unceasing** manner as its empty essence that has a heart of wisdom, its innately present nature that is luminosity's own glow, and its compassionate responsiveness that is **the dimension** of shining as the outer **lucidity of** the wisdom of **awareness**. Nevertheless, just like the sun and its light rays, its **essence** {497}—the wisdom that is present as the ground, in which the three kāyas are inseparable—**is** not going beyond evincing its [own true] makeup, which consists of the **single** dharmatā.

Among the situational characteristics that are [merely] isolates[287] [of this wisdom, which has a single essence], (1) within the wisdom of the stainless dharmadhātu, (2) on the surface of the mirror-like wisdom that unimpededly provides space for the dawning of the appearances of luminosity, (3) no matter how lucidly manifest this [dawning] may be, there is nothing that is not perfect as this wisdom's own qualities, and therefore it is present as the mode of [the wisdom of] the equality of good and bad. Nevertheless, (4) since this wisdom is not obscured by any nescience of lacking the capacity to distinguish, [all] its own characteristics are clearly manifest in an unobscured and unconflated manner. Therefore, it is [also] endowed with discriminating knowledge. (5) Since those [four wisdoms] are not contingent on any effort, the intrinsic perfection of the power of innate presence constitutes all-accomplishing **wisdom**. Thus, this [wisdom with a single essence] bears these **five** characteristics.[288]

These five wisdoms are not merely some new names that are superimposed onto the sheer emptiness of each one of them lacking any qualities whatsoever. Rather, the clear realization of unity that is inseparable from the appearance dimension **matures** as the kāyas, in which the major and minor marks are clearly manifest and perfectly complete. **From that**, in the Akaniṣṭha that is a self-appearance [of wisdom] and constitutes the maṇḍala of the vajra expanse, the **buddha**[hood] that is [nothing but] the self-appearance of the self-arising wisdom that represents **the primal** protector **springs forth** as the **five families**: the *vajra* family of being immovable by change or transition, the *ratna* family of the perfect completeness of [all] qualities, the *padma* family of stainlessness, the *karma* family of the perfect completeness of [all] activity and seeking, and the *cakra* [family] of innate presence.[289]

From each one of **these** [buddha families], {498} the four **wisdoms** [except dharmadhātu wisdom] radiate and **fully unfold** in the manner of a [spinning] wheel. [Thus,] each one [of these five buddha families] is divided into five kinds of self-awareness. **Through** that, they each arise as a fourfold assembly of bodhisattvas. Garab Dorjé says this:

> Vajra Akṣobhya dwells in the center,
> surrounded by the four of Kṣitigarbha,
> Maitreya, Lāsyā, and Puṣpā.
> This is the first assembled maṇḍala.

As exemplified by this model, the maṇḍalas of the five families [are constituted] in an analogous manner in the other [four] directions. [Also,] by virtue of the compassionate responsiveness that is a self-appearance [of wisdom] and occurs simultaneously with the appearance of the impure gateway to saṃsāra, there arise the six teachers, who appear as the six sages to guide beings and thus promote their welfare. [Furthermore, there are] the four great gatekeepers[290] including their female counterparts, as well as the male and female forms of Samantabhadra [and Samantabhadrī], who are the radiance [of innate presence] and abide in the manner of the ground of the arising [of the ground manifestations]. [In this way,] **the forty-two buddhas** who represent the peaceful deities **originate**.[291]

From them, just as the light of a fire within a vase illuminates the space [around it, once the vase is broken], the maṇḍala of wrathful nature that is stirred up by **the dynamic energy of the five wisdoms**—the wisdom of the awareness of compassionate responsiveness—**dawns** on its own. **Through that,** [there further appear] the five[292] *heruka*s of freeing the [five] wisdoms that are present as the reversal of this saṃsāra of the five [mental] poisons [into or as] the expanse, together with their female counterparts of the expanse, the eight [*gaurī*] mothers of the abodes, who appear as the primordial freedom of the subjects that consist of the eight consciousnesses, the eight female [*piśācī*s] of the areas, who appear as the complete freedom of the appearance of objects, the four [female] gate guardians of unobstructed wisdom, and the twenty-eight *īśvarīs*, who are perfectly complete as the enlightened activities that are appearances of [wisdom's] dynamic energy. [In that way,] all **the sixty blood-drinkers come to life** as self-appearances.[293] {499}

Therefore, though his own essence is originally pure, Samantabhadra as the perfection of innate presence's own dynamic energy is solely the **ground** of freedom—self-arising **awareness**—but **was never** impaired by the ground of **delusion** that is unawareness. Hence, **since I am the primal buddha**—the awareness that is connate with dharmatā, which has the character of being primordially pure of contingent, conventional phenomena that appropriate and are appropriated, without its own essence increasing or decreasing—this, **my** very dharmatā, abides in an intrinsic and innately present manner, even in the mind streams of sentient beings at the time of adventitious delusion. By virtue of this essential point, [I am] **making** [my aspiration prayer] without any **aspiration** for a result that is accomplished through engaging in efforts from now on [but] in the form of the wisdom of the **path**[294] of nonlearning—the complete freedom of the three buddhakāyas. **Through** this, **may** all **the sentient beings who cycle through the three realms** of karma, afflictions, and maturation due to the coarse and subtle [forms of] apprehender and apprehended in terms of their body, speech, and mind **recognize self-arising awareness's own face,** may realization and freedom be simultaneous through that alone, and may the basic nature of the perfection of [awareness's] own dynamic energy as the **great** maṇḍala of the kāyas and **wisdoms**, which are the self-appearances [of awareness], **unfold** as the great freedom from **extremes.**[295]

2.1.2.2.1.2. The aspiration prayer in terms of the manner in which emanations unfold as other-appearances

Simultaneously with the first victor [Samantabhadra]'s full awakening within the primal ground, the infinite arisen beings who have sprung from the ground of delusion—which consists of [awareness's] not being aware of its own face and devolves into the increasingly coarse minds and mental factors that represent the flourishing of the power of apprehender and apprehended—{500} experience the *duḥkha* of pain.[296] Seeing this through the unobscured wisdom of knowing variety, self-arising compassion without any reference point or effort springs forth, and thus an array of lamps for the welfare of beings manifests. Without departing from the realm of the dharmakāya ([the realm] Vajra Heart of Luminosity, which is the inseparability of alpha-purity and innate presence), the realm of the sambhogakāya (the ground for the arising of the self-appearances [of the dharmakāya] that consist of [the realm] Sound of Brahmā's Drum, which is definite as the ornamental [realm] Richly Adorned Akaniṣṭha) is arranged. By virtue of that, from the ocean [of realms] that consists of the boundless clouds of the five families of [Great] Glacial Lake [of Wisdom], the infinite worlds in the ten directions of [the Realm Whose] Ground and Center Are Adorned with Flowers [arise]. In them, **my** countless **emanations** who guide beings issue forth in **an uninterrupted flow**. Also, in the cardinal and intermediate directions of this realm Endurance, [there are] the sixty-four protectors of the fortunate, and in each distinct abode in each of its realms with the four continents [we find] the twelve fully perfected teachers and so on.[297] Thus, I am **unfolding as** all kinds of countless and **inconceivable billions** of emanations who guide beings **and displaying as a vast array of** illusory manifestations of **guiding** certain beings to be guided through certain **suitable** means of guidance.

In the future, **through** [the power of] the wisdom of **my** great **compassion**, which consists of those appearances of [my] dynamic energy that occur in a self-arising manner as the unceasing play of nirmāṇakāyas who guide beings (such as Maitreya) and diversified nirmāṇakāyas,[298] {501} as well as through the power of [my] innately present[299] **aspiration prayer, may** the bondages of the karmas and afflictions of **all** these **sentient beings who cycle through the three realms** as the six [kinds of] mind streams[300] become free in themselves, may they then **leave** the impregnations of the negative tendencies **of the six families** as the matured appearances of delusion **behind**, and may they thus proceed directly to the undeluded ground of Samantabhadra.

2.1.2.2.2. The aspiration prayer for the pit of saṃsāra to be emptied [from its depths] that is based on the mode of delusion of unaware sentient beings

This has two parts:

1. Detailed explanation of the characteristics
2. Summary of the topic at hand

2.1.2.2.2.1. Detailed explanation of the characteristics

This also has two parts:

1. The aspiration prayer for awareness to be free as wisdom, through teaching that the shortcomings of the Peak of Existence arise from unawareness
2. The aspiration prayer for this very [unawareness] to become free in itself, in terms of the manner in which the dependent origination of delusion arises from this [unawareness]

2.1.2.2.2.1.1. The aspiration prayer for awareness to be free as wisdom, through teaching that the shortcomings of the Peak of Existence arise from unawareness

This has two parts:

1. The aspiration prayer for unawareness to be free as the wisdom of awareness, through teaching the manner in which the two

subsequent unawarenesses evolve from the unawareness that has the same identity as the cause

2. The aspiration prayer for knowing the two unawarenesses to be of the essence of the wisdom of awareness, through clearly teaching their presentation

2.1.2.2.2.1.1.1. The aspiration prayer for unawareness to be free as the wisdom of awareness, through teaching the manner in which the two subsequent unawarenesses evolve from the unawareness that has the same identity as the cause

Dharmatā, which is without beginning and end, is the primordial ultimate ground of all—the sugata heart. Due to not knowing its nature, it is present as the object condition of linking saṃsāra and nirvāṇa. From it, **at first**, the adventitious apprehender and apprehended of not being aware of its own face rise, and thus {502} the manner in which **deluded sentient beings** are deluded [is as follows]. **Since** the **awareness** that is superior insight—perfect prajñā—**does not dawn in the ground** of all (the primordially pure ground), the indistinct cognizance of **being absolutely mindless** about apprehender and apprehended that is as **oblivious** as deep sleep represents the all-ground of diverse latent tendencies. **Exactly that is the cause of** both connate **unawareness** and imaginative **delusion**. Therefore, this is called "the unawareness that has the same identity as the ground."[301]

From **that** [basic unawareness], an oblivious cognizance, which is a **dazed** coming to at the brink of waking up to [perceiving] objects[302] and resembles the state of mind immediately after having woken up from sleep or from having **been unconscious**, arises as that which discerns. With an agent of clinging not having arisen [yet], the all-ground consciousness is present as mere lucidity: without identifying [anything clearly], **a cognizance** that involves an element of being **fearful and anxious** (similar to wondering, "What's going on? What is this?") **stirs**[303] in a **vague** manner without being able to hold its ground. This is called "the connate unawareness that is connate with objects."

From that [connate unawareness, the notions of] **self and others** (wondering, "Has what is over there arisen from me, or have I arisen from what is over there?") **arise and**, from that, **the** mental consciousness bound by attachment and hatred that **clings to enemies** [arises]. This is called "the unawareness of imagining apprehender and apprehended."

Through the gradual blossoming of the dense **latent tendencies** of mistakenness in terms of dharmatā serving as the ground of the delusion of objects, the five lights[304] as the ground of the delusion of the container and its contents, latent tendencies as the ground of the delusion of bodies, and awareness as the ground of the delusion of mind, the **saṃsāra** of the appearances of the delusion of clinging to places, referents, and bodies—the whirl of delusion of unawareness,[305] {503} whose nature is to be without termination and without increase—**unfolds, taking its natural course. By virtue of that, the five poisons of the afflictions** (such as attachment) **flourish, and** based on the power of **the karmas of these five poisons**, suffering is experienced in **an incessant flow. Thus, the** initial **ground of** adventitiously deluded **sentient beings' delusion**, in the form of apprehender and apprehended or the utter **lack** of any cause of being **mindful, is** nescient **unawareness.**

Hence, through this aspiration prayer of the self-abiding awakened mind **of myself, the** primal **buddha**, Samantabhadra, in whom unawareness is pure from the ground, being made in the mind streams of sentient beings, **may** they **all know awareness**'s **own** face—Samantabhadra—and may their unawareness be dispelled through the power of that, in such a way that it no longer has an object.

2.1.2.2.2.1.1.2. The aspiration prayer for knowing the two unawarenesses to be of the essence of the wisdom of awareness through clearly teaching their presentation

The **unawareness** that is **connate** with the beginning of the arising of adventitious delusion from the basic state of the ground that is dharmatā **is** the nescience that is present as the means of being

distracted toward objects through the **mindlessness** of conceptual **cognizance.** The **unawareness** of **imagining** apprehender and apprehended **is the clinging to the duality of self and others**—the conceptual delusion of creating a split into distinct sides and parts. **This** kind of **twofold connate and imaginative unawareness is the ground of** appropriating the **delusion of all sentient beings** in the three realms.[306]

Therefore, **through** the potent power of the reality of the originally pure dharmatā **of myself—the buddha** who is the freedom of the ground, primordially perfect {504} Samantabhadra—having matured as **this aspiration prayer, may** the **darkness of** the connate unawareness (being oppressed by **dull** oblivion, due to the lack of luminosity of **mindless** cognizance, whose nature consists of the essence of nescience) of **all sentient beings** without exception, who **cycle**[307] through the abodes of latent tendencies and unawareness, **be dispelled** as the freedom from extremes. May the movements of **their** stirring and discursive **cognizance of clinging to** the **duality** of hope and fear **be translucent** as the wisdom of being free in itself **and** may the superior insight of fully knowing the nature of self-**awareness**—which is without change or transition since the very start and whose **essence** is the wisdom of the inseparability of the three kāyas—be revealed.

2.1.2.2.2.1.2. The aspiration prayer for this very [unawareness] to become free in itself in terms of[308] teaching the manner of cycling in the realms of saṃsāra under the sway of the five poisons that constitute the dependent origination of delusion [arising] from this [unawareness]

This has five parts.

2.1.2.2.2.1.2.1. The aspiration prayer in terms of introducing the conceptions of desire as being discriminating wisdom

Thus, the root of the afflictions of the desire [realm]—**the mind of** the imaginative delusion of **clinging** to the **duality** of self and others—arises from the connate unawareness that appears as dual-minded **doubt**, which [actually] consists of the latent prajñā of differentiating the nature [of awareness as what it is]. **Due to the arising of** the **subtle fixation** of the latent tendencies for the flourishing of the power of this [doubt], the adventitious delusion of something appearing while it is [actually] nonexistent, which is similar to [what one sees with] blurred vision, {505} **gradually unfolds** as the **dense latent tendencies** that rise[309] as places, referents, and bodies. Attractive objects, which serve as nourishment and [favorable] conditions necessary for our own body, appear as **food, wealth, clothing, places** (regions, countries, realms), **companions** (dear friends), **the five sense pleasures** (necessary as the enjoyments of the sense faculties), **or beloved relatives** (such as siblings, parents, and children). **We are tormented by the desire** of being **attached to** and craving for **what is** highly **attractive** in these objects. **These** appropriations of such object conditions **are** deceiving, changing, and find their end by perishing in a momentary manner, and the **delusion** of being lost in the domain of the conditional formations that are based on [these objects] brings about [all kinds of] unpleasant sufferings. This resembles clinging to [licking] the honey that sticks to a razor blade. In [Saraha's *Dohakoṣagīti*] it says this:

> Regard this as in the case of fish,
> butterflies, elephants, bees, and deer.[310]

Thus, **the karmas of apprehender and apprehended**, which consist of the incessantly occurring series of causes and results, in which earlier results of concordant outflow form later sufferings, arise in an uninterrupted manner. **When the results of** the maturation of the **clinging** to those [karmas] that **is never exhausted ripen**, they are established **as** the bodies of **hungry ghosts tortured by craving** and turn into the dominated result that consists of a **birth**place that is an unpleasant and destitute location, where not even the names of food and drink are known.[311] {506} Then these [beings there] are continuously tormented by unbearable sufferings of **hunger and thirst** and plagued by **pitiful** [conditions in terms of] time, being burned, being distorted, and so on.[312]

Through this aspiration prayer for being inseparable from great bliss **of myself, the buddha** Samantabhadra, in whom the fixation of the delusion of dualistic clinging has been awakened as the native freedom of the ground of nonduality, **may** the **sentient beings** who are under the sway of **the clinging of desirous attachment**, unlike śrāvakas and pratyekabuddhas of the causal yāna of characteristics, [not] relinquish it through putting themselves at a great distance from the objects of **desire** and cultivating the yoga of mentally engaging in the remedy for **the torment of** fixating [on these objects]. Unlike bodhisattvas, may they also **not cast out** desire through bringing it onto the path in such a way that the seven actions of body and speech [normally] to be relinquished are allowed, in cases when it is certain that they serve the welfare of others, once the craving of one's own desire has become exhausted, while still being dependent on the purification and transformation [of these actions] through the illusion-like samādhi. [On the other hand,] according to the resultant yāna of secret mantra, if **the** very **clinging of** the affliction of **desirous attachment** is embraced by [skillful] means, to the same extent that its afflictive power (its dimension of appearance) blazes, the dynamic energy of the wisdom of bliss and emptiness (its dimension of freedom) is perfected. Thus, by virtue of possessing the ability to bring desire onto the path through that, similar to a strong wind aiding a fire blazing in a large forest, such practitioners deliberately engage in [certain] objects at [certain] times. [However,] may beings **not welcome** desire **within** through such an approach [either].

Rather, in the system of the natural Great Perfection, **through letting** all bondages of clinging to any factors to be relinquished, remedies, purity, or freedom settle and **relax in the** awakened mind's **own state**, which is the wisdom of the uncontrived and native perfect ground, {507} or by letting them relax directly within naturally settled freshness, **may awareness take its very own seat**, without moving away from its own dimension and without being stirred by any thoughts of conditional formations, **and may** the great, unceasing, and self-arising **discriminating wisdom** of great bliss **thus be attained**.

2.1.2.2.2.1.2.2. The aspiration prayer in terms of introducing hatred as being luminosity

A subtle, unpleasant **mind of fear stirs around the appearance of outer objects** that involve unpleasant harm. Through this, **the unfolding of** the power of the **latent tendencies of** the **hatred** of wishing to remove such conditions (the mental factor malice) reveals **fixation on enemies** (resentment), which **leads to** motivating **powerful** karmic formations of **beating** (hitting and so on) **and killing. When the results** of the maturation **of hatred ripen, we suffer through** [experiencing the painful] feelings of **being boiled** in heated [liquids] and so on **in** the miserable sphere of the **hell** realm **and** being **burned** in [hells] such as Avīci.[313]

Therefore, **through this aspiration prayer** of the unceasing compassion **of myself, the** primal **buddha**, who is never disturbed, **when fierce hatred flares up in** the mind streams of the entirety of **all sentient beings who migrate in six ways, may it relax** at ease **in its own** primordially free and effortless **state without** any **adopting or rejecting** that involves effort, may the **awareness** that is present as the ground **take its very own seat** through simply letting it be in its own way, in a fresh manner, {508} **and** may naturally **lu**minous mirror-like **wisdom thus be attained.**

2.1.2.2.2.1.2.3. The aspiration prayer for pride being free as equality

[Due to] proponents of philosophical systems holding **their own** views and spiritual disciplines to be paramount, or **due to** ordinary people's **minds having become haughty** through their ancestry, power, or wealth, there arises a **mind** of **vying with others** who are superior **and** a **mentality** of **dismissing** those who are [deemed] inferior. **Through the arising of** such **arrogant pride, we experience** the cause of **the suffering of fighting and struggling** through clinging to **ourselves** and **others** as being separate. And even if we engage in a little bit of contaminated virtue that is motivated by holding [our views and spiritual practices] to be paramount, or by pride, **when the results of those actions ripen,** we will **be born as gods experiencing** the suffering of change as our **transition and downfall.**

Therefore, **through this aspiration prayer of myself, the buddha** of nonconceptual equality, which arises as the fulfillment of all wishes and makes all hopes come true, **when sentient beings give rise to a haughty,** prideful **mind, may their** unmodified native **cognizance relax in its own place**—dharmatā—or in a naturally settled, fresh manner, may **awareness** thereby **take its very own seat, and** may the unbiased wisdom of **equality** [without any] good or bad be attained, or **the actuality of** this [equality] **thus be realized.**

2.1.2.2.2.1.2.4. The aspiration prayer in terms of introducing envy as being unobstructed wisdom

Through the latent tendencies of the **rampant** power of imaginative unawareness—the **clinging** to the **duality** of self and others—{509} and through the karma that gives rise to the suffering of **the pain of praising ourselves** due to being attached to ourselves **and** the malice of **disparaging others** due to hating them, **the** prowess **of** our **fighting and struggling** and of a **competitive mind** is perfected, and the envy of being afraid of others being superior **blossoms.** No matter whether wrongdoings or ostensible virtues result **thus,** it is by virtue of the ripening of such [karma] that we **are born in the asura realm**—the land **of** uninterrupted **killing and slashing.** There, through the coming together of the actions and experiences that are the concordant outflows [of envy], the revived [karmic] seeds [of the hell realm] become powerful, due to which **we** [eventually] **take a deep plunge into the hell realms.**

Through this aspiration prayer of the natural accomplishment of [all] activity and seeking **of myself, the buddha** who is the effortless fruition, **may any arisen competitive mind, fighting, struggling,** and envious thoughts, while **not** following the dualistic **clinging** of separating **enemies** from friends, **relax in** dharmatā's **own place** that is the awakening of the awareness of the one who clings as the freedom of the ground, may **cognizance** thereby **take**

its very own seat, and may the fruition that consists of the innate presence of all moving and scattered thoughts as **the wisdom of unobstructed enlightened activity thus be** attained.

2.1.2.2.2.1.2.5. The aspiration prayer in terms of introducing nescience as being the dharmadhātu of nonconceptual[314] wisdom

Meditative absorptions of utter **mindlessness**, the **indifference** of not distinguishing any standpoints, **distraction** toward objects, {510} the **obtuseness** of the active consciousnesses' being indistinct, the **dullness** and sleep of the mental sense faculty's not being awake to [perceive] objects, **forgetfulness** of the points to be adopted and to be rejected, cognizance's helplessly becoming **unconscious**, the **laziness** of remaining heedless about what is profitable and what is detrimental, **and** so on are [all forms of] **nescience. Through** forming such karmas, **as** their **result, we roam** the realms of the **animals,** who are sentient beings **without shelter.**

For these [animals] who experience the difficult-to-bear sufferings of being dull, obtuse, and bound into servitude, **through** the power of **this aspiration prayer** of nonreferential inner luminosity, which constitutes the wisdom of the absorbed yet unoblivious awakened mind[315] **of myself, the buddha** Samantabhadra, who has revealed the dharmadhātu, **may the radiance of** the **mindfulness** of the all-encompassing dharmatā—**lucid** and unimpeded awareness, free from [all] chains of entanglement—**shine in** [their state of] being completely covered by their oblivious latent tendencies, which represent **the darkness of** their **nescience and dullness and may** the inconceivable **nonconceptual wisdom** of not abandoning the locus of effortless samādhi, despite lacking any operation of mind, mentation, and consciousness, **thus be attained.**[316]

2.1.2.2.2.2. The aspiration through a summary of the topic at hand

If this dharmatā—the sugata heart, which is self-arising as the ground of freedom that consists of the originally pure nirvāṇa—does not recognize its own face, it is justified as the indeterminate ground from which the two of saṃsāra and nirvāṇa diverge, and this represents a suitable [basis] for the unawareness of dualistic appearances to arise. From that, {511} there arises the ground of delusion of the saṃsāra of diverse latent tendencies, which is the first occurrence of the dormant latent tendencies of oblivion. From that, while the conceptions of apprehender and apprehended gradually evolve into increasingly coarser forms, within the one-pointed all-ground that represents the meditative absorption of the Peak of Existence, there manifest the formless [realm] (the city of mind that does not appear), the form [realm] (the city of speech that appears halfway), and the desire [realm] (the city of the body that appears).

Even during the times when **all sentient beings of the three realms** are being deluded, bodhicitta—**the ground of all**, whose own face is without any change or transition—is primordially untainted by any goodness, badness, flaws, or qualities. Therefore, it abides as the great nondual **equality with myself, the buddha** Samantabhadra. However, since the nature of this wisdom has not been experienced[317] but remains dormant, **it has become the ground of** the **delusion** of **mindless** unawareness. Then, under the sway of clinging to self, others, container, and contents, **right now**, [sentient beings] **engage in meaningless** worldly **activities**, and **the karmic** appearances of the six formations of afflictions that manifest as the **six** classes [of beings] have the nature of being deluded about latent tendencies. They **are** groundless delusive appearances, **like the** arising of appearances of **delusions in a dream** due to being intoxicated by sleep, or the appearances of strands of hair for someone with blurred vision who has a phlegm disorder. Yet the naturally all-illuminating wisdom in these beings, who are conceived as such under the sway of temporarily occurring thoughts, is lucidly present as the compassionate responsiveness that has a heart of awareness. Therefore, {512} since I am omniscient [about this] in an unobscured manner, **I am the original** one of all **buddhas** because the very essence of changeless dharmatā and the wisdom of awareness are connate in an inseparable manner.

Therefore, **in order to guide** the sentient beings of **the six realms through** the diverse plays of my **emanations** who provide suitable guidance, because the continuous stream of my great non-referential compassion is uninterrupted, based on the power of **this aspiration prayer of** glorious **Samantabhadra**—the effortless and naturally accomplished wisdom of unimpeded compassionate responsiveness—**may** the deep sleep of unawareness [of] **all sentient beings without exception** in this saṃsāra of apprehender and apprehended, which obscures the primordially free, alpha-pure **dharmadhātu** without reference points, **become** pure and **awakened in** its own abode, and thus may the full **unfolding**[318] of the qualities of the kāyas and wisdoms that are Samantabhadra's own dynamic energy be perfectly complete, in an innately present manner.

[All] applications of terms and thoughts [such as] the above should also be regarded as being [nothing other than] Samantabhadra's own face—the awareness that is peaceful as dharmatā, free from speech, thought, and expression.

2.2. Teaching the benefits and the performances

This has two parts:

1. [Teaching] the timeless, continuous yoga of supreme persons free from reference points, including its [benefit and] performance
2. Teaching the yoga of persons with reference points [that is practiced] at certain times, including its benefit and performance

2.2.1. [Teaching] the timeless, continuous yoga of supreme persons free from reference points, including its benefit and performance

"**A HO!**" [indicates that] since Samantabhadra's enlightened activity appears in an effortless and self-arising manner, this Dharma of emptying the pit of saṃsāra with its three realms—so that it is great, complete freedom—{513} is amazing![319] The characteristic of the persons who recite this [aspiration prayer] in [such an amazing] manner refers to [all] **yogic practitioners from now on** who are endowed **with great power** in their view, awakened mind, and spiritual discipline. As for the manner or performance of reciting it, [such yogic practitioners recite it] **through making this aspiration prayer** for emptying the pit of saṃsāra—which possesses the **great power** of freedom—**from within** the natural state of resting in meditative equipoise in **self-luminous awareness free of delusion.**

The benefit of reciting it in this way is that **all sentient beings who hear this** special Dharma of buddhahood without meditation that is endowed with the fourfold freedom **will fully** display the signs that are the gauge of freedom and thus **awaken within** [a period] that is no longer than **three lives.**

2.2.2. Teaching the yoga of persons with reference points [that is practiced] at certain times, including its benefit and performance

The times when [this aspiration prayer] is recited refer to specific, distinctly crucial times, such as **during the times of** either **solar or lunar eclipses, at the occurrence of loud noises or earthquakes** in the world, **at the** summer and winter[320] **solstices, at the turn of the year,** or at the equinoxes.[321]

As for the manner of reciting, **if we let ourselves arise as Samantabhadra and,** through focusing on all sentient beings (such as the creatures in our immediate surrounding who are able to hear this), **recite this** aspiration prayer **within the hearing of all** of them, **all sentient beings of the three realms, through** the power of **the aspiration prayer of such yogic practitioners, will gradually become free from suffering and then,** through their power of having assumed sovereignty over dharmatā, {514} **attain buddhahood in the end.**

The detailed manner in which this [happens] is elucidated in the volumes on freedom through wearing in our own texts.[322]

3. Summary of the topic at hand

This is the explanation of **the nineteenth chapter, which teaches that through making this aspiration prayer of great power, all sentient beings are powerless not to awaken, in the** ***Tantra That***

Teaches the Great Perfection as Samantabhadra's Unobstructed Awakened Mind.

This yāna of Atiyoga, which is the supreme secret
of all philosophical systems of the paths of gradually applied effort,
being at peace within the expanse of inconceivable wisdom,
consists of the direct perception of wisdom but not of gradual efforts.

The scriptures of the awakened mind, awareness, and ear-whispers[323]
are the quintessential treasures of the minds of the three kinds of emanated awareness-holders.[324]
They were entrusted by the ḍākinīs to the Rock of Snakes[325]
and revealed by Ngödrub Gyaltsen's seal of karmic destiny.[326]

Through the wisdom of Samantabhadra, which is awareness,
the aspiration prayer of the definitive meaning of the complete freedom of the three realms flourishes,
and the joy of the amazing supreme *siddhi* of condensing it
into the single sphere of the all-embracing consummation of existence and peace dawns.[327]

Through the excellent accomplishment due to having practiced this[328]
for billions of eons, the beryl gem of the Dharma
of the heart of luminosity, which is not just found as a trinket,
beautifies the crowns of the heads of us with virtuous, fortunate karma.

Through this virtue, {515} may the supreme secret—the teachings of Samantabhadra's mind
that represent the great illumination of the vajra sun—
completely lift the darkness of unaware sentient beings
and unfold the wisdom of perfect realization.

For the sake of fulfilling the wish of the all-pervasive lord, the great treasure revealer Lama Silnön Namké Dorjé,[329] *who exhorted me [to write this commentary], Kakyab Rangjung Dewé Dorjé,*[330] *the monastic awareness-holder who obtained the blessings of the name of Buddha Karmapa, composed it in the manner of condensing the essence [of this aspiration prayer] by summarizing it in a few [words. He did so] in the year of the Fire Dragon in the fifteenth sexagenary cycle [1916] at the very top of the great Dharma palace at which the successive [embodiments of] Lokeśvara*[331] *have arrived and which is the cakra of the enlightened mind of the supreme bliss of the ḍākinīs' web.*[332] *The erudite śramaṇa Karma Tubten Jampel Tsültrim Tragpa*[333] *served as a scribe. May virtue and excellence increase.*

For the time being, GUHYA GYA.

An Exposition of The Aspiration Prayer of Samantabhadra *Found in the* Great Tantra of the Unobstructed Awakened Mind *of the Northern Treasures, Called* The Lamp That Clearly Illuminates the Short Path of Samantabhadra

Tsültrim Sangpo

{1b} I bow to dharmatā, free from reference points, which does not transcend
the nature of great, all-encompassing wisdom and has the form of space—
unobstructed, free from dawning and setting, and thus unconfined,
free from the stains of delusion's dimension, and endowed with twofold purity.

This mighty wish-fulfilling [jewel] of the supreme path of ground, path, and fruition,
having reached the very top of the precious gems of the progression of yānas,
is the excellent quintessence of the ocean of the Dharma collection of Divine Rock.
I shall elaborate on it here in accordance with the profound treasures of Padma.

Now, the buddhas who have gained ultimate mastery over Samantabhadra's true reality possess no activity other than that through which sentient beings become free from their stains. Therefore, the point to which all enlightened activities of the path free from stains lead is this ultimate {2a} aspiration prayer of Samantabhadra, or this short path of abruptly merging with the stainless, original expanse through the supreme path that consists of the ground, path, and fruition of the Pith Instructions Series of the Great Perfection.

[My] concise explanation of this [aspiration prayer] has three parts:

1. The initial instruction of briefly presenting ground, path, and fruition
2. The detailed explanation of this through finely differentiating it further
3. Teaching the benefit of reading and hearing this aspiration prayer

1. The initial instruction of briefly presenting ground, path, and fruition

The first point is taught through the [first] six lines of verse beginning with "**HO! All that appears and is possible**." "HO" appears as an expression of nonreferential loving-kindness for saṃsāric sentient beings who, rendered powerless by their delusion, are greatly tormented by [all kinds of] undesired, terrible flaws and problems. {2b} This [syllable] is an exclamation of exhorting [beings to enter] this profound, short path of the appearances of delusion being pure in their own place.

Thus, since the phenomena that are suitable to be taken as objects of the mind are not truly established from their own side, they are nothing but mere **appearances**. Since what appears is present in a nondeceptive manner as mere conventions, it **is possible** and exists as mere appearances. Such appearances include what is impure (these containers and contents of [our] **saṃsāra** of afflicted phenomena and delusion—the arrays of all kinds of magical creations of causes and results) **as well as** what is pure (the freedom of the **nirvāṇa** of purified phenomena—the inconceivable, playful dance of the wisdoms, qualities, and enlightened activities of liberation).

All these phenomena of delusion and freedom **have a ground** of origination from which they arise and unfold, as well as a ground of absorption into which they dissolve and are withdrawn. Ultimately, this is the subtle and native fundamental mode of being of sentient beings' own minds—the vajra of mind, bodhicitta. From the perspective of its essence, it is empty and alpha-pure. Therefore, it is free from all elements of the reference points of [independent,] specifically characterized entities. From the perspective of its nature, it is inseparable from the qualities of the innately present nature of unceasing depth-lucidity. Therefore, it never abandons its own essence, which consists of the shining of primordial radiance. From the perspective of compassionate responsiveness, these two [essence and nature] have a single essence. Therefore, the awareness of compassionate responsiveness in which appearance and emptiness are nondual is the unimpededly spacious ground of arising that unfolds as the all-encompassing and impartial knowledge of wisdom. {3a} In its being inseparable from these three qualities of luminosity (essence, nature, and compassionate responsiveness), [this ground] does not shift away from being of a single taste to any other [state]. Hence, it lacks any counterpart and is strictly **single**.

The **paths** that are the tracks of traveling and voyaging[334] to their own specific results are **two**: the path of unawareness, karma, afflictions, and delusion that is the great causal root of [all] the flaws that consist of the contaminated skandhas and *dhātu*s of the impure saṃsāra of sentient beings, as well as the uncontaminated reality of the path—the wisdom of self-arising awareness that is the genuine, great means to gain mastery over the ocean of qualities of the original inner expanse (the liberation that is the pure result [of this path]).

The final **results** that are attained and accomplished through the functions of these two paths are [also] **two**: the phenomena of saṃsāra (the reality of suffering, which consists of the contaminated impure appearances of delusion) and the phenomenon of stainless liberation, whose nature is uncontaminated pure wisdom. These impure and pure paths and respective results of saṃsāra and nirvāṇa represent **the** mere **miraculous displays of** attaining mastery, by way of the primal ground's basic nature itself recognizing and becoming **aware** of its own face, **and** the body of delusion growing in power, by way of being deluded about self-appearances as being something else and thus being **unaware** of these [appearances'] own face. Thus, [both] are definitely contrary to any phenomena that are established as some permanent, everlasting, and immutable entities or characteristics other than that [primal ground].

In this way, the ultimate vision of the basic nature of the ground of freedom and delusion—the treasure vault in which [all] inexhaustible qualities of the fruition {3b} are universally [**samanta**] present, the treasury of [all] excellent [**bhadra**] dharmas, which constantly overflows in an all-pervasive and innately present manner—is the **path**[335] of **the** profound **aspiration of** the awakened mind of stainless wisdom. It is **through** the buddha who himself travels [this path] and guides others on it that this crowning peak of the nine yānas—the secret path of the unsurpassable, ultimate secret—is taught. Therefore, through coming face to face with the actuality of the ground that is taught on such a supreme path, **may all** flaws and faults, which consist of the stains of delusion of deluded persons, vanish within the great, original locus of freedom—**the palace of the dharmadhātu.**[336] Through thus **fully perfecting** the dharmas that consist of the qualities of freedom and maturation[337] **in** the ultimate Akaniṣṭha, free from stains, may the state of **awakening** be swiftly attained.

2. The detailed explanation of this through finely differentiating it further

This has three parts:

1. The ground
2. The path
3. The fruition

2.1. The ground

This has three parts:

1. Detailed explanation of the basic nature of the ground
2. Teaching Samantabhadra's mode of freedom through taking the recognition of the [ground] as the path
3. The manner in which sentient beings are deluded in saṃsāra due to not knowing the actuality of the ground

2.1.1. Detailed explanation of the basic nature of the ground

This is explained through the seven lines of verse beginning with "**the ground of all.**" The *Great Tantra of the Universes and Transformations of Sound* says this:

> What is the beginning of sentient beings' saṃsāra?
>
> . . . .
>
> From what does sentient beings' delusion originate?
> What is the foundation of self-aware wisdom?[338]

Accordingly, **the ground** is explained by many names, [such as] "the general ground **of all** delusion and freedom," "the great expanse of the mother-ground of all,"[339] "the hollow space of mother innate presence," {4a} "the general locus that has not obtained[340] a name," and "the intermediate state of saṃsāra and nirvāṇa." As for the basic nature that is the essence of [this ground], the *Garland of Pearls* says this:

> Though the basic nature is inconceivable,
> it consists of the three kinds of wisdom.
> Though the aspects of the ground of delusion are explained as
> many,
> they consist of innate presence and compassionate
> responsiveness.[341]

Accordingly, the ascertainment of the basic mode of being of this general ground has two parts: (1) the six flawed positions and (2) the one flawless position.[342]

(1) Among the six flawed philosophical positions concerning the basic mode of being of the ground, (a) the position that the ground is innate presence is mistaken. Since the ground is the ground of both the causes and results of saṃsāra and nirvāṇa, if the causes were innately present in the ground, the results would also have to be established in that way. Therefore, in that case, [this position] is invalidated through it [absurdly] following that causes and results would be one, and it following that the production of results would be needless and endless. The *Sixfold Expanse* says this:

> Since cause and result are different,
> yet again, it is not innate presence.
> Likewise, if cause and result were one,
> efforts would become unnecessary.[343]

As for our own system, since we hold the ground to be alpha-purity, it is not established as saṃsāra. Since we hold its nature to be diversity, it is not established as nirvāṇa.

(b) The position that the ground is indeterminate is also mistaken. Just as the ground is indeterminate, what arises from it—referents (the objects of expression) and {4b} words (the means of expression)—would also be indeterminate. Therefore, it would follow that the means of expression do not indicate the objects of expression and that these two have no connection. Furthermore, the presentations of good and bad karma and of different causes and results could not be put forth. Alternatively, it would follow that, just like its results, the ground is intermittent; or, just like the ground, solid material phenomena are cognizance. Just as the presentations of saṃsāra and nirvāṇa are determinate, the ground would also be determinate. Just as the ground is indeterminate, the phenomena of saṃsāra and nirvāṇa would then be in disarray. The [same] tantra says this:

> Its results would vacillate,
> or it would become its opposite.

> What is indeterminate would become determinate,
> and what is determinate would become indeterminate.[344]

(c) The position that the ground is the determinate ultimate ground is also mistaken. Is the actuality of the ground determinate after it has been realized, or is it determinate without realizing it? In the first case, if the basic nature of the ground were determinate after it has been realized, it would be through the power of the path [that leads to its] being without stains that it would become the very fruition, but this would contradict its being asserted as the ground. In the second case, without realizing the ground, its [consequently] being determinate as saṃsāra would contradict the presentations of both the path that brings this [saṃsāra] to an end and the fruition of that [path]. If this ground were determinate as both saṃsāra and nirvāṇa independently of the distinction of whether it is realized or not realized, it would follow that one is not able to differentiate [this position] from the one of the tīrthikas who propound permanence, because nirvāṇa would be permanently present, even at the time of saṃsāra. The [same] tantra says this:

> Therefore, this is not the true actuality either.
> Or, with a determinate cause and a determinate result, {5a}
> it would be no different from a permanent self.[345]

(d) The position that the ground is capable of transforming into anything whatsoever is also mistaken. If its mode of appearing is capable of transforming into anything whatsoever, is it the mode of appearing of a permanent ground that transforms or the mode of appearing of an impermanent [ground] that transforms? In the first case, since conditions cannot affect something permanent, this would contradict its transformation. In the second case, is this [hypothetical] impermanent ground something existent or something nonexistent? If it exists, does it exist after it has arisen or does it exist without having arisen? If it exists after it has arisen, did it arise from itself or did it arise from something other? If it arose from itself, it would follow that its arising is pointless and endless. If it arose from something other, are cause and result one or different? If they are one, this ruins the thesis of its arising from something other. If they are different, they have no connection, and hence it would follow that fire [can] arise from water. If, according to the second case [of existing], it were to exist without having arisen, its not having arisen would contradict the thesis of its being capable of transforming, just as space is something that cannot be transformed by colors. [Finally,] a phenomenon that is other than either permanent or impermanent is definitely not possible among knowable objects. The [same] tantra says this:

> If its own basic nature were capable of transforming,
> this would be similar to its being indeterminate.
> Since the very fruition would revert to the cause,
> [all] efforts would be unnecessary.
> [Also,] this would entail repeated reversals.
> Hence, it resembles material phenomena's incapability of
> turning into something that possesses awareness.[346]

(e) The position that the ground can be asserted as anything whatsoever {5b} is also mistaken. Is the ground asserted in terms of being existent or is it asserted in terms of being nonexistent? If it exists, is it permanent or impermanent? If it were permanent, this would contradict its being suitable to be asserted as anything whatsoever. If it is impermanent, has this impermanent ground arisen or not arisen? If it has arisen, did it arise from itself or from something other? If it had not arisen, this would contradict its being impermanent. If it were nonexistent and yet suitable to be asserted [as anything], what would invalidate the assertion that the child of a barren woman has been born and so on? It would follow that [such an assertion can] not be invalidated [by anything]. If [the ground] were asserted as a knowable object that is neither existent nor nonexistent, this would definitely be highly contradictory.

The tantra teaches the invalidation of this position such that it would follow that the factors that establish a truly established ground [that can be asserted as anything] would be endless:

> Because it would be established from the perspective of being everything,
> there would be the flaw of its being endless.[347]

(f) The position that the ground is diversity is also greatly mistaken. Is the ground posited as diversity due to diverse aspects of appearance, or is it posited as diversity due to diverse cognizances? In the first case, though mere appearances appear as different [appearances], if that were to establish the essence of the ground as diversity, it would follow that this is similar to [the flawed position of] the Naiyāyika tīrthikas, who speak of different distinctive features of the [single] self, due to distinctive features of karma. In the second case, if the ground is posited as diversity in accord with the [diverse] enumerations of cognizance, then, just as many [kinds of] cognizances arise in a single person in each moment, the ground would also exist as many different [kinds of] essences in the mind stream of that person. Therefore, [the ground] would consist of different continua of cognizance. {6a} In that case, there would also be the flaws of it following that efforts on the path are pointless, or that [beings] are free without any effort. The [same] tantra says this:

> With a single cause having different results,
> this essence would appear through that [diversity].
> Hence, this would be equivalent to meaning different results.[348]

The defining characteristics that represent these six [positions concerning the] ground are not definite as the complete defining characteristics of the ground. Without taking into account the essential point of the ground being free from reference points, [in each case, a certain] defining characteristic that is [only] a fraction of the phenomena that are its innately present qualities is taken to be the defining characteristic of the ground. However, it is an error to conceive of parts as that which possesses these parts. This resembles the example of seven blind people [each] mistaking certain parts or limbs of the body of an elephant for its body, which possesses [all these] parts, and [the examples of] a single human or a single cairn appearing differently due to [distinct] conditions of delusion in different onlookers.

(2) As for the one position that is flawless, the *Tantra of the Universes and Transformations of Sound* says this:

> The primal [ground] is present as the three aspects
> of essence, nature, and compassionate responsiveness.[349]

Self-Arising [Awareness] states this:

> The ground is called "great alpha-purity," which is present as the three aspects of essence, nature, and compassionate responsiveness.[350]

Thus, [the ground is] the maṇḍala of the nature that is innate presence, the inner luminosity that is the original buddha, the wisdom of self-arising awareness that is the youthful vase body whose outer seal has not been rent open,[351] the essence that is alpha-purity, {6b} the **unconditioned** wisdom free from reference points—which is identityless and empty of any characteristics and entities of karmic winds and reference points of apprehender and apprehended that are established by a nature of their own—and the great dharmakāya. The *Universes and Transformations [of Sound]* says this:

> Apart from the wisdom of the alpha-pure essence,
> there is not [even] the name of [saṃsāric] existence that is
> "unawareness."
>
> . . . .
>
> Apart from dharmatā, which is not differentiated as anything,
> there is not even anything that is established as mere wisdom.[352]

The nature that is innate presence consists of the kāyas, pure realms, wisdoms, and qualities being absorbed within the inner luminosity that is equal to the dharmadhātu—the ocean of the qualities of the three secrets—in an all-encompassing manner, yet it is empty without any oblivion, having the form of space. Just like the sun and its rays, without anything to be removed or to be added, it is primordially lucid in a **self-arising** manner. The *Universes and Transformations [of Sound]* states this:

> "The wisdom of the nature that is innate presence"
>
> . . . .
>
> is the ground of diversity's perfect completeness,
> due to what appears as a sheer play
> through its unimpeded dynamic energy and qualities.[353]

Since the awareness of compassionate responsiveness unfolds as wisdom, free from any confinement or bias, it abides as the dharmatā of the entirety of [saṃsāric] existence and peace. Therefore, it is **vast spaciousness**. The above [tantra] declares this:

> The gateways that arise as the diversity of nonactivity
> from the wisdom of all-pervasive compassionate responsiveness
> are perfectly complete as the essence of what looks like activity.
> From within the nature of the empty dharmakāya,
> the dimension of the perfect knowledge of wisdom
> automatically appears for sentient beings. {7a}
> Without this, the hub of saṃsāra and nirvāṇa would be severed—
> therefore, this knowledge is aware of and illuminates [them].[354]

As for this wisdom that is present as the ground, since its essence is to transcend any characteristics of reference points, it does not fall into the one-sided extreme of being permanent. Since its nature is to be innately present as lucidity, it does not fall into the one-sided extreme of becoming extinct. Since its compassionate responsiveness is all-pervasive and lucid yet empty awareness, it does not fall into the one-sided extremes of being both permanent and extinct or being neither. Therefore, it is the wisdom of the Madhyamaka free from extremes,[355] which is free from any one-sided [reference points] of clinging to extremes. Since it is free from any expression and clinging due to one-sided [reference points] of clinging to extremes, it is **inexpressible**. The *Tantra of Awareness's Being Free in Itself* says this:

> It is the very self-dissolution of the stains of the four extremes.[356]

Thus, the wisdom of the alpha-pure essence is the inseparability of emptiness and lucidity, similar to a completely pure sky. The wisdom of the innately present nature is [its] inseparable natural luminosity, similar to an ocean free from silt. The wisdom of all-pervasive compassionate responsiveness is the inseparability of awareness and emptiness, similar to a stainless gem. What does not transcend the nature of these three wisdoms is called "the dharmatā of the ground." The *Garland of Pearls Tantra* says this:

> Though the basic nature is inconceivable,
> it consists of the three kinds of wisdom.[357]

The *Sixfold Expanse* states this:

> Through the three kinds of wisdom, {7b}
> the ground's distinctive features are taught as words.[358]

Unrealized, the dharmatā of the ground, which is endowed with these three wisdoms, is present as the ground of saṃsāra, but its own essence does not fall into the one-sided domain of saṃsāra. Therefore, it is [still] suitable as the ground of nirvāṇa. Realized, it is present as the ground of nirvāṇa, but its own essence does not fall into the one-sided domain of nirvāṇa. Therefore, it [can also] serve as the ground of saṃsāra. Hence, it is the general ground of all phenomena of saṃsāra and nirvāṇa—original buddhahood itself. It abides as the basic nature of all the particulars that are the phenomena of saṃsāra and nirvāṇa, free from anything to be removed or added. Therefore, it cannot be expressed [in accordance with] delusion (the stains of the phenomena of **saṃsāra**) or its remedy (the realization of the path to **nirvāṇa**); that is, [it cannot be expressed] in accordance with the particulars of the one-sided domains **of the dyad** that consists of the paths of factors to be relinquished and their remedies, [both of which] arise from effort. Consequently, it is **without the names** [of any of those phenomena]: it is present in such a way that it is free from the one-sided domains of both saṃsāra and nirvāṇa.

However, the flaws and qualities of delusion and freedom, or saṃsāra and nirvāṇa, respectively, arise merely due to the ground's basic nature not having been revealed or having been so. Thus, they are present [just like] food and clothing in our hands. **If there is** the ability to undeludedly recognize and be **aware of just this** actuality of the ground on the basis of its own true face, firmly decide on this one thing, and gain confidence in being free, **it is** the time when [the ground] is present as the **buddhahood** that consists of the ground's having been rendered free from stains, because all consummate, innately present qualities are perfectly complete in their own place.[359] [On the other hand,] due to being **unaware** of this mode of being of the ground, just as it is, and its not having been revealed, the entire [scope] of apprehender and apprehended {8a} is readily acquired [through] the power of delusion, and thus **sentient beings** torment themselves through the actions that they themselves have committed, as well as their results. Thus, they will endlessly **wander in saṃsāra** at all times. The *[Pramāṇa]vārttika* says this:

> Through what could the result be stopped
> in the case of its fully complete causes?[360]

Therefore, through relying on this function of the supreme secret path of Samantabhadra, **may all** innumerable **sentient beings** included in **the three realms** and the six classes [of beings], who are under the sway of unawareness, karma, and afflictions, **be** nakedly **aware of the actuality** or basic nature **of** the mode of being of **the** primordial **ground** of **inexpressible** alpha-purity, and let it be revealed.[361]

2.1.2. Teaching Samantabhadra's mode of freedom through taking the recognition of the [ground] as the path

This has two parts:

1. The actual mode of freedom

2. The manner of promoting the welfare of others after having become free

2.1.2.1. The actual mode of freedom

This is taught through the six stanzas[362] and the one line that begin with "**I, Samantabhadra.**" While at all [**samanta**] times never rising from the spaciousness of the dharmadhātu, which is endowed with the twofold freedom from stains, **I**, or myself, the primal buddha—these fruitional phenomena of having gained mastery over the unbiased array of the excellent [**bhadra**], miraculous displays of wisdom that are the self-appearances [of the dharmadhātu]—surely neither arose through being fabricated in dependence on **causes and conditions** in terms of what is to be adopted and to be discarded, or to be blocked and accomplished, through the path of the conceptual mind that involves effort, {8b} nor am I something permanent and truly established that is causeless and self-arisen **without** depending on any cause.

Nevertheless, at the time of either the ground or the path, all these boundless qualities of the self-radiance of the innately present, luminous brilliance of cognizance deep within the expanse **of the** alpha-pure and primal primordial **ground** are enclosed within this expanse, together with the dimension of the delusion of the impure mind and winds. By virtue of prajñā's maturing the energy of the primordial winds of the native wisdom of awareness into becoming powerful, the seal of the innately present youthful vase [body] is rent open, and thus the appearances of the expanse dawn as outer luminosity. [In this process,] it is compassionate responsiveness's awareness itself, [which is aware] of the basic mode of being that is **the actuality** of [those appearances] (**these very** empty appearances, which have the form of space), that undergoes a slight shift through simply dawning as the dimension of unawareness. [However,] in the very moment of **being** inwardly **aware** that [all] that appears **from the ground**'s own expanse dawns in a **self-arising** manner, [there is no] clinging to any of these appearances as being objects that are established over there from the **outside**, [or] to the awareness that appears as these [appearances] as being a subject that is established over here from the **inside.**[363] [There are also no] **superimpositions** of what is pleasant, unpleasant, and neutral that evolve from the self-inflated cognizance of thinking, "I am here and that is over there" **and** [no] **denial** in the form of thinking that existing empty appearances, [which are reified] due to clinging to them as entities and characteristics, do not exist as [mere] empty appearances.

Thus, [the ground] is not obscured **by the** mental **flaws** of imaginative unawareness, which has the character of all kinds of superimpositions and denials. Hence, it is **unaffected** and untouched by any superimposition or denial. It is [also] unimpaired **and untainted by the stains** that resemble **darkness**—[the unawareness of] identical character, whose nature consists of the dense and dull **mindlessness** that is the sheer oblivion of the true reality of the expanse, {9a} as well as connate unawareness. **Therefore**, it is free from the bondage of unawareness and clinging. The *Universes and Transformations of Sound* says this:

> What appears on its own through the power of rising
> from the ground is known to be without any nature of its own.
> Mentations of examination and analysis do not deviate to the
> outside,
> and there is a firm decision on the basis of movement itself.[364]

The *Tantra of the Wheel of Self-Arising Bliss* states this:

> If awareness wells up from a slight caress,
> being radiantly lucid, it is free from superimposition and denial.[365]

Thus, once the uncontaminated self-arising remedy of self-appearances' recognizing their own face clearly differentiates [them as what they actually are], without being contingent on any remedy other than just this differentiating, and with the qualities that are [the ground's] **self-appearances being untainted by any flaws** of clinging and delusion, this is the unfolding of the wisdom of being free from delusion including [all] its aspects. The *Blazing Lamp Tantra* states this:

What matures the very ground as the fruition is prajñā:
through[366] prajñā's maturing as kāyas,
the essence dharmakāya
is matured as the wisdom dharmakāya.
The wisdom of this [kāya] is uninterrupted—
kāyas and wisdoms are innately lucid.[367]

At which time is Samantabhadra free? Master Vimala[mitra] declares this:

As for the natural ground of primal alpha-purity,
its essence is that it is not established as anything whatsoever,
while its nature is that it appears as anything whatsoever.
Its compassionate responsiveness is to be free in dawning as anything whatsoever.

Accordingly, {9b} Samantabhadra is free at the time when the seal of the inner expanse's sphere of innate presence is rent open, [this sphere of innate presence] rises from the ground and is seen as the ground manifestations.

Through what is Samantabhadra free? The same [master] states this:

By virtue of knowing the basic nature of entities,
one's own welfare is realized and the stream of delusion is thereby exhausted.

Thus, Samantabhadra is free through the prajñā of self-appearances being realized and appearing as the play of wisdom and their being differentiated from the characteristics of entities, which are other-appearances.[368]

How is [Samantabhadra] free? He is free by way of realizing self-appearances to be self-appearances through differentiating them from other-appearances.

What is freedom? Through the power of being without adventitious stains, freedom does not arise from anything other, but merely consists of revealing primordially free wisdom as complete freedom.[369] The *Garland of Pearls* says this:

> Everything becomes fully awakened as the abode
> of alpha-purity, which is free from stains.[370]

In which location is Samantabhadra free? The [same] tantra says this:

> The very locus of freedom is the beginning.[371]

And:

> Once the primordially present heart of the matter itself
> has been revealed through cognizance,
> it has arrived at the locus of phenomena's exhaustion.[372]

Accordingly, the primal alpha-purity that rests in its very own place[373] is free as the original inner expanse. Through the prajñā winds' dissolving [back into this expanse], prajñā travels within space. Through the impure elements' dissolving, the elements become dormant within the mother[-ground]. Through the temporary {10a} wisdom of the path dissolving, wisdom dissolves within the expanse. Original wisdom dissolves but is not oblivious. It is lucid but nonconceptual, and yet lacks any identity. Through thoughts' not making any distinctions within [natural] distinctness,[374] prajñā swirls within space. Thus, at the time of the unceasing wisdom that is like eternity, the changeless dharmakāya—the kāya that is like a vajra—is endowed with the water of uninterrupted samādhi that is like nectar and the light of the unobscured awakened mind that is like the sun and the moon. Therefore, this is called "having seized awareness's very own place." The *Tantra Without Letters* states this:

> They have gone beyond to the place without going
> . . . .
> the single buddha without thoughts is seen.[375]

Accordingly, the dharmakāya of having come face to face with realization abides as the completely perfect primal buddha—Samantabhadra, whose character consists of the three dharmas[376] and who is self-arising as the sphere of innate presence, which is the consummate fruition.

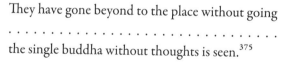

Thus, within the spaciousness of the wisdom of the empty inner expanse, lucid **self-aware** prajñā seizes **its** very own **seat**. That is, without deliberately clinging to whatever appears, and without being distracted from the yoga of simply letting [this self-aware prajñā] be, it is **resting** [just as it is]. **Within** this [state], **even if** there dawn appearances like the simultaneous **destruction** of **the threefold existence** (which consists of the appearance dimension of the intermediate state of dharmatā—the triad of sounds, lights, and rays), through understanding that these sounds are the sounds of the mother-ground of all, there is no **fear** of these sounds. {10b} Through knowing that the lights are the five wisdoms' own lights, there is no fright of these lights. Through knowing that the illumination of [light] rays represents the dynamic energy of awareness—the emanations of compassionate responsiveness—**there is no anxiety.**

Nor is there any impairment through the fixation of clinging **attachment to** what consists of **the five** kinds of **sense pleasures** that appear, filling [the entirety of] space and making up the riches of the saṃsāric and nirvāṇic realms of gods, humans, and so on. Unimpeded **nonconceptual** wisdom free from reference points is allowed to sustain [itself] as such, in its own **self-arising** and self-settled way, which is the attainment of consummate stability. **In** this state, through knowing that the [self-arising] appearances of saṃsāra and nirvāṇa, which have the nature of being pleasing or frightening, contradict the makeup of the five objects (such as **forms** and sounds) that seem to be **solid** material phenomena, the stirring and scattering of the thoughts that consist of **the five poisons**—the afflictions of hoping to block, accomplish, adopt, or reject these [objects]—are severed at their root. Thus, **neither** [real objects nor the ensuing afflictions] **exist.**

Without thus being bound by any clinging to the appearances of objects, the wisdom **of** self-luminous **awareness** without clinging is present as **the unceasing dimension of lucidity** in an undisturbed and clear manner. Due to that, it **is of a single essence and yet** will unfold as the impartial knowledge of **fivefold wisdom**, which is classified merely in terms of its aspects, which are isolates. In that way, the appearances of **the five primal buddha families** of the victors and the five mothers (which serve as the ground of the arising of nirmāṇakāyas or the ground of their emanation) **spring forth** and thrive as the self-appearances of these five wisdoms **from the maturation** and unfolding **of these** very **five wisdoms. Through** the power of the dynamic energy of **wisdom** endlessly **unfolding from that,** {11a} its appearances expand even further, and thus the maṇḍala of **the forty-two** [deities] ([the principals of] the five **buddha** families, the five mothers, the sixteen male and female bodhisattvas, the six sages, and the eight male and female gatekeepers) **originates** and unfolds. At the time of the impartial unfolding **of the five wisdoms, the dynamic energy of** the maṇḍala of these peaceful [deities] that is primordially appearing [further] **dawns** in a wrathful form. **Through** this, **the sixty** glorious, great herukas, who **drink** the **blood** of the clinging to duality, also appear and **come to life** in an innately present manner. In this way, due to delusion's becoming pure and due to delusion-free wisdom's unfolding, these primordial appearances expand in an unbiased fashion. **Therefore**, the **ground**—the wisdom of alpha-purity, which is the self-arising **awareness** that **was** primordially **never deluded**—has arrived at being completely free within the spaciousness of being primordially free.[377]

At that point, **since I, the primal buddha**, Samantabhadra, have become revealed, **through** the power of **making** and relying on this **aspiration prayer** of the profound, secret awakened mind of **myself** (Samantabhadra), or the path of realizing it, in their own mind streams with the pair of devoted and constant vigor, **may** all **sentient beings, who** are included in six classes and **cycle** powerlessly **through** the abodes of **the three realms** by virtue of their karmas and afflictions, **recognize the** ground's own **face** (the wisdom **of self-arising awareness**'s [own face] together with its primordial appearances), may they, based on that, endlessly **unfold** the orb of the **great** self-appearances of **wisdom**, and may they thus be able to seize the original stronghold free from stains.

2.1.2.2. The manner of promoting the welfare of others after having become free

{11b} This is taught through the stanza and the two lines that begin with "**my emanations**." The alpha-pure expanse of **my**self, Samantabhadra (the dharmakāya's having come face to face with realization), is the realm of the dharmakāya. While not departing from it, the compassionate responsiveness that [arises] from the gates of innạte presence and involves the enlightened activity of promoting the welfare of sentient beings in accordance with their modes of appearance represents the **emanation** bodies. Since the time during which these [emanations] remain is as long as [saṃsāric] existence lasts, they **are a** constant, **uninterrupted flow**. Since their number is equal to [the vastness of] space, they consist of **billions**; that is, they are unlimited. Since they cannot be calculated as objects that are assessable by the mind, they are **inconceivable**. Thus, having the nature of being permanent and pervasive, without depending on being created newly through the power of any effort, they **unfold** and are displayed **as** simply arising on their own, in an effortless and innately present manner.

Now, [Samantabhadra's] essence displays as the [three] kāyas. The dharmakāya is the truly established kāya. To always experience it through compassionate responsiveness is the sambhogakāya. The nirmāṇakāya is this very dharmakāya as it promotes the welfare of beings through the omniscient wisdom that arises as all kinds of rūpakāya displays whatsoever, from the perspective of the appearances of those to be guided, in accordance with their [individual] fortunes in terms of their constitutions, faculties, and thinking. The *Tantra Without Letters* says this:

> The mode in which the kāya abides is threefold:
> Since it is free from phenomena that are characteristics,
> it is not [established] as any delineated form.
> Since the nature of lucidity is perfect, {12a}
> its appearances lack any nature of their own.
> Since it trains the mind streams of those to be guided,
> it abides in the great, immovable meditative equipoise.[378]

[Samantabhadra's] nature displays as the wisdoms. The wisdom of the dharmakāya—the ultimate wisdom that is present as the ground and is endowed with the three distinctive features[379]—pervades [both] ground and fruition without any partiality. The wisdom of the sambhogakāya—the great, vast, and unimpeded inseparability of emptiness and lucidity—has the nature of the five wisdoms. The wisdom of the nirmāṇakāya—knowing the basic nature of how things are, as well as the presentations of their entire variety—has the function of bestowing siddhis in conformity with the fortunes of [individual] sentient beings. The *Universes and Transformations of Sound* declares this:

> The wisdom that is present as the ground
> functions as the ground for nature's automatic dawning.
> The wisdom of apprehending characteristics
> matures the pure ones through conditions.
> The wisdom of knowing and knowable
> bestows siddhis upon those with devotion.[380]

[Samantabhadra's] compassionate responsiveness displays as the deeds of enlightened activity. Thus, all the kāyas, wisdoms, and qualities mature and function for sentient beings as the single means that matures them, in [countless] temporary and lasting ways, until saṃsāra is empty. The *Universes and Transformations of Sound* states this:

> Thus, by virtue of the mode of arising of compassionate
> responsiveness,
> the kāyas who guide them are just as numerous
> as the various beings to be guided.[381] {12b}

In that way, enlightened deeds have the nature of compassionate responsiveness, compassionate responsiveness has the nature of wisdom, wisdom has the nature of the kāyas, the three kāyas have the nature of the dharmakāya, and the dharmakāya is something like the general ground of all kāyas. The *Array of Inlaid Gems* says this:

> From within the appearance of the dharmakāya,
> the appearances of the three kāyas are simultaneously perfect.[382]

Thus, from within the natural state of the dharmakāya, **a vast array of** means of **guiding** those to be guided, through any **suitable** means, **displays.** This constitutes the enlightened deeds of the nirmāṇakāya. The *Abhisamayālaṃkāra* states this:

> The perpetual nirmāṇakāya of the sage
> is the one through which various benefits
> for the world are performed equally,
> until the end of [saṃsāric] existence.[383]

The *Mañjuśrīnāmasaṃgīti* says this:

> You who send out infinite myriads
> of nirmāṇakāyas of the buddhas[384]

And:

> You who send out all kinds of emanations in the ten directions,
> acting in accordance with the welfare of the world.[385]

Thus, the perfection of the two welfares comes down to buddhahood alone. Therefore, the genuine, ultimate heart of all **my** or his (that of Buddha Samantabhadra, who solely thinks about the welfare of sentient beings) **compassionate** enlightened activity, which appears as the glory of sentient beings, combines the instructions of [all] sūtras and tantras in the form of their single quintessence. It represents the sole destination of the paths of hundreds of **aspirations** of the awakened minds of the victors in the three times and the supreme **path**[386] of the Great Perfection, which is the unsurpassable, ultimate secret. {13a} Based on this, **through** revealing the consummate qualities of the innately present three kāyas, **may** these **sentient beings** without end, **who cycle** without beginning **through** the birthplaces of **the three realms** and are fettered by the traps of threefold suffering, **leave the** three [kinds of] births due to the afflictions **of the six families** that constitute appearances of delusion (the paths that consist of both causes and results) as well as the four paths that are states (the state of birth, the state of dying, the intermediate state, and the state of the previous time)[387] **behind** and thus attain mastery over the enlightened deeds that empty the pit of saṃsāra [from its depths].

2.1.3. The manner in which sentient beings are deluded in saṃsāra due to not knowing the actuality of the ground

This has two parts:

1. General instruction on the mode of delusion
2. The particular distinct instruction on the [mode of delusion]

2.1.3.1. General instruction on the mode of delusion

This is taught through the three stanzas and the three lines that begin with "**at first, since deluded sentient beings.**"

There is no delusion in the primal **first** ground. However, as far as **sentient beings** under the sway of many sorts of adventitious **delusion** are concerned, at the time when the ground manifestations dawn **in the ground**, they are not aware of these self-appearances' own face, which [for them] **does not dawn as** the **awareness** that is the play of wisdom. **Since** they therefore possess the root of indeterminate unawareness, they compartmentalize the ground manifestations. Therefore, sentient beings are deluded. The *Garland of Pearls* says this:

> From the appearance of the great uniqueness,
> both existents and nonexistents arise.
> The general locus becomes called "the ground of delusion."
> Since it is polluted by unawareness itself, {13b}
> exactly that which is to be known appears as stains.[388]

Furthermore, the same [text] states this:

> The sky-like dharmakāya
> is obscured by the clouds of adventitious sentient beings.
> The undeluded dharmatā as well

is associated with the mode of adventitious delusion—
the momentariness that involves causes and conditions.[389]

Thus, among the causes and conditions of delusion, the causes are the three [kinds of] unawareness. Among them, [the first one] is the [causal] unawareness that serves as something like the initial ground for the evolution [of further unawareness and delusion]. The *Tantra [of the Universes and Transformations of Sound]* states this:

Unawareness is of three kinds:
The one of same identity functions as the root of delusion.
The connate one has the two conceptions.
Through the imaginative one, it turns into objects.[390]

Master Vimalamitra says this:

As for the "causes," definitely, the one of same identity
is the first of the [three] unawarenesses.
From it, the connate one
appears because of being contingent on pure wisdom.
Therefore, the appearing of objects is the imaginative one.

The threefold unawareness [described] in this way consists of the three kinds of unawareness that are contrary to the three dharmas of the ground [essence, nature, and compassionate responsiveness].[391] Among these [three kinds of unawareness], the first one is the unawareness that operates in a manner that is contrary [to the ground] by way of its sheer oblivion about the actuality of the [ground's] essence free from reference points. It lacks [all] qualities, such as the revelation of the mindfulness and alertness of the native state of this [essence] free from reference points. Given its **absolute lack** of any appearance of being **mindful** of objects, it is [completely] **oblivious** and dull. **Exactly that** is called "the unawareness that has the same identity as the cause." For it is the **unawareness** that serves as **the cause of** [both] connate and imaginative unawareness, as well as all kinds of deluded appearances in terms of karma, afflictions, and **delusion.** {14a}

Within the state of that first unawareness, a multitude of appearances, consisting of the triad of sounds, lights, and rays and filling [all] space, arise in a progressive manner. Upon becoming initially distracted toward these [appearances] and discerning them, they appear as self and other, as well as subject and object, and the clinging to an apprehender [of these appearances] first arises. Then, through initially being very afraid of **those** appearances of objects, a **dazed unconsciousness** and passing out occur. **From** that [state], due to differences in terms of greater or lesser fright, a **fearful and anxious cognizance** evolves gradually, arising in a **vague** and languid manner. Once again, with regard to all **those** appearances of a multitude of indistinct objects, just as before, the duality of **self and others** (thinking, "I am over here, and what is over there is over there"), **as well as the clinging to** attractive friends and repellent **enemies, arises.** From such clinging to a personal self, [all] primary and secondary afflictions such as desire and hatred evolve, and thus propelling karmas are newly accumulated, again and again. Also, the karmas that have been accumulated since many eons ago are revived through craving and grasping and thus **gradually** unfold and **blossom** as powerful karmic **latent tendencies. Through** those that serve as completing karmas, the dependent origination of propelled results and completed results in the form of the birthplaces of the six classes [of beings] in **saṃsāra** is accomplished in **its natural** progression. Thus, {14b} saṃsāra **unfolds**, powerlessly **taking** its **course** in the form of the spokes of the wheel of delusion that make up the great mountain of suffering, such as misery and wailing.

Again, **by virtue of that** ground of suffering consisting of the results of prior dependent origination, **the five poisons of the afflictions** (such as attachment and hatred) arise by **flourishing** with intense force in their many facets. Due to their arising, **the karmas** that are accumulated through **these five poisons** of the afflictions arise in each moment as a multitude within the basis of their karmic allotment, in such a manner that they **become an incessant flow.** In that way, the three paths of dependent origination[392] are linked[393] in their sequential progression in time, and **thus** keep revolving as the single, sharp point of a weapon that involves a host of flaws.

[In sum], **the ground** that serves as the root **of** the flaws of the appearances of **delusion of sentient beings**—who are overwhelmed by it without waking up from it—**is** the **unawareness** that consists of the sheer, **mindless** oblivion of not seeing the actual mode of being of the essence that was taught above. Therefore, if this cause that is the root [of delusion] does not come to an end, all suffering will flow uninterruptedly. If this cause does come to its end, its results—[all] flaws and sufferings—will naturally come to their end.

Hence, through the power of relying on **this** ultimate Dharma of the awakened mind of **myself, the buddha** Samantabhadra—the quintessence of all **aspirations**, the **path** of the Great Perfection that is the ultimate secret—**may the** very expanse of the alpha-pure essence of the **awareness of all** sentient beings be able to **know** and see in **its own** place.

2.1.3.2. The particular distinct instruction on the [mode of delusion]

This is taught through the two stanzas and the three lines that begin with "**connate.**" {15a} Given that delusion thus comes about through the coming together of the three [kinds of] unawareness and the four conditions, the pair of connate unawareness and imaginative unawareness evolves from (1) the unawareness of same identity—the oblivion about the essence free from reference points—that was taught above.

In due order, (2) the **unawareness** that operates in a manner that is contrary to the phenomena which have the nature of the ground, and thus originates as the distracted delusion of what dawns as other-appearances, **arises** on its own **simultaneously**[394] or together with the phenomena that are the [self-appearing] qualities of [the ground's] nature dawning as outer luminosity. This [unawareness] **is** precisely the **mindless cognizance** of being oblivious about the basic mode of being of the ground's essence, and it has the nature of being **distracted** toward the appearance of objects.

From that [connate unawareness], (3) there arises the **unawareness of imagining** and analyzing [all kinds of] negations and affirmations with regard to all appearances of objects—which operates in a manner that is contrary to the awareness of compassionate responsiveness. This [unawareness] thereby arises as the essence of clinging to subject and object, and thus has the nature of all kinds of superimpositions and denials in terms of distinct apprehenders and what they apprehend. [This imaginative unawareness] is nothing but the clinging to a [real] identity of phenomena. Based on this [clinging to such an identity], through observing the self-appearances [of the ground] as **the duality of self and others**, the clinging to a [real] identity of persons—**the clinging to** [oneself and others as] being established as [independent,] specifically characterized phenomena—**is** arising.

Thus, **this twofold unawareness—connate** unawareness **and imaginative** unawareness—and the unawareness of same identity, as the third one, constitute the causes of delusion.

Not only that but there are [also] {15b} the following four conditions [from which delusion arises]:

(1) The first among them is called the *causal condition*. For just as in the example of the actual face of a person serving as the causal condition for becoming deluded about its reflection [in a mirror] as being that [actual] face, we here speak of the causal condition in the sense that the delusion consisting of the afflictions (such as the clinging to a self), karma, and its results arises from the three kinds of unawareness.

(2) The miraculous displays of the appearances that are the ground manifestations constitute the *object condition*. For just as in the example of the reflection [of a face] that appears in a mirror being the object condition for being deluded about it as being the [actual] face, the dimensions of the ground's appearances serve as the object condition for the delusion of apprehending these [appearances] as focal objects that are other-appearances.

(3) Thus, when the appearances of objects and the conceptions that constitute the subjects which take those [appearances]

as objects come together, these subjects individually discern those objects as "this is this" and "that is that." This examining [of objects by subjects] represents the *dominant condition*. For just as in the example of a face, a mirror, and a reflection [of that face], which appear and are conceived as being distinct, being the dominant conditions for being deluded about that reflection as being the [actual] face, [likewise,] the ground manifestations (the objects) and the conceptions (the subjects) that take these [ground manifestations] as objects and discern them as being their own objects serve as the dominant conditions for the arising of delusion, such as the clinging to a self.

(4) The coming together of the triad of the causal condition, the object condition, and the dominant condition in this way constitutes the *immediate condition* for the arising of delusion. This corresponds to the example of the coming together of these three [conditions] in the case of a face [reflected in a mirror] {16a} serving as the immediate condition for being deluded about that reflection as being the [actual] face.

Thus, by way of unawareness itself serving as both the causes and the conditions for the **delusion of all sentient beings**, it **is the** basic **ground of** delusion.[395]

Therefore, **through** relying on the function of **this** ultimate **aspiration** of the awakened mind **of myself, the buddha** Samantabhadra, which is the **path**[396] of the Ati Great Perfection, **may** the **darkness of** the **mindless**, oblivious, and **dull** unawareness of the all-ground that serves as the root **of all** flaws of delusion and constitutes the origin of [all] **sentient beings** who roam through **saṃsāra be dispelled**. May **their awareness**—in which **their cognizance of** grasping thoughts that **clings to** the **duality** of self and others' distinctness and is rooted in the flaws of connate and imaginative unawareness has vanished in[397] the original inner expanse—be able to nakedly **recognize** and see **its own face**, which is the great emptiness of the natural state without reference points.

2.2. The explanation of the path of delusion's coming to its end once the ground has been revealed

Among the two paths of maturation and freedom, in the beginning, the mind stream is matured through the power of the means of maturation and the stable life-vein that consists of the *samaya* vows including their basis [is adopted].[398] Through that, we enter this path that frees. On it, if the unmistaken introduction that consists of introducing the actuality of the ground—the path's outlook with which to familiarize and which is made into the path—is not planted [properly into the mind stream] at the beginning, we will not be able to go beyond the narrow passages of deviating, erring, and going astray during the time of cultivating that path in the middle. Due to that, {16b} we will not go beyond anything, but simply distance ourselves from the qualities of the fruition. Therefore, though there are many methods of introducing the outlook with which to familiarize that are contingent on the differences in the faculties of [different] persons, it is crucial in the beginning to excellently drive the nails of the essential points of the clear distinctions of the all-ground not becoming the dharmakāya, mentation not becoming wisdom, and mind not becoming awareness into our own mind stream. Consequently, the wisdom of awareness, which is the dharmakāya free from [all] coarse and subtle turbidities of the all-ground, mentation, and mind, must be identified on the basis of its own face. The *Garland of Pearls* says this:

> The wise need to understand
> the distinction between mind and wisdom.[399]

The *Sixfold Expanse* states this:

> If mind's and wisdom's own essences are not distinguished,
> this is similar to the sun being obscured by cloud banks—
> it cannot perform the function of illuminating what is outside.[400]

The *Universes and Transformations of Sound* declares this:

> As for the essential point of the all-ground and the
> dharmakāya...[401]

Accordingly, the all-ground represents the ultimate ground and support of mentation, mind, and their latent tendencies, thus being characterized by unawareness. The dharmakāya is the wisdom free from reference points that is completely pure of all [forms of] mind, mentation, and their latent tendencies, thus being characterized by unawareness having come to its end. The *Garland of Pearls* says this:

> Because the all-ground has been accumulated,
> the dharmakāya is the termination of contamination.
> It is empty and lucid, lucid and pervasive,
> unpolluted by thinking, {17a} devoid of minding,
> and free from any reference points.[402]

Mind is the phenomenon that is associated with unawareness and possesses stains—ordinary saṃsāra, which resembles clouds obscuring the sun of wisdom. Wisdom is associated with the dharmakāya and is stainless, resembling the sun that is free from [the clouds of] mind's minding and thinking. The *Garland of Pearls* states this:

> Mind is the ground of all latent tendencies.
> It represents the stains of sentient beings,
> being both the apprehended and the apprehender.
> Therefore, it is the very nature of saṃsāra.[403]

Since awareness's own dharmatā does not transcend the empty expanse, once the expanse free from reference points is revealed, it is through its own power that wisdom appears as awareness. Since the appearing of wisdom as awareness does not transcend the expanse either, once the wisdom of the actuality that is the freedom from reference points is revealed, both the all-ground (what pervades) and the mind (what is pervaded) simply disappear by vanishing on their own. The [same] tantra says this:

> Wisdom is free from the very ground of minding.[404]

Therefore, once the true face of the wisdom without reference points and free from thoughts—which is not impaired by the dimension of the delusion of the all-ground, mind, and mentation—is identified on the basis of itself, by being free from all doubts of searching for any path other than this, there will be a firm decision on this one thing. If there is such a firm decision on this, and certainty is induced [in that way], {17b} there arises the ability to sustain exactly this natural state without losing it. By virtue of the arising of that [ability to sustain this state], the ability to gain confidence in being free will come about as well.[405]

Thus, when adventitious, ordinary delusion wells up in an abrupt fashion, the progression of the manner in which this [delusion] becomes free consists of the path of the five poisons' being free as the five wisdoms without relinquishing them. The explanation of this has five parts.

2.2.1. The manner in which desire is free as discriminating wisdom

This is taught through the four stanzas and the two lines that begin with "**the mind of dualistic clinging.**" Among the five poisons of the afflictions, it is from the point of view of its appearance that desire is explained to be delusion.

Therefore, the state of mind of thinking whether the appearance of an object is attractive or not attractive[406] is **the mind** that involves **clinging** to **dualistic** items, which **is** called "a dual mind" or "**doubt.**" From the perspective of what appears to be attractive, as this [doubt] gradually evolves from this primary affliction, craving and **fixating** clinging only arise in just a **subtle** form at first; but without relying on a remedy for this, it is attached fixation's own force that makes this [fixation] **arise** and increase further. **Due to**[407] **that**, the **latent tendencies** of the craving of attached fixation in their subtle forms are progressively accumulated and thus will **gradually unfold** and expand into **dense** or stable latent tendencies. Thus, **be it** tasty, delicious **food**; accumulated, protected, and sustained **wealth**; expensive ornaments and **clothing**; stable and joyful **places**; long-acquainted **companions** and friends; {18a} and the riches of **the five**

sense pleasures that are the glory of the higher realms; **or**, furthermore, assemblies of **relatives** for whom we feel heartfelt affection and with whom we are mutually connected through **love** and kindness—without seeing the shortcomings of such objects, they appear to have **attractive** forms, and **we** will thus **be** greatly **tormented** and plagued **by the desire** of being **attached** and clinging **to** them.

This kind of desire and its objects **are** contaminated **mundane** phenomena (the reality of suffering that consists of the appropriated skandhas), whose sole nature is **delusion**. In this world, through such desire, there is not only no satisfaction but also craving increases excessively. The clinging to the mere names and designations of those objects of craving, and to the mere essence of what is expressed [by them] or the mere generalities of their meanings, [is called] "the mind that is the **apprehended** object." What finely differentiates the particular distinctive features of these objects' means of expression and of the objects of expression is called "the mind that is the **apprehending** subject." Through the attached fixation that has evolved into having the essence of such a mind with apprehender and apprehended, we are tormented in a very intense manner, **and the** [countless] specifications of volitional and volitioned **karmas** accumulated through this attached craving **are never exhausted.**[408] Rather, in each moment, they have been accumulated and will be accumulated naturally, on their own.

In future times, **when the results of clinging** and craving **ripen** and are thus experienced, {18b} **we are born in** the abodes of **hungry ghosts** such as the city Kapila, experiencing the [many] sufferings of being **tortured by craving** for food, drink, and so on. As those who have outer obscurations, those who have inner obscurations, and those who have specific obscurations,[409] we will experience many **pitiful** and unbearable sufferings, such as **hunger**, **thirst**, heat, cold, exhaustion, and fear, for a long time.

When such suffering arises through being lost in this kind of ordinary delusion, the ultimate of all **aspirations** of the awakened mind **of myself, the buddha** Samantabhadra, is the short **path**[410] of the very heart of the matter—that is, the awakened mind of delusion's not being relinquished, but being primordially free as wisdom. Within that [awakened mind], and without depending on any other remedy, object, or time, delusion [simply] is pure in its own place **through** the power and the blessings of the secret, profound miracle of the skill in the means to allow this stainless wisdom to sustain itself in such a manner that it is stripped naked, uncontrived, and naturally settled. The *Garland of Pearls* says this:

> Though cycling sentient beings
> are bound by their own thoughts,
> freedom is certain due to their lack of nature.[411]

Apart from what only looks like delusion, due to being under the sway of the power of being confused about not moving away from self-abiding wisdom, there is no being tainted by any [independent,] specifically characterized phenomena, nor any being under the control of what seems to have the nature of delusion. Rather, it is [simply] by virtue of wandering away from awareness's own domain, and thus straying based on its dynamic energy, that the power of delusion {19a} is encountered in an unobstructed manner and can thus be overcome [through recognizing this]. Since this is what is taught [here], on this supreme path, the manner of delusion and freedom is not to become pure through something like relinquishment as in [the paths of] śrāvakas and pratyekabuddhas, purification as in [the path of] bodhisattvas, transformation as in the creation and completion [stages], taming through a remedy as in the outer [tantras], mind's settling within its own natural way as in the Mind Series, or taking everything to be the single dharmatā as in the Expanse Series. Rather, this is the unblemished method to overcome the source of the life-force of saṃsāra all at once through merely revealing [its actual] nature—the self-abiding wisdom that is beyond mind. The *Kiss of the Sun and the Moon* states this:

> If suchness is not realized,
> yoga is like a body and its shadow.
> Since one is self-arising from the other,

> it is not relinquished through relinquishment.
> Likewise, it is neither [purified] through purification,
> nor will it change through any transformation.[412]

This is the essential point of being free in itself, like a drawing on water. In terms of different faculties: (1) Being free through effort represents "the mode of freedom that is like meeting a person with whom we were acquainted before." That is, though we may fall under the sway of thoughts that arise, it is through the power of the effort of mindfulness that they are reabsorbed back into the spaciousness that is their own abode and thereby become free. (2) Being free without effort is twofold. (a) First, the mode of freedom that consists of thoughts' having become free in themselves and resembles a snake's knots untying [themselves on their own is as follows]: at the very time when thoughts arise, {19b} they become free [immediately] by sinking right back into the wisdom of the native state through their own power. (b) Second, the mode of freedom that consists of thoughts' being without benefit or harm and resembles a thief's entering an empty house [is as follows]: no matter which abrupt thoughts may arise, given that they cannot be stolen away from the spaciousness of dharmatā, which is their own abode, they are empty of any [independent,] specifically characterized arising, though it may seem as if they arise—that is, at the very time when they arise, they are [already] free in their own place.[413]

Thus, **may sentient beings** in whom the intense craving and **clinging of desire** for, and the **attachment** to, the objects of attached fixation taught above has arisen, and who have fallen under its sway, **neither cast** it off, as in the case of the general yāna, through not relying on tiresome activities that involve effort (such as casting **out the torment of** the craving of **desirous** attached fixation from their own mind streams through the power of other remedies), **nor** openly **welcome** it, and thus bring it about **within**, as in the case of ordinary persons (such as relying on it in their mind streams as **the** pervasive and seemingly uninterrupted **clinging of** the attached craving of **desire** and **attachment**, based on the objects of attachment).[414]

Rather, the native nature of the **cognizance** that manifests as desirous fixation and so on does not become free in a sudden manner, but it abides as the essence that is [already] primordially free, since the primordial beginning. Thus, there are no stains to be purified or to become free from by delivering them to stainless wisdom—the empty expanse without any reference points, which is free from the referential phenomena that consist of the adventitious stains that involve arising and ceasing (such as some ground of supporting, some root of arising, or some characteristics of abiding). {20a} Therefore, desire is free from any ground to be delivered to.

In that way, as the fundamental ground of the adventitious stains, the wisdom whose own face is not blemished by any dimension of delusion is devoid of any meeting and parting and thus represents these stains' actual dharmatā. Hence, these stains are revealed as their very own remedy, through **letting** them **relax** in an uncontrived manner **in their own state**, as the self-arising wisdom that is their own native dharmatā. It is **through** exactly this that the [stains] are free; they are not contingent on any other remedy that makes them free. Therefore, they are devoid of any remedy.

Thus, this freedom does not [occur] in such a way that the dharmatā of the stains (attachment and so on) is revealed and they thus become free thereafter. Rather, in the very first instant of seeing the basic nature of these stains, **awareness takes** its own domain, which is its own state—the wisdom that is dharmatā—as **its very own seat**, and thus [these stains] are free immediately upon the very instant of revealing [awareness's] sheer nakedness, or of its sheer being seen. Consequently, appearances [are free in themselves] right from their sheer appearing and based on that very appearing, and cognizances are free in themselves immediately upon their sheer moving and based on that very moving. They vanish within the place of their being seen.

In that way, even in a single stain, such as desire, the basic nature is present in the manner of pervading all stains without any bias. Therefore, without [needing to] rely on different remedies equal in number to the divisions of stains, they will be free just as [described] above through the power of the single nonconceptual wisdom that is the fundamental being of each one [of these stains]. **Thus**, this is called "knowing one, all is free"[415] and "the pith instruction of effortless innate presence." {20b}

In that way, once primordially free wisdom sees its own face, in the instant it is seen, the essence of the freedom of becoming nakedly free absolutely does not transcend the dharmatā of being free from any extremes of reference points, such as arising, ceasing, sameness, difference, being, and nonbeing. The *Universes and Transformations of Sound* says this:

> Since it is primordially free, there is no ground to be delivered to.
> Since it is free by itself, there is no remedy.
> Since it is nakedly free, all vanishes in the place of its being seen.
> Since it is completely free,[416] there is no effort.

Accordingly, by way of thus being endowed with those five qualities of being free,[417] **may** there be the ability to reveal and thus **attain** the distinctly **discriminating** and knowing **wisdom** of desire's being free in its own place.

2.2.2. The manner in which hatred is free as lucid wisdom or mirror[-like] wisdom

This is taught through the three stanzas that begin with "**a subtle mind of fear.**" Hatred is explained [here] as delusion by virtue of its progressive arising.

Therefore, through focusing on **objects** that bring harm, such as inner phenomena without mind (diseases caused by an excess of wind, bile, and so on), **outer** phenomena without mind (harm through the four elements), and harm through inimical sentient beings, **appearances of** a displeasing nature arise from the factors that consist of the nine [kinds of] hostile attitudes, such as thinking, "this one has harmed me in the past," "this one harms me in the present," or "this one will harm me in the future."[418] {21a} By virtue of that, an unpleasant, **subtle mind of fear stirs** and arises in us. Through its power, the **latent tendencies of** the **hatred** that focuses on those objects that harm gradually evolve and **unfold.** What we find [in us] due to that is the powerful force of the hateful and angry thinking that sees and **fixates on enemies** who inflict harm. This **leads to** the **powerful** malice that results in [nonlethal] beatings of the bodies of those objects [that are perceived as harmful] **and** [even] the [kind of] **beating and killing** that takes their lives. In that way, we destroy the roots of virtue from many eons, our loved ones become weary and sad, we cannot gather followers, and throughout the day and the night we lack any notion of our body or mind being happy. Therefore, we do not experience the pleasures of the senses and so on. All of this serves as the basis for a plethora of our own suffering and that of others in this life.

In future [lives] as well, **when** this **hatred's results** of maturation, concordant outflow, and so on **ripen**, we plunge **into** the hot or cold **hells** and thus experience an abundance of harm through heat and cold (such as **being boiled, burned**, beaten, and cut) in an incessant manner. At that time, **oh how we suffer** and how we faint [as a result of all this, again and again]**!** Nevertheless, apart from [simply] experiencing [all this suffering] while not wanting to, what means are there that we could apply to our being rendered powerless through the actions that we ourselves committed? [In fact,] we lack any means to do anything [about this]. Thus, when reflecting on the shortcomings of the delusion of hatred, it appears to be the greatest bringer of harm.

Therefore, the ultimate remedy to eliminate this [hatred] so that it lacks any object {22a}[419] is **this aspiration prayer of myself**, or himself, **the buddha** Samantabhadra—the realization that is the knowledge of [my] awakened mind, the path of the luminous Great Perfection. **Through** the power of its functioning, **when** the cause that thus represents the root of many flaws and degenerations—the **fierce hatred** that is triggered by improper mental engagement—suddenly **flares up in all sentient beings, who** constitute the guests powerlessly roaming and **migrating** through the paths of [saṃsāric] existence and experiencing the many sufferings of the **six** types [of beings], **without** either **rejecting** [this hatred] through relying on a path that involves effort (and thus not relinquishing it) **or** [doing] something like letting it arise as ordinary hatred in just the way it comes, just as before, **may** the dharmatā of hatred—the essence of awareness—**relax** within the expanse of primordial freedom **in its own state**, in a naturally settled way. Due to that, may it be free merely by virtue of the face of awareness being revealed as being free in itself. May **awareness take its very own seat** within its own basic nature, **and** may its own dharmadhātu—the mirror-like wisdom that is **lucid** and aware in itself—**thus be attained** by being revealed.

2.2.3. The manner in which pride is free as the wisdom of equality

This is taught through the two stanzas and the three lines that begin with "**due to our own mind having become haughty.**" It is from the perspective of the view that the affliction of pride is explained [here] as delusion.

Therefore, pride arises from the views about a self. By focusing on our own lofty and vast qualities in a higher realm, such as our ancestry, looks, erudition, youth, and power, {23a} **our own mind** arises in the form of **being haughty** or self-inflated. **Due to** its **having** arisen [in that form], through focusing on the qualities of **other** persons who are equal in qualities to our own, there arises from this [haughty] form [of mind] a **vying mind** that wishes for ourselves to be superior **and** a bad **mentality** that wishes to criticize those [other persons] and **dismiss them**. Under the influence of that, and **through** focusing on our own qualities, **a mind of** haughty and **arrogant**[420] **pride**, which has the form of clinging [to ourselves as] being superior to others, **arises** with intense force. **Through** that, **we** are tormented in this life by way of **experiencing the** many **sufferings of our fighting and struggling with others** who are inferior or equal in qualities to **us**.

In future lives as well, **when the results of those** bad **actions ripen** in a direct manner, we must experience [many] sufferings in the hell realms. Not only that, but even if we are born as beings like gods in the desire [realm] as the result of the maturation of other merits and virtues, even while having taken birth in such [a state], as a result of concordant outflow that is an experience, **we are born as** beings like **gods** who must **experience** the many intense sufferings of **transiting** away from the glories of the higher realms **and falling down** into the miserable realms and so on. Thus, pride serves as the basic ground for [all kinds of] flaws in both this and future [lives].

Therefore, **through** the power and the blessings of **this** genuine **aspiration** of the awakened mind **of myself**, **the** primal **buddha**, Samantabhadra, the supreme **path**[421] of Ati, {23b} **when** the **sentient beings** who are rendered powerless through **giving rise to** the intense, negative mental state of **a** proud and **haughty mind** have developed pride and a haughty mind, **may their cognizance relax** without contrivance **in its own state** as the dharmatā of that [pride]—the wisdom of awareness. By virtue of its having thus settled, may **awareness take its very own seat** in its own domain **and the wisdom of equality** (the inseparability of emptiness and lucidity) **thus be attained** by being revealed.

2.2.4. The instruction that envy and a competitive mind are free as the wisdom of effortless all-accomplishment

This is taught through the two stanzas and the two lines that begin with "**through the latent tendencies of rampant dualistic clinging.**" It is from the perspective of nonrealization that envy is explained [here] as delusion.

Therefore, due to not realizing the actuality [of the equality] of the clinging to real existence and the equality of good, bad, and so on, we take ourselves and others to be two, **clinging** to the qualities of this **duality** as being good and bad, respectively. **Through** the power of **the latent tendencies** consisting of the dense latent tendencies implanted by the evolving, **rampant** clinging to a self and what belongs to this self, [which results from clinging to duality,] we **praise ourselves and disparage others. From** having planted **the pain of** such attachment and hatred into our minds, we become fully immersed in avoiding and accomplishing [the negative and the positive counterparts among] the eight worldly dharmas.[422] Thus, the **competitive mind**

of fighting and struggling with **our** enemies and rivals, as well as the mind of clinging to and craving for the assembly of our friends, **blossoms** and expands. Due to that, we are tormented in this life. {24a}

In future [lives] as well, **through** the power of such envy, the karmas accumulated by it, and their motivations, [their results] of concordant outflow that are experiences and their results produced by persons[423] mature as the state of **being born in the asura realm** of being tormented by the sufferings **of killing and slashing**. Thus, through the envy of such asuras' competing and struggling with the gods, they will suffer mental agony and so on. The result of maturation [of that] is the experience of suffering through **taking a deep plunge into the** hot and cold **hell realms**. They may also assume displeasing human bodies [such as those of] servants who hope for the food of others and [humans with] dull minds and bad complexions. In that way, [envy] is the root of [many] flaws in this and future [lives].

Thus, **through** the power of **this** genuine treasury of the qualities of the three secrets **of myself, the** primal **buddha**, the destination of all the **aspirations** of my mind, the supreme **path**[424] that is the pinnacle of [all] yānas, at the time when the latent tendencies of envy—the single fundamental cause of sentient beings' naturally engaging in the actions of **a competitive mind, fighting, and struggling**—flourish[425] and their power ripens, **without** either [letting] envy arise in just the way it comes and thus letting the mental factor **enmity** triumph or relying on relinquishing it through the functions of a contrived path as in the general yānas, **may** envy **relax in its own place** within its own basic mode of being—the single sphere of alpha-purity, free from reference points. {24b} Due to that, by way of the **cognizance** that is the native state—the wisdom of the awareness of compassionate responsiveness—**taking its very own seat**, may **the** all-accomplishing **wisdom** that is endowed with effortless and innately present **enlightened activity** in an **unobstructed** manner **be** revealed.

2.2.5. The manner in which nescience is free as nonconceptual dharmadhātu wisdom

This is taught through the two verses that begin with "**through mindlessness, indifference, distraction.**" Unawareness is explained [here] as delusion [by virtue of its being] the ground that retains the dimension of deluded thoughts and by virtue of nescience being the mere opposite of prajñā and awareness.

Therefore, since such unawareness is the nonrecognition of the ground awareness's own face, it is **mindlessness**—the oblivion of being deluded about [awareness] itself as being something other—the fundamental unawareness that consists of mind [as opposed to awareness]. Since it does not understand appearing objects' essence, which lacks any specific characteristics, it is the oblivion of **indifference**—the delusion that is the unawareness about objects. The delusion due to the condition that consists of the ground manifestations is the oblivion of **distracted** cognizance, which resembles being deluded about a cairn being a person—the ground of delusion, which is unawareness of the ground. While the essence of awareness lacks any self, there is **obtuseness** about this, which is the oblivion [that takes on] the form of a self—the unawareness of thoughts about an apprehender. The **dullness** of being deluded about what is not the path as being the path is the unawareness of the contrived path, which does not bestow freedom due to the antidote's having turned into poison. The ignorance due to **forgetting** the actuality of natural luminosity is the unawareness of ignorant oblivion. {25a} The **unconscious** mind [that occurs] due to the internal withdrawal of this unawareness, as well as of the coarse sense consciousnesses and mental consciousness that are included in its dimension is the mind of deep sleep. Furthermore, there are the laziness that is the lack of effort, which does not allow us to engage in the Dharma, or the **laziness** of procrastination, **and** the **nescience** of being oblivious about the basic mode of being of what is and what isn't this Dharma.

The **result** of the karmas and afflictions that are triggered **through** [all] these [aspects of unawareness] is that the general and specific saṃsāric sufferings of lacking protection and **shelter** through the power of others, and of being **without** the time to become liberated through one's own power, are experienced as the many sufferings in the realm of **animals** or beasts who have fallen into deception, such as being stupid, oblivious, bound into servitude, hungry, thirsty, hot, and cold. Thus, **we** are born **as** animals in the birthplaces of animals. From there, we will further continue to **roam** the places of [other] miserable realms, such as those of hell beings and hungry ghosts.

Thus, **through** the power and the blessings of **this** ultimate awakened mind **of myself, the buddha** Samantabhadra—the essential point of what must be **aspired** for, the destination of the **path**[426]—**may the radiance of** the **mindfulness** consisting of the awareness of compassionate responsiveness effortlessly settled in itself (the uncontrived prajñā that is **lucid** in its very own place) **shine** in a direct and naked manner **in** the expanse of the wisdom of self-arising awareness—the basic nature of **the** manifestly arisen **darkness of our nescience** that consists of **dull** and obtuse oblivion (the root of the conglomeration that constitutes delusion's whirling host of flaws of which the mind streams of sentient beings have never been free)—{25b} **and may** dharmadhātu **wisdom—nonconceptual** alpha-purity free from reference points, which transcends [all] characteristics of reference points—**thus be attained** by being revealed.[427]

2.3. Teaching the manner in which the qualities of the fruition free from stains are to be revealed just as they are

This is taught through the two stanzas and the two lines that begin with "**all sentient beings of the three realms.**" The qualities of the ground—the expanse of inner luminosity that is alpha-purity free from reference points—have the character of being [as vast as] the ocean. The buddha qualities that are the ultimate fruition—the outer luminosity of the great expanse free from stains—have the nature of being inconceivable. These [qualities that seem to be] twofold are [absolutely] equal in their having the [same] character of the single set of qualities of the empty wisdom without reference points that abides possessing the character of all qualities and whose own essence is pure of [both] delusion and the lack [of delusion], in that it is without any decrease in delusion or increase in freedom.

Therefore, by virtue of the general **ground of all** phenomena of saṃsāra and nirvāṇa, which consists of primal alpha-purity and, from the perspective of its own essence, has the nature of changeless innate presence, **all** lowly **sentient beings** deluded in **the** impure **three realms are** abiding as being of a type that is **equal to** the fruition—the phenomena that constitute the qualities of **myself, the buddha** Samantabhadra. Nevertheless, for sentient beings who have been rendered powerless through delusion, {26a} by virtue of [this ground's] being associated with the stains of **mindless** oblivion, **it has become the** general **ground of delusion** and freedom. Due to that, these sentient beings lack the fortune of gaining mastery over the phenomena that are [this ground's] own qualities. Rather, in this state of delusion's own time **right now**, under the influence of mistaken motivations and their applications since [time] without beginning, **they engage in activities** of causes and results that consist of nothing but suffering, while being **without** any [trace of the] essential **meaning** and the principal purpose.[428] Thus, there arises[429] this whirl of delusion that involves [all] general and specific sufferings—the propelled results of the causes that consist of **the sixfold karmas**, which propel [sentient beings] into the six abodes of saṃsāra that give rise to suffering, with [all of this] **being like the delusive** appearances of illusive figments **in a dream.**

When the ground, through the power of the accumulation of the virtue of recognizing its own uncontaminated face, has become devoid of stains, and is thus simultaneously revealed as the qualities of the ultimate fruition, which have the character of being [as vast as] the ocean, it is called "**I,** Samantabhadra." Thus, this wisdom of primordially free alpha-purity, which lacks the stains of adventitious delusion and oblivion, abides as the attainment of mastery over the phenomena that are the ultimate qualities, which have the character of the ocean of the three kāyas, the qualities, and the enlightened activities of **the buddha**, who is endowed with twofold purity. Having revealed this [buddhahood already] before [the passage of] eons [whose number is] even more countless than countless, any starting point of Samantabhadra is completely beyond reach. Therefore, he is called "without **origin**."[430] {26b} This is the time of the dharmakāya, which is the origin when compared to the times of the sambhogakāya and nirmāṇakāya.

The recurrent displays of all kinds of enlightened actions of pure and impure **emanations** for the sake of guiding the endless sentient beings of **the six realms** for as long as saṃsāra remains is simply equal to [the vastness of] space. Therefore, **in order to guide** these endless sentient beings, **through** the power and the blessings of **this** heart of all **aspirations** of the awakened mind, which represents the bodhicitta[431] **of** Buddha **Samantabhadra**, the supreme **path** of the luminous Great Perfection, **may all** the hosts of individual **sentient beings** whose number equals space, **without** even a single **exception**, reveal the wisdom that abides within themselves. May they thus **become awakened in** the realms that consist of the ultimate Akaniṣṭha—the palace of **the dharmadhātu**—and the innately present Richly Adorned Akaniṣṭha, which is its self-appearance, thereby attaining mastery over the host of qualities consisting of the ten powers.

3. The benefits of reading and hearing the text of this aspiration prayer

This has two parts:

1. The actual benefit of reading and listening to these words of aspiration and application as they are intended by yogic practitioners who have attained stability in the path of the Great Perfection
2. Instruction on the crucial points in time

3.1. The actual benefit of reading and listening to these words of aspiration and application as they are intended by yogic practitioners who have attained stability in the path of the Great Perfection

This is taught through the five lines that begin with "**E MA HO! From now on, through yogic practitioners with great power.**"

{27a} "**E MA HO**" is an utterance of amazement about the benefits that will be explained [in what follows]. **From now on**, during these latter times of the degenerate age, through their striving to benefit [all] sentient beings, yogic practitioners **with** the **great** realization of having attained the consummate **power** of stability in making the **yoga** of this path a living experience for the sake of those of inferior fortune[432] arouse the vigorous dimension of the **self-luminosity** of self-arising **awareness free of delusion. From within** [that state], they utter the text of **this aspiration prayer** of the triad of ground, path, and fruition, whose nature it is to have qualities **of great power** and whose benefits cannot be fully described, even if the victors of the three times and their children were to speak of them for eons. **Through making** this aspiration prayer in such a way, even through merely **hearing the** words of proclaiming this aspiration prayer, **all sentient beings who hear** it **will fully awaken within** the course of only **three** successive **lives**, without [their awakening's] being contingent on a long series of lifetimes. Given this declaration [of such a benefit through merely hearing this aspiration prayer], there is no need to mention the vast manifestation of benefits for those who, other than just hearing it, [actually] familiarize themselves with [this aspiration prayer] and practice it by making it a living experience in accordance [with its words].

3.2. Instruction on the crucial points in time

The following is taught concerning the transient crucial points in time in the world that appear as signs of excellence and defects. This means [that the aspiration prayer is to be primarily recited] **during the times** when **solar or lunar eclipses** take place, {27b} **at** times when **loud noises** resound from mountains or space, at times when **earthquakes occur, at the solstices** of [the sun's reaching its most] northerly or southerly [excursion], **or at the turn of the** previous into the following **year**.

If we recite this aspiration prayer while **we let ourselves** who make this aspiration prayer **arise** and clearly manifest **as**

Samantabhadra, and while **all** people in a place where many assemblies of persons have gathered **hear** it—by virtue of the completely pure time, intention, and application having come together internally, as well as **through** the power of **the** completely pure generation of bodhicitta and the potent **aspiration prayer of such yogic practitioners**, in either a direct or indirect manner, **for all sentient beings**, as the persons who wander through **the three realms**—temporarily, [those beings] **will gradually become free from** suffering, through the progressive arising of the remedies for coarse saṃsāra's **suffering** including its causes (the paths that accord with [those beings'] individual faculties). **In the end**, through this yāna that is the ultimate of all paths, they will **then attain** the precious state of **buddhahood**—the knowledge of all aspects, free from the all-ground and [all] its dimensions. May[433] [all] sentient beings be able to receive these benefits as they were explained, in a proper manner without any obstacles.

Furthermore, I say this: {28a}

Marvelous is this pathway of excellent explanations, which is
embraced
by hundreds of thousands of lotuses of scriptures and reasoning,
and enters
this pleasure grove of the supreme location of the profound
treasure that displays
as the great feast of the excellent aspiration prayer of
Samantabhadra's awakened mind.

Nevertheless, for those polluted by the stains of nonrealization,
it is difficult to explain the true reality of profound enlightened
speech.
Hence, I confess my mistakenness, errors, and flaws to those who
possess the eye of knowledge,
while any excellent parts present constitute the kindness of the
genuine protector.

Through the luminous shine of the merit of making effort in this
Dharma,
may the accumulation of the dense darkness of [saṃsāric]
existence's flaws, degenerations, and delusions
vanish within the empty sky of the alpha-pure inner expanse,
and the empty lights of its innately present qualities thus blaze
brightly.

By virtue of the power and the blessings of the victors and their
children,
and through this function of the path of the unsurpassable
ultimate secret,
may I, too, mature my skandhas, which are the dross, as the
vajrakāya, which is the pure essence,[434]
and thus become the glory of beings, in accordance with the
duration of [saṃsāric] existence.

This Exposition of The Aspiration Prayer of Samantabhadra *Found in the* Great Tantra of the Unobstructed Awakened Mind *of the* Northern Treasures, *Called "The Lamp That Clearly Illuminates the Short Path of Samantabhadra" [was composed as follows.] The venerable genuine guru, who has gone to the ultimate level of an awareness holder on the secret path of the unsurpassable Atiyoga, is the omniscient mighty Dodrub.*[435] *Though it is difficult to [even] utter his name, if I refer to him by name [just] for the sake of its meaning, he is [called] Jigmé Tenpé Nyima. [I shall furthermore mention] the precious treasure revealer,*[436] *Sangdzin Gönpo Wangyal,*[437] *as well as* {28b} *many other genuine [gurus] of the Rimé [movement]. It is through their kindness and by way of combining my fulfilling the wish of Lhatra Lama Trinlé Tudob*[438] *with my being exhorted by the attendant Dorjé Gyaltsen*[439] *[to write this commentary] that the crazy beggar who is named a tulku and called Tsültrim Sangpo [completed it] on the full-moon day of the victor in the year of the "wrathful" Wood Ox.*[440] *The quintessence of the ocean of Guru Padma[sambhava]'s profound treasures, which represents the single refuge that protects the kings of Tibet, is well-known to all as "The Northern Treasure." The location of this treasure is a slope that resembles many poisonous snakes worshiping deities on the east side of Rock Mountain Sangsang Deity Rock Resembling a Cluster of Poisonous Snakes, or White Rock Mountain Resembling a Divine Stūpa,*[441] *in the middle of Nyenyül Sangsang,*[442] *to the north of Glorious Samyé.*[443] *On [that slope, there is] the practice cave of the guru, called "the cave of taming demons and overpowering whatever appears and is possible," which is beautified by an abundance of self-arisen marvelous signs and awe-inspiring great magnificence, all of which represent the blessings of the three vajras of the vajra of speech, Padmasambhava. It was in [that cave] that I composed this [commentary] in an excellent manner.*

Appendix 1

The Outlines of the Commentaries

Clearing the Guide to **The Aspiration Prayer of Samantabhadra** *with the Lancet of a Ṭīkā*[444]

The arising of two paths and two results from the ground that is undetermined (1–7)
Awareness and unawareness of the ground that is alpha-purity (8–14)
The ground lacks any causes, conditions, and duality of apprehender and apprehended (15–25)
The single ground matures as five wisdoms, one hundred kinds of deities, and countless emantions (26–45)
The essential point of the causes of delusion and freedom: cutting through nonrecognition (46–71)
Letting afflictions rest directly within the place of their arising without contrivance (72–140)

A Commentary on the Meaning of **The Aspiration Prayer of Samantabhadra** *Called* **Ketaka**

1. The initial composition [of this aspiration prayer]
2. [Explaining] the actual meaning of the text
2.1. Making the special aspiration prayer of saṃsāra and nirvāṇa being pure within the ground
2.1.1. Brief introduction to the essence (1–7)
2.1.2. Detailed differentiation of the nature
2.1.2.1. Brief introduction to linking the ground with the fruition (8–14)

2.1.2.2. Detailed explanation of the way in which saṃsāra and nirvāṇa diverge

2.1.2.2.1. The aspiration prayer for wisdom to fully unfold that is based on Samantabhadra's mode of freedom

2.1.2.2.1.1. The aspiration prayer in terms of the manner in which awakening is found as self-appearances

2.1.2.2.1.1.1. [The aspiration prayer in terms of] the manner of truly becoming a buddha in the form of being endowed with the six distinctive features of alpha-purity (15–25)

2.1.2.2.1.1.2. The aspiration prayer in terms of the manner of fully and perfectly becoming a buddha through the array of the self-appearances of the kāyas and wisdoms of innate presence (26–39)

2.1.2.2.1.2. The aspiration prayer in terms of the manner in which emanations unfold as other-appearances (40–45)

2.1.2.2.2. The aspiration prayer for the pit of saṃsāra to be emptied [from its depths] that is based on the mode of delusion of unaware sentient beings

2.1.2.2.2.1. Detailed explanation of the characteristics

2.1.2.2.2.1.1. The aspiration prayer for awareness to be free as wisdom through teaching that the shortcomings of the Peak of Existence arise from unawareness

2.1.2.2.2.1.1.1. The aspiration prayer for unawareness to be free as the wisdom of awareness through teaching the manner in which the two subsequent unawarenesses evolve from the unawareness that has the same identity as the cause (46–60)

2.1.2.2.2.1.1.2. The aspiration prayer for knowing the two unawarenesses to be of the essence of the wisdom of awareness through clearly teaching their presentation (61–71)

2.1.2.2.2.1.2. The aspiration prayer for this very [unawareness] to become free in itself in terms of teaching the manner of cycling in the realms of saṃsāra under the sway of the five poisons that constitute the dependent origination of delusion [arising] from this [unawareness]

2.1.2.2.2.1.2.1. The aspiration prayer in terms of introducing the conceptions of desire as being discriminating wisdom (72–89)
2.1.2.2.2.1.2.2. The aspiration prayer in terms of introducing hatred as being luminosity (90–101)
2.1.2.2.2.1.2.3. The aspiration prayer for pride being free as equality (102–12)
2.1.2.2.2.1.2.4. The aspiration prayer in terms of introducing envy as being unobstructed wisdom (113–22)
2.1.2.2.2.1.2.5. The aspiration prayer in terms of introducing nescience as being the dharmadhātu of nonconceptual wisdom (123–30)
2.1.2.2.2.2. The aspiration through a summary of the topic at hand (131–40)
2.2. Teaching the benefits and the performances
2.2.1. [Teaching] the timeless continuous yoga of supreme persons free from reference points, including its benefit and performance (141–46)
2.2.2. Teaching the yoga of persons with reference points [that is practiced] at certain times, including its benefit and performance (147–55)
3. Summary of the topic at hand

An Exposition of **The Aspiration Prayer of Samantabhadra** *Called* **The Lamp That Clearly Illuminates the Short Path of Samantabhadra**

1. The initial brief instruction of briefly presenting ground, path, and fruition (1–7)
2. The detailed explanation of this through finely differentiating it further
2.1. The ground
2.1.1. Detailed explanation of the basic nature of the ground (8–14)
2.1.2. Teaching Samantabhadra's mode of freedom through taking the recognition of the [ground] as the path
2.1.2.1. The actual mode of freedom (15–39)

2.1.2.2. The manner of promoting the welfare of others after having become free (40–45)
2.1.3. The manner in which sentient beings are deluded in saṃsāra due to not knowing the actuality of the ground
2.1.3.1. General instruction on the mode of delusion (46–60)
2.1.3.2. The particular distinct instruction on the [mode of delusion] (61–71)
2.2. The explanation of the path of delusion's coming to its end once the ground has been revealed
2.2.1. The manner in which desire is free as discriminating wisdom (72–89)
2.2.2. The manner in which hatred is free as lucid wisdom or mirror[-like] wisdom (90–101)
2.2.3. The manner in which pride is free as the wisdom of equality (102–12)
2.2.4. The instruction that envy and a competitive mind are free as the wisdom of effortless all-accomplishment (113–22)
2.2.5. The manner in which nescience is free as nonconceptual dharmadhātu wisdom (123–30)
2.3. Teaching the manner in which the qualities of the fruition free from stains are to be revealed just as they are (131–40)
3. The benefits of reading and hearing the text of this aspiration prayer
3.1. The actual benefit of reading and listening to these words of aspiration and application as they are intended by yogic practitioners who have attained stability in the path of the Great Perfection (141–46)
3.2. Instruction on the crucial points in time (147–55)

Appendix 2

The Ground, Its Manifestations, and Samantabhadra's Freedom

The first chapter of Longchenpa's *Precious Treasury of Words and Their Meanings* discusses (A) the primordial ground of being, (B) the eight kinds of ground manifestations that naturally emerge or unfold from it, and (C) the freedom of Samantabhadra that takes place through the immediate recognition of these manifestations for what they are—the self-appearances of original awareness.[445]

(A) Longchenpa's text lists seven ways of asserting the ground in the literature of the Great Perfection: (1) the ground as being innately present, (2) the ground as being indeterminate, (3) the ground as the determinate ultimate foundation, (4) the ground as being capable of transforming into anything whatsoever, (5) the ground as being assertable as anything whatsoever, (6) the ground as diversity, and (7) the ground as alpha-purity. He refutes the first six views, said to be held by those who adhere to philosophical systems, through showing that, despite containing some elements of truth, they are liable to misinterpretations with absurd consequences, especially when understood too literally or dogmatically. Thus, only the ground as alpha-purity, said to be asserted by those who adhere to the path, is determined as the correct view.[446]

> As for the first vajra point, what is to be determined is the fundamental mode of being of entities before buddhas emerge due to realizing it and sentient beings emerge due to not realizing it, as well as the ground manifestations' mode of appearing from it. ... The instruction on this has three parts:

1. The primordial primal ground's mode of being
2. The ground manifestations' mode of appearing from it
3. Samantabhadra's mode of freedom

1. The primordial primal ground's mode of being

This has two parts.

1.1. General instruction on the list of the seven [assertions about the] ground

. . . .

1.1.1. The assertion of the ground as being innate presence

The assertion: The innately present basic nature is completely unconfined, without any bias whatsoever, and has the character of all qualities' being primordially innately present.

Its refutation: If all qualities existed in an innately present manner, it would follow that the fruition of being free from adventitious stains also exists in an innately present manner right from the start, because all qualities would already be primordially established in an innately present way. If that were accepted, such would not be tenable either because it would follow that it is impossible for anyone to become deluded about this ground, it would be unreasonable for this delusion to be purified, and it would follow that the result is [already] present within the cause. If everything were innately present, even saṃsāra would be innately present, and thus freedom would be unreasonable. For, since cause and result are different, it follows that [the result] is not innately present [at the time of the cause]. The *Sixfold Expanse* says this:

> This ground of innately present diversity
> is not the true actual ground itself.
> If it were, it would be as follows:

through making efforts, sentient beings
would not become free
because of being polluted by [naturally present]
unawareness.
If you say that freedom [occurs] due to the existence of
awareness,
wouldn't the result be double freedom?
[For] this resembles the example of being unable
to change black coal into having
a white color through cleaning it.
Since cause and result are different,
again, [the ground] is not innate presence.[447]

Summary of the refutation: We do not assert such [a position] here. Since the [ground's] essence is alpha-pure, saṃsāra is not established. Since its nature is completely pure, nirvāṇa [as a new attainment] is not established [either]. Since the ground is nondual [in being neither saṃsāra nor nirvāṇa] and beyond thought and expression, it abides as having the character of being primordially beyond flaws. [When we call this ground "innate presence,"] we merely indicate that it is the ground of the arising of innate presence, but apart from that it is not [innate presence] in the sense of an [independent,] specifically characterized such entity ...

1.1.2. The assertion of the ground as being indeterminate

The assertion: Since the [ground's] essence isn't anything at all, it is indeterminate as having a single nature. It appears simply as whatever the mind imputes it to be.

Its refutation: If the ground were something that is imputed by the mind, it would be unsuitable as nirvāṇa when it is imputed as saṃsāra [and vice versa]. It would [likewise] be untenable to be many when it is [imputed as] one [and vice versa]. Since [such opposing] determinacies would become mutually conflated, it would follow that delusion and freedom would interchange their states. If there were no determinacy, it would follow that there is a return to delusion after having become free. It would [also] follow that freedom already exists at the very time when there is no freedom. It would [furthermore] follow that everything is conflated, because determinacy and indeterminacy would interchange their states. If [the ground] were indeterminate, it would not be suitable as the ground—it would entail the flaw of not standing its [own] ground. The same [tantra] states this:

> What is taught as the indeterminately abiding ground
> is also not sufficient as the ground itself;
> I understand it in this way [when explained according to] degrees of intelligence.
> Its results would vacillate
> or would revert back [to their causes].
> What is indeterminate would become determinate
> and what is determinate would become indeterminate.
> Since its own indeterminacy existed in itself,
> in its being determinate, it would be like the outcome of karma.[448]

Summary of the refutation: We do not assert such [a position] here. By virtue of names and their referents not being differentiated as anything [within the ground], primordially unarisen dharmatā is ascertained as lacking arising, abiding, and ceasing. Thus, we assert that space-like dharmatā lacks any determinacy in terms of biased fixation.

1.1.3. The assertion of the ground as the determinate ultimate foundation

The assertion: The [ground's] essence is changeless like space. Its mode of appearance cannot be transformed, just like fire and water.[449]

Its refutation: If the ground were absolutely unchanging, it would follow that it is the same as the self that is asserted to be permanent. It would [also] follow that freedom through making efforts is impossible, because impure awareness could not be transformed into being pure. If that is accepted, there would be the flaws of it following that there is no need for realizing the ground and cultivating the path, and it following that it is impossible to counteract delusion through realizing the ground. The *Sixfold Expanse* declares this:

> Its being taught as "the determinate ground"
> is not the true, actual heart either.
> Just as in the example of a conch shell's
> appearing yellow to those with jaundiced eyes,
> due to the feature of its own status's becoming inverted,
> it lacks both self and other, being free from any extreme
> of determinacy.
> Therefore, this is not the true actuality either.
> Or, with a determinate cause and a determinate result,
> it would be no different from a permanent self.[450]

Summary of the refutation: We do not assert such [a position] here. Rather, we say that alpha-pure dharmatā lacks any change or transition because from the intrinsically pure perspective of realization, its nature is nondual,[451] even if this is not realized. However, we do not accept that it does not become pure through making effort.

1.1.4. The assertion of the ground as being capable of transforming into anything whatsoever

The assertion: Since the [ground's] essence is without any bias or partiality, it is capable of transforming into any mode of being whatsoever.

Its refutation: If the basic nature were capable of transforming, it would follow that it is not the basic nature. It would [also] follow that despite already having attained freedom (the result), this result could revert back to its cause, or that this cause—the appearances of delusion—at the very time of its own plain state, without having undergone even the slightest change, could interchange its state with the state of being already free, [simply due to] having transcended [delusion] previously.[452] For the ground has this capability of transforming into anything whatsoever. If that were accepted, it would follow that there is no need [for realizing the ground and cultivating the path], and that a freedom that can revert back is not real [freedom]. It would [also] follow that matter and awareness are capable of transforming into each other. The same [tantra] says this:

> As for its being taught before as capable of transforming,
> if its own basic nature were capable of transforming,
> this would be similar to its being indeterminate.
> Since the very fruition would revert to the cause,
> [all] efforts would become unnecessary.
> [Also,] this would entail repeated reversals.
> Hence, it resembles material phenomena's incapability of turning into something that possesses awareness.[453]

Summary of the refutation: Since [the ground] itself lacks any change or transition, it does not change into anything else. Once delusion has become pure as [its own basic] state, the [ground's] essence is referred to as "seizing its own place."

1.1.5. The assertion of the ground as being assertable as anything whatsoever

The assertion: It can be asserted as anything whatsoever, because as the essence of all entities, it appears in a way that is baseless and unrestrained.

Its refutation: If the ground were assertable as anything whatsoever, just as entities are endless, the ground would [also] be endless. If that were accepted, there would be the flaw of it following that an end of this endlessness [can] not be established. Since it would follow that such a ground [could be described in many contradictory ways, such as] being existent, nonexistent, permanent, and extinct, it would follow that such a ground is not suitable as the ground that is the basic nature. The same [tantra] says this:

Since the teacher himself taught previously
that it is associated with assertions,
all these are only partial conjectures.
Since it would be established from the perspective of
being everything,
there would be the flaw of its being endless.[454]

Summary of the refutation: Since the ground transcends existence, nonexistence, permanence, extinction [and so on], it is without any assertions whatsoever. Nevertheless, any approaches of illustrating [the ground] that [are used to] point to it in a partial way are referred to as "metaphorical indications."

1.1.6. The assertion of the ground as diversity

The assertion: "Since the [ground's] essence is self-arising as everything, it appears as diverse modes of appearance."

Its refutation: Since the ground would be diverse, it would be a plurality. However, since it would not be suitable as the ground of purity and freedom, [all] efforts [toward freedom] would [just] be pointless hardships. Since [the ground's] plurality would be infinite, without any end, it would follow that there is no time at which certainty [about it] is found and no time at which it is realized. It would [also] follow that just as its mode of appearance involves change and transition, the ground too involves change and transition. Yet if it involved change and transition, it would not be tenable as the ground because it would follow that, just as many constellations of thoughts stir in a [single] instant, the ground would involve flickering movement and afflictions. The same [tantra] says this:

> The teacher previously taught it as variegated,
> yet this is not tenable in terms of [our] position either.
> For, with a single cause having different results,[455]
> this essence would appear through that [diversity].
> Hence, this would be equivalent to meaning different results.
> [This is untenable] because of being invalidated by the term "plurality."[456]

Summary of the refutation: We do not assert such [a position] here. Since the [ground's] essence is not established as anything whatsoever, it is devoid of any illustrating example. Since its nature is free on the basis of its appearance, it is devoid of any definiendum. Since the basic nature is without any reference points, it is devoid of any definition. Since it is not found as the designations of this triad of example, definiendum, and definition, it transcends [all] flaws of [particular] modes of being [something], despite its [serving as] the unimpeded ground of the appearing of diversity.

1.1.7. The instruction that alpha-purity is flawless, [which is found] in our own texts [and given] by those who adhere to the path

This has three parts:

1. Identifying the essence of alpha-purity
2. Rebutting the flaws of disputing this
3. General instruction on the manner in which the ground of arising flows forth

1.1.7.1. Identifying the essence of alpha-purity

The alpha-purity of the primordial primal ground is the great transcendence of speech, thought, and expression that is beyond the extremes of existence and nonexistence.

It is free from the extremes of existence and permanence by virtue of its essence being alpha-purity and thus not being established as phenomena that are entities and their characteristics. It is [also] beyond the extremes of nonexistence and extinction by virtue of its nature being innate presence.[457] Thus, it is the luminous and empty pure dharmatā, self-lucid original buddhahood, the awakened mind of the changeless dharmakāya, the great primordially empty and self-arising wisdom that is not established as either saṃsāra or nirvāṇa and is present like space from the very origin. …

1.1.7.2. Rebutting the flaws of disputing this

… It may be said, "Since all stains would be primordially exhausted if [the ground's] essence were alpha-purity, it would not be reasonable for sentient beings to be deluded in saṃsāra. Since the fruition would already be innately present if [the ground's] nature were innate presence, it would be reasonable for sentient beings to be primordially free without any effort."

The answer is taught as follows. [First,] since beings are already free primordially, stains are [indeed] not to be purified in a way that actually fulfills the definition [of purification], nor is there any [independent,] specifically characterized phenomenon [that exists] as delusion or freedom. Similar to delusion and freedom in a dream, they have never been established from the very time of their appearing as the mere play of awareness. Therefore, there is no flaw in [the ground's] being alpha-purity. [Second,] since the ground is innate presence, it is primordially perfect as the pure nature of the kāyas and wisdoms of the expanse. However, similar to awakening from sleep, by virtue of the factor of becoming free from adventitious stains, these kāyas and wisdoms exist as the dimension that is clearly revealed within the primordial primal [ground]. Therefore, there is no flaw.

1.1.7.3. General instruction on the manner in which the ground of arising flows forth

The expanse, the original ground, can be described as the triad of its essence, nature, and compassionate responsiveness, the triad of its natural state, nature, and character,[458] as well as its alpha-purity and innate presence. Thus, if [the ground's] single essence is divided by way of isolates, it is present as these eight. When [these manifestations] dawn from within its natural state as the ground manifestations, it is called "the general ground" in light of its functioning as the ground of both freedom and delusion. It is referred to as "the ground of freedom" by virtue of its functioning as the ground of freedom. It is referred to as "the ground of delusion" by virtue of its functioning as the ground of sentient beings' delusion. [Thus,] if the aspects of freedom and delusion are distinguished within the ground manifestations' single essence, the [ground] is present as this triad [the general ground, the ground of freedom, and the ground of delusion].[459] The *Garland of Pearls* ... explains this in detail:

> The essence is alpha-purity, free from any basis for
>   expression.
> The nature is innate presence—perfect as however it may
>   appear.
> Compassionate responsiveness is all-pervasive
>   self-arising.
>
> I am spontaneously arising:
> My nature is uncontrived universal illumination.
> Therefore, my character is all-encompassing
>   inclusiveness.
>
> Alpha-purity is the self-purity of stains.
> Innate presence is the arising of diversity.
> Therefore, the general ground appears to be
>   established.[460]

Since these are very important and intrinsic essential points of the ground, they are to be understood through having the eye of prajñā.

1.2. Distinct explanation of the primordial ground of alpha-purity

This has three parts:

1. Identifying the way its essence is
2. Detailed explanation of its nature
3. Rebutting sources for being mistaken about the aspects [of the ground]

1.2.1. Identifying the way its essence is

It is the self-arising wisdom that is awareness, the primordially empty primal dharmakāya, the ultimate reality that is the expanse, and the basic nature of luminosity that is dharmatā, which is not established as anything whatsoever, such as saṃsāra or nirvāṇa, happiness or suffering, existent or nonexistent, being or nonbeing, freedom or delusion, awareness or unawareness. ... Furthermore, it is called "alpha-purity," "purity from the outset," "primal purity," "primordial purity," and "original purity." ...

1.2.2. Detailed explanation of its nature

This has two parts:

1. Explaining it as being endowed with two wisdoms
2. Explaining it as being endowed with three wisdoms

1.2.2.1. Explaining it as being endowed with two wisdoms

Since awareness lacks any entity, based on the inseparability of awareness and emptiness, the wisdom of the alpha-pure essence is free from any perspective of conceivability and the wisdom of the innately present nature is present as depth-lucidity's primordial radiance. ... In terms of the isolate of the [ground's] essence, it is beyond the extremes of being existent or nonexistent. In terms of the isolate of its nature, it is present as the sheer dimension that is the ground of arising. Thus, they abide as the Great Perfection free from extremes, in which these two [essence and nature] are inseparable in their own essence. ...

1.2.2.2. Explaining it as being endowed with three wisdoms

This has two parts:

1. Brief introduction to their essence
2. Detailed explanation of their nature

1.2.2.2.1. Brief introduction to their essence

Self-Arising Awareness says this:

> What is called "the great alpha-purity that is the ground" is present as the three aspects of essence, nature, and compassionate responsiveness.[461]

...

1.2.2.2.2. Detailed explanation of their nature

As for the threefold basic nature that consists of the triad of essence, nature, and compassionate responsiveness, the position of this Unsurpassed Secret [Cycle][462] is as follows. Since the originally pure essence of the dharmakāya abides as the kāyas, it is present as the ground of the arising of the three kāyas without meeting or parting. However, it is not in the slightest bit established as faces, hands [and such] that represent segregated characteristics. Since its lucid nature abides as the five lights, its threefold radiance[463] is primordially self-lucid. However, it is not established as any distinct segregated colors. Since its compassionate responsiveness abides as the wisdom of awareness, its aspect of knowing is unceasingly and distinctly lucid. However, it lacks any appearance of subject and object in the form of an agent and what is acted upon. ...

1.2.3. Rebutting sources for being mistaken about the aspects [of the ground]

(1) In the context of the teaching that the alpha-pure ground is endowed with three wisdoms, due to being mistaken about the essence being present as the [three] kāyas, some assert that [these kāyas] have the mouths, eyes, and ears of prajñā and self-luminosity and so on. However, they conflate this teaching with the Secret Cycle and fail to relinquish the pitfalls of Mahāyoga. If [the kāyas] had mouths and eyes, they would exist either in a coarse way as sense organs that possess form or merely as the factor of formless mind. In the first case, there would be no difference [between the essence] and the coarse [realms of] desire and form. In the second case, there would be no difference [between the essence] and the four types of āyatanas.[464] *Self-Arising* [*Awareness*] says this:

> Since in the wisdom of the pure dharmakāya,
> no entity is to be apprehended,
> it cannot be imputed as having characteristics.
> If it had any characteristics,
> the dharmakāya could be apprehended.[465]

(2) Due to being mistaken about the explanation of the [ground's] nature as the five lights, some assert that these five lights exist as [independent,] specifically characterized phenomena. However, [in that case,] there would be no difference between the dharmakāya and the rūpakāyas, and the expanse would not be empty dharmatā. ...

(3) Due to being mistaken about the explanation of the [ground's] compassionate responsiveness as being unceasing, all-pervasive, and free from reference points, some assert that wisdom is discontinuous. However, if the ground of the arising of wisdom did not exist, the knowledge aspect

of buddhas would not exist, and thus the ground would be like completely void space or else like matter. ... The two-fold wisdom [of knowing suchness and variety] exists within the alpha-pure primordial ground as a mere source but does not exist in any coarse form. Therefore, it is justified that the twofold wisdom arises at the time of buddhahood. ...

"But how is it then that awareness is explained as being endowed with a mansion of light and as a cognizing subject of limitless light?" This is explained as follows. Within the primordial ground, at the respective times of the alpha-purity of the expanse [as the ground] and the alpha-purity of the final state of freedom, apart from the sheer dimension that is the ground of their arising [from within the ground's] depth-lucidity, they do not actually exist as the dimension of the kāyas, lights, and lucid awareness as they engage objects. For the utterly immovable state of the dharmakāya does not exist as being observable as anything whatsoever or as any characteristics. This is similar to a transparent crystal ball at the time of its not being[466] in the sun [at all] and at the time of its being in the shadow separated from the condition [of the sun's light]: at both [times], apart from the sheer dimension that is its depth-lucidity, the five lights do not appear outside [of it].[467] However, when awareness has risen from within the ground and thus emerges as the ground manifestations during the time of its presently dwelling within the body and during the intermediate state of dharmatā, awareness is present in a mansion of light [or a halo]. Thus, once self-awareness rises from within the ground, it remains within the ground manifestations until it embraces the final state [of freedom]. Therefore, [until then] it resembles a butter lamp sitting in the middle of its own light, or the appearances [of the five lights] when a crystal comes into contact with the sun's rays.

In brief, when awareness exists within the internal expanse that is present as the ground, apart from its depth-lucidity, the kāyas and lights do not actually exist at either the beginning [the ground] or the end [buddhahood]. Then, when awareness rises [from the ground], it is endowed with the radiance of its own light.

Though [awareness] is said to be present within the ground in its temporary state[468] when it is present within our hearts, it rises from the expanse as saṃsāra and thus has not arrived at the state of freedom. Therefore, it is still asserted as being the ground manifestations. In view of that, awareness is present in an immature form (resembling a peacock chick) within the space of self-radiance's five lights (resembling a peacock egg), and it shines like a rainbow in space at the time of the four visions,[469] which are the appearances of the path. Once this very awareness has matured as the kāyas through having been brought to its culmination, when all corporeality has become pure, it resembles [a peacock's] presence after having emerged from its egg.[470] The *Lion's Perfect Prowess* states this:

> The awareness that is present within the ground
> is perfect as the three kāyas within the expanse of
> wisdom,
> just as in the example of a peacock's egg,
> lucidly displaying the wisdom of inner light.
>
> The awareness that shines forth on the path
> is taught to resemble the example of a rainbow.
> The awareness that is brought to its culmination
> resembles the example of a peacock's chick
> that bursts open its egg and emerges from it.[471]

It is important to distinguish between the ground that is the expanse and the ground in its temporary state. These two times, during which awareness respectively is and is not situated within an actual mansion of light, represent a crucial, essential point. Thus, the ground abides such that its essence

> is inseparable emptiness and lucidity, its nature is inseparable lucidity and emptiness, and its compassionate responsiveness is inseparable awareness and emptiness. What is analogous to its way of abiding [like that]? The wisdom of its alpha-pure essence abides like the completely pure sky. The wisdom of its innately present nature abides like a clear, transparent ocean. The wisdom of its all-pervasive compassionate responsiveness abides like a stainless jewel.[472]

(B) After this description of the characteristics of the ground, there follows an explanation of how the eight kinds of ground manifestations naturally emerge or unfold from this ground, as its own appearances.

2. The ground manifestations' mode of appearing from the ground

This has three parts:

1. Brief introduction to their essence
2. Detailed explanation of their nature
3. Concluding summary through their aspects

2.1. Brief introduction to their essence

The seal of the youthful vase body—the primordial ground of the alpha-pure internal expanse—is rent open, and thus the wisdom winds stir [from the ground]. Through that there dawn the eight gateways that represent the innately present self-appearances of awareness's rising from the ground. At that time, the alpha-pure dharmakāya's manifestation that is like a cloudless sky [is present] above. Directly in front, the sambhogakāya's manifestations of luminous pure realms pervade the sky's expanse. Through the dynamic energy of that, the great ground manifestations are present below. Through the dynamic energy of that, the nirmāṇakāya's manifestations are also present below, while the manifestations of the natural nirmāṇakāya's pure realms are present in the intermediate directions.[473] Further below, through the gate of saṃsāra, the infinite realms of the self-appearances of the six forms of existence manifest. Since all of this is self-arising from the manifestations of the eight gateways of innate presence, it is called "the simultaneous dawning of the great manifestations of saṃsāra and nirvāṇa." When [these manifestations] dawn as outer luminosity from within inner luminosity, the manifestation of their essence is self-luminosity in its unimpeded flow, the manifestation of their nature is primordial radiance in the form of the five lights, and the manifestation of their compassionate responsiveness is like a cloudless sky, thus providing space. It is from this dimension that those self-appearances [manifest].

2.2. Detailed explanation of their nature

This has two parts:

1. General instruction on the manner in which the ground manifestations of innate presence dawn
2. Distinct explanation of their great mode of appearing

2.2.1. General instruction on the manner in which the ground manifestations of innate presence dawn

With the seal of the inner youthful vase body being rent open, the precious amulet-box's basic nature is self-arising as the manifestation of the eight gateways of innate presence.[474] *Auspicious Beauty* declares this:

> Alas, though I lack delusion, delusion emerges from my dynamic energy. With the nature arising in an unceasing manner from the unchanging ground, unawareness arises on its own from within compassionate responsiveness's indeterminacy. For example, while clouds do not actually exist in the sky, clouds emerge in an adventitious manner. Similarly, unawareness does not exist at all within the ground, but unawareness emerges from what dawns

like compassionate responsiveness. Thus, the ground is called "the basic nature of innate presence." This is present as the great indeterminate manifestation [before saṃsāra or nirvāṇa]. Its being endowed with an eightfold mode of arising is called "the basic nature of the precious amulet-box," which provides the unimpeded spaciousness for sense objects. It is present as the great establishment of not being established [as anything at all]. (1) The spaciousness of its dawning as if it were compassion is unimpeded. (2) The illumination of its dawning as if it were light is unimpeded. (3) The enjoyment of its dawning as if it were wisdom is unimpeded. (4) The essence of its dawning as if it were the kāyas is unimpeded. (5) The view of its dawning as if it were nonduality is indeterminate. (6) The means of its dawning as if it were the freedom from extremes is unimpeded. (7) The gateway of the purity that is wisdom is what is ultimate. (8) The gateway that arises as if it were impurity is unimpeded compassionate responsiveness. These [eight gateways of innate presence] resemble a precious jewel that is a pleasure for the senses.[475]

Mound of Jewels declares this:

From undifferentiated great compassionate
responsiveness,
pure yet indeterminate innate presence
springs forth in the manner of the eight [gateways] that
cause arising.

1. Since its mode of manifesting is unimpeded,
through its manner of arising as if it were compassion,
it is the place of refuge for all sentient beings.
2. Since its self-lucid manifestation is unimpeded,
it manifests in the manner of the five lights' illumination.

3. Since its appearance dimension of knowing is unimpeded,
it is as the very gateway of pure wisdom
that its unimpeded manifestation dawns as if it were the path.

4. Because its self-appearance is the full completion of all bodies,
it manifests as if it were the kāya of all dharmas.

5. Since the essence of cognizance is a single one,
it dawns as if it were nonduality.

6. Since it itself[476] does not dwell in any place of its own,
it is as the manifestation of the great freedom from extremes
that it appears within the ground of indeterminate innate
presence.

7. Because unobstructed awareness is perfect in its oneness,
it is as the gateway to the purity that is wisdom
that it is connected with the very essence itself.

8. Because its mode of arising is unimpeded,
from its dimension of pervasive appearance,
it also dawns as the source of all sentient beings,
as if it were the gateway to the impurity that is saṃsāra.

All this manifests as the eight [gateways] that cause arising.
Since they are self-arising in the manner in which they come
about,
"the manifestations of innate presence"
appear in the manner of a jewel.[477]

2.2.2. Distinct explanation of their great mode of appearing

At the time of [the ground manifestations'] dawning in these ways, all that appears and is possible manifests as lights and kāyas. Therefore, this is referred to as "everything manifests as the realm of innate presence." The manifestations of the sambhogakāya dawn from the dynamic energy of the essence of these [ground manifestations], the manifestations of the natural nirmāṇakāya realms [dawn] from the dynamic energy of its qualities, and the self-appearances of saṃsāra [dawn] like a dream from the dynamic energy of its compassionate responsiveness. ... Since the gateways of innate presence exist in the ground manifestations, the essential point of seeing pure realms or impure appearances of delusion also comes down to this.[478]

2.3. Concluding summary through their aspects

Though these ground manifestations' own essence appears in such modes of manifesting, this essence is not established at all as either delusion or nondelusion. The *Garland of Pearls* states this:

> Within this great ground manifestation,
> nothing can be imputed as "unawareness."
> Hence, it is not established as delusion.
>
> Since there is nothing imagined as a "mental state,"
> it lacks even the names "stains" and "delusion."
> Since there are no collections of names and letters,
> it [also] lacks the delusion of imputations.
>
> Since there is nothing known as the name "dharma,"
> there is not even the name "mentally imputed delusion."
> Since it is not established as mind and mentation,
> it naturally lacks any delusion that causes movement.
>
> Since both subtle and coarse stains are absent,
> it naturally lacks delusion due to the conditions of the elements.
> Since both agent and what is acted upon are absent,
> how could there be any delusion of apprehending objects?[479]

However, from the perspective of functioning as the condition for being free in that they recognize themselves, these [very ground manifestations] are labeled as "the ground of freedom." From the perspective of their functioning as the condition for delusion if they do not recognize themselves, they are labeled as "the ground of delusion." Since these ground manifestations themselves are the ground of freedom, while alpha-purity is the locus of freedom, it is very crucial to distinguish these two, though their proper distinction is quite rare [in other texts].[480] Thus, the ground manifestations are labeled as delusion because they function as the condition for delusion based on this [nonrecognition of themselves]. This is similar to a white conch shell's functioning as the condition for being deluded [about it by seeing it] in the form of a yellow [conch shell]: though it is not the actual delusion, it is labeled [as delusion] when it functions as the condition [for delusion]. ...

Within such ground manifestations, their own essence's innately present manifestations consist of the vast appearances of saṃsāra and nirvāṇa to the very ends of space, and saṃsāra and nirvāṇa emerge from awareness and unawareness, respectively. Therefore, since [it appears that] this expanse [of the ground manifestations] is [even] larger [than the expanse in its primordial state], this unprecedented vast [expanse] that accommodates [the entire plethora of] the self-appearances [of saṃsāra and nirvāṇa] is called "the great marvel."[481] ...

(C) Finally, "the freedom of Samantabhadra" refers to the instantaneous buddhahood that occurs through the immediate recognition of the ground manifestations as what they are—the self-appearances of original awareness—before any trace of delusion is able to stir.

3. Samantabhadra's mode of freedom

At the very moment in which they rise from the ground, the ground manifestations—the eight gateways of innate presence—dawn as [the ground's] self-appearances. An impartial state of mind without grasping [at these ground manifestations] as something other will recognize them as [the ground's] natural self-radiance. Through that, this stirring [of the ground manifestations] is [immediately] cut through, right within itself: through what dawns as self-appearance recognizing its own face in the first instant, realization arises, and thus [the ground manifestations] are differentiated [as what they actually are]. In the second [instant], through delusion's having been purified (Tib. *sangs*) and wisdom's having expanded (Tib. *rgyas*), the ground is matured as the fruition. Thus, the essence—primordial awakening [purity and expansion]—is said to be re-awakened [re-purified and re-expanded] through realization. The teacher who has thus awakened prior to everything right within the ground, through its self-appearances' dissolving within alpha-purity, is called "Samantabhadra." ...

The seed-like awareness that rises from the ground [as the ground manifestations] is indeterminate in terms of whether it causes freedom or delusion; therefore, it is called "nonmatured awareness." Its maturing into awakening is caused by the prajñā of realization. ... When this awareness is realized as itself, by virtue of not straying outward into discernment, through joining the dissolution process [of the ground manifestations] with an impartial state of mind, it remains within inner luminosity.[482]

Appendix 3

The Arising of Delusion and the Unchanging Inherent Purity of All Saṃsāric Manifestations

The second chapter of Longchenpa's *Precious Treasury of Words and Their Meanings* presents (A) detailed explanations on how delusion stirs from the primordial ground and (B) the perpetual inherent purity of all manifestations of saṃsāra, which never changes no matter how these manifestations may appear.

(A) The manner in which delusion arises from the ground is through not recognizing the ground manifestations for what they are due to three kinds of unawareness and four conditions. Thus, delusion is not rooted in these ground manifestations or in awareness's dynamic energy per se, but in reifying and identifying with certain of their aspects as self, other, subject, object, and so on.

1. Brief introduction to the essence [of delusion]

Delusion arises by virtue of the factor of the ground manifestations not [having the ability of] recognizing themselves ... In what manner does it arise? When the ground dawns as the ground manifestations, the dynamic energy of compassionate responsiveness is self-arising as a lucid and aware cognizance that is able to discern objects.[483] Based on not recognizing its own face, this [cognizance] dawns as being associated with threefold unawareness. (1) The unawareness that has the same identity as the cause consists of [the factor of] not recognizing this arisen cognizance as this [dynamic energy of compassionate responsiveness] itself. (2) Connate unawareness consists of [the factor of] the simultaneous arising of this cognizance and [its] non-recognition of [its] own face.[484] (3) Imaginative unawareness consists of the factor of discerning the self-appearances [of the ground manifestations] as something other. These three [aspects of unawareness] exist within that single cognizance as different isolates with a single essence.[485] Once this [cognizance together with its threefold unawareness] discerns self-appearances, the appearances of [both] the ground (essence, nature, and compassionate responsiveness) and the ground manifestations (innate presence's mode of arising) are not recognized as having the nature of the ground and the ground manifestations but are apprehended as being something other. It is due to this distinctive feature that there is delusion.

[Thus,] by virtue of the factors that consist of this cause—the threefold unawareness—and the impure observation [of the ground manifestations] that consists of the four conditions,[486] that cognizance becomes deluded about the appearances [of the ground manifestations] as being apprehender and apprehended.[487] At that time, through the six mentations'[488] emerging as unceasing clinging, the six afflictions dawn as the factors that are their latencies, whereby awareness is fettered and thus deluded in terms of the appearances of the six objects. [This is described] in the *Illuminating Lamp*:

> From within the ground that abides in this way,
> the cause and the seed of delusion
> is a highly lucid and aware cognizance
> [that arises] through the lucidity dimension's straying
> outward.
>
> By virtue of the three unawarenesses,
> a slight stir to the outside occurs, whereby mind
> apprehends

objects within the appearance dimension as identities
[other than itself],
thus becoming deluded about the ground and the
ground's appearance dimension[489]
as the distinction between the ground and the cognizance of the ground.[490]

Through the cause of delusion, the conditions of objects
are encountered.
By virtue of impure observation in terms of the four
conditions,
the lucidity dimension that appears as diversity is blocked.

Through the unceasing clinging of the six mentations,
the six afflictions fetter awareness as a self-identity
and the distinct appearances of the six objects dawn.
In this way, objects are grasped as identities.[491]

The six objects consist of forms, sounds, smells, tastes, tangibles, and phenomena. The six afflictions are unawareness, desire, hatred, nescience, pride, and envy. Since unawareness pervades all of the five poisons, while nescience is [simply] one among the five poisons, the two are explained separately [here].[492] If unawareness is classified, the causal triad was already explained [above], while the six aspects of its essence are listed in *Self-Arising Awareness*:

> Unawareness is as follows: (1) the fundamental unawareness of mind, (2) the unawareness of objects, which is delusion; (3) the unawareness of the ground, which is the basis of delusion; (4) the unawareness of thoughts, which is clinging; (5) the unawareness of the path, which is fabrication; and (6) the unawareness of oblivion, which is nonrecognition. In this way, six kinds of unawareness emerge and thus self-appearances are not seen [for what they are].[493]

These [six kinds of unawareness] are explained separately because these individual factors occur as six kinds of oblivion. As for the six mentations, [*Self-Arising Awareness* says this]:

> The six clinging mentations emerge: (a) the mentation associated with unawareness, (b) the mentation of the mental consciousness, (c) the mentation of searching, (d) the mentation of ascertainment, (e) mentations whose aspect is coarse, and (f) the mentation of determination.[494]

In due order, these refer to (1) the mentation that involves movement, (2) self-awareness through cognizance, (3) apprehending objects, (4) determining objects, (5) being distracted toward objects, as well as coarse afflictions, and (6) one-pointed internal fixation.[495] These are the six aspects of oblivion.

2. Detailed explanation of the nature [of delusion]

This has two parts:

1. [Detailed explanation of] the factor that is the essence of the manner of delusion
2. Detailed explanation of the factors that consist of the conditions that are its aspects

2.1. [Detailed explanation of] the factor that is the essence of the manner of delusion

When the general ground of delusion[496] appears, through the stains of awareness not [having the ability of] recognizing its own face, this very awareness is polluted[497] as delusion. Due to that, stainless awareness itself (what is to be known) has become stained. Having become trapped in the mind's snare, this awareness whose essence is alpha-purity has become polluted by conceptions. Thus, by virtue of being fettered by the six mentations, the body becomes incorporated into a web of partless minute particles and its luminosity becomes dormant. Delusion manifests in terms of four conditions due to (1) not recognizing that the ground manifestations are self-arising (the causal condition), due to (2) the dawning as objects of these very [ground manifestations] (the object condition), due to (3) the clinging [to these objects] as a self and what belongs to this self (the dominant condition), and (4) due to the simultaneity of these three [conditions] (the immediate condition)[498]...

[Through] the cause of delusion (unawareness), the condition [of delusion] (the appearances of objects for cognizance), and the agent of delusion (what appears as the cognizance of the ground from within the ground), the awareness that stirs and expands [outward] is fettered in the form of apprehender and apprehended[499] ...

2.2. Detailed explanation of the factors that consist of the conditions that are its aspects

The cause of the delusion of seeing what is nonexistent[500] as existent consists of the threefold unawareness: (1) Through the factor of ultimate nondelusion itself being unaware of its own face, it becomes deluded by way of its being imagined [as what it is not]. This is called "the unawareness that has the same identity as the cause." (2) To not recognize this very [unawareness for what it is] is connate unawareness, which emerges as the appearance dimension of both saṃsāra and nirvāṇa. (3) Through the arising of distinctly imagining and discerning the appearances of different objects, there is imaginative unawareness.[501]

This threefold unawareness has four conditions: (1) The causal condition is the arising of delusion through the conjunction of threefold unawareness, just as when a person has a physical form and its limbs [complete], [that person's] face[502] appears as a matter of course.[503] (2) Due to that, the object condition resembles the appearing [of that person] as an external object in something like a mirror, and since that [person] has a face, this face also appears in that mirror, which is the condition [for such an appearance]. Similarly, the focal object consists of the external appearance of self-luminosity [as if in a mirror].[504] (3) Due to that, the dominant condition resembles [that person's] direct perception of the mirror, their face [reflected in it], and their actual self, and thereby having thoughts about that mirror, their face [in it], [and themselves]. Similarly, the dominant condition here consists of entertaining thoughts about the triad of the [five] lights, awareness, and their dharmatā. Therefore, one speaks of "the dominant condition."[505] (4) Thus, by virtue of the simultaneity of the cause (threefold unawareness) and those [first] three conditions, there is the immediate condition, whereby delusion directly emerges.[506]

The *Mirror of Vajrasattva's Heart* states this:

> All these sentient beings of the three realms first become deluded as anything whatsoever from within the ground that is nothing whatsoever. This ground is empty in its essence and lucid by its nature, and its compassionate responsiveness is capable of appearing for sentient beings. Then the cognizance that is the inner apprehender and arises from the factor of unawareness stirs for just an instant, and thereby this dim cognizance thinks, "Have I arisen from what is over there, or has what is over there arisen from me?" Through the sheer arising of this cognizance, delusion arises. This unawareness does not exist in the ground [itself] but is present as the [subjective] experience or the dream[-like] aspect [through which the ground is misperceived].
>
> From the appearance of this aspect, the [four] conditions arise: (1) The ground's presence in the manner of a luminous mansion is called "the causal condition," which is the actual unawareness.[507] (2) Due to that turning into clinging thoughts, one speaks of "the dominant

condition." (3) Due to taking that as subject [and object], one speaks of "the object condition," like in the example of a person's face showing in a mirror. (4) Due to the simultaneity of these three, one speaks of "the immediate condition."

This [dim cognizance] is deluded in its own nonrecognition of what its own ground is,[508] whereby saṃsāra with its three realms is established. Proceeding from there into coarse afflictions, the different forms of sentient beings emerge. Delusion [arises] from such a ground.[509]

Auspicious Beauty says this:

Manifestations are unceasing from within the basic nature of the amulet-box of precious innate presence. By virtue of that, these manifestations [keep] changing while the ground does not change [at all]. Pursuing the plurality of objects, cognizance conceives of all [of them]. Though the manifestations of the dharmakāya involve no change, the manifestations of delusion arise as if they involved constant change. Though Vajrasattva lacks any delusion, he displays the manner of delusion in sentient beings. In the end, [awareness's] self-appearances are returned to the ground that is their own condition.

(1) Delusion emerges through not recognizing that nondual appearances are self-arising and this delusion is taken to be the owner [or sovereign of those appearances]. Therefore, this is the dominant condition. (2) Not recognizing that the fruition of self-awareness is self-arising, the very cause is taken as something that involves dependence. This is the causal condition.[510] (3) Not recognizing that objects and cognition are empty, what is observed is taken to be [real] objects. Therefore, this is the condition of the object's own state. (4) In terms of time, [awareness's] light is not recognized as being self-arising. [Thus,] there emerges the cognizance that apprehends what is

> not [an object] as being [an object]. Therefore, this is the immediate condition.[511]

This is followed by an explanation of how the initial arising of delusion extends and ramifies into the twelve links of dependent origination, the five skandhas, the twelve āyatanas, the eighteen dhātus, the five primary afflictions, and so on.[512]

(B) The complete inherent purity of all of saṃsāra's manifestations, no matter how they may appear, is discussed in a general manner and in very specific detail:

> Apart from their mere arising from within the natural state of awareness, dwelling within this state, and playing within this state, the impure phenomena of saṃsāra do not even the slightest bit move toward something other, just as dreams do not move away from the state of sleep. The teaching that these appearances are ultimately empty forms that are mere miraculous displays of clearly appearing nonexistents represents the complete purity of saṃsāra ...
>
> **1. [Saṃsāra's] complete purity in general**
>
> Primordially empty self-appearances manifest as the sheer play [of awareness]. For example, though a rope may appear as if it were something coarse, in its own actuality it consists of its individual filaments, which in turn consist of partless minute particles, [all of] which are empty. Likewise, though the appearances of delusion may manifest as if they were coarse, ultimately, they are empty self-appearances free from arising, abiding, and ceasing ... Within the natural state of awareness, phenomena such as the skandhas resemble clouds in the sky: though they appear within awareness, they are just floating [within it] as empty forms without [ever] tainting awareness. Thus, they are like illusions and magical creations. *Uttaratantra* [I.159cd] says that the skandhas are like the magical manifestations in an illusion.

Where do these [phenomena] abide? Just as the [world's] container and its contents rest within space, skandhas, dhātus, āyatanas, karmas, and afflictions are merely the self-appearances of conception, which rests within the natural state of empty mind as such. Therefore, they are empty at first, empty at present, and also empty in the end, being present in such a way that they are free from any arising, abiding, and ceasing. The *Uttaratantra* states this:

> Earth rests upon water, water on wind,
> and wind on space,
> [but] space does not rest on the elements
> of wind, water, or earth.
>
> Likewise, skandhas, dhātus, and faculties
> rest on karma and afflictions,
> and karma and afflictions always rest on
> improper mental engagement.
>
> Improper mental engagement
> rests on the purity of the mind,
> [but] this nature of the mind does not rest
> on any of these phenomena.[513]

Though they appear to arise, abide, and cease, at the time of their [seeming] abiding, they are not [actually] established as these [phenomena] ... From the very time of their appearing, all phenomena that appear and are possible are free from the extremes that are the reference points of arising and ceasing.

2. [Saṃsāra's] complete purity in its specific details[514]

Since all appearances of saṃsāra with its three realms are right from the start embraced by the dimension of the expanse, each one of their aspects exists in such a manner that it is intimately linked [with the expanse]. Therefore, ultimately, they are present as empty dharmatā, just like reflections. When they appear at present, the skandhas, elements, and so on are intimately linked with the dimensions of the kāyas and wisdoms. The nature of the three gates [of our ordinary body, speech, and mind] is their being free as the awakened body, speech, and mind [of a buddha]: the appearances of birth, aging, sickness, and death arise as the play of dharmadhātu wisdom. All agents, objects, and appearances are explained as the complete purity that appears as the great self-arising view and meditation of dharmatā.[515]

Appendix 4

How Buddha Nature and Its Pure Qualities Pervade All Sentient Beings

The third chapter of Longchenpa's *Precious Treasury of Words and Their Meanings* is in a sense an extension of the final topic in the second chapter—saṃsāra's complete purity—because this chapter here explains (A) how *tathāgatagarbha* pervades and dwells within all sentient beings at all times[516] and also describes (B) the pure qualities of buddha nature and their corresponding impure saṃsāric counterparts.

(A) Longchenpa first adduces a range of Dzogchen and general sources from the sūtras and tantras on buddha nature's inherent existence in all beings' mind streams, and then deals with objections about how tathāgatagarbha relates to emptiness and the notion of a self.

1. General instruction on the manner of its pervasion

This has two parts:

1. The actual qualities of pervasion[517]
2. Eliminating doubts about that

1.1. The actual qualities of pervasion

The *Tantra of the Mirror of Vajrasattva's Heart* says this:

> The tathāgata heart exists inherently in all sentient
> beings of [all] worldly realms.
> It is present just as [sesame] oil pervades sesame seeds.[518]

The *Array of Inlaid Gems* states this:

Just as oil is primordially innately present
within sesame seeds or mustard seeds,
the seed of the tathāgatas
and its corresponding light [dwell] inherently
within what appears as if a sentient being's body.[519]

Universes and Transformations [of Sound] says this:

Self-aware wisdom dwells within the body,
just like oil within a sesame seed.
The body's luster and radiant glow
represents its being pervaded by wisdom's moisture.[520]

Self-Arising [Awareness] declares this:

The awakened mind of perfect buddhahood
dwells in the manner of the kāyas and wisdoms
within all sentient beings' own mind stream.[521]

This is also stated in the sūtras and tantras of the common yāna. The *Hevajra[tantra]* says this:

Great wisdom abides within the body.
It has left behind all thoughts
and is what pervades all entities,
residing in the body, yet not born from the body.[522]

...

The *Uttaratantra* declares this:

Since the perfect buddhakāya radiates,
since suchness is undifferentiable,
and because of the disposition,
all beings always possess the buddha heart.[523]

The *Two-Chaptered [Hevajratantra]* says this:

Sentient beings are buddhas indeed
but they are obscured by adventitious stains.

> due to the removal of these, no doubt,
> beings are definitely buddhas.[524]

[Saraha's] *Doha[koṣagīti]* states this:

> The existence of buddhahood within the body is not realized
> through the explanations in the treatises of any scholars.[525]

The *Uttaratantra* speaks of nine examples and their nine meanings, such as [the one of a treasure beneath the house of a pauper] ... The *Avataṃsaka[sūtra]* declares by way of many examples (such as a huge silk cloth [the size of] a trichiliocosm)[526] that the basic element—the sugata heart—exists in the mind streams of sentient beings.

1.2. Eliminating doubts about that

This has three parts:

1. Presenting the doubts
2. Eliminating them
3. Giving rise to joyful enthusiasm through this special certainty

1.2.1. Presenting the doubts

Those who have neither procured roots of virtue in the past nor met a genuine spiritual friend in the present and [thus] have not heard the profound Dharma of the definitive meaning say, "How could it be possible for the so-called 'nature or heart of a buddha' to exist as the qualities such as the major and minor marks or the powers within mind as such—emptiness? Since it is taught in all [sūtras] such as the intermediate Mother[527] that the basic nature—identitylessness—is similar to empty space, the sūtras that teach the [tathāgata] heart are of expedient meaning. If that were not the case, this [tathāgata heart] would just not be different at all from the permanent self of the tīrthikas." Thus, it appears that they have turned their back on the Dharma of the definitive meaning.

1.2.2. Eliminating them

Since this approach is not good, for now I shall reject it by taking the scriptures themselves as valid authority. From among the three cycles of the Bhagavān's words, this topic [of the tathāgata heart] was taught in the final cycle that ascertains the ultimate but you did not understand it. If sheer emptiness alone were the ultimate, how would it be justified [for the Buddha] to teach these three cycles as [three] distinct ones?[528] Rather, he taught emptiness to be of expedient meaning, with the underlying intention of merely refuting the clinging to [real] identities by beginners and those afraid of this basic nature [that is tathāgatagarbha]. In a [dharma] specification in the *Āryamahāparanirvāṇasūtra*, the Buddha first gives the simile of a woman who cures her breastfed infant[529] and then says the following.

> Oh son of noble family, similarly, in order to free all sentient beings, the Tathāgata teaches by strongly emphasizing the identitylessness of all sentient beings. Through strongly emphasizing this, they will lack a mind of [thinking about] any identity and thus pass into parinirvāṇa. He teaches thus in order to dispel the bad view of the Lokāyatas, in order to show that [his teaching] transcends the dharma of the Lokāyatas, in order to furthermore show that the view of the Lokāyatas about a self is not correct, and in order to transform [beings] into a completely pure body through their meditating on the dharma of identitylessness.
>
> Just as that woman smeared her breasts with bile for the sake of her son, the Tathāgata likewise spoke of the identitylessness of all phenomena so that sentient beings

> would meditate on emptiness. Just as that woman [later] washed the bile off her breasts and called her son to her with the words, "Drink the milk from my breast," I have similarly taught the tathāgata heart. Oh bhikṣus, without becoming frightened, just like the son who was called by his mother and then drank her breast milk sip by sip, oh bhikṣus, you should understand the difference [here]: the tathāgata heart is not said to be nonexistent.[530]

And:

> The teaching that all phenomena are emptiness in what I said in the prajñāpāramitā sūtras previously was given in order to lead childish beings away from their clinging to any identity. Actually, however, it is the tathāgata heart alone that is ultimate reality.[531]

Thus, this [tathāgata heart] is not like the permanent self of the tīrthikas. Though this heart is primordially luminous and present within the body, it transcends permanence and impermanence and hence is not held to be just permanent. Since its luminosity can become visible through the pith instructions of the guru, it is not held to be something hidden that no one at all can see. Since its empty and lucid essence is free from all extremes, it is not correlated in terms of its attributes with any [independent,] specifically characterized entity such as a thumb.[532] Since it does not exist as any entity or characteristics, this heart is not held to be of larger or smaller size in larger or smaller bodies, respectively, or to be better or worse [in certain beings]. There are very many distinctions such as these [between the self of the tīrthikas and the tathāgata heart].

Though what the tīrthikas say is completely dissimilar to the buddha heart, you may be deluded about this by thinking that they are alike by virtue of mere [similarity in certain] names or verbal expressions, through which we [can] see that you have the intellect of a fool. It resembles [the story of] how once the sword of a king appeared to be lost and a pauper who then dreamed of this sword went into meaningless ramblings [about it in his sleep]. Disputing about that sword [on the basis of these meaningless ramblings], the king's ministers were trying to establish [the whereabouts and characteristics of] a sword they had not [ever] seen, since apart from mere names [such as "sword" being mumbled], they did not [ever] see the referent [of these names][533] ...

1.2.3. Giving rise to joyful enthusiasm through this special certainty

This has three parts: (1) It is appropriate to be joyful because the heart of the matter that is not suitable to be seen if it is not shown by an authentic spiritual friend is found through a genuine guru. (2) One gives rise to joyful enthusiasm because the secret of the buddhas alone is a vajra topic in that it is a topic that is difficult to realize even by bodhisattvas who dwell on the bhūmis, so what need is there to speak of those who see just this life? (3) It is also appropriate to give rise to enthusiasm because [pure wisdom or] awareness is directly seen if shown by an authentic guru, and its self-appearance will naturally dawn in the intermediate state ...[534]

(B) Longchenpa explains tathāgatagarbha's qualities of pervading all sentient beings in detail by way of presenting six sets of five pure elements and their corresponding five impure elements:

(1) The five kāyas, (2) the five wisdoms, (3) the five lights, (4) the five qualities of the [five buddha] families, (5) the five wisdom winds, and (6) the five qualities [each] of essence, nature, and compassionate responsiveness are primordially present within the wisdom of the [tathāgata] heart. What are present as the [corresponding] signs of these [sets of five] within impure appearances are (1) the five skandhas, (2) the

five afflictions,[535] (3) the five elements, (4) the five sense faculties, (5) the five sense objects, and (6) the five natural qualities of [each of] the three gates ...

(1) Regarding the [primordial] presence of the wisdom of awareness as the five kāyas, (a) the wisdom of awareness innately brings forth the shine of primordial radiance from within the dimension that is its own object—dharmatā. Therefore, it emerges as the kāya of Vairocana. (b) Since the wisdom of awareness is unshakable and unchangeable like a vajra, it emerges as the kāya of Akṣobhya. (c) Since the qualities of luminosity exist primordially in the wisdom of awareness, they shine forth in an increasing manner when [this wisdom] is made a living experience. Therefore, it emerges as the kāya of Ratnasambhava. (4) Since the wisdom of awareness's own light is infinite, it emerges as the kāya of Amitābha. (5) Since the wisdom of awareness primordially makes the actuality of buddhahood a living experience, the two welfares are innately certain. Therefore, it emerges as the kāya of Amoghasiddhi. It is by virtue of these five kāyas' primordial presence within awareness in such a way that they dawn as the five skandhas at present ...

(2) [Awareness] is also primordially present as the five wisdoms. (a) Since the reflections of phenomena in general as well as in their specific individual forms are clearly present within awareness, it is mirror-like wisdom. (b) Since awareness itself lacks any distinctions such as good and bad or large and small, it is [everywhere] equal just like space or a jewel. Therefore, it is the wisdom of equality. (c) Since [all] the specifics of phenomena and faculties are clearly present within awareness without being conflated, it is discriminating wisdom. (d) Since awareness itself is free in itself without any obstruction or impediment, it is all-accomplishing wisdom. (e) Since awareness itself is free from all reference points, it is dharmadhātu wisdom. It is by virtue of these five

wisdoms' primordial presence within awareness in such a way that they dawn as the five afflictions at present[536] ...

(3) As for the five lights: (a) Since awareness is not tainted by any karma or afflictions whatsoever, it dawns as if being white. (b) Since its qualities are primordially and perfectly complete, it dawns as if being yellow. (c) Since the four empowerments that are present without being sought are perfectly complete within [awareness] itself, it dawns as if being red. (d) Since awareness transcends movement and effort, it dawns as if being green. (e) Since it is unchanging, it dawns as if being blue. It is by virtue of these five colors' [primordial] presence [within awareness] in such a way that they dawn as the five elements at present[537] ... These [five elements] are also correlated with the purity of the five mothers[538] ...

(4) As for the five families, (a) the buddhas of the past have become buddhas previously through seeing awareness itself, having thus gone to the buddhabhūmi. Therefore, [it is in this sense that] awareness is the buddha family. (b) Awareness itself is without change or transition even at the times of being born in any of the [six] forms of existence. Therefore, it is the vajra family. (c) Since its qualities are innately present within awareness, it is the ratna family. (d) Since [awareness] is not tainted by any flaws despite its being present in saṃsāra, it is the padma family. (e) Since enlightened activity is innately present within awareness, it is the karma family. By virtue of these five families' primordial presence [within awareness] in such a way, they dawn at present as the five sense faculties that symbolize [these families][539] ...

(5) The five winds are correlated with the experience of objects as the five sense objects ... (a) Since awareness brings down the heat of the wisdom of awareness, it is called "the fire-accompanying wind." (b) Since it sustains the life-force of saṃsāra and nirvāṇa, it is "the wind that sustains the life-force." (c) Since the five lights of wisdom are inherently

present [in awareness], it is "the wind that produces luster and radiant glow." (d) Since it delivers to the level of perfection, it is "the propelling wind." (e) Since it frees saṃsāra as nirvāṇa, it is present as the wind that mercilessly functions [to usher in a new] eon[540] ...

(6) As for the five qualities [each] of essence, nature, and compassionate responsiveness, their meaning is summarized as the three wisdom kāyas that are present in the ground.[541] (a) The five [qualities] of the essence are correlated with the [five] kāyas in terms of their fivefold ground of arising.[542] (b) The five [qualities] of the nature are correlated with the manifestation of the five lights. (c) The five [qualities] of compassionate responsiveness are correlated with the five wisdoms. Therefore, on the buddhabhūmi, compassion emerges in five forms: (1) the compassion that is [a buddha's] natural power, (2) the compassion when encountering the condition of an object,[543] (3) the compassion when exhorted and supplicated, (4) the compassion that manifests as various activities, and (5) the compassion for those to be guided that is unchanging.[544] [These five kinds of compassion] emerge [at buddhahood] due to the fact that the dimension that is their ground of arising [already] exists in an innately present manner in the wisdom of awareness right now [in every being].

Awareness itself is also primordially present as the following five [kinds of] prajñā. (1) Since it is present as the differentiating prajñā, it distinguishes between appearances and cognizance as being different. (2) Since it exists as the incorporating prajñā, everything is perfectly complete within itself. (3) Since it pervades all appearance and cognizance, it emerges as the pervading prajñā. (4) Since awareness is propelled into space in dependence on the wisdom winds, it is present as the propelling prajñā. (5) Since it cuts off the life-force of saṃsāra and nirvāṇa through dharmatā, it emerges as the freeing prajñā.

Furthermore, awareness itself is present as the threefold stack of kāyas, lights, and wisdoms. (1) By virtue of its essence being present as the kāyas, what is to be known [awareness] dawns as self-lucidity. (2) By virtue of its nature being present as the lights, it expands as luminous spaciousness. (3) By virtue of its compassionate responsiveness being present as wisdom, it emerges as impartial activities.

When considering a yogic practitioner in the present, the dharmakāya [is present] during meditative equipoise, the sambhogakāya when there is no distinction at all between meditative equipoise and subsequent [attainment], and the nirmāṇakāya during subsequent [attainment]. *Self-Arising [Awareness]* says this:

> Nonconceptual awareness is the essence of the dharmakāya.
> Awareness's unceasing lucidity is the sambhoga[kāya].
> Awareness's manifestation as anything whatsoever is the nirmāṇakāya.[545]

In this threefold manner in which [awareness] is present, it is [also] present as having the character of the three jewels' being primordially complete in itself ... *Self-Arising [Awareness]* states this:

> Likewise, the buddhas of the three times
> are explained to be great self-appearances.
> They constitute the triad of body, speech, and mind:
> speech represents the buddha of the past,
> mind represents the buddha of the future,
> and the body represents the buddha of the present.
> This is how the three kinds of buddhas are present.[546]

...

When [impure phenomena] are correlated with their concordant pure [counterparts], all phenomena of saṃsāra and nirvāṇa that appear and are possible are said to be complete within the body and the mind ... If [all phenomena] were not complete within ground awareness, they would not be complete within the appropriated body and mind. If they were not completely present within that [body and mind], they would not be complete in [the sphere of] the external objects that appear to the mind. This is similar to a barren woman's not having a child, [her nonexistent child's] thus not having a face, and that face's not appearing in a mirror due to its nonexistence. Rather, appearances emerge from the [preexisting] completeness of these appearances within the body and the mind, which [in turn] emerge by virtue of their completeness within awareness. This is similar to Devadatta's having a head, his thus having a face, and its reflection's emerging in a mirror due the existence of that [face].[547]

Appendix 5

The Distinctions between All-Ground and Dharmakāya as well as Mind and Wisdom

In the fourth chapter of Longchenpa's *Precious Treasury of Words and Their Meanings*, we find discussions of the important distinctions between (A) the all-ground (*kun gzhi*) and the dharmakāya, and (B) mind (*sems*) and wisdom (*ye shes*). Both are closely related to the famous distinction between mind and basic awareness.

(A) Regarding the general distinction between the all-ground and the dharmakāya, Longchenpa says this:

> Since the all-ground is the root of saṃsāra, it is the support of all latent tendencies, just like a pond.[548] Since the dharmakāya is the root of nirvāṇa, it is free from all latent tendencies and therefore the termination of contamination ... *Self-Arising [Awareness]* gives an example that clarifies these two ... Within the state of the dharmakāya that abides as the ground and resembles the clear ocean, the all-ground is like a ship filled with the passengers of the multiple collections of mind and consciousness and with the many provisions of karmas and latent tendencies. This is the manner in which the path arises from within the state of awareness, the dharmakāya.[549]
>
> In some sūtras and tantras, the aspect that is the ground is labeled with the name "all-ground." There are some who do not understand the intention behind that and assert the two as being one. Since this is a very grave error, there is a multitude of flaws [that it entails]. Since the all-ground possesses latent tendencies, it would follow that the dharmakāya [also] possesses latent tendencies. Since the all-ground must

> undergo the fundamental change, it would follow that the dharmakāya must also undergo the fundamental change. Since the all-ground is dependent on the temporary phenomena of saṃsāra and thus is transitory, it would follow that the dharmakāya is also transitory. There are many flaws such as these.[550]

In more detail, the specific distinctive features of the all-ground are explained in terms of its (1) essence, (2) hermeneutical etymology, (3) classification, (4) function, and (5) the rationale for using the term:

> (1) Its essence is that it serves as the support of all karmas and latent tendencies of saṃsāra and nirvāṇa because it consists of minds and mental factors; it is the dimension of unawareness [or ignorance] that is neutral ...
>
> (2) As for its hermeneutical etymology, it is the all-ground because it is the ground of a multitude of latent tendencies ...
>
> (3) When classified, it is fourfold: (a) The primordial ultimate all-ground is the dimension that has simultaneously arisen within awareness since primordial primal time from the start, just like gold and tarnish—unawareness contingent on awareness. It is the original ground of all saṃsāric phenomena. (b) The ultimate all-ground of linking is the ground that is the dimension of karma; it is the indeterminate basic support of linking with and propelling into saṃsāra or nirvāṇa through individual karmas. (c) The all-ground of diverse latent tendencies is the neutral dimension of the diverse latent karmas of minds and mental factors that are the factors that are [eventually re]produced as saṃsāra. (d) The all-ground of the bodies of latent tendencies is the dimension that is the support of unawareness that is the ground of the distinct appearance of three [kinds of bodies]—the coarse bodies [in the desire realm] that appear as the parts that consist

of the minute particles of main and secondary limbs, the lucid bodies of light [in the realm of form], and the bodies [in the formless realm] that appear in accordance with [certain] samādhis[551] ...

(4) Its function is to serve as the support of earlier and later latent tendencies, the cause of karmas and afflictions, the source of a multitude of bodies and collections [of attributes], and the factor of linking with a distinct form of a body, a mind, saṃsāra, or nirvāṇa[552] ...

(5) As for the rationale of using the term ["all-ground"], one speaks of "all" because of its linking earlier and later latent tendencies, connecting earlier and later maturations, and functioning as the support of the individual positive and negative powers of causes and results. One speaks of "ground" because it is the foundation in which [all these processes] come together ...

"Though [the all-ground] is tenable as the ground of saṃsāra, how is it the ground of purified phenomena?" In general, in terms of [being] the ground [of saṃsāra], it is the actual ground, similar to the sun [being the ground of sunlight] due to its rays. However, as the ground of linking with those [purified phenomena], it resembles the functioning of virtues as the ground of higher realms. Due to that, this [all-ground] is labeled with the name "the ground of linking." This is due to the factor that the virtues conducive to liberation that link with nirvāṇa and are accumulated through the three gates exist within the all-ground. The karmas that are conducive to liberation function as the causes for dispelling the stains that obscure the dimension of nirvāṇa. It is [this karma] that is labeled as the cause of nirvāṇa but [this karma and nirvāṇa] are not asserted as a producing cause and a produced result, respectively, because the essence of nirvāṇa is unconditioned and thus is contradictory to being newly produced through causes and conditions.[553] The *Uttaratantra* says this:

> Being unconditioned, effortless,
> not being realized through other conditions,
> and possessing wisdom, compassion, and power,
> buddhahood is endowed with the two welfares.[554]

Therefore, [it is only in the above sense of being the ground of purified phenomena that] the foundation that is the all-ground and the dharmakāya bear a resemblance within [the natural ground's] cognizance. [However,] through mistaking them as being a single ground, the assertion "Stained awareness is the all-ground, and stainless [awareness] is the dharmakāya" represents a failure to distinguish them due to conflating them. Due to not understanding the particular meaning that they are of a single essence but different isolates, there is no benefit even when one distinguishes them through [mere] words[555] ...

The dharmakāya is likewise explained in detail in terms of its (1) essence, (2) hermeneutical etymology, (3) classification, (4) function, and (5) the rationale for using the term:

(1) The essence of the dharmakāya is the space-like awareness that is untainted by saṃsāra ...

(2) As for the hermeneutical etymology, *Universes and Transformations [of Sound]* says this:

> The hermeneutical etymology: *Dharma* is the perfect path
> and *kāya* is the accomplishment due to that.[556]

(3) When classified, it is threefold. The same [text] states this:

> Its classification consists of dharma-, sambhoga-, and nirmāṇakāya.

> Through this threefold division, its distinctions are comprehended.[557]

(4) Its function is to operate in a stainless manner through the play of view, meditation, conduct, fruition, qualities, and enlightened activity. *Self-Arising [Awareness]* declares this:

> Without ceasing, without clinging, and without attachment—
> this is the conduct of the dharmakāya.
> Lucid, naked, and without distraction—
> this is the meditation of the dharmakāya.
>
> Unviewable, already viewed, the perfect view—
> this is the view of the dharmakāya.
> Unproduced, unarisen, and not arising—
> this is the fruition of the dharmakāya.
>
> Unaccomplishable, already accomplished, the perfect accomplishment—
> this is the enlightened activity of the dharmakāya.
> A single one arising, two arising, all arising—
> this represents the qualities of the dharmakāya.[558]

(5) As for the rationale for using the term ["dharmakāya"], it is called "dharmakāya" because the dharmas that consist of the qualities of the powers, fearlessness, and unique [buddha attributes] are perfected within the kāya that is empty and without entities and characteristics ... The dharmakāya in this context [of the Great Perfection] is asserted as the naturally pure dharmakāya that abides as the ground and has the characteristics of essence, nature, and compassionate responsiveness.[559]

(B) Longchenpa presents the distinction between mind and wisdom first in a general way in terms of the following five points:[560]

(1) Regarding the actual difference [between mind and wisdom], mind refers to saṃsāric phenomena, that is, the flaws that arise as the stains whose nature consists of karma and latent tendencies. At the time when awareness is associated with it, [awareness] is labeled as a "sentient being" (Tib. *sems can*; lit. "having mind"). It is this mind that causes delusion in the form of the individual six forms of existence. At the time when awareness has become free from mind, it is called "buddhahood free from adventitious stains." Wisdom refers to nirvāṇic phenomena: since it burns up karma and latent tendencies, it resembles a fire, and it has the nature of empty lucid space free from all imagination ...

(2) As for the flaws of not understanding [this difference], if mind and wisdom are not distinguished, there is the flaw of not cutting the root of appearing objects and thus not being free from saṃsāra—the appearances of delusion that are mind's objects ... In brief, [the appearances of delusion] are six: forms, sounds, smells, tastes, tangible objects, and phenomena. They appear from mind's latent tendencies, like the aspects of [imaginary] strands of hair [in eyes with floaters]. To what do they appear? They appear to the deluded mind. The objects of wisdom consist of space-like pure dharmatā and the appearances of luminosity—the vast appearances of the realms of the kāyas and wisdoms.[561]

[We find] explanations [in the scriptures such as the following]: "If mind recognizes its own face, it is wisdom," "These present appearances are the luminosity of wisdom," and "If mind is realized, it is wisdom." When deluded about the words of such explanations, there are many assertions such as that wisdom is nothing but the nonconceptual aspect of mind. Since this is also a very grave point of error, there are infinite flaws to be dispelled, but roughly speaking, [there are the following].

Since mind involves clinging, the same would follow for wisdom. Since mind possesses stains, the same would follow for wisdom. Since mind appears as saṃsāric phenomena, which are to be relinquished, the same would follow for wisdom ... Furthermore, since these appearances appear in a deluded manner, it would follow that luminosity consists of the appearances of delusion. Since appearances exist as what appears for ordinary sentient beings in common, it would follow that luminosity is established as a common appearance. If that is accepted, it would follow that, just like yogic practitioners, all [beings] are free. Since appearances and mind appear to arise, change, and alter, the same would follow for wisdom and its appearances.

Since many flaws such as these are observed, we are instructed not to rely on the positions of those who are much more ignorant than ignorant dimwits. Thus, we are taught that if we wish for the fruition of buddhahood by taking mind as the ground, we will search for cause and result or ground and fruition [within that framework]. Consequently, this is [completely] mistaken ...

Since mind represents the adventitious obscurations, it is not suitable as the support and cause of buddhahood. Since wisdom exists primordially, it is buddhahood's own nature. To take these two as one and the same is very inappropriate, just like clinging to the sun and clouds as being the same. Here it is not asserted that the fruition [lies] in the mind, while it is held that it stems from empty, lucid, and pure wisdom ... The *Mirror of Samantabhadra's Mind* says this:

> Asserting that appearances are the dharmakāya
> obscures me.

> Asserting that whatever appears is mind obscures me.
> . . . .
> Asserting that wisdom is mind obscures me.[562]

Nowadays some ordinary dull people say that appearances are one's own mind, that appearances are the dharmakāya, and that wisdom is mind. This is no different from crazy people who say just anything that comes to their mind, [such as] "The head is the ass," "Fire is water," or "Darkness is light." ... There are many [absurd consequences] such as the following.

If appearances were mind, it would follow that mind has color and so on. It would follow that when you are not [at a given location anymore], your mind [still] exists at this location because the appearances [there continue to] exist. Furthermore, it would follow that all [appearances] are born by virtue of one [sentient being] being born and that all [appearances] die by virtue of one [sentient being] dying. It would follow that when ten million people see a single vase, all these people have a single mind, like having a single collective mind. It would follow that saṃsāra is buddha wisdom because all phenomena appear as the objects of the buddha knowledge of variety. It would follow that when a sentient being sees a buddha, that buddha is a delusion because of being the mind of that sentient being. It would follow that that sentient being is a buddha because this buddha is the mind of that sentient being. It would follow that just as mind moves in a vacillating manner in a [single] instant, appearances [also] vacillate in a [single] instant.

If appearances were the dharmakāya, it would follow that appearances are beyond appearance and nonappearance because the dharmakāya is beyond appearance and nonappearance. It would follow that the dharmakāya represents appearances of delusion and it would follow that the dharmakāya is apprehended as an entity and its characteristics, because these appearances are the appearances of delusion and are apprehended as entities and their characteristics. It would follow that it is impossible for these appearances to appear from the perspective of delusion because it is impossible for the dharmakāya to appear from the perspective of delusion since it is the ultimate ... It has already been refuted that wisdom is mind.[563]

(3) The manner of the instruction to understand [this difference] is that intelligent people should understand the difference between mind and wisdom. The *Garland of Pearls* says this:

> Since mind arises as a gathered collection,
> it is filled with stains.
> Mind gathered as the all-ground and so on
> represent the enumeration of stains.
> Therefore, the distinction between mind and wisdom
> is to be understood by those with expertise.[564]

(4) As for the two essences of these two, the essence of mind is what presents itself as the appearances of delusion, which have the form of the three realms ... The essence of wisdom is nonconceptuality ...

(5) Their locations are two: the location of mind is the all-ground and the location of wisdom is the dharmakāya. The *Sixfold Expanse* states this:

> Oh mahāsattva, the location of mind is the all-ground. Why is that? Because the all-ground gathers all conceived objects and entertains the notion of a [perceiving] mind. The location of wisdom is the dharmakāya. Why is that? Because the dharmakāya does not have any thought processes and lacks any cognition of clinging to subject [and object] as being different.[565]

> Thus, there is no identical location for these two—cloud-like mind that obscures wisdom and sun-like wisdom. That is, what obscures and what is obscured abide distinctly. Due to that, at the time when mind and what appears to mind are understood as delusion, externally appearing objects and the mind that apprehends them are realized to be adventitious and without base. At the time when wisdom and the appearances of wisdom are known to be nondelusion, mastery is gained over the maṇḍala of the dharmakāya that is awareness. Therefore, mind and wisdom are to be distinguished. If they are not distinguished, there is the flaw that wisdom, through being obscured by mind, is not able to appear as its own essence of linking [with nirvāṇa or the dharmakāya]. The same [text] states this:
>
>> Oh mahāsattva, if the essences of mind and wisdom are not distinguished, wisdom is like the sun obscured by cloud banks: it is unable to perform the function of illuminating what is outside. Therefore, yogic practitioners who are experts in mind realize that outer objects are identityless. Yogic practitioners who are experts in wisdom are able to gain mastery over wisdom through awareness itself.[566]

As for the detailed explanation of the points of mind that are difficult to realize, Longchenpa first presents the common specifications of mind in terms of its essence, hermeneutical etymology, and classifications as they are also found in the abhidharma and Yogācāra (such as pure and impure states of mind and the eight kinds of consciousnesses).[567]

Then he explains the special points of mind as understood in Dzogchen in terms of its (1) essence, (2) location, (3) pathway, (4) function, and (5) fruition:

> (1) Mind's essence consists of the imagination of those in the three realms that cognizes apprehender and apprehended.

It includes mind (the all-ground consciousness), mentation (what is omnipresent and experiences objects), and consciousness (the five consciousnesses of the five [sense] gates).[568] Thus, it is the cognition that is the single essence of these three, which is unaware of its own face and is the root of the five poisons.

(2) Mind's location is that it abides within the channel that connects the lungs to the heart, which has the width of the hollow tube of a straw. [The winds] in the heart [that come] from the lungs, [which could be described as being] like its dynamic aspect, mix in that [channel] with the self-radiance of the dimension of awareness, which is like an eye. Through that, [our] "mind of dazzling variety" arises in an adventitious manner from these conditional factors.[569]

(3) Its pathway is that it moves upward because it moves from that [channel at the heart] upward along the spinal column in the single [life-force] channel and connects with the mouth and the nose via the "small tip" [channel].

(4) Its function is to gather [all kinds of latent tendencies] through different karmic actions.

(5) Its fruition is to mature as saṃsāric appearances of delusion. This is called "the stack of threefold impurity": the radiance of awareness [mounted] on the horse of the breath in the channel petals between the heart and the lungs represents the threefold collection of unawareness (its essence), mind (its aspect [of appearance]), and what is called "mentation" (its conception).[570]

As for the detailed explanation of the points of wisdom that are difficult to realize, Longchenpa first presents the common specifications of wisdom in terms of its (1) essence, (2) hermeneutical etymology, and (3) classification:

(1) The essence of wisdom is luminous awareness, the sugata heart ...

(2) As for its hermeneutical etymology, it is wisdom (*ye shes*) because it is the genuine cognition (*shes pa*) that is present primordially (*ye nas*). The same [text, the *Universes and Transformations of Sound*,] says this:

> As for its hermeneutical etymology, it is wisdom because it cognizes the primordially present heart of the matter just as it is.[571]

(3) Its classification is threefold: the wisdom that is present as the ground, the wisdom of apprehending characteristics, and the wisdom that pervades [all] objects ... The wisdom that is present as the ground consists of the three wisdoms of essence, nature, and compassionate responsiveness. The wisdom of apprehending characteristics consists of five: dharmadhātu [wisdom], mirror[-like wisdom], [the wisdom of] equality, discriminating [wisdom], and all-accomplishing [wisdom]. The wisdom of pervading [all] objects consists of the two [wisdoms of] knowing suchness and variety.[572]

Finally, Longchenpa explains the special points of wisdom as understood in Dzogchen in eight points:

> (1) The essence of wisdom is the ground explained above, the sugata heart. (2) Its support is the skandha of form. (3) Its location is the precious citta. (4) Its palace is the mansion that is comprised of all five colors of light.[573] (5) Its pathways consist of the quartet of the rasanā, lalanā, avadhūti, and crystal tube channels, and in particular the pathway through which it appears as [visual] objects—the channel that resembles a white silk thread and connects the heart with the far-reaching lasso [water lamp].[574] (6) Its appearance [or illumination] consists of the following two lamps:

the essence of the lamp of the pure expanse is what fills [the entire] space through expanding from the [initial] deep blue that appears like the [Tibetan] letter *naro*. The essence of the lamp of empty spheres consists of self-luminous circles enclosed by a fivefold rim that appear like the eye of a peacock feather. (7) Its function is to seize the primal state of dharmatā through freeing saṃsāra as nirvāṇa and maturing awareness as the kāyas. (8) Its fruition is the attainment of the dharmakāya—the ultimate inseparability of expanse and wisdom.[575]

Appendix 6

The Kāyas and Wisdoms

I. *The Precious Treasury of Words and Their Meanings*

The eleventh chapter of Longchenpa's text discusses the ultimate fruition of buddhahood by way of (A) the three kāyas[576] and (B) three main kinds of wisdom.[577]

> (A) Each kāya in the standard triad of dharmakāya, sambhogakāya, and nirmāṇakāya is presented in terms of its (1) essence, (2) hermeneutical etymology, (3) defining characteristic, (4) nature, (5) mode of abiding, (6) pure realm, (7) who or what is to be guided, (8) function, (9) full measure of confidence, and (10) classification.
>
> (1) The essence of the kāyas in general is that they serve as the body or the supporting basis of the buddha qualities. The essence of the dharmakāya is great alpha-purity because it is free from thinking and expression. The essence of the sambhogakāya is great innate presence because it is self-lucidity free from all extremes of thoughts. The essence of the nirmāṇakāya is whatever arises as suitable guidance from compassionate responsiveness as its ground of arising.
>
> (2) As for the general hermeneutical etymology of kāya, *Self-Arising Awareness* says this:
>
>> It is a kāya by virtue of abiding as the essence of self-lucidity without clinging.
>> It is a kāya by virtue of bearing the characteristics of distinct appearances of colors.

> It is a kāya by virtue of being endowed with the actuality
> that is the vajra heart of the matter.[578]

As for the specific hermeneutical etymology of the three kāyas, (a) *dharma* refers to empty luminosity endowed with twofold purity and beyond characteristics, and *kāya* to what is without change and transition. (b) As for the sambhogakāya, *bhoga* ("enjoyment") refers to the major and minor marks, *sam* to their being complete, and *kāya* to their appearing but lacking any nature. (c) *Nirmāṇakāya* refers to what appears in all kinds of forms and promotes the welfare of beings.

(3) The general defining characteristic of each of the kāyas is to abide as the buddha body that is a supporting basis and is endowed with ultimate twofold purity. As for the specific defining characteristics, the *Lion's Perfect Prowess* states this:

> The defining characteristic of the dharmakāya is freedom
> from thinking.
> The defining characteristic of the sambhogakāya is non-
> conceptual lucidity.
> The defining characteristic of the nirmāṇakāya is the
> display of diversity.[579]

(4) The nature of the kāyas is as the *Universes and Transformations of Sound* says:

> The nature of the kāyas is dharmatā;
> their nature is empty and lucid, as well as
> the manifestation of unimpeded knowing awareness.
> The dharmatā of the kāyas is perfect;
> irreversible; without coming and going;
> and lacking speech, thought, and expression.[580]

(5) As for the kāyas' modes of abiding, the dharmakāya abides free from all characteristics, as exemplified by space. The sambhogakāya abides free from materiality, as

exemplified by a rainbow. The nirmāṇakāya abides as diversity without anything being definite, as exemplified by an illusory play.

(6) The pure realm of the dharmakāya is alpha-purity beyond thinking. The pure realm of the sambhogakāya consists of the five kāyas' lucidity as wisdom. The pure realm of the nirmāṇakāya consists of the appearance of containers and contents for all kinds of beings to be guided, which reaches to the limits of space. This will be explained in more detail under the tenth item on this list.

(7) As for who or what is to be guided, in terms of its own completely pure essence, what is to be guided by the dharmakāya is awareness beyond movement and effort. What is to be guided by the sambhogakāya consists of the clusters of the primary buddhas and their retinues, all of whom are self-appearances. What is to be guided by the nirmāṇakāya consists of the individual states of the six classes of beings.

(8) As for the functions of the three kāyas, by virtue of one's own welfare being perfected as the dharmakāya, within the state of abiding without moving away from the expanse, the welfare of others rises as the rūpakāyas. Through leading beings upward, the two welfares are effortlessly promoted for as long as saṃsāra lasts. This function is called "turning the wheel of Dharma." The welfare of others arises on its own while not moving away from the expanse, similar to a reflection of the moon in water.

(9) As for the full measure of confidence, once the qualities of relinquishment and realization have been completed, one arrives at the three kāyas of buddhahood. This is similar to having arrived at the full measure of confidence in a wish-fulfilling jewel given that what is needed and desired has come about through it. The full measure of confidence in the dharmakāya is the immovable freedom from reference points. The full measure of confidence in the sambhogakāya

is self-lucidity's perfection as the major and minor marks. The full measure of confidence in the nirmāṇakāya is the innately present promotion of the two welfares. The perfection of all kinds of welfares while being nonconceptual is always present in an innate manner in the expanse of the dharmakāya without change and transition.

(10) The classification of the kāyas is twofold: (a) the general classification of the five states of the three kāyas and (b) the specific classification of their permutations.

(a) Each one of the three kāyas is divided into five: body, speech, mind, qualities, and enlightened activity. The *Universes and Transformations of Sound* declares this:

> The dharmakāya consists of body, speech,
> mind, qualities, and enlightened activity.
> Its body's nature is being empty, lucid,
> and without any characteristics.
> Its speech is free from sounds, words, and names,
> and thus lacks expression and discourse.
> Since its mind lacks thinking and movement,
> it is beyond proliferation and discernment.
> Its qualities neither regress nor come to an end,
> consist of pervasive expanse and wisdom,
> and have an uncontrived nature.
> Its enlightened activity is unarisen, unborn,
> automatically arising, unimpeded,
> uncreated, and unproduced.
>
> The sambhogakāya also consists of the five of body,
> speech, mind, qualities, and enlightened activity.
> Its body is appearing yet without any nature,
> lucid, illuminating, and pervaded by awareness.
> Its speech is self-arising and self-appearing—
> the wheel that appears as radiating and withdrawing.
> Its mind consists of uninterrupted vision
> and the dynamic energy and awakened mind of knowing.

Due to the perfection of the major and minor marks as
its qualities,
lucid awakened mind and supernatural knowledges are
perfect.
From the wheel of Dharma as its enlightened activity,
the outer, inner, and secret issue forth.
They also issue forth from the self-arising tongues
of the buddha's and bodhisattvas
of the individual families,
and teach the retinues through their own essence.

The nirmāṇakāya also consists of the five of body,
speech, mind, qualities, and enlightened activity.
Its body consists of the major and minor marks,
and emanates bodies that guide those to be guided.
Its speech consists of the sixty[581] branches
of Brahmā's voice for the sake of excellent eloquence.
Its mind refers to the wisdom of what is to be known
remaining in having the two welfares of oneself and others in mind.
Its qualities consist of the perfection of knowledge.
Its enlightened activity is present as the perfection of all
outer, inner, and secret deeds without exception
and also as the five excellences.[582]

(b) The specific classification of the permutations of the three kāyas is as follows.

(1a) As for the dharmakāya of the dharmakāya, its pure realm is inconceivable, its abode is dharmatā beyond thinking, its samādhi is the great state of being unwavering, its retinue is the diversity whose nature is nondual, its teaching is the inexpressible[583] true nature, and its time is that of dharmatā, which does not change into anything whatsoever. (1b) As for the sambhogakāya of the dharmakāya, its pure realm is free from blemishes and without stains, its abode is the severance of all thought processes, its samādhi consists of mind and mental factors being pure as the expanse, its retinue is the emptiness that has the function of self-appearance, its teaching is the complete purity of focus, and its time is the lack of imputation. (1c) As for the nirmāṇakāya of the dharmakāya, its pure realm is unlimited emptiness, its abode is the ground of the arising of everything, its samādhi is self-lucidity in its great unimpededness, its retinue consists of oceans of unbiased buddhas and wisdoms, its teaching is its uncontrived nature, and its time is the self-appearance of the full awakening of the tathāgata heart.

(2a) The dharmakāya of the sambhogakāya is the mode of abiding of Glacial Lake Vairocana: he is inner luminosity if viewed from the outside, and outer luminosity if viewed from the inside, his body is without front or back, and his face is all-pervasive in the ten directions. His pure realm consists of the twenty-one realms in the palm of his hand, his abode is the pure Richly Adorned,[584] his retinue is not different from himself, his teaching is the self-appearance of self-arising wisdom, and his time is realization's having become manifest. (2b) The sambhogakāya of the sambhogakāya consists of the primary buddhas of the five families. Their defining characteristic is that their essences are different, while their natures are the same. Their pure realms are the countless maṇḍalas of the individual buddha families, their abode is [Richly Adorned] Akaniṣṭha, their retinues consist of the individual [buddha] families, their teaching is the enjoyment of the five wisdoms, and their time consists of the unfolding and withdrawing of appearances. (2c) The nirmāṇakāya of the sambhogakāya consists of the principal buddhas of the five families and their individual retinues. Their defining characteristics are to appear but lack any nature and to be lucid but nonconceptual. In their pure realms, they enjoy inconceivable millions of gods and goddesses, their abodes consist of the five innately present wisdoms of Alakavatī,[585] their retinues consist of countless buddhas and bodhisattvas,[586] and their time is the time of self-appearing awareness.

(3a) The dharmakāya of the nirmāṇakāya is glorious great Vajradhara. His defining characteristic is the commitment to arise as all kinds of bodies through the four kinds of birth and to complete the thirty-six enlightened deeds. His pure realm is Mahābrahmā[587] surrounded by a billion trichiliocosms, his abode is Endowed with Open Lotus Flowers, his retinue consists of the beings who are born through the four kinds of birth, his teaching is the root of all piṭakas—the *Universes and Transformations of Sound*—and his time is to have a lifetime of countless years. (3b) The sambhogakāya of the nirmāṇakāya is glorious Vajrasattva. His pure realm consists of the billion worldly realms of the largest cosmos in a trichiliocosm, his abode matches the essence of those to be guided, his retinue consists of bodhisattvas on the eighth bhūmi [and above], his teaching is the yāna of the definitive meaning, and his time is uncertain. (3c) The nirmāṇakāya of the nirmāṇakāya is Buddha Śākyamuni. His defining characteristic is to engage in the twelve deeds such as going forth into homelessness. His pure realm is our world, Endurance, and his abodes are Vulture Flock Mountain[588] and so on. His common retinue consists of bhikṣus, bhikṣuṇīs, upāsakas, and upāsikās; his uncommon retinue of countless great bodhisattvas on the bhūmis; and his diversified indefinite retinue of countless gods, humans, asuras, and so on. His teaching consists of various causal and resultant yānas, and his time is the time of cutting through [doubts with] great certainty, thus benefiting each individual being to be guided.

(B) The wisdom of buddhahood is explained in three main points: (1) its essence, (2) its hermeneutical etymology, and (3) its classification.

(1) The essence of the wisdom of awareness is that sunlike awareness abides primordially as the dimension of omniscient awareness, which is free from all clouds of

adventitious obscurations. Therefore, it is the awakened mind of stainless prajñā that is present as the very heart of the kāyas.

(2) As for the hermeneutical etymology [of *ye shes*], this innately present dimension of being primordially (*ye nas*) lucid as omniscient awareness is cognized (*shes*) in the form of a directly manifest realization, whereby it is free in itself from all obscurations and thus unfolds as the maṇḍala of all qualities without exception. Therefore, it swirls in the expanse of bliss as the inseparability of kāyas and wisdoms. Since wisdom is present as the very heart of the kāyas, the gist of this is that the inseparable kāyas and wisdoms have a connection of identical essence.

(3) The classification of wisdom is twofold.

(a) Its common classification is threefold. (i) The dharmakāya wisdom that is present as the ground is like the core of the sun and functions as the ground of the arising of the two wisdoms of the sambhogakāya and nirmāṇakāya, which resemble the rays of the sun. (ii) The mirror-like sambhogakāya wisdom of apprehending characteristics displays the reflections of perfect wisdom and clearly apprehends all characteristics without conflating them. (iii) The all-pervasive wisdom of the nirmāṇakāya is like a water-moon and thus performs its functions in accordance with the vessels in which it appears.

The wisdom that is present as the ground is present as the dimension that is the empty and lucid ground of arising, similar to the way a crystal ball is present in its own natural condition. From within the state of that wisdom, apart from its being the sheer dimension that makes both the wisdom of apprehending characteristics and the all-pervasive wisdom emerge, nothing shines forth in a directly manifest manner. At the time of apprehending characteristics, the wisdom that is present as the ground is just the mode in which the ground of arising is complete, while the all-pervasive wisdom radiates like rays. Therefore, at that time, the latter two wisdoms do not exist in a directly manifest manner. In its own essence, the wisdom of apprehending characteristics is present like the appearance of five-colored lights from a crystal. At the time of the wisdom of the nirmāṇakāya, the wisdom that is present as the ground does not stir from the expanse, similar to the core of the sun or moon, while the wisdom of apprehending characteristics is present in the sambhogakāya realms similar to rays and rainbows. Thus, at that time, the latter two wisdoms do not exist in a directly manifest manner. Similar to a water-moon's appearing in contingence on the vessels it is reflected in, the all-pervasive wisdom appears from the perspectives of individual beings to be guided.

This threefold classification of wisdom is only made in terms of the manner in which these three appear as bearers of dharmatā. In terms of their actual nature (dharmatā), they are said to simply be of the very same essence that is beyond being one or being different. Furthermore, those three wisdoms arise from the existence of the eight gateways of innate presence in the dharmakāya that is awareness: The wisdom that is present as the ground arises from the dharmakāya's own essence that does not exist as any entity or characteristics, that is, from the gateways of nonduality, freedom from extremes, and pure wisdom, as well as from [the fact that] the ground's ground of arising remains in its very own place. The sambhogakāya wisdom of apprehending characteristics amounts to the three gateways of light, kāyas, and wisdom. The nirmāṇakāya wisdom arises in connection with the gateway of impure saṃsāra.

(b) There follows the detailed explanation of the individual nature of these three wisdoms in terms of the three kāyas.

(i) Regarding the dharmakāya wisdom that is present as the ground, the alpha-purity of the dharmakāya that represents freedom within the locus of freedom is of a single taste, just like space. At that time, it is endowed with three wisdoms. (1) The wisdom of the alpha-pure essence is beyond all extremes of reference points and expression, like an utterly transparent crystal ball. (2) The wisdom of the innately present nature is the sheer subtle depth-lucidity that is the ground for the arising of the qualities of the appearance dimension but does not exist as any segregated entity. (3) The wisdom of all-pervasive compassionate responsiveness is present as the sheer dimension that is the unimpeded ground of the arising of the rūpakāyas from the dynamic energy of the essence, while its cognizant awareness does not directly discern objects. If the dharmakāya existed as something coarse, it would become an entity and characteristics. Hence, it would not be tenable as the peace that is free from all reference points. On the other hand, if the dharmakāya did not exist as the subtle dimension of the depth-lucidity that is the ground of arising, it would be a space-like blank emptiness. Therefore, contrary to both of these extremes, the dharmakāya is the wisdom of subtle emptiness and lucidity that is present as the ground of arising. In that way, the empty wisdom of the dharmakāya is called "the ground of arising's remaining in its own natural state."

(ii) The sambhogakāya wisdom of apprehending characteristics is fivefold. (1) The essence of dharmadhātu wisdom is the inseparability of the triad that consists of the empty dimension of the alpha-pure expanse that is the ground of freedom, the ground of self-luminous wisdom's own light, and the expanse of cognizant awareness. (2) The essence of mirror-like wisdom is the lucidity that is the unobstructed mode of arising within empty and lucid awareness. (3) As for the essence of the wisdom of equality, within the great equality of being primordially free as the expanse of saṃsāra and nirvāṇa (the twofold cause of equality), the triads of the three gates; the awakened body, speech, and mind; and essence, nature, and compassionate responsiveness abide as great equality (the threefold condition of equality). Therefore, this wisdom is completely unconfined and unbiased. (4) The essence of discriminating wisdom is the direct realization of all phenomena without conflating them. (5) The essence of all-accomplishing wisdom is that after one's own welfare has been accomplished within the natural state of awareness, the welfare of others arises innately and effortlessly as in the case of a wish-fulfilling jewel.

(iii) The all-pervasive wisdom of the nirmāṇakāya is twofold. The nirmāṇakāyas that appear from the perspective of those to be guided are not like some dead empty reflections; rather, they promote the welfare of beings through these two wisdoms in an effortless manner. (1) The wisdom of knowing suchness realizes ultimate reality—the infallible essence of all phenomena. Through it, buddhas teach that dharmatā free from the reference points of arising and ceasing is like space. (2) The wisdom of knowing variety realizes seeming reality—the aspects of all phenomena—without conflating them. Through it, buddhas instruct on the bearers of dharmatā—faculties, phenomena, actions and their results, the path, and so on—in the manner of the eight examples of illusion.[589]

II. *The Treasury of Precious Qualities*

Jigmé Lingpa's text describes the innately present fruition of the Great Perfection as the five kāyas (the vajrakāya, the abhisaṃbodhikāya,[590] the dharmakāya, the sambhogakāya, and the nirmāṇakāya) as well as the five wisdoms (dharmadhātu wisdom, mirror-like wisdom, wisdom of equality, discriminating wisdom, and all-accomplishing wisdom).

Kangyur Rinpoche's commentary on Jigmé Lingpa's work explains the first three of the five kāyas as the ultimate expanse's three kāyas of inner luminosity: (A) The vajrakāya is the emptiness that constitutes the changeless essence of the dharmakāya or dharmadhātu endowed with twofold purity (equivalent to dharmadhātu wisdom). (B) The abhisaṃbodhikāya consists of all distinct buddha qualities in terms of relinquishment and realization (equivalent to mirror-like wisdom). (C) The dharmakāya is the wisdom of the very subtle inner luminosity that is the unceasing dimension of knowing that serves as the foundation of all kāyas and wisdoms.

> (A) [The vajrakāya] What is taught by the term "vajra" is emptiness—the essence of the dharmakāya in which the three kāyas are inseparable. From the point of view of the dharmadhātu endowed with twofold purity, this is the changeless vajra. From the point of view of the appearance dimension of its qualities' individual distinction, this is fully perfect awakening—the unimpeded self-radiance of the unity of appearance and emptiness that is free from all operations of dualistic appearances. This is dharmadhātu wisdom.
>
> If the three kāyas of inner luminosity are classified as this single wisdom, what obscures the primordial ultimate ground of all[591]—the dharmadhātu free from obscurations, whose essence is awareness—is the all-ground that is the support of diverse latent tendencies (the two obscurations and their latent tendencies). These are eliminated in their entirety through the two accumulations. Within the primordially pure essence, the two [kinds of] adventitious stains in all their aspects are relinquished, which represents [this essence's] purity of what is adventitious. This ultimate fruition endowed with twofold purity is the actual supreme awakening that has the character of an ocean of kāyas and wisdoms. Through the dharmatā of the original expanse having been revealed, buddhahood, in its great purity and equality, is the expanse of wishlessness. For example, the radiance of the light of the full moon with its outward luminosity sinks into the expanse at the new moon and thus its light is not visible [though it is still present in that it has only withdrawn into its depths]. Likewise, in its being the

dimension of the dharmatā of not conceiving of any aspect of subject and object at all, which is free from any change and transition, lacks any nature, and constitutes the expanse of all kāyas and wisdoms, the unconditioned permanent essence that has a heart of wisdom represents the changeless vajrakāya.

(B) [The abhisaṃbodhikāya] The entire ocean-like mode of being of the qualities such as the ten powers that result from the adventitious stains' having become pure in their own place within the emptiness of the meditative equipoise of the noble ones that is endowed with all supreme aspects of qualities—the expanse in which all discursiveness is at peace, which is the dimension of the unity of appearance and emptiness—represents the awakening at the moment of buddhahood. However, since the appearance dimension of kāyas and wisdoms exists in such a manner that their own essences remain distinct, the buddha qualities such as the ten powers, the four fearlessnesses, the eighteen unique [qualities], great compassion, and the thirty-seven dharmas concordant with awakening are evaluated from the perspective of relinquishment and realization. This is the abhisaṃbodhikāya—the mirror-like wisdom that is the unimpeded dimension of knowing.

(C) [The dharmakāya] Through the subsiding of mind's (the subject's) engagement in outer knowable objects such as form, all clinging to the real existence of the inner mind as the knower, in terms of taking it to have [certain] characteristics, dissolves into the expanse and thus seeming [reality] in all its aspects is relinquished. Then the lucidity dimension of wisdom—the personally experienced true reality that is present as the ground, the actuality of being free from extremes without falling into any extremes of permanence or extinction—is absorbed into the expanse. Though it thus dwells in peace, [Jigmé Lingpa says that] it is "not oblivious." It is not that its dimension of knowing has become absolutely nonexistent; rather, the wisdom of the extremely subtle inner luminosity that is the unceasing dimension of knowing remains. This foundation of the ocean of kāyas and wisdoms that constitutes the experiential sphere of the buddhas alone is seen by the buddhas, who lack any greatly resting or not resting in meditative equipoise, but not by others. The isolate of this foundation or ground of arising is called "the peaceful dharmakāya."

These three kāyas of inner luminosity that are something to be personally experienced are called "the basic element of the victors" (*jinadhātu*).[592] In actuality, since [this basic element] is not established as either one or many, it is not an entity. Since its dimension of knowing variety is lucidly present on the inside, it is also beyond being a nonentity. Since it is completely pure by nature, just like space, it is inconceivable as kāyas, wisdoms, and so on, and is untainted by any impure characteristics. Outer luminosity—the radiation of its modulations—has subsided within the expanse. Its nature is beyond being an object of speech because it consists of the ultimate reality that is dharmatā. Thus, it cannot be illustrated by any examination, analysis, conventional example, argument, and so on. Because of being incompatible with any state of mind or thinking (mind and mental factors), examples, and so on, the entirety of the qualities of the victors lies not even within the scope of the mighty [bodhisattvas] on the tenth bhūmi.

This state that is directly perceived by the guides (the buddhas) alone is the dharmadhātu—emptiness free from [all] reference points. Since it is inconceivable, it is profound. Since it is naturally completely pure of all thoughts of mind and mental factors, it is peaceful. Since it is free from all reference points of unity, this nature's dimension of knowing is unceasing or without transition and therefore it is youthful. It abides as the inner luminosity that does not radiate [outwardly] as the sambhogakāya that is outer luminosity.

> Or its radiance that appears as the ocean-like realm of buddha qualities is unceasing. Therefore, [Jigmé Lingpa] labels it with the conventional expression "the beautiful interior of the mansion of the vase" ...
>
> The buddhas of the three times always reside within this kind of spaciousness with an equal awakened mind. However, when this is evaluated from the perspective of the aspect that self-appearances have been absorbed into the expanse, these buddhas do not see each other ... Dharmatā remains as having the character of being free from the reference points of being one or many. Those with the ultimate realization of the expanse as being this nature are the tathāgatas. Therefore, from the perspective of dharmatā, as all buddhas constitute an expanse of awakened mind that is of a single taste, they do not see [each other] because there is no seer or seen, just as the azure sky is not able to [look at itself and] say about itself, "My own essence exists in this way."[593]

By contrast, outwardly radiating luminosity manifests as the sambhogakāya and the nirmāṇakāya. (D) The sambhogakāya is endowed with the five certainties of (1) place, (2) time, (3) teacher, (4) Dharma, and (5) retinue. (E) The nirmāṇakāya is of three kinds: (1) the natural nirmāṇakāyas whose essence accords with the sambhogakāya, (2) the nirmāṇakāyas who guide beings as the teachers of the six realms, and (3) the diversified nirmāṇakāyas who appear in both animate and inanimate forms (both can be pure or impure).[594]

> (D) [The sambhogakāya] At first, through merely not recognizing the essence of the ground manifestations that arise from the ground, [these ground manifestations] appear as saṃsāra. Finally, when free, they have become of a single taste with the peaceful expanse. Therefore, this is [called] "what is self-arising [from the ground] is reabsorbed into [the ground] itself." Though [inner luminosity's wisdom] never moves away from the state of inner luminosity free

from reference points, by virtue of the self-radiance of this wisdom that is [inner luminosity's] unceasing dimension of knowing, the eight gateways of innate presence manifest as the outwardly luminous compassionate responsiveness that is the sambhogakāya of enjoying the Mahāyāna Dharma.[595]

[The sambhogakāya] arises as being endowed with the five certainties: (1) the place is [the pure realm] Richly Adorned Luminosity, (2) the time is the inconceivable expiration in the ground,[596] (3) the teachers consist of the buddhas of the five families, (4) the Dharma is the natural Great Perfection, and (5) the retinues are not different from [these buddhas] themselves. The principal [buddhas], their retinues, and so on, [all of whom] manifest in a distinct and lucid manner, are present with their character of being an ocean of qualities, such as awakened bodies, pure realms, and major and minor marks ...

As for the manner of [all] these being present as self-appearances, from within the natural state of unconditioned dharmakāya wisdom, which is permanent by nature, its self-radiance that manifests as outward luminosity is innately present as the abodes of its perfection as the sambhogakāyas endowed with the five excellencies, that is, the pure realms that are permanent in terms of their continuity. From there, this [outer luminosity] is [furthermore] present as the ground of the arising of [all] nirmāṇa[kāya]s, who are permanent in terms of an uninterrupted series.[597] At the time when the end of the paths of learning has been reached, it is the play of wisdom, which consists of solely a buddha's mind stream wherein all stains that obscure the basic element have been relinquished, that manifests as the places, teachers, retinues and so on [of the sambhogakāya]. Therefore, though [this play of wisdom] appears as pure realms and palaces (the support) as well as the principal [buddhas] and their retinues (the supported), there is nothing outer or inner, higher or lower [in any of these appearances]. All of them are equal as the display of Samantabhadra—the single self-arising wisdom.

Since the minds of all sambhogakāyas, who are self-appearances, never move away from the natural state of the dharmakāya, they are nonconceptual. Since their speech is beyond any characteristics of sounds and words, it is free from expression. Since their bodies appear in great splendor, all their major and minor marks are perfectly complete in a clearly manifest manner. With their eyes of the pure vision of the wisdom [of seeing] all self-appearing phenomena, the rūpakāyas behold each other in a way that is never obscured at any time.

Since the experiential sphere of the basic element and the qualities of the victors of the three times is inconceivable, just like space, it is unsurpassable. Since there is nothing higher, it does not fall into the extremes of permanence and extinction. Since it is not included in the domains of [saṃsāric] existence or nirvāṇa, even noble bodhisattvas—the great pure sentient beings from the first to the tenth bhūmis—are not able to see it. For they have not yet relinquished the obscuring factors of the basic element that are incompatible with the victors' inconceivable wisdom of knowing suchness and variety. In the self-appearing Great Akaniṣṭha, which is beyond the definiteness of all three seeming and conditioned times (past, present, and future), the awakened minds of the principal buddhas and their retinues, who have the character of the fourth inconceivable time of the dwelling of the buddhas in the wheel of everlasting continuity, are equal. Therefore, since there is no difference in terms of good or bad in their essence, they are [all] self-appearances that are concordant as one.

(E) [The nirmāṇakāya] From within the natural state of the self-appearing sambhogakāya, in order to guide the pure and impure sentient beings who are to be guided, the three [kinds of nirmāṇakāya] teachers who provide guidance effortlessly array themselves from the compassionate responsiveness of the [sambhogakāya] teachers: (1) the natural nirmāṇa[kāya]s whose mode of being accords with the sambhogakāya, (2) the nirmāṇa[kāya]s who guide beings and appear as the teachers of the six [kinds of] being, and (3) the diversified nirmāṇa[kāya]s who appear as animate, inanimate, and so on.

(1) Regarding the natural nirmāṇakāyas among these three, it is the wisdom of the dharmakāya of the victors appearing as outer luminosity that abides in the realm Akaniṣṭha in the form of sambhogakāyas who are appearances of the expanse. Their major and minor marks appear as if projected into a transparent crystal. These reflections that appear to the noble children of the victors who are the supreme ones to be guided partly resemble the [sambhogakāya] teachers who are peaceful self-appearances. Therefore, they are [likewise] counted as sambhogakāyas. [However,] since they are included in what appears to those to be guided, they are also counted as nirmāṇa[kāya]s. Hence, their status is half nirmāṇakāya and half sambhogakāya. From the perspective of those to be guided, they appear similar to the following example: when the autumn moon appears in the clear sky, it is reflected in vessels containing water in accordance with the clarity or turbidity of that water ...[598]

Though the five teachers [such as Vairocana] appear separately in their five pure realms, their mind streams are not different but appear as the display of the single wisdom of buddhahood. Each one of the five kinds of wisdom of the minds of the five [buddha] families possesses four attendant wisdoms, such as dharmadhātu wisdom (the mind of Vairocana) possessing the mirror-like wisdom of dharmadhātu wisdom and so on ... Thus, [there are] twenty-five wisdoms.

(a) In accordance with all phenomena not being different in dharmatā, dharmadhātu wisdom is not stirred by any apprehending of characteristics. It pervades the entirety of containers and contents, and its essence is inexpressible. For example, the form of space is beyond speech and expression. Likewise, though [this wisdom] knows in a manner that pervades all phenomena and is ineffable, it is beyond [all] extremes of knowable objects. Therefore, it is of a single taste as the dharmadhātu.

(b) As for mirror-like wisdom, for example, though the surface of a mirror is so clear that it is suitable for reflections to appear [in it], it lacks any effort. Likewise, the wisdom that is the unceasing dimension of knowing is free from the dust of apprehender and apprehended. While it lacks any movements and labors of exertion, it is in terms of the classification of the isolates of the evolving manner in which knowable objects are known that [this mirror-like wisdom] serves as something like the ground for the arising of the last three wisdoms.

(c) The nature of equality is that all phenomena of saṃsāra and nirvāṇa are without good or bad but of equal taste. The wisdom of knowing that knows this realizes the inseparability of [saṃsāric] existence and peace in the manner of the mind's dwelling in the expanse in which all reference points are at peace, without any phenomena having any characteristics such as good or bad, or what is to be adopted or to be rejected.

(d) Discriminating wisdom means that all dependently originating phenomena appear as distinct causes and results. The wisdom of knowing this always knows, in an unobstructed manner, [both] identitylessness (the suchness that is dharmatā) and [all] knowable phenomena from the skandhas and so on up through the knowledge of [all] aspects (the variety that consists of the bearers of that nature).

(e) As for the fifth wisdom, its activities are the deeds for the welfare of others. The approach of the wisdom of accomplishing and knowing these in an effortless way is to bring about [all] the enlightened activities of body, speech, and mind that are of vast benefit to others. Its deeds, in which any attachment and obstruction[599] as the factors that obscure [this all-encompassing approach] have been relinquished, are innately present until saṃsāra is empty.

If these [five] wisdoms are summarized, dharmadhātu [wisdom] represents the wisdom of knowing suchness, while the other four constitute the wisdom of knowing variety ...

(2) [As for the nirmāṇakāyas who guide beings,] from the six centers of the bodies of the sambhoga[kāya] buddhas who appear from within the natural state of the dharmakāya free from reference points, light rays that consist of garlands of syllable clouds stream forth. Through that, the supreme nirmāṇakāyas who guide beings in the worlds of the six classes [of beings] appear [in forms] ... such as the six sages [in those worlds] ... the lords of various god realms (such as Indra, Brahmā, and Viṣṇu) ... śrāvakas, pratyekabuddhas, bodhisattvas ... cakravartins, kings, ministers ... animals ... and so on.

As for the appearance of all kinds of nirmāṇa[kāya]s who guide certain beings to be guided, by virtue of the coming together of the blessings of the buddhas who have realized their stainless nature and individual sentient beings' aspiration prayers and virtuous karmic appearances, there appear the two rūpakāyas of pure wisdom and enlightened activity who constitute the dawning of the compassionate responsiveness of the three kāyas of the expanse of inner luminosity as outer luminosity. In particular, from the perspective of ordinary beings, certain supreme nirmāṇakāyas such as the lion of the Śākyas appear. These are nothing but appearances of our own mind, similar to seeing buddhas in a dream when having gone to sleep. These nirmāṇa[kāya]s' teachings of the Dharma are [also] like in a dream. Both lack any essence, while a second nature [called] "buddha" is not established. The minds to which they appear are likewise identityless and luminous, while the buddhas who appear [to them] are emptiness without any nature of their

> own. Therefore, the profound sūtras say that they are to be understood as delusive ...
>
> Therefore, all phenomena of saṃsāra and nirvāṇa are a dream-like play. Though the buddha nirmāṇa[kāya]s who constitute what appears to those to be guided never move away from the essence—the dharmakāya that is primordially endowed with twofold purity—the reflections of the nirmāṇa[kāya]s appear in accordance with those to be guided as if they were included in the reality of suffering. For these reasons, with all of saṃsāra and nirvāṇa lacking any nature of its own and thus being like an illusion or a dream, from the perspective of impure beings, nirmāṇakāyas who are the play of compassionate responsiveness appear. They appear as the uninterrupted welfare that accords with those to be guided for as long as saṃsāra is not emptied. Thus, while both those to be guided and those who guide never move away from the single expanse, they are [nothing but] the basic nature that appears in the form of saṃsāra during its phase of being associated with stains and in the form of nirvāṇa when it is free from these stains. Those who arrive within this fundamental ground are called "the persons who see true reality" ...
>
> (3) The natural nirmāṇakāya explained here represents the sambhogakāya [as it is presented] in the context of the sūtras. Therefore, from within the natural state of this [natural nirmāṇakāya], though not different in essence, the diversified [nirmāṇakāyas]—animate ones (such as the six sages), inanimate ones, and so on—emanate.[600]

Finally, Kangyur Rinpoche explains how the nirmāṇakāya and the sambhogakāya as the manifestations of outwardly radiating luminosity gradually dissolve into the dharmakāya once their activities have been accomplished. He also discusses how the dharmakāya naturally remains as or within the dharmadhātu (the ultimate expanse of inner luminosity) and clearly distinguishes this from the *Prāsaṅgika view of the dharmakāya.

This kind of enlightened activity [of the sambhogakāya and nirmāṇakāya] first arises from the expanse, and in the end its proliferations subside within the expanse. As for the manner [in which this happens], once the time for an actual [nirmāṇa]kāya's guidance [of beings] has come to its end and their welfare has been promoted, when there are no more beings to be guided in general and in particular, the rūpakāyas who guided them merge back into the expanse. An example that illustrates the way [in which this takes place] is as follows. When there are no more vessels with water at all on the ground, the reflections of the moon that appeared in these [vessels before] dissolve back into the basis from which they were emanated—the moon in the sky. Though it is not like these reflections become blended with the moon, they vanish where they went without a trace. Likewise, [all] appearances from the nirmāṇa[kāya]s who are included in what appears to pure and impure beings to be guided up through the natural nirmāṇa[kāya]s dissolve into the self-appearing ultimate Akaniṣṭha—the expanse of the sambhoga[kāya]—and thus become inseparable from it. In that way, the appearance dimension [of the nirmāṇakāya] is no longer perceptible.

The example for the manner in which the self-appearing sambhogakāya dissolves back into the dharmakāya is as follows. From the sixteenth day [of a lunar month] up through the new moon, it is not that one moon is poured out and is absorbed into another one or that it becomes nonexistent altogether. Rather, the radiance of outward luminosity is absorbed back into the state of the depth-lucidity of inner luminosity from which no light is projected outwardly. Likewise, the sambhogakāyas and their pure realms that have dawned as self-appearances are gathered back into the inner expanse—the great wisdom of the dharmakāya that is without any projections.

As for this state of the awakened mind of the three kāyas having become of a single taste, the *Prāsaṅgika Mādhyamikas assert that when even the most subtle dualistic appearances of the operations of mind and mental factors have subsided in the dharmadhātu free from all reference points, just like a fire having died out once its fuel is consumed; this is "the genuine ultimate cessation of the victors" and not just the limited cessation of someone like an arhat of the Hīnayāna, in which subtle latent tendencies have not become exhausted yet. The *Madhyamakāvatāra* says this:

> With the dry firewood of knowable objects without exception
> being burned, this peace is the dharmakāya of the victors.
> At this point, there is neither arising nor cessation.
> The cessation of mind is revealed through this kāya.[601]

[However,] the manner in which the dharmakāya is gathered back into the dharmadhātu here in the system of the Great Perfection is as follows. Though [the entirety of] the adventitious stains together with the eight collections [of consciousness] (all minds and mental factors included in the three realms) ceases, personally experienced wisdom does not cease. That is, the way in which all [buddha] qualities [of the dharmakāya] exist in an uninterrupted and hidden manner [already at the time of the ground], just like the sun and its rays, is stated in the *[Tantra of] the All-Illuminating [Bindu]*:

> Though the moon in the night of the new moon is [already] perfectly complete,
> it is through the power of the sun that it does not appear in a visible manner.
> Therefore, from the first until the fifteenth day, the moon becomes full,
> but then there is no more growing of it after that.
> Likewise,

> those who are inseparable from the precious sphere
> are unable to clearly reveal it due to the power of their
> delusion.[602]

Thus, those on the paths of learning gradually eliminate the obscurations and become buddhas. What is revealed at that time is the youthful vase body (inner luminosity), in which the rūpakāyas (the dimension of outer luminosity) remain absorbed in the dharmadhātu (the subtle and difficult-to-realize wisdom that is inner luminosity) so that they are inseparable, while this vase body's own nature is not dull. All qualities of relinquishment and realization have become consummate, similar to the full moon. Thus, there is nothing higher to proceed to. Still, immediately when beings as the objects to be guided appear in any place or at any time, the rays or the radiance of compassionate responsiveness serves as the ground for the uninterrupted and effortless unfolding of the kāyas and wisdoms (the wisdom that is outer luminosity) [as they manifest] from this unceasing radiance of compassionate responsiveness.

This inconceivable dharmatā of utterly resting in meditative equipoise, in which all dualistic appearances have dissolved into the expanse, constitutes the fruition that is the unique feature of the buddhas alone—the state of the great innate presence of [all] qualities that never lacks resting in meditative equipoise. In this natural state of the unborn expanse that is like space, kāyas and wisdoms abide in an innately present manner without any increase, decrease, change, or transition, just like the sun and its rays.[603]

Appendix 7

The Many Facets of the Single Freedom

The teachings of the Great Perfection discuss a number of sets of three, four, and five "modes of freedom."

The Three Modes of Freedom

"The three modes of freedom" consist of (1) being free upon arising (Tib. *shar grol*), similar to a person recognizing an old friend in a crowd of people; (2) being free in itself (Tib. *rang grol*), similar to a snake uncoiling and untying its own knots; and (3) being free without benefit or harm (Tib. *phan med gnod med du grol ba*), similar to a thief entering an empty house.[604]

The Four Modes of Freedom

The most common set of "the four great modes of freedom" usually includes being (1) primordially free (Tib. *ye grol*), (2) free in itself, (3) nakedly free (Tib. *gcer grol*), and (4) free from extremes (Tib. *mtha' grol*). Sometimes being free upon arising, being completely free (Tib. *yongs grol*), or being free as one (Tib. *gcig grol*) replace one of the other four kinds of freedom (usually, freedom from extremes) or are added to this list (thus making five; see below).

On "the four great modes of freedom," Jamgön Kongtrul's TOK[605] says the following: (1) Awareness is primordially free because its own face is not tainted by any saṃsāric phenomena whatsoever since beginningless time, and thus all causes for appropriating saṃsāric existence are exhausted right from the start. (2) It is free in itself because, without being fixed or contrived by any remedy whatsoever, everything that arises is like a knot in a snake that dissolves on its own and thus does not depend on any other means for being free. (3) It is nakedly free because all eight kinds of consciousnesses are naturally free without any duality of subject and object in an instant with great lightning-like suddenness. (4) It is free from extremes because it does not abide in the three times or as any knowable object. Self-arising wisdom—one's own awareness that abides within the natural state of these four great modes of freedom—is the distinctive feature of this path of the Pith Instructions Series.

The *Great Tibetan-Chinese Dictionary*[606] says that these four constitute the four great modes of awareness's freedom as the dharmakāya, which is an instruction of Cutting through Solidity. (1) Since time without beginning, self-arising awareness itself is untainted in its own essence by any saṃsāric phenomena whatsoever, and therefore all substantial causes of saṃsāric existence are exhausted from the start. Hence, it is called "primordially free." (2) In its own essence, this very self-arisen awareness is not mended (or contrived) by any remedy whatsoever—without depending on anything else, it allows everything that may arise to be free (Tib. *'grol byed*), just as the knots in a snake come undone on their own. Hence, it is called "free in itself." (3) Within self-arisen awareness, all cognitions of the eight collections of consciousness are naturally free with great lightning-like suddenness in the single instant of the duality of subject and object falling away. Hence, it is called "nakedly free." (4) This very self-arisen awareness does not abide as any of the three times or any knowable object whatsoever. Hence, it is called "free from extremes."

The list of the four modes of freedom in the context of mind being free through confidence that is found in the *Tantra of the Universes and Transformations of Sound* replaces "free from extremes" with "completely free":

> Since it is primordially free, there is no ground to be delivered to.
> Since it is free by itself, there is no remedy.
> Since it is nakedly free, all vanishes in the place of its being seen.
> Since it is completely free, there is no effort.[607]

Later, in the context of describing the dharmatā of being free, the tantra lists these four again, repeating the two lines about "being free by itself" and "being nakedly free," while explaining the other two modes of freedom as follows:

> Since it is primordially free, there is no need for repetition.
> Since it is free by itself, there is no remedy.
> Since it is nakedly free, all vanishes in the place of its being seen.
> Since it is completely free, its nature is pure.[608]

Dzogchen Ponlop Rinpoche (born 1965) explains these four in detail as follows:

> *Primordial Liberation*
> When a moment of passion arises in a vivid and sharp manner, the nature of that passion is primordially liberated. In this sense, "primordial" refers to the ground, to the fundamental state of emptiness of that passion. At the moment when passion arises, it is already in the state of selflessness, or shunyata. Its nature has never been tainted by any trace of samsaric confusion. It is already free from concepts; therefore, it is primordially and utterly free. We do not need to re-create that ground of emptiness, because it is already there. That basic state is simply a brilliant experience of unceasing clarity ...
>
> *Self-liberation*
> With regard to self-liberation, that vivid passion is not liberated by anything outside of itself. Like a snake that simply uncoils itself from its own knot, passion returns to its natural state independent of any external antidotes. It is self-liberated. It is already in the nature of transcendence, of rigpa, the true nature of mind. Even in the relative sense, passion arises, changes constantly and ceases by itself. As much as we may desire to solidify and hold on to it for another moment, it will not stay. That is why, from the Vajrayana perspective, it is taught that we cannot purify or transform passion except through passion itself ...

Naked Liberation

Naked liberation occurs when the mind observes itself. When passion arises and we look at it nakedly and straightforwardly, we do not see anything that truly exists in a substantial way. The bare experience of passion is simply the "isness" quality that is left when we look at passion without concepts. It is called naked liberation because when we look nakedly and directly at the passionate mind, that very process of looking liberates the experience of passion. The true nature of rigpa is naturally free from the dualistic experience of consciousness. In the absence of our solid concepts, there remains a sense of vivid energy and movement, like the flickering of a flame. That vibrant, radiant quality shows us the actual insubstantial nature of mind, which is not what we generally experience in our mundane, relative world ...

Complete Liberation

Complete liberation occurs when passion is further liberated as mind observes the experience of passion again and again. In the first moment of the arising of passion, we look at it directly, and it liberates itself. In the second moment, we look directly again and it liberates itself further. As we continue to look nakedly and straightforwardly at this world of passion, moment after moment, it liberates itself further and further, or more completely. This method needs to be applied repeatedly and in short sessions. In this way, we can see that the essence of rigpa does not abide in any of the three times—past, present or future—and is perfectly free. This process is similar to working with "the watcher" in shamatha practice. The watcher is the self-conscious aspect of mind that participates in our practice as an "observer." When we look at the watcher, it dissolves. Then it returns again, and we look [at] it, and it dissolves again. Eventually, the watcher does not return ...

> Fundamentally, these are the instructions on the nature of mind and how we look at it. As far as primordial liberation is concerned, it is important to look without artifice or further fabrication. For self-liberation, it is important to look without engaging too much in concepts and mental discernments, such as labeling thoughts "good" or "bad" ... When you are actually in a session of Dzogchen or Mahamudra meditation, it is important to disengage completely from all movements of conceptual mind and simply rest. For naked liberation, it is important to observe the nature of mind while resting naturally. Whatever arises, let it rest in its own place. For complete liberation, it is necessary to go through all the stages of the path and their meditation practices.[609]

Yet another explanation of the four kinds of freedom, by Dongag Chökyi Gyamtso (1903–57), consists of being free in itself, being free upon arising, being primordial free, and being nakedly free:

> At the time of being truly convinced, (1) being free in itself means being free within awareness's own domain without searching for any remedy outside of it. (2) Being free upon arising means that everything that arises is free right at the sheer point of its arising. (3) Being primordially free means that each and every one in the [entire] collection of thoughts is free within its own natural and primordial way of being. (4) Being nakedly free means that the collection of thoughts does not merely return to its own ground but dissolves into the natural ground of mind-as-such, the dharmakāya. Through identifying this process again and again from within the essence of awareness, naked awareness-emptiness is enhanced by being stripped bare [repeatedly].[610]

The Five Modes of Freedom

The *Garland of Pearls* speaks of five modes of freedom, which consist of being primordially free, being free in itself, being nakedly free, being free from extremes, and being free as one:

Apart from unimpeded awareness,
there is no delusion and thus no thoughts.
Since it is primordially free, it is absolutely supreme.
Since it is free in itself, object conditions are exhausted.
Since it is nakedly free, appearances are pure.
Since it is free from extremes, the four possibilities cease.
Since it is free as one, it is empty of many.[611]

Longchenpa's *Precious Treasury of the Supreme Yāna*[612] discusses the same five modes of freedom in the context of gaining confidence in being free in order to clear dangerous passages. This is explained in three points: (A) general instruction on the meaning of being free in itself, (B) particular explanation of the basic nature of being primordally free, and (C) detailed discussion of the intention behind being free in itself.

(A) In this king of paths that delivers from the afflictions, the vajra heart of Ati, the afflictions are not relinquished but are pure in their ground. Therefore, this is unlike their becoming pure through relinquishing them as śrāvakas and pratyekabuddhas do, relinquishing them as bodhisattvas do, transforming them as in the creation stage and making them subside on their own as in the completion stage of the lower mantrayāna, taming them through remedies as in the general common yāna, settling them within their own natural way as in the Mind Series, or taking the afflictions themselves to be dharmatā as in the Expanse Series.

If it is not understood how the afflictions primordially never existed, they cannot be relinquished through any form of relinquishment. If the afflictions were relinquished through mind, since what is to be relinquished and what relinquishes would be of the same substance, it would not be feasible for the afflictions to become pure. If they were relinquished by wisdom, since mind does not see wisdom and wisdom does not see mind, these two are directly opposed in that they cannot exist simultaneously; and in that case, the conventional notions of what is to be relinquished and what relinquishes it are not feasible. Nor is there any relinquishment of a former affliction through a later remedy: since the past and the future are of opposing substance, at the time when the one exists, the other one has already ceased. But if they were simultaneous, they would tamper with each other, and thus it would follow that what is to be relinquished is the remedy and the remedy is what is to be relinquished, because they exist at the same time in a single mind stream. Moreover, given that afflictions arise from the mind itself, which resembles a body and its shadow that accompanies it, there is no time for their relinquishment through any form of relinquishment. The same applies to the notion of purification and so on. Therefore, this is to be understood as the essential point of being free in itself by itself, just like a drawing on water.

In terms of two levels of mental capacity and in terms of what looks like a progression, there are two kinds of being free in itself: with and without effort. (1) Regarding being free in itself with effort, whichever afflictions may arise are identified and allowed to settle in their own place. Through that, within the natural state of their evanescence of having vanished on their own, there occurs the training in the dynamic energy of awareness as being the great equality of awakened mind free in itself in which movement and stillness are pure, without being distracted for even an instant. (2) Being free in itself without effort refers to being the dharmatā of the vanishing of afflictions on their own without anything that arises being able to stand its own ground. Therefore, without needing to relinquish the method of looking at the afflictions, they are naturally or automatically free.

(B) The particular explanation of the basic nature of being primordally free has three parts.

(1) Regarding the teaching that everything has already been free primordially and therefore is free in itself right now, thus not needing any remedy that involves effort, the *Garland of Pearls* says this:

> It does not become free through effort—
> it primordially abides as being free.[613]

And:

Since unawareness is self-arising,
the very cause of delusion is primordially awakened.
Since the all-ground is self-arising as the dharmakāya,
any birth of a mind stream is severed at its root.
Since what is wish-fulfilling primordially abides as awakened mind,
the factors that cause stirring are self-settled.
Since the breath has been primordially interrupted,
there is no birth and death from the origin.
Since the sense objects are primordially perfect,
meditation itself is the end of clinging.
Since there is primordial arrival without having moved any limbs,
the very path to travel has been traversed primordially.
Since spoken words are inexpressible,
objects of speech and thought are transcended primordially.
Since the proliferation and withdrawal of thinking[614] is primordially empty,
it primordially abides as the great dhyāṇa.
Since the stains are self-pure,
they abide as great unobstructed stainlessness.
Since what is produced is without arising,[615]
there is freedom of producer and produced from the beginning.
Since there are no phenomena other than the ground,
this is the sole originally self-arising state.
Since the numbers of one and two are exhausted,
this is the sphere without any counterpart.
Since darkness is originally pure,
the manifestations of awareness are pervasive luminosity.
Since saṃsāra without a cause[616] has already ceased,
it is the buddhabhūmi primordially.[617]
Since entities with characteristics are purely empty,
the mind of clinging to a self has been exhausted primordially.

Since conditions are free in themselves through these conditions,
dependent phenomena are resting directly.[618]

(2) As for the instruction that nothing goes beyond the nature of this basic state, the *Universes and Transformations of Sound* states this:

The culmination of the natural Great Perfection
is that phenomena are settled in their own place.
Since the dharmatā of appearances and cognizance is their unity,
they meet directly within primordially free letting be.
The awakened mind is beyond mental states
and what bears characteristics is pure in its own place,
free from the extremes of emptiness and entities.
Movement is exhausted, there are no thoughts,
mental states are exhausted, and mentation is transcended.[619]

The *Garland of Pearls* declares this:

Since the five elements are primordially limpid,
appearances are free as luminosity.
Since the five sense faculties are nakedly settled,
the five objects of clinging are free in their own place.[620]

(3) As for the firm resolve that everything never went anywhere else than merely vanishing on its own without a base within that natural state, the *Universes and Transformations of Sound* says this:

What is called "one's own mind being free"
is without any succession from one to another.
As for this mind that is not to be freed (*bkrol*) through anything,
since it is perfect in the ground, it lacks any coming and going.
It is not found through examination and thus lacks any reason.
Since it is without base and root, it is present as being empty.
It is the mind that is present as self-lucidity.
Since it is free through the essential point, it is unbiased.
Since it is free of time, it lacks any basis to depend on.
Since it is free without toil, there is no exerting or accomplishing.

> Since it is free through confidence, there is no effort.
> Here, its being free through confidence is explained:
> Since it is primordially free, there is no ground to be delivered to.
> Since it is free by itself, there is no remedy.
> Since it is nakedly free, all vanishes in the place of its being seen.
> Since it is completely free, there is no effort.[621]

Since the three gates of body, speech, and mind are primordially free, there is no need for them to become free through effort at some point later. Without any need whatsoever for transforming anything through body gestures and so on, the elements are free by virtue of their own essential point. Therefore, there is no returning to the six forms of existence. Without needing to make any efforts through speech, such as reciting an essence mantra, expressions are free as pure lucidity. Therefore, all that is said is free by virtue of the essential point of sounds and their referents (or meanings). Without needing to make any efforts of the mind, such as cultivating samādhi, whatever is thought is free by virtue of the essential point of being the awakened mind. Since it does not arise from anywhere else, it is free in itself—the existence of a remedy is impossible. Thus, this is the essential point of there being no remedy within being free in itself.

As for "being free," there are many aspects such as being free through merely letting be, being free directly within the essential point through merely knowing, being primordially free, being free in itself, being nakedly free, and being completely free. However, this "being free" is taught here to be without any need for effort because there is no remedy in the great freedom in itself.

(C) The detailed discussion of the intention behind being free in itself has three parts.

(1) As a brief introduction to its essence, the *Garland of Pearls* says this:

> Apart from unimpeded awareness,
> there is no delusion and thus no thoughts.
> Since it is primordially free, it is absolutely supreme.
> Since it is free in itself, object conditions are exhausted.

> Since it is nakedly free, appearances are pure.
> Since it is free from extremes, the four possibilities cease.
> Since it is free as one, it is empty of many.[622]

In the naked unimpeded awareness in which outer and inner are not two and which resembles a stainless crystal ball, by virtue of the essential point of its being without any basis, there is no cause of delusion right now and therefore there is no path in this awareness that lacks any root. Since there is no path, there is no fruition right now either; there is no place in this awareness where it would regress into the three realms. Awareness has already been free primordially and has already been innately present as the awakened mind that is like space. Therefore, this is the essential point of its eminence relative to all the common yānas: it is endowed with the five great modes of freedom.

(2) The distinct explanation of the nature of each of these five modes of freedom is as follows.

(a) As for being primordially free, based on the essential point that primordial freedom lacks any basis for repetition, the freedom of awareness is taught as not contingent on any effort in terms of view or meditation. This means that it is unproduced and uncontrived due to the general pervasiness of wisdom. It never changes from not arising from anywhere, not going anywhere, and not abiding anywhere. Since being free (*grol*) is not like freeing or liberating (*bkrol*), there is no need for any effort through view or meditation. "Being free" means simply being present in its own natural condition while lacking any modification or contrivance. Since that is the case, "being free" refers to body, speech, and mind being relaxed in their own natural condition, and mind as such resting in its genuine state. Since primordially being free always remains this way, it is more distinguished than the common yānas. The example for being primordially free is the primordially ripe *ālika* fruit, in which there is nothing to be ripened right now.

(i) Regarding the understanding of being primordially free, the essential point is that since it refers to already having been free from the very beginning and not suddenly at some point, there is nothing to become free again right now.[623] Awareness arises from never having experienced delusion.

(ii) This being presented as being primordially free is tenable through reasoning: the essential point of the primordial freedom of awareness is that since awareness is without any basis, there is no place of its regressing. Since it lacks any root, there is no place where it arises. Since it lacks any characteristics, it is not ascertained. Since it is without arising, there is no cause to become free. There is no characteristic that could serve as a sign of its being primordially free and that is to be seen through any meditation or practice whatsoever. This is tenable through the reasoning of causes and results leaving no trace: in awareness, there are no causes and therefore there are no results. Thus, the existence of karma and its maturations is impossible. This is also tenable through scripture, as *Meaningful Exertion* says:

> For mind as such, which is primordially free,
> how could there be any conditions for its becoming free later?

This is furthermore tenable through the argument that both focusing the mind and its vanishing settle on their own. By virtue of focusing being primordially free, it is free in its own place because it is free from the very start. It is to be understood as being primordially free through the essential point that mind has no place where it arises, no place where it abides, and no place where it goes.

(iii) As for the mode of being free, since mind is empty, it cannot even be designated as the mere conventional terms "being free" or "not being free." Therefore, as a sign that it has already been free primordially, there is no need for it to become free again right now because mind is primordially awakened. Thus, it is understood that there is nothing to become free in what has already been free primordially.

(b) Regarding being free in itself, based on the essential point that it lacks any remedy, it is taught to not be contingent on any instructions of the guru. For when all phenomena of sight and sound arise, they are self-arising and when they are free, they are free in themselves, similar to the sky and clouds. Therefore, since this is unlike the flawed forms of meditation, view, and conduct that rely on other objects, "ultimate freedom" refers to the exhaustion of phenomena.

(i) The understanding of being free in itself means that there is no remedy. Appearances are free in themselves from the very moment of their appearing. Therefore, other than appearances, there are no phenomena whatsoever. Likewise, there is nothing besides emptiness and so on being free by virtue of themselves, similar to overcoming poison through poison or breaking iron through iron. Since the afflictions are free by virtue of these very afflictions, we speak of their "being free in themselves."

(ii) This being presented as being free in itself is tenable through reasoning by virtue of the principle of dharmatā.[624] Since all being free is free in itself, it is tenable that it is unlike being freed or liberated (*bkrol*) through something else. If it became free through something else, this would be as impossible as a single entity appearing as different forms. In fact, the characteristics of an entity are determined by that very entity. This is also tenable through scripture; the Mind Series says that being free arises on its own and not from anything else. It is furthermore tenable through the argument that there is no basis for disputing the great being free in itself. Thus, appearances are free in themselves because this is not contingent on any other remedy.

(iii) As for the mode of being free, there is no other way to be free apart from being free in itself through itself. Other texts such as the *Hevajratantra* also explain that those with desire are free through making this very desire into the path. Appearances are free within these very appearances themselves. Apart from these appearances, there are no other causes or conditions for becoming free. They are free in that they have no basis, lack any support for abiding, and are without a base or root. For these reasons, mind as such is without a base or root. According to the *Guhyagarbhatantra*, this mind as such is neither male, nor female, nor neutral; neither a color nor a shape; not the lack of characteristics; and not any family lineage either. Apart from this very mind as such itself, there is no place where it might regress to and no place where it might go. For these reasons, it has never arisen. There is no place where it arises; it is called "free in itself" because there is no separate phenomenon that is not this very mind as such. This resembles the example of a knot in a snake; it is free in itself without anybody untying or freeing it.

(c) Regarding being nakedly free, based on the essential point of vanishing upon sight, it is taught that it is not contingent on tantras and scriptures;[625] merely through seeing nakedly, appearances and cognizance are free in themselves. Since mother and child are free through meeting, these very appearances are not altered by cognizance, nor is cognizance cut off by appearances; simply letting them be in that way, they are free as being pure in themselves.

(i) Regarding the understanding of being nakedly free (vanishing upon sight), merely through seeing nakedly, appearances and cognizance are free in seeing themselves; they are free merely through seeing themselves, hearing themselves, or being aware of themselves in the first moment. This is the gauge of "the perception of dharmatā."[626]

(ii) This being presented as being nakedly free is tenable through reasoning by virtue of the essential point that focusing and vanishing are not observable as anything whatsoever. It is merely through their appearing that appearances are free within their appearing, and it is merely through its moving that cognizance is free within its moving. By virtue of the essential point of its own seat that consists of its being empty, form is seen nakedly. Through that, form is shown to be nothing but conceit and thus is free through this very form itself. The same goes for sound and so on. How does one know that form is free? Through seeing form as form, all reference points that indicate it is not form are severed. Through nakedly settling within that, this very form is free because there is no arising of any cognizance that engages in anything else. This is also tenable through scripture, as the *Tantra of the Essence of Gold* states:

> Through the gaze of great naked freedom,
> both buddhas and sentient beings are free.

This is furthermore tenable through the argument of self-purity free from any sides. Thus, appearances are nakedly free because they are allowed to settle in their place of being naked, thus are free in the place where they are allowed to settle, and vanish in their place of being free.

(iii) As for the mode of being free, through having trained in certain parts of phenomena, they are free as those parts in their place of being naked; they are without going anywhere or coming from anywhere, and there is also no place to go. Nor do they change from not[627] abiding anywhere. Through having trained in phenomena in general, all appearances are nakedly free.

(iv) The example for being nakedly free is an impartial person entering a temple—their seeing is unbiased.

(d) Regarding being free from extremes, based on the essential point of lacking dependence, the key point is not to entertain any dependence whatsoever. Through being free from the first extreme, there is no dwelling in the second, and through being free from the second, there is no dwelling in the first either. The same goes for both extremes and neither. It is the cessation of the four extremes—the extreme of existence (appearing), the extreme of nonexistence (not appearing), both, and neither—that is referred to as the conventional term "being free."

(i) The understanding of being free from extremes consists of not entertaining any dependence on the extremes of existing, nonexisting, appearing, and being empty whatsoever. Ultimately, being free from extremes is beyond any assessments in terms of being or not being something.

(ii) This being presented as being free from extremes is tenable through reasoning by virtue of the very essence of lacking any depending. Since being devoid of extremes is due to not depending on anything whatsoever, there is no dwelling in any extreme whatsoever. Hence, this is called "the view of lacking extremes and not observing any middle."[628] This is also tenable through scripture, as the *Perfection of the Qualities of Great Dynamic Energy* says:

> We speak of "being free" because of lacking extremes.

This is furthermore tenable through the argument of all being free through knowing one. Through knowing that a single one is devoid of extremes, there is thus freedom from all appearances and imputations because there is no depending whatsoever to be entertained.

(iii) As for the mode of being free, through not dwelling in the extreme of existence, there is freedom from the extreme of nonexistence. Through not dwelling in the extreme of nonexistence, the extreme of existence is free. Through not dwelling in both existence and nonexistence, the extreme of both is free. Through not dwelling in neither, the extreme of neither is free.

(e) As for being free as one, based on the essential point of there being no counterpart in it, it is taught that this is not contingent on means and prajñā. "One" refers to the single sphere of the Great Perfection free from all reference points. Since being free occurs within this natural state, it is empty of all numerical extremes of many.

(i) Regarding the understanding of being free as one without any counterpart, it is not untenable; there is no being free whatsoever apart[629] from one being free as one. Therefore, awareness is primordially beyond any conventions of being or not being free.

(ii) This being presented as being free as one is tenable through reasoning. All being free is not different; we speak of "being free" because there is only one and nothing other, and this "one" is awareness itself. For there is no separate phenomenon that is not this sole self-awareness. This is also tenable through scripture, as the *Tantra of the Essence of Gold* states:

> For dharmatā free as one
> is the single taste of the many.

This is furthermore tenable through the argument of all being free through knowing one. For, through knowing that a single one is awareness, all of saṃsāra and nirvāṇa is free.

(iii) The mode of being free is that all appearances and cognizance are free through recognizing them as being the single dharmatā.

(iv) The examples of being free are (1) having determined the taste of all salt if the taste of a single grain of salt has been determined, because the many are known to have a single taste, and (2) recognizing all fires through having recognized one fire.

These five modes of freedom are not evaluated within a single person. Rather, due to their distinct faculties, different persons become free through whichever one among these five they aspire for.

(3) To summarize the meanings of these five modes of freedom, they all lack any basis to depend on.

(a) Due to being free in itself, there is no depending on any phenomena of view, meditation, and conduct that involve any focal objects; conditions are free through these very conditions. Just as stains wash away stains, bad conditions are free through these bad conditions and thus dawn as the aids of wisdom. Alpha-purity is free through alpha-purity, and awareness is free through awareness.

(b) Being primordially free is devoid of any depending in terms of the unity of apprehender and apprehended. Therefore, objects are free through these very objects, similar to poisons overcoming poisons.

(c) Since being nakedly free does not depend on either saṃsāra or nirvāṇa, causes are free through these very causes, just as iron cuts through iron.

(d) Since being free from extremes does not depend on any conventional expressions, phenomena are free through these very phenomena, just as a fire arising from wood consumes this very wood.

(e) Since being free as one does not depend on any state of mind that causes being free, mind itself is free through mind, just as stones break stones.

It is not the case that anything is not perfect as awareness. By virtue of this essential point, at the time when awareness is free, all phenomena are free. Through the perishing of a supporting basis, the phenomena that are supported by it perish as well. Likewise, in their being free in themselves and perishing by themselves, all phenomena diffuse into the expanse in an even and pervasive manner. The *Garland of Pearls* says this:

> Therefore, in the awareness that is present as the ground,
> appearances are perfect because they are self-dawning.
> The ground itself is perfect because it is self-arisen.
> Objects are perfect because they are self-appearing.
> The ground of delusion is perfect because it is free in itself.
> All paths are perfect because they are self-pure.
> Knowable objects are perfect because they are self-awareness.
> The fruition is perfect because it is self-pervasive.
> Causes and conditions are perfect because of what is their own place.
> Dharmatā is perfect because it is self-realizing.
> Saṃsāra and nirvāṇa are perfect because they are self-reversing.
> Tantras and scriptures are perfect because they are self-abiding.
> The single time is perfect because it is self-expired.
> The instructions are perfect because they are self-knowing.
> Dhyāna is perfect because it is self-settled.
> The expanse is perfect because it is self-abiding.[630]

Since this perfect and free awareness is alpha-pure from the very beginning, it is stainless. Since it is the awakened mind, any mind stream is exhausted. It is the single great bliss that is beyond speech, thought, and expression. It is the genuine primordial purity that is empty in its being pure of materiality. It is the generic appearance that is not tainted by the proliferating dimensions of saṃsāra and nirvāṇa. It is the exhaustion of phenomena and the vanishing of movement. Beyond matter and awareness, it abides as the buddhahood of the native ground. The *Garland of Pearls* states this:

> The dharmakāya of great self-perfection
> is the exhaustion of stains because it is alpha-pure.
> Since it arose at the beginning, any continuum is exhausted.
> Since it lacks any counterpart, it is beyond calculation.
> It is the great bliss devoid of any causes of suffering.
> It is beyond speech and thought, lacking any causes of expression.
> It is the pure awareness that is primordially self-aware.
> It is not material because contaminations are exhausted.

It remains empty because entities are exhausted.
It is the very essence without any proliferation through duality.
Since it is free from dharmas, it is beyond extremes.
Since it is nonconceptual lucidity, movement has vanished.
It is the perfection of the two accumulations without both matter and awareness.
It is letting be itself, without any rival.
Since it cannot be altered by words,
it lacks any words of contrivance and is all-pervasive.
Without a thinking mind and free from any minding,
it is sheer freshness—the native state itself.
Being the supreme uncontrivedness, it abides as true naturalness.[631]

Jigmé Lingpa's *Treasury of Precious Qualities* lists the same five modes of freedom as Longchenpa's text. In the course of its explanations of these five, Yönten Gyatso's commentary[632] also links being primordially free and being nakedly free with the notion of being free upon arising.

According to this commentary, in general, awareness, which is the basic nature of the sugata heart's own face and is not seen due to being obscured by thoughts, must become free based on the essential point of being free in itself. However, there is no ground whatsoever to be *made* free. If the ground that is obscured by stains is taken to refer to awareness's essence, dharmatā—the fundamental state of bodhicitta—is not visibly manifest in terms of being existent, not limited in terms of being nonexistent, not partial in terms of either one, and not apprehendable as any middle either. Therefore, it is beyond any beginning, end, arising, ceasing, coming, going, the three times, a middle, extremes, and so on. Thus, what is to be freed? If "the ground to be freed" is taken to refer to the obscuring stains, dharmatā is omnipresent and it is not the case that all thoughts are not free from the moment of their sheer arising. Therefore, if "thoughts" are not established as any ground, they are devoid of any notion of "some obscuration being free through some means."

Hence, if awareness, which lacks any ground of direct superior insight's depending on the unimpeded radiance of self-lucidity and any root that would give rise to such insight, is allowed to settle in an uncontrived manner in the natural state of its self-lucidity within the spaciousness of alpha-purity, all thoughts disintegrate in their own place, and thus natural dhyāna is accomplished on its own.

Based on the progressive mental engagement of different persons, there are two kinds of being free in itself—(a) with effort and (b) without effort. (a) Within the natural state of not stirring from the basic nature that is the fundamental ground, no matter which afflictions and thoughts may arise, they are identified by the superior insight of recognizing their nature. Thoughts are allowed to settle without moving away from this natural state, not fettered by any remedy, and not pursued. Through that approach, since thoughts are not established as such in the ground of awareness, their magical display of movement becomes transparent in that it lacks any nature of its own, just like muddied water becomes transparent when it is allowed to settle. (b) As for effortlessly being free in itself, since the place of arising and that which arises are of one taste, dharmatā and thoughts—the essence and the appearances of its dynamic energy—arise such that they are not established as two separate things. Since they are free in themselves by themselves, whatever arises is unable to stand its own ground.

Let's revisit once again what the *Garland of Pearls* says about the five kinds of freedom:

> Apart from unimpeded awareness,
> there is no delusion and thus no thoughts.
> Since it is primordially free, it is absolutely supreme.
> Since it is free by itself, object conditions are exhausted.
> Since it is nakedly free, appearances are pure.
> Since it is free from extremes, the four possibilities cease.
> Since it is free as one, it is empty of many.[633]

(1) Regarding being primordially free, in the middle of the cloud-like appropriations of the five skandhas and the eight consciousnesses,

awareness lacks any nature of its own, just like the sky. Therefore, it is untainted by the flaws of being fettered in saṃsāric existence, and its own face is free from all reference points. Hence, its being free is not produced or contrived subsequently through any conditions for its being free. Rather, it exists as being primordially free right from the very start. As we saw before, the *Garland of Pearls* states this:

> It does not become free through effort—
> it primordially abides as being free.[634]

Therefore, ordinary sentient beings who cling to "me" and what is "mine" fixate on the adventitious appearances of delusion that never existed, and thus are deceived. Hence, no matter how the appearances of awareness's dynamic energy may unfold from the natural state of the space-like essence of awareness—which is primordially empty, rootless, beyond any basis to depend on, and in which causes and results leave no trace—yogic practitioners need to make the firm resolve to simply let awareness's own empty forms, which lack existence yet appear, be transparent as being free upon arising in an impartial manner, while they have never expressed themselves in any other way. This resembles the following example: when a mirage appears as water, since it never existed as water primordially, it is already free in its not being water. Apart from simply understanding this and deciding that it is in fact so, there is no need for this mirage to become free of being water newly. Thus, the *Precious Treasury of the Dharmadhātu* says:

> In changeless awareness free from reference points,
> arising is primordial arising, abiding is primordial abiding,
> and being free is primordially being free, just like space.

(2) Being free in itself means that there is no relying on antidotes. The Mind Series says that being free manifests on its own and not through anything else. Accordingly, all sights and sounds are self-arising from awareness's own dynamic energy. Right upon their arising, they are already established within the dharmatā that is beyond existence, nonexistence, permanence, and extinction. Therefore,

they are neither made free through other conditions nor do they themselves perform the action of freeing themselves. Rather, they exist as being free in themselves, just like a gently flowing river that remains free in its flow by its own nature. Common naive beings are fettered through clinging to a self and also allow themselves to be marred by the flawed notions of contrived forms of view, meditation, and conduct (such as regarding the five skandhas to be empty). Therefore, just like water frozen into ice, the essence of being free in itself is obscured. Even what is taught as the reality of the path that has a conditioned nature and involves the conventions of view, meditation, and conduct for the type of persons who do not right from the start realize the essential point of being free in itself must in the end become free in itself in the expanse of the dharmakāya.

Hence, it is the very lack of any essence of its own that constitutes the basic nature of being free in itself. Therefore, all other conditions of the path, such as the kinds of means and prajñā that involve cognizance (Tib. *rnam par rig pa*), simply represent superimpositions that are the opposite of being free in itself; thus, it does not depend on them. Consequently, if the fortunate ones who have entered this path of the Great Perfection recognize that genuine awareness abides nakedly and in an alpha-pure way in the expanse of the dharmakāya, and seize its own place, all thoughts that arise from its dynamic energy vanish on their own without a trace and thus become pure, just like a knot in a snake. The *Precious Treasury of the Dharmadhātu* declares this:

> In the unmoving awareness of great equality,
> at the time of arising, what is self-arising seizes its own place.
> At the time of abiding, what is self-abiding seizes its own place.
> At the time of being free, what is free in itself seizes its own place.

(3) As for being nakedly free, awareness always exists in an uninterrupted manner like the flow of a river. When the eyes see any objects of attachment, objects of aversion, and so on due to the unceasing dynamic energy of this awareness, thoughts of attachment, aversion, and so on begin to proliferate. At that point, with great

lightning-like suddenness, one intensely focuses on the moment of mind and the gaze of the eyes, nakedly directing one's attention to them and thus settling directly within awareness in a bare manner. Through that, in the very first moment, all reference points of visible forms are severed and thus the perceiving mind does not cling to objects, nor is this mind tainted by appearances. Still, while the appearing object does not go anywhere, the perceiving mind vanishes completely. This is called "the nonobservation of the feeling that is conditioned by contact based on the eyes." The same applies when the ears hear sounds, the nose smells odors, the tongue tastes flavors, the body touches tangible objects, or the mental faculty focuses on the objects of the five senses or on object generalities and so on.

If there is familiarity with letting all the different appearances of fragmented phenomena be nakedly free through the essential point of instantaneous great lightning-like suddenness, gradually, all appearances are pure in their being nakedly free. Through this, one will be rid of the entire foundation of causes and results in terms of accumulating the latent tendencies of saṃsāra through the connection of apprehender and apprehended due to the mutual dependence of subject and object. In that way, being free upon arising will occur automatically as a matter of course.

(4) As for being free from extremes, from the perspective of the unborn essence of awareness, it is free from the extreme of existence. However, from the perspective of its being without ceasing, it does not dwell in the extreme of nonexistence. Since it is an uninterrupted flow, it is free from the extreme of nonexistence. However, since it is not a permanent entity, it does not dwell in the extreme of existence. Since it dawns as all kinds of appearances of its dynamic energy, it is not established as anything singular. Since its essence lacks any reference points, it is free from the extreme of being designated as many. This nature is what represents Samantabhadra. That is, through remaining without change or transition within the natural state of recognizing the vast spaciousness of Vajrasatta by virtue of its unobstructed emptiness and lucidity, buddhahood is found

within oneself through stripping awareness bare, without pondering over there on outer objects, without thinking over here about inner mind, and without intentionally settling in what is unborn as its own place in between.

(5) As for being free as one, in this nonreferential awareness that is the inseparability of the two realities, one and many are not established. However, there are no phenomena whatsoever that are not nakedly free as the single unobstructed wisdom that is conventionally designated as "the single sphere of the dharmakāya" within the natural state of awareness, without depending on conditions such as the means and prajñās of the lower paths. If this natural state is not lost, all movements and postures of the body, expressions of speech, and thoughts of the mind are nothing but nonexistents that clearly appear but are not established as the essence of awareness and therefore lack any characteristics. They are self-arising as the awakened body, speech, and mind of the victors. Ultimately, since there is no departing from the natural state of awareness, awareness remains beyond the objects that consist of the entirety of physical movements and postures, expressions, and thoughts. Thus, if there is no stirring from the natural state of this single awareness, the awakened mind of the three kāyas does not exist anywhere else than that either. The *Precious Treasury of the Dharmadhātu* states this:

> Not existing yet arising as anything whatsoever, it is the nirmāṇakāya.
> Itself enjoying itself, it is the sambhogakāya.
> Not having any actual ground, it is the dharmakāya.
> The fruition is the spaciousness of the innate presence of the three kāyas.

Therefore, if one understands that the above four modes of freedom, which are presented due to the progression of the different faculties of people, share the characteristic of ultimately being free as the single dharmatā of personally experienced awareness, one will be truly convinced that all phenomena of saṃsāra and nirvāṇa are the emptiness of the great primordial infinity free from any restrictions.

The commentary on Jigmé Lingpa's *Treasury of Precious Qualities* by the late Kangyur Rinpoche, Longchen Yeshe Dorjé, explains these five modes of freedom as follows.[635]

Since everything is without beginning, end, arising, and ceasing, the ground to be freed—the dharmatā of mind as such—has never been established as anything. Just as there is no need for a dam to keep back a mirage that appears as if it were water, the bodhicitta that lacks any ground whatsoever is devoid of anything that obscures it, anything that is to be freed, and any extrinsic means to do so. As the unceasing appearance of objects that is the unimpeded radiance of awareness's own lucidity, it is not like some utter void—rather, it has primordially never ever ceased. Therefore, though it needs to be seen as being empty, the self-radiance of awareness, which lacks any ground of being empty and any root that would make it abide, is self-lucid within the spaciousness of alpha-purity.

This awareness is endowed with the distinctive features of fivefold freedom.

(1) Regarding being primordially free, in the middle of the cloud-like eight consciousnesses, just like the sky, awareness is untainted by the flaws of saṃsāric existence and free from all reference points. Therefore, no matter which thoughts may arise through conditions, awareness itself lacks any subsequent kind of production or contrivance. Hence, it exists as being primordially free right from the very start.

(2) Regarding being free in itself, there is nothing but letting just that which the guru introduced on the basis of itself simply be, in a naturally settled way. Nevertheless, there is the temporary need to rely a little bit on remedies for the ongoing continuity of coarse thoughts. Still, in the final picture, all such phenomena of thoughts and their remedies are free in themselves through awareness itself. This process does not depend on any conditions, just as running water does not need to be driven on.

(3) Regarding being nakedly free, when thoughts have become a profusion of delusion, they become free through looking at awareness's face. Rather than running after thoughts like a dog chasing

after a stone that someone throws, thoughts are free through nakedly looking at awareness's face like a lion chasing the person who throws the stone. Therefore, both awareness and thoughts lack any depending and a basis to depend on.

(4) Regarding being free from extremes, from the perspective of the unborn essence of awareness, it is free from the extreme of existence. From the perspective of its being without ceasing, it does not dwell in the extreme of nonexistence. Since it is an uninterrupted flow, it is free from the extreme of nonexistence. Since it is not a permanent entity, it does not dwell in the extreme of existence. Since it dawns as all kinds of appearances of its dynamic energy, it is not established as anything singular. Since it lacks any reference points, it is free from any possibility to be designated as many. This is Samantabhadra free from all extremes.

(5) Regarding being free as one, in this nonreferential awareness that is the inseparability of the two realities, one and many are not established. However, all thoughts are free within the spaciousness of awareness as the single unobstructed wisdom that is conventionally called "the single sphere of the dharmakāya." Therefore, without any phenomena at all, there are no characteristics, similar to clear and transparent space.[636]

Furthermore, the entire twelfth chapter of Longchenpa's *Precious Treasury of the Dharmadhātu* and its autocommentary *A Treasure Trove of Scriptures* consists of an extensive discussion of being primordially free, which also includes brief explanations of being free in itself, nakedly free, free from extremes, free as one, and completely free. In addition, both texts refer to many other kinds of freedom, such as unchanging freedom, self-arising freedom, innately present freedom, freedom as utter lucidity, and freedom as dharmatā.[637]

The Five or Six Methods to Gain Freedom without Meditation

The Great Perfection also speaks of a set of five or six kinds of freedom or "methods that lead to freedom without the need for meditation," which were originally concealed as termas by Padmasambhava.

These consist of (1) freedom through seeing (Tib. *mthong grol*) sacred pictures, diagrams, paintings, statues, and so on; (2) freedom through hearing (Tib. *thos grol*) mantras, dhāraṇīs, or texts such as *Freedom Through Hearing in the Intermediate State* (*The Tibetan Book of the Dead*); (3) freedom through tasting (Tib. *myong grol*) specially prepared pills or nectar; (4) freedom through recollection (Tib. *dran grol*), such as through phowa; and (5) freedom through wearing (Tib. *btags grol*). Sometimes (6) freedom through the touch of sacred objects (Tib. *reg grol*) is added.

There are numerous devices for the freedom through wearing, mostly amulets with mantras in the form of diagrams (Skt. *yantra*, Tib. *srung 'khor*) that are related to tantras or Dzogchen teachings.[638] Handing over such diagrams can be part of a detailed empowerment or constitute a simple form of empowerment on its own in order to bestow longevity, protection from obstacles, diseases, negative influences, and so on. Tantra texts are also used in this way by wearing them on the body (such as at the heart or in a locket on top of the head). Such diagrams and texts are also placed onto the heart cakra or the crown of the head of dying persons and either buried or burned with them in order to create a positive karmic connection, alleviate their suffering during the intermediate state, and provide conducive conditions for freedom.[639]

Appendix 8

An Aspiration Prayer for Ground, Path, and Fruition

Jigmé Lingpa

I pay homage to glorious Samantabhadra.

The original basic nature is naturally free from reference points.
It is not existent—the victors have not seen it.
It is not nonexistent—it is the ground of all of saṃsāra and nirvāṇa.
It is not self-contradictory—it is beyond being an expressible object.
May the basic nature of the ground of the Great Perfection be realized.

Because its essence is empty, it is free from the extreme of permanence.
Because its nature is luminous, it is free from the extreme of extinction.
Its unimpeded compassionate responsiveness is the ground of all kinds of emanations.
Though it is divided into three, these are not different in actuality.
May the basic nature of the ground of the Great Perfection be realized.

With its being inconceivable and free from all superimpositions,
biased clinging to existence and nonexistence falls apart.
In expressing this heart of the matter, even the tongues of the victors become exhausted.
It is the expanse of the great depth-lucidity without beginning, middle, or end.

May the basic nature of the ground of the Great Perfection be realized.

In its own pure essence, unborn alpha-purity,
the radiance of unconditioned innate presence dawns.
Not apprehending it as something separate but realizing it as the great unity
of awareness and emptiness is the full measure of the ground's awakened mind.
May there be no straying from the essential points of the path.

By virtue of being primordially pure, it lacks even the name "view."
By virtue of being aware of its own face, it emerges from the sheath of what is meditatable.
By virtue of being without any focal point, it is freedom from the chains of conduct.
Residing in the natural womb, it is the state of naked nonreferentiality.[640]
May there be no straying from the essential points of the path.

Not falling into the partiality of thoughts about good and bad
and not spacing out into neutral indifference,
being free upon arising is impartial, carefree, and boundless spaciousness.
Within the state of realizing the nature wherein adopting and rejecting are primordially exhausted,
may there be no straying from the essential points of the path.

Within the sky-like state of the primal general ground,
the awareness of the ground manifestations resembles clouds disappearing in the sky.
By virtue of the cognizance of outer luminosity turning back inside,
may the sphere of the youthful vase body endowed with six distinctive features—
the fortress of the king of fruitions—be seized.[641]

In primordial awareness, Samantabhadra,

all wishing for something to be attained vanishes within the expanse.
The fundamental ground of the Great Perfection beyond a mind with effort
is the sphere of Samantabhadrī's open spaciousness of expanse and awareness.
May the fortress of the king of fruitions be seized.

Not abiding anywhere at all is the heart of the matter of Great Madhyamaka.
All-encompassing innate boundlessness is the natural state of the Great Seal.
Vast spaciousness free from extremes is the essential point of the Great Perfection.
The perfection of the qualities of the paths and bhūmis in the ground is the sphere of innate presence.
May the fortress of the king of fruitions be seized.

This profound aspiration prayer that represents a summary
of the seal of the profound expanse of the heart essence[642]
was composed at the urging of the protector of the teachings,
the seer Rāhula, who assumed the form of a monk.
So that the dissemination of the profound heart of the matter may be meaningful
and this aspiration prayer of auspicious connections may come to its fruition,
I opened the profound seal and entrusted it
to the hidden awareness-holder Madman from Kong,[643]
who has received the blessings of Namké Nyingpo.[644]
May the welfare of all beings become equal to the sky.[645]

Appendix 9

The Essential Point of Practice[646]

Patrul Rinpoche

I pay homage to the guru.

I pay homage at the feet of the omniscient father, his heirs,
and their lineage,
as well as the glorious protector, the guru,
who teaches the reality of the inconceivable Great Perfection—
the nature of primordial freedom—in a naked manner.

Beyond eliminating flaws, accomplishing qualities, adopting
and rejecting,
the present cognition, naturally settled and relaxed,
is the wisdom of awareness without contrivance and change.
If it rests directly within that state, that's the unity of view and
meditation.

With knowing how to meditate but not knowing how to be free,
meditative concentration is like that of the gods, it is taught.
Thus, it is crucial to gain the firm confidence of realization
directly within being free.

Through settling the restless mind—the meditative concentration of its still aspect—
afflictions may be suppressed temporarily,
but without knowing the secret essential point of realizing
that they are free in themselves,
upon encountering certain circumstances, the rotten corpse of
thoughts will rise again.

If the essential point of realizing self-arising and being free in
itself is known,
thoughts of adopting and rejecting are like sketches on water.
Even if they arise temporarily, they are unable to hold their
ground and dissolve.
With their arising and their freedom being simultaneous, they
cannot stand their own ground—
even if bad thoughts come up, there is no accumulating of bad karma.
Since they are realized instantly, for whom would there be any
benefit or harm?

When lacking the essential point of being free in its own place,
even if the mere self-recognition of the infinite flow
of undercurrent thoughts and afflictions is seized with mindfulness,
good and bad thoughts will give rise to hope and fear.
Through this, formational karma is accumulated and becomes
saṃsāra's cause.

Therefore, a single instant of awareness free in itself
is superior to a thousand experiences of a still mind.
Thus, all the essential points of view, meditation, and conduct—
such as primordial freedom, freedom in itself, freedom upon
arising, and naked freedom—are one.
Hence, familiarize with the essential point of realizing this
freedom in itself.

If this essential point is understood, there is no need for any
other view or meditation.
All good thoughts emerge as a continuous stream without fixation—
even if efforts in virtue are made, there is no presumptuous
mind of clinging to being supreme.
All bad thoughts dissolve like knots in a snake.
Even if the five poisons arise, they are instantaneously free in
their own place.
The hosts of neutral thoughts are settled in themselves—the
expanse of awareness;

self-appearing and free in themselves, they resemble the traces
of a bird in the sky.

The root of saṃsāra consists of deluded thoughts.
If thoughts are brought onto the path and there is confidence
that they are free,
this is called "saṃsāra's freedom as the expanse of nirvāṇa."
Through confidence in the scope of liberation, bad circumstances rise as the path.
Without this essential point, through platitudes and empty talk,
you may speak of your object of understanding as being your
realization,
but that will just naturally bring the faults of your own bad
character to light.

Being worse than the ordinary solid fixation of the five poisons,
such represents the flaw of not knowing the scope of being free.
Therefore, the gist of the essential point of view, meditation,
and conduct
comes down to this firm confidence of realizing the way of being free.
Thus, it is crucial to bring it onto the path of realization
through fusing it with any circumstance.

Though what I said here is not present in my own mind stream,
I have written it down unmistakenly through relying on the words
of the omniscient guru, the embodiment of the Buddha.
This is the essential point of practice, so keep it in mind!

Sarva maṅgalam!

Appendix 10

Afflictions as Wisdom, Skandhas as Avalokiteśvara[647]

Patrul Rinpoche

Do not chase after the object of your hatred—look at the
angry mind.
This anger's appearance, self-arising and free in itself, is the
natural state of lucid emptiness.
Apart from that, there is no mirror-like wisdom—lucid emptiness.
Right within hatred's being free in itself, recite the six syllables.[648]

Do not hold on to the object of your pride—look at the grasping mind.
Fixating on supremacy, self-arising and free in itself, is the
natural state of primordial emptiness.
Apart from that, there is no wisdom of equality—primordial
emptiness.
Right within pride's being free in itself, recite the six syllables.

Do not cling to the object of your desire—look at the clinging mind.
This clinging's appearance, self-arising and free in itself, is the
natural state of blissful emptiness.
Apart from that, there is no discriminating wisdom—blissful
emptiness.
Right within desire's being free in itself, recite the six syllables.

Do not pursue the object of your envy—look at the assessing mind.
Examining and assessing, self-arising and free in itself, is the
state of empty intelligence.

Apart from that, there is no all-accomplishing wisdom—
empty intelligence.
Right within envy's being free in itself, recite the six syllables.

Do not get inflated by the object of your ignorance—look at
its own face.
The hosts of thoughts, self-arising and free in themselves, are
the state of awareness-emptiness.
Apart from that, there is no dharmadhātu wisdom—awareness-emptiness.
Right within ignorance's being free in itself, recite the six syllables.

The skandha of form is primordially empty, unborn, the natu-
ral state of space.
This bindu of emptiness-awareness is Avalokiteśvara.
Apart from that, there is no noble King of Space.[649]
Right within beholding emptiness, recite the six syllables.

Feeling is the lasso that ties mind and object together.
When nondual equality is realized, that is Avalokiteśvara.
Apart from that, there is no noble Meaningful Lasso.[650]
Right within realizing equal taste, recite the six syllables.

Discrimination—holding on to characteristics—is the mind
of delusion.
If all beings are held with compassion, that is Avalokiteśvara.
Apart from that, there is no noble supreme One who Empties
Saṃsāra's Pit.
Right within nonreferential compassion, recite the six syllables.

Through formation—the karmas of saṃsāra—the six kinds
[of beings] are cycling.
When the equality of saṃsāra and nirvāṇa is realized, that is
Avalokiteśvara.
Apart from that, there is no Great Compassionate One[651]
who guides beings.
Right within the single flavor of benefiting others, recite the six syllables.

Consciousness is the portion of mind's nature that comes in
eight collections.
When mind as such is realized as dharmakāya, that is Avalokiteśvara.
Apart from that, there is no noble and supreme Ocean of Victors.[652]
Knowing that your own mind is buddhahood, recite the six syllables.

Chart

The Ground, Its Manifestations, and the Resulting Freedom or Delusion

primordial ground—basic awareness

eight isolates: essence, nature, compassionate responsiveness, natural state, nature, character, alpha-purity, and innate presence

ground manifestations

eight gateways (general ground): compassion, light, kāyas, wisdom, nonduality, freedom from extremes, saṃsāra, and nirvāṇa

ground of delusion = all-ground	ground of freedom
primordial ultimate all-ground ultimate all-ground of linking all-ground of diverse latent tendencies all-ground of the bodies of latent tendencies	Samantabhadra's freedom with six features
five afflictions as the aspects of delusion	**five wisdoms as the nature of freedom**
ignorance desire hatred pride envy	dharmadhātu wisdom discriminating wisdom mirror-like wisdom wisdom of equality all-accomplishing wisdom

Notes

1 Throughout, I use either the Tibetan *rig pa* (arguably *the* hallmark term of Dzogchen, well-known and evocative) or render it "awareness." Sometimes I also use "basic awareness," "primordial awareness," or "pure awareness." Alternative translations abound, including "intrinsic awareness," "intuitive awareness," "awakened awareness," "immediate awareness," "wakefulness," "knowledge," and "pure presence."

2 Tib. Klong chen rab 'byams pa dri med 'od zer.

3 In these commentaries, I have for the reader's reference offered the page or folio numbers of the original texts in curly braces, e.g., "{592}" or {23a}, and bolded the words and phrases that come directly from *The Aspiration Prayer*.

4 Tib. Dpal sprul o rgyan 'jigs med chos kyi dbang po.

5 The Sanskrit name Samantabhadra has been translated in a number of different ways, such as "Universal Excellence," "All-Good One," "Completely Excellent One," "Ever-Excellent One," "Ever-Perfect One," "that which is wholly positive," "the Omnibeneficent," and even "everything is fine." Literally, *samanta* means "having the ends together," thus meaning "contiguous," "adjacent," "in conjunction with," "all around," "on all sides," "universal," "whole," "all," and "completely." *Bhadra*'s range of meanings includes "blessed," "auspicious," "fortunate," "prosperous," "happy," "gracious," "friendly," "kind," "good," "excellent," "fair," "beautiful," "pleasant," "dear," "good at or skillful in," and "great." If I were to translate Samantabhadra, I would tentatively choose "Universal Goodness" or "Universal Excellence." However, "goodness" here means a transcendent goodness that leaves behind all ordinary dualistic notions of both goodness and badness, as well as any other reference points, be they moral, psychological, or philosophical. As Dowman (2003, 114) says, "His name means All-Good, where his goodness is transcendent and supramoral." In any case, since both components of this Sanskrit name have such a wide range of connotations, it is impossible to cover all of them in a single English rendering. Therefore, I will simply retain the Sanskrit.

Note also that this buddha Samantabhadra is not to be conflated with the bodhisattva of the same name who is well-attested in the common Mahāyāna literature. One of the eight major bodhisattvas, this Samantabhadra is considered to be one of the closest disciples of Buddha Śākyamuni and appears in sūtras such as the *Saddharmapuṇḍarīkasūtra*,

Gaṇḍavyūhasūtra, and *Avataṃsakasūtra*. In the latter sūtra we find Samantabhadra's famous and often-recited *Aspiration Prayer for Excellent Conduct*. It is not the case that this bodhisattva has somehow evolved or transformed into the primordial buddha, Samantabhadra, or vice versa, because both are clearly distinguished in the Tibetan tradition. As Turpeinen 2016 (104n292) points out, Germano's forthcoming *Prophetic Histories of Buddhas, Ḍākinīs and Saints in Tibet* contains a detailed discussion of Samantabhadra's appearances as a bodhisattva and as a buddha in Buddhist literature.

6 *Buddhahood Without Meditation*, revealed by Düjom Lingpa (1835–1904; Bdud 'joms gling pa 2004, 345), glosses *Dzogchen* as follows: "It is the perfection (*rdzogs pa*) of the triad of saṃsāra, nirvāṇa, and the path. It is great (*chen po*) because it represents the general ground of all yānas through subsuming all yānas into the single heart of the matter and into a single point of condensation." Dzogchen Ponlop Rinpoche (2002, 25–26) explains:

> "Dzog" means "to perfect" or "to complete" as well as "to exhaust." "Chen" means "great." So, Dzogchen means "great perfection," "great completion," or "great exhaustion." It is a state of being totally free. At this stage, you have exhausted every tiny bit of ego-clinging, every element of emotional disturbances. Therefore, it is called "great exhaustion." It is also called "the great completion" because in that state, all the wisdom of buddha is complete, all the elements of enlightenment are complete. There is nothing missing in this state. Finally, because your mind has never been polluted, it has always been in this state of complete purity. ... To convey fully the meaning of Dzogchen in English, the expression "full stop" is quite good. Full stop. Period. This period is a little but very powerful dot called the full stop. There is the sense of being full in that this dot has a circular form that is complete and full. At the same time, everything stops here: it doesn't go beyond this period. Dzogchen has a similar meaning. On the one hand, it has this meaning of fullness, which is why we use the term "completion." It also has this meaning of stopping, which we express as exhaustion. Your whole expression of samsara has been exhausted, so it stops right here. It does not go beyond this. Therefore, Dzogchen is a giant full stop.

7 Typically, especially the early Dzogchen tantras (found in several compilations of the Nyingma tantras [Tib. *Rnying ma rgyud 'bum*]) are unlike the better-known classical Indian Vajrayāna tantras (found in the Kangyur) with their detailed teachings on the elaborate rituals and yogic practices of the creation and completion stages (Skt. *utpattikrama* and *utpannakrama*).

In essence, these Dzogchen tantras primarily teach the natural innate freedom of primordial awareness and the very unelaborate practices to rediscover and remain in it. However, some later Dzogchen tantras of the Pith Instructions Series that were revealed as treasure texts (said to have been hidden by Padmasambhava) include more extensive tantric techniques of yoga, visualization, and ritual. In addition, they teach other practices that are based on the tantric view of nāḍīs, vāyus, and bindus but without direct parallels in the classical Vajrayāna. For details of the Mind Series, Expanse Series, and Pith Instructions Series, see below.

8 *Buddhahood Without Meditation* (Bdud 'joms gling pa 2004, 346) glosses the Vajra Heart of Luminosity (Tib. 'Od gsal rdo rje snying po) as one of six synonyms of Dzogchen as follows:

> It is luminosity (*'od gsal*) because the natural state of awareness—the sugata heart—is transparent, lucid, and free from anything that may sully it. It is a vajra (*rdo rje*) because it is endowed with the seven vajra qualities of indestructibility. It is a heart (*snying po*) because it is present as the vital essence of all phenomena of saṃsāra and nirvāṇa.

The seven vajra qualities of indestructibility are (1) uncuttable, (2) indestructible, (3) real, (4) solid, (5) stable, (6) completely unobstructable, and (7) completely undefeatable. More specifically, in terms of the ground, emptiness or mind's true nature is (1) uncuttable by the afflictive obscurations and (2) indestructible by the cognitive obscurations. In terms of the path, (3) its essence is real, (4) its nature is solid, and (5) its function is stable. In terms of the fruition, it is (7) unobstructable by the cognitive obscurations and (6) undefeatable by the afflictive obscurations.

9 For more details on these three aspects of the primordial ground or basic awareness, see *Ketaka*, *Lamp*, and section 1.1 in appendix 2.

As for rendering the third aspect or essential characteristic here as "compassionate responsiveness," while a literal rendering of the Tibetan *thugs rje* as "compassion" is not entirely wrong, the term in the specific context of Dzogchen involves much more than our ordinary notion of compassion. Germano (1992, 852ff.) explains:

> Thugs rJe in this special technical use clearly signifies how this radiant empty energy is also inherently characterized by "intelligence" (Rig Pa'i sNying Po), such that rather than being mere static light energy, it is ceaselessly self-organizing as in-formed by this intelligence, and thus is "all-pervading" ... "Compassion" being that which drives the Buddha from his absorption in emptiness to manifestation, it is the "energy" behind his/her actions, and is an inherently active term ... Additionally, "compassion" involves being "tuned into" other

> such that we "vibrate" in resonance with their plight ... it possesses this natural uncontrived responsiveness to others rather than being flat, uninspired, unresponsive, like a candle blown out by the wind; compassion is the ability to empathize, when your own spirit "resonates" in tune with the other, transcending the distance between two lives ... Thus when the original creator[s] of this terminology searched for terms to express their insight, they began with the standard terms "essence" (Ngo Bo) and "nature" (Rang bZhin): reality's quintessential essence is empty, yet its very nature is simultaneously radiant dynamism ... It was then necessary to find a third term to express how this empty luminosity is also intrinsically intelligent, and how that intelligence is naturally self-organizing without any need for the external hand of a godhead, adventitious accidents, or some other extrinsic force. They found this term in Thugs rJe (a term that in its ordinary meaning signifies intelligence, responsiveness, and action, this inner heart resonating within the enlightened state), and defined it as "the heart-nucleus of awareness" (Rig Pa'i sNying Po) which is "all-pervading" (Kun Khyab) as the Universe dynamically expands, just as the Buddha's compassion naturally self-organizes the enlightened energy into a vast array of particular emanations and enlightened activity permeating the cosmos ... Its translation as "resonance" connotes that this dimension is "vibrant" with energy shaping itself into various forms, yet remains capable of response and awareness (as opposed to sterile, inert forms characterized by solidity and lack of resonance), while "compassion" connotes that this dimension is experienced as caring, as something with which your own relationship is quite intimate; additionally, this "responsiveness" implies an Other not in the sense of the alienated Other, but rather in the sense that a profound dialogue is ongoing in the heart of reality.

In addition, Germano matches essence, nature, and compassionate responsiveness with the dharmakāya, sambhogakāya, and nirmāṇakāya, respectively. Dowman (2003, 37) renders the term as "responsiveness" and comments as follows:

> It is the third and final denominator in the list of categories or aspects by which emptiness can be defined: essence, nature, responsiveness. It appears anomalous, an attribute rather than a category. The third logical category is function, or *manifest function*, and the attribute found in its stead is responsiveness and its qualifier is *all-pervasive*. Viewed as a functional

> attribute of inner space [*dbyings*], total presence [*rig pa*], and light [*gsal ba*], the implication is that the dynamic, the intentionality, the purpose of being is compassion, which is a synonym of responsiveness and demonstrable as the responsive aspect of love. It is this compassion that is coextensive with space, the buddha-heart pervading all beings. Viewed as the potential form or manifestation of emptiness, the implication appears to be that every vibration of body, speech, and mind is a form of compassionate energy, nothing excluded. Consider the distinction between responsiveness and compassion. In Dzogchen, compassion is much more than the virtue of loving-kindness. Nor does the word *compassion* in the Dzogchen context denote its English etymological meaning, "suffering together" or "empathy," although both these meanings may be inferred. Essentially, compassion indicates an open and receptive mind responding spontaneously to the exigencies of an ever-changing field of vibration to sustain the optimal awareness that serves self-and-others' ultimate desire for freedom and well-being. The conventional meaning of compassion denotes the latter, active part of this definition, and, due to the accretions of Christian connotations in the West, response is limited to specifically virtuous activity. *Responsiveness* defines the origin and cause of selfless activity that can encompass all manner of response. On this nondual Dzogchen path, virtue is whatever action optimizes presence [*rig pa*]—loving-kindness is the automatic function of primal awareness [*ye shes*]. (Emphasis by Dowman; insertions of Tibetan equivalents in [ ] by the present author.)

The Padmakara Translation Group (Jigme Lingpa and Kangyur Rinpoche 2013, xxviii–xxix) explains this term as follows:

> [T]he etymological sense of the Tibetan words ("lordship, or power, over the mind") gives them a range of meanings in other places that the English word "compassion" cannot possibly cover. In the context of the Great Perfection, *thugs rje* means, in the words of Yönten Gyamtso, "pure and unadulterated awareness that has not yet stirred from its own true condition or state," but which has the potential to do so. In this case, therefore, we have decided to translate *thugs rje* (tentatively and without much euphony), not as "compassion," but as "cognitive potency."

In sum, the term in question refers to the ultimate nonreferential compassion that is the natural and unimpeded manifestation of the boundless energy and awareness of the unity of the open and spacious alpha-purity and the innately present luminosity of mind's nature. Thus, it is usually referred to as "all-pervasive compassionate responsiveness with a heart of awareness" (Tib. *kun khyab thugs rje rig pa'i snying po can*). When this internal quality becomes perfectly manifest in buddhas and bodhisattvas, it keeps radiating outwardly throughout space and time, thus accomplishing the welfare of countless beings in the most appropriate and skillful ways possible.

10 In general, there are three kinds of Akaniṣṭha ("Nothing Higher")—(a) the ultimate Akaniṣṭha (the formless sphere of the dharmakāya), (b) the Richly Adorned Akaniṣṭha (the sphere in which the sambhogakāyas manifest), and (c) the highest pure level of the form realm (the natural sphere of nirmāṇakāyas). Attributing the anonymous *Vajrasattvamāyājālatantraśrīguhyagarbhanāmacakṣuṣṭīkā* (P4756) to the Indian master Buddhaguhya, TOK (1:297–99) cites its enumeration of six forms of Akaniṣṭha:

> (1) The ultimate Akaniṣṭha is the dharmadhātu because it is the residence of the buddhas and there is nothing higher than it. (2) The symbolic Akaniṣṭha is what appears as the shapes and colors of a palace as the symbol for the inseparability of expanse and wisdom because it is the residence of the sambhogakāya and there is no other symbol higher than this that illustrates the dharmadhātu. (3) The Akaniṣṭha of awareness is the wisdom of awareness that is the realization of the basic nature of entities, just as it is, because it is the residence of the dharmakāya endowed with twofold purity and there is no other awareness higher than this. (4) The secret Akaniṣṭha is the space of the Mother because it is the residence of the secret kāya and there are no qualities of any other abode that are higher than this. (5) The conceptual Akaniṣṭha is the palace of Akaniṣṭha as it is meditated on by beginners because it is the residence of the maṇḍala of superior samādhi and there are no other conceptions apprehending an object generality that are higher than this. (6) The Akaniṣṭha that is a mundane abode is even above the five [kinds of] gods in the pure regions [of the form realm] because it is the residence of the noble ones and there is no other abode in the form realm that is higher than this.

TOK adds that Longchenpa summarizes these six into three: (1) "The Akaniṣṭha of ultimate true reality" is the essence that cannot be presented as any dimension in terms of center, circumference, or direction and is free from all reference points—the final *buddhabhūmi* or the genuine destination. (2) "The Great Akaniṣṭha that is Richly Adorned" is self-arising as the appearance of great wisdom from the expanse of the dharmakāya. It consists of what appears as palaces of light, principal deities, and their retinues, which are innately present as the families of the five wisdoms and are without change or transition at all times. These self-appearances consist of the group formations that are the maṇḍalas of the five buddha families and reach to the very ends of space. (3) "The Akaniṣṭha that is a natural nirmāṇakāya realm" is twofold: (a) The first appears as the realms of the five buddha families (such as Vairocana), with Akaniṣṭha's multistoried palace in the middle and so on, for the sake of those to be guided who are on the bhūmis; and (b) the second is the widely known Akaniṣṭha that is a pure abode—the supreme abode that accords with the appearances of sentient beings in world-systems such as ours, the Sahā world (Skt. *Sahāloka*, Tib. *mi 'jed 'jig rten*; lit: "unbearable"), for the sake of both those on the bhūmis and ordinary beings. This Akaniṣṭha is the abode of the five kinds of gods in the pure regions at the highest dhyāna level of the form realm within each individual world-system. This Akaniṣṭha is not a coarse entity but an abode that consists of the nature of clear light and is adorned by various specific structures, such as a palace. (1) and (2) represent the abodes of the dharmakāya and sambhogakāya, respectively, while the two realms under (3) represent the abodes of the nirmāṇakāya. Compare also Jigme Lingpa and Kangyur Rinpoche 2013n538.

11 Tib. *chos nyid*. Though this term is usually translated as "the nature of phenomena" or the like, in the Great Perfection it does not simply refer to the generic nature of all phenomena in general but specifically represents an equivalent of primordial awareness as mind's own ultimate nature. Thus, it is only by extension that it can also be understood as the nature of all other phenomena, in that awareness ultimately is the nature and source of all that appears and is experienced.

12 Longchenpa calls this the "fourth time," as the equality of the three times of past, present, and future. Thus, Smith 2016 (16–17) rightly says the following about the timelessness of the primordial ground ("basis"), which also applies to Samantabhadra's freedom ("liberation") as the timeless presence of awareness ("vidyā"):

> Since time does not apply to the original basis, we must regard the use of terms such as "original," "primordial," and so on, as indicating a state in which time is irrelevant, rather than an actual conventional historical epoch or starting point that existed countless eons ago. From such a perspective, placing the original basis on a temporal spectrum is therefore a didactic myth ... The basis can only be self-arisen and self-originated if temporality is not a factor. In other words, the constant references in Great Perfection texts to self-origination, self-arising, and so on only make sense in light of the absence of

time. Vimalamitra's perspective excludes even pointing to a "now," since the past, present, and future are undifferentiated. This also applies to the presence of the basis in sentient beings as vidyā. Since time is not a factor when it comes to the analysis of the basis, Great Perfection texts can define the liberation of sentient beings as timeless, meaning that the state of liberation is their unconditioned essential state. It is not something to gain; it is something to discover. More importantly, the basis is buddhahood and functions as buddhahood.

13 "Alpha-purity" (Tib. *ka dag*) and "innate presence" (Tib. *lhun grub*) are two of the most crucial Dzogchen terms and are often used in conjunction to fully describe the nature or basic quality of rigpa. "Alpha-purity" refers to the original and beginningless purity or emptiness of all phenomena in general and of rigpa in particular.

"Innate presence" (full Tibetan *lhun gyis grub pa*) is one of many Dzogchen terms that are difficult to translate. Krang dbyi sun et al. 1985 (512 and 3107) explains *lhun* to mean "natural state," "power," or "nature" (*ngang ngam shugs sam rang bzhin*), while *'grub pa* (intransitive verb; past tense *grub pa*) means "to be well finished, completed, or accomplished," "to exist," "to abide," "to be established," or "to occur" (*legs par tshar ba dang/ chags pa* and *yod pa dang/ gnas pa'am 'byung ba*). Thus, *lhun gyis grub pa* is explained as "accomplished/established/existing effortlessly by nature" (*'bad med rang bzhin gyis grub pa*). The most common English translation of this term is clearly "spontaneous presence." Additional renderings include "spontaneously accomplished," "spontaneously (self-) perfected," "spontaneously existent," "spontaneous fulfillment," "natural spontaneity," "immanently spontaneous," "inherent presence," "self-perfection," "self-existence," "natural achievement," "effortless manifestation," and "formed all at once."

However, "spontaneous" for *lhun gyis* is somewhat problematic, because its English definitions refer to either (1) being performed or occurring as a result of a sudden inner impulse or inclination and without premeditation or external stimulus (thus often involuntarily) or (2) involving some form of arising, growing, or being produced. In its technical use, this Dzogchen term obviously does not refer to spontaneous unplanned or involuntary actions due to sudden impulses, nor does it refer to any kind of arising, growing, or being produced. Rather, the point is that the innate qualities of the luminosity of basic awareness are naturally and intrinsically complete and utterly perfect without any need for increasing, evolving, or improving them through any kind of effort or path.

Given that, the rendering "presence" for *grub pa* may seem too weak an expression to denote the innate qualities of awareness that are not just there but already perfect as the natural richness and fulfillment of primordial freedom and awakening. Thus, words such as "perfection" or "accomplishment" would convey this sense better. However, "perfection" (Tib. *rdzogs pa*) is already taken by "Great Perfection" and there also exists the term *lhun rdzogs* ("innate perfection"). "Accomplishment" can be too easily misunderstood as the result of an active act of having accomplished, achieved, or created something, which is obviously not the point here.

Therefore, I chose the renderings "innate presence" and "innately present." I understand "presence" here in the sense of saying that someone or something has a great or impressive presence, which also conveys a sense of perfection, power, and richness. Similarly, *Webster's Third New International Dictionary* says this about one of the meanings of "presence": "a quality of poise and effectiveness and ease of performance that enables a performer to achieve a close and sympathetic relationship with his audience." In this sense, rigpa's innate presence is its perfectly effective and yet completely relaxed way of being, which is utterly at ease with itself and displays an abundance of wisdom, compassion, and power.

Finally, in its nontechnical Dzogchen use, Tib. *lhun grub* also means "effortless" (such as in effortless buddha activity).

14 For a detailed discussion of the fivefold excellences of the teacher, teaching, disciples, place, and time as they vary in the contexts of the basic nature, practicing the path, the ultimate fruition, and the common yānas, see Smith 2016, 38–47.

15 Tib. Lhag sems can.

16 This is the second-highest level of the god realms in the desire realm, ruled by Indra.

17 The Sanskrit equivalent of the Tibetan name Garab Dorjé (Tib. *Dga' rab rdo rje*) is often given as Prahevajra, though Germano (1992, 4) points out that the form Vajraprahe may be the oldest attested Indic version of this name appearing in the Seventeen Tantras of the Pith Instructions Series of Dzogchen Atiyoga.

18 As van Schaik (2004a, 167n6), Kapstein (2008, 283), and Smith (2016, 2) note, this classification of the three series of Dzogchen is not attested before its appearance in the *Vima Nyingtig*, which was revealed in the early twelfth century by Shangdön Dashi Dorjé (Tib. Zhang ston bkra shis rdo rje; 1097–1167). Thus, this classification appears to originate in the tantras of the Pith Instructions Series, and it is unknown in any other system of Dzogchen.

19 Vairocana passed on the Mind Series to Yudra Nyingpo (Tib. G.yu sgra snying po; eighth–ninth century). Both transmitted it to the translator Nyag Jñānakumāra (Tib. Gnyags ye shes gzhon nu; eighth–ninth century), who also studied with Vimalamitra. Jñānakumāra in turn instructed Sogpo Balgyi Yeshé (Tib. Sog po dpal gyi ye shes), whose main disciple was Nup Sangyé Yeshé (Tib. Gnubs sangs rgyas ye shes; ninth to tenth century),

who also studied with a number of other masters in India, Gilgit, and Nepal. Later Mind Series proponents include the masters of the Nub, Sur (Tib. Zur), and Rong (Tib. Rong) clans, the followers of the Kham and Nyang lineages, as well as Aro Yeshé Jungné (Tib. A ro ye shes 'byung gnas; born thirteenth century). It seems that the scriptures of the Expanse Series appeared only from the eleventh century onward: the primary lineage was the system of *The Vajra Bridge, the Ear-Whispered Lineage of the Dzogchen Expanse Series* (Tib. *Rdzogs pa chen po klong sde'i snyan brgyud rdo rje zam pa*) as transmitted by Dzeng Dharmabodhi (Tib. 'Dzeng dharma bodhi; 1052–1168), which counts Śrī Siṃha and Vairocana among its founders. This approach is related to tantras such as *The Tantra of Secret Wisdom* and also contains a number of treatises on the nine expanses of the Expanse Series (see note 268) as well as ancillary texts attributed to Śrī Siṃha (for more details, see Anspal 2005a and 2005b and Smith 2016, 2–3). Just as the texts of the Expanse Series, those of the Pith Instructions Series began to appear in the eleventh century. However, according to the traditional reports, the Seventeen Tantras of this series were concealed earlier by Vimalamitra's main disciple Nyang Tingdzin Sangpo (Tib. Myang ting 'dzin bzang po; 760–815) in the Hat Temple (Tib. Zhva'i lha khang) about eighty kilometers northeast of Lhasa, after he taught them to Drom Rinchen Barwa (Tib. 'Brom rin chen 'bar ba). They were then rediscovered by Dangma Lhüngyal (Tib. Ldang ma lhun rgyal) in the eleventh century, who passed them on to his disciple Jetsün Sengé Wangchug (Tib. Lce btsun seng ge dbang phyug); see the colophon of *Self-Arising Awareness* (Anonymous 1973–77, 1:852–55). The Mind Series and Expanse Series were both eventually eclipsed by the Pith Instructions Series after the fourteenth century and are not often taught or practiced today (the contemporary Dzogchen master Namkhai Norbu [born 1938] appears to still transmit these two series). As Smith 2016 (1, 4) says, by all accounts, Padmasambhava did not teach Dzogchen widely during his stay in Tibet but instead hid many cycles of the Pith Instructions Series to be rediscovered later. Traditionally, the first treasure revealer is said to have been Sangyé Lama (Tib. Sangs rgyas bla ma; 1000–1080). Also, apart from the Mind Series and that of the *Vajra Bridge*, all later developments of the tradition of the Great Perfection are based on revelations of treasure texts.

20 Tib. 'Jigs med gling pa. He is held to be a reincarnation of the earlier treasure revealers Sangyé Lama and Chöjé Lingpa (Tib. Chos rje gling pa; 1682–1720).

21 The Tibetan Nyingma School classifies the entire Buddhist teachings into nine yānas: *Śrāvakayāna*, *Pratyekabuddhayāna*, *Bodhisattvayāna*, *kriyātantra*, *caryātantra*, *yogatantra*, *mahāyoga*, *anuyoga*, and *atiyoga*. The last three are also known as generation stage (Skt. *utpattikrama*, Tib. *bskyed rim*), completion stage (Skt. *utpannakrama*, Tib. *rdzogs rim*), and Great

Perfection, respectively. Mahāyoga (Tib. *rnal 'byor chen po*; "great yoga") has its name because it trains the mind in the actuality of nonduality and thus is greatly superior to the three outer tantras (kriyātantra, caryātantra, yogatantra). Anuyoga (Tib. *rjes su rnal 'byor*; "subsequent yoga") is so called because it primarily teaches the path of passion (Skt. *anurāga*, Tib. *rjes su chags pa*) as it is related to *prajñā*. As van Schaik (2004a, 179ff.) and Cabezón (2013, 29n57) point out, the terms *anuyoga* and *atiyoga* (or their Tibetan equivalents) are found in a number of tantric works in the Kangyur. However, they usually do not refer to distinct classes of tantras, let alone yānas, but different stages of tantric practice.

By contrast, in Nyingma tantras such as *The All-Creating Monarch* (Tib. *Kun byed rgyal po*), the terms indicate distinct systems of tantric practice. Also, in at least two Dunhuang texts, these terms clearly refer to distinct tantric systems or yānas. Atiyoga (Tib. *shin tu rnal 'byor*; "utmost yoga") bears its name because it is the pinnacle of all yānas and represents the ultimate completion stage of both the creation and completion stages. Eventually Atiyoga, or Dzogchen proper (for these two terms' range of meanings, history, and relationship, see van Schaik 2004a, 167–90), was classified as three—the Mind Series, Expanse Series, and Pith Instructions Series.

According to Longchenpa, the view of the Mind Series is to be free from all extremes of factors to be relinquished, because all phenomena do not exist outside of mind as such. Based on twenty-one major tantras (such as *Soaring Great Garuda*), this series has seven main distinctions, such as its result arising from nothing but mind.

The view of the Expanse Series, which is free from anything to be done, is to be free from all extremes of remedies, because all phenomena (the bearers of dharmatā) are contained and perfected in the expanse of Samantabhadrī (dharmatā). Said to be based on many tantras, such as *The Vast Array of the Expanse*, this series is classified as fourfold: (1) the black expanse of speaking in terms of the lack of causes, (2) the multicolored expanse of speaking in terms of diversity, (3) the white expanse of speaking in terms of mind, and (4) the infinite expanse of having passed beyond cause and result (with each of the first three being subdivided into three). The texts also speak of the nine expanses of the Expanse Series (for details of these nine, see note 268; according to Anspal 2005a, 89–91, the set of scriptures that was considered to make up the Expanse Series has been highly variable in different periods, has evolved significantly over time, and includes texts of substantially different character).

The view of the profound Pith Instructions Series is to be free from all extremes of both factors to be relinquished and remedies, because it is determined according to the actual way of being of the specific characteristics of the essential nature itself. This series is divided into three categories: (1) scattered instructions, (2) oral instructions, and (3) the texts of the tantras themselves, which are subdivided into four cycles: (a) the Outer Cycle that resembles the body, (b) the Inner Cycle that resembles the eyes, (c) the Secret Cycle that resembles the heart, and (d) the Unsurpassable Ultimately Secret Cycle that resembles everything being complete. In particular, the view of the fourth cycle is that since its essence is not a knowable object, it does not depend on a knower. Since its nature is seen directly, dharmatā does not remain an assumption. Through the four visions that are its characteristics, the original expanse of the ground is arrived at in this very lifetime, without any hope for a result at a later time (for more detailed descriptions of these four cycles, see Longchen Rabjam 1989, 64–66).

The Unsurpassable Ultimately Secret Cycle, to which the teachings in *The Aspiration Prayer* belong, is based on the famous Seventeen Tantras—from *The Tantra of the Universes and Transformations of Sound* as the root tantra, the following further tantras derive: *Self-Arising Awareness, Awareness Free In Itself, Self-Arising Perfect Power, The Lion's Perfect Prowess, Auspicious Beauty, The Array of Inlaid Gems, The Garland of Pearls, Without Letters, The Mirror of Samantabhadra's Mind, The Mirror of Vajrasattva's Heart, The Kiss of the Sun and the Moon, The Pure Realm Adorned with Precious Introductions, Glorious Spaceless Blazing Relics, Mound of Jewels, Blazing Lamp*, and *The Sixfold Expanse*. To this list, Śrī Siṃha (Thondup 1996, 362) adds *The Tantra of the Mantra Protectress Wrathful One*, while Padmasambhava adds *The Blazing Sun of the Luminous Expanse of Samantabhadrī*. Thus, one also finds lists of eighteen or even nineteen tantras of this cycle.

The pith instructions that comment on the first eighteen tantras listed above are contained in the *Vima Nyingtig*, transmitted by Vimalamitra (revealed by Shangdön Dashi Dorjé in the twelfth century), while the pith instructions on *The Blazing Sun of the Luminous Expanse of Samantabhadrī* as transmitted by Padmasambhava are known as the *Khandro Nyingtig*, revealed by Pema Ledreltsal (Tib. Padma las 'brel rtsal; born 1248). Longchenpa's main works include his famous seven treasuries (*The Precious Treasury of Wish-Fulfillment, The Precious Treasury of Pith Instructions, The Precious Treasury of Philosophical Systems, The Precious Treasury of the Supreme Yāna, The Precious Treasury of Words and Their Meanings, The Precious Treasury of the Dharmadhātu*, and *The Precious Treasury of the Basic Nature*), the *Trilogy of Resting at Ease* (Tib. *Ngal gso skor gsum*), the *Trilogy of Being Free In Itself* (Tib. *Rang grol skor gsum*), and the *Trilogy of the Innermost Essence* (Tib. *Yang thig skor gsum*), which is part of the *Fourfold Heart Essence* (Tib. *Snying thig ya bzhi*). For an overview of these texts by Longchenpa, see Higgins 2013 (50–52). Jigmé Lingpa's major works include *The Heart Essence of the Great Expanse* (Tib. *Klong chen snying thig*), *Wisdom Guru* (Tib. *Ye shes bla ma*), and *The Treasury of Precious Qualities* (Tib. *Yon tan rin po che'i mdzod*). For details on the nine yānas, see Kongtrul Lodrö Tayé 2005 (301–57). For details on the main lineages of Dzogchen, see Bdud 'joms 'jigs bral ye shes rdo rje 1991 (447–57 and 538–880), Thondup 1996 (48ff), Nyoshul Khenpo 2005, Kongtrul Lodrö Tayé 2010 (183–96 and 324–32), and Jigme Lingpa and Kangyur Rinpoche 2013 (323–31). For lists of the eighteen, twenty, or twenty-one tantras of the Mind Series and some major tantras of the Expanse Series, as well as more details on most of the above texts, see Longchen Rabjam 1989 (32–35) and 2007 (333–36 and 364–77), Nyoshul Khenpo 2005 (559–65), and Lopez 2018.

22 Klong chen rab 'byams pa dri med 'od zer 1999a?, 214–15. In general, my translations of quotes from the Seventeen Tantras follow Anonymous 1973–77, here 1:545–46.

23 Tib. *rang ngo shes pa* can be read as any of these three related meanings. I usually chose the more poetic rendering "recognizing its own face" throughout because *The Aspiration Prayer* is a poem and this rendering implicitly includes the other two meanings. Also, sometimes the honorific term *rang zahl* is used for *rang ngo*, which clearly means "own face" and not "own essence."

24 The *Longchen Nyingtig* represents one of the most popular collections of treasure texts and commentaries, revealed and authored by Jigmé Lingpa.

25 Usually, the Tibetan term for "unawareness" (*ma rig pa*) is rendered as "ignorance." However, since it is the direct opposite of the most crucial Dzogchen notion of "awareness" (*rig pa*) and thus is simply the failure to recognize this primordial basic awareness just as it is, I render the term throughout as "unawareness."

26 The three terms "dynamic energy" (Tib. *rtsal*), "play" (Tib. *rol pa*), and "radiance" (Tib. *gdangs*) are often connected with all three or one of the aspects of mind's true nature (essence, nature, and compassionate responsiveness), awareness, the primordial ground, or its ground manifestations in a general manner. They are also often used as synonyms and sometimes combined (such as *rtsal gyi rol pa* or *gdangs kyi rtsal*). *Gdangs* usually means "tone," "pitch," "manner of doing," and "manner of functioning." However, in the Great Perfection, it is used in the sense of "radiance." Thus, it is similar in meaning to *mdangs* ("glow") or sometimes simply a misspelling of the latter. As Germano (1992, 866) points out, these two terms as well as "dynamic energy" (Tib. *rtsal*), "play" (Tib. *rol pa*), and "adornment" (Tib. *rgyan*) "are all highly technical terms used to describe the way in which the entire macrocosmic and microcosmic Universe derives from awareness, and as such are clearly defined and differentiated by Longchenpa. While these five terms are used in a variety of ways in previous texts such that their mutual relationships and differences become quite blurred, Longchenpa's typical terminological precision is quite clear in his use of these terms as well as in his incisive innovative explanations of

each. However, only a full analysis would do this issue justice." According to Germano, Longchenpa strictly differentiates between "glow" (*mdangs*) and "radiance" (*gdangs*), with the former signifying a nonmanifest internal glowing that is associated with "inner luminosity" (Tib. *nang gsal*; the nonmanifest innate potential of the ground), while the latter indicates the externally manifest radiance as the actualized forms that are associated with "outer luminosity" (Tib. *phyir gsal*; the ground manifestations as the seeming "exteriorization" of the ground's innate dynamic qualities; see appendix 2B).

Still, it seems that Longchenpa is not always consistent in applying this distinction, and other Dzogchen authors clearly do not make such a distinction at all. According to Namkhai Norbu (1996, 54–55 and 2006, 68–70), among the three characteristics of the ground (essence, nature, and compassionate responsiveness), it is primarily compassionate responsiveness that manifests as radiance, play, and dynamic energy, and these three terms are explained in terms of how compassionate responsiveness manifests as saṃsāra or the qualities of awakening:

(1) In its dharmakāya aspect, compassionate responsiveness is called "radiance." During meditative equipoise, the compassionate responsiveness of the ground manifests like a crystal ball. If such a globe is placed on a red surface, it appears red, while it appears blue on a blue surface, and so on. However, its own basic state of being pure and transparent never changes into any of these colors. Similarly, when resting in meditative equipoise in awareness, it is not altered or influenced by any conditions extrinsic to it. Thus, the natural condition of compassionate responsiveness in itself remains the same no matter how it may manifest. Sometimes, "adornment" is used instead of "radiance" because in meditative equipoise all manifestations of compassionate responsiveness are perceived as adornments of the primordial state of the ground.

(2) In its sambhogakāya aspect, compassionate responsiveness shows as its "play" or "playful display," which is illustrated by rainbow-colored lights appearing within a crystal ball. Likewise, the compassionate responsiveness of the primordial ground is able to manifest within its own dimension "subjectively." This happens, for example, in the intermediate state between two lives when the hundred peaceful and wrathful deities appear for those with prior training: these deities are not external entities but manifestations of the ground's innately present qualities. Another example for compassionate responsiveness's play is a mirror and its reflections. Whatever is in front of a mirror is immediately and unimpededly reflected in it. However, yogic practitioners are not influenced or conditioned by what appears in the mirror of awareness because they understand that whatever appears is only a mental reflection and not something real or external. Just as a mirror does not care about or react to reflections that we

deem good or bad, beautiful or ugly, ultimately, there is no difference whatsoever between any of the reflections that are simply the dynamic play or display of awareness's compassionate responsiveness. Anything can appear but nothing has any independent reality—within awareness, everything is self-arising and free in itself.

(3) In its nirmāṇakāya aspect, compassionate responsiveness is referred to as "dynamic energy" or "creative display." This is exemplified by a crystal that is struck by the rays of the sun. Such a crystal, which in itself is completely pure and transparent, refracts these rays and projects infinite rainbow-colored displays of light onto the walls of the room in which it is placed. These displays of light are not inherent to the crystal itself but manifest when the secondary condition of sun rays is present. Also, none of these displays appear inside of the crystal: though they arise from it, they are only visible outside of it. The crystal symbolizes the primordial ground consisting of essence, nature, and compassionate responsiveness. The light displays in the room stand for compassionate responsiveness's natural manifestations, which look like external objects when not recognized for what they are. Thus, through not recognizing this dynamic energy of the ground's compassionate responsiveness, all impure appearances of saṃsāra arise as if they involved the duality of subject and object. On the other hand, when recognized through skillful techniques such as Cutting through Solidity and Direct Leap, this dynamic energy manifests as the expression of the ground's original qualities in its pure form and thus leads back to its very source, the ground itself as undifferentiated and nondual primordial awareness. In this way, the cause of both saṃsāra and nirvāṇa is the single manifestation of the luminosity of the primordial ground.

27 This could also be read as "the tantras of ground, path, and fruition." The ground tantra consists of buddha nature, basic awareness, or the mind of Samantabhadra, while the fruition tantra is buddhahood or the dharmakāya. This threefold classification of tantra is also found in the *Guhyasamājatantra* and is similar to the classification of causal tantra, method tantra, and resultant tantra that is used in the new translation schools, particularly in the Sakya Lamdré system (Tib. *lam 'bras*).

28 Here and in the following two instances, some versions of this text say *rtogs* instead of *rtog*. However, as the last line of this quote makes clear, the text speaks of mistaken thoughts about what Samantabhadra is and not any kind of realization.

29 'Jigs med gling pa mkhyen brtse 'od zer 1973, 3:97–98 and 100–101.

30 Ibid., 3:84. "Contaminated virtue" is any virtue of body, speech, and mind that is based on dualistic perception, clinging to a self, and the ensuing basic afflictions and karmic actions.

31 The Tibetan for "diverging" literally says "separating their backs" (*rgyab gyes*), somewhat similar to Siamese twins being separated into two individual bodies.

32 Ibid., 3:79–80.

33 The eight gateways of innate presence are the inner mechanism of the emergence of the ground manifestations from the alpha-pure potency of the primordial ground. These eight are often further classified as the six manifestations (or modes of appearing) and the two gateways through which these manifestations may pass. That is, awareness manifests from within the ground as (1) compassion, (2) light, (3) kāyas, (4) wisdom, (5) nonduality, and (6) freedom from extremes, while the two gateways are those to (7) impure saṃsāra and (8) pure nirvāṇa. Thus, the two gateways represent the two possibilities to interpret the six manifestations, which hinge upon awareness's recognition or nonrecognition of its own self-appearances. If awareness recognizes this sixfold efflorescence as its own self-arising dynamic energy or display, the six manifestations pass through the gateway to nirvāṇa. If awareness fails to recognize this display as its own self-arising appearances, these manifestations pass through the gateway to saṃsāra, which means that the six manifestations of innate presence become systematically mistaken as the six realms of beings and become increasingly solidified. In the case of awareness's self-recognition, the eight gateways immediately reverse into a corresponding eightfold dissolution as the entire unfolding of outer luminosity returns to inner luminosity as the full awareness of awakening. This is what is referred to as "Samantabhadra's mode of freedom" (see appendix 2C). In the case of nonrecognition, the five lights of innate presence become solidified and distorted as the corresponding five material elements and so on, which represents "the delusion of sentient beings" (for more details, see appendices 2A–B, 3A, and 4B).

34 Tib. *sangs rgyas* is the rendering of "buddha(hood)."

35 Klong chen rab 'byams pa dri med 'od zer 1999b?, 35–36. For more details and descriptions of the six distinctive features of Samantabhadra's freedom, see appendix 2C. "Inner luminosity" refers to the nonmanifest innate potential of the ground, while "outer luminosity" refers to the ground manifestations as the seeming "exteriorization" of the ground's innate dynamic qualities (see appendix 2B).

36 Tib. Padma las 'brel rtsal (born 1248).

37 As translated in Longchen Rabjam 1989, 63. As here, Dzogchen texts sometimes speak of "freedom and delusion" (as opposed to the reverse order "delusion and freedom"), in particular with regard to the primordial ground of both because freedom is what is supposed to manifest naturally or first through the self-recognition of the ground manifestations as what they truly are before any kind of delusion or nonrecognition can arise. This

is what the notion of Samantabhadra's freedom is all about (see part 1 and appendix 2C).

38 Tib. *gzhi snang*. Depending on how this compound term is grammatically unraveled, it could more literally be translated as "the ground's appearance(s)," "the appearance(s) of the ground" (*gzhi'i snang ba*), "appearance(s) within the ground" (*gzhir snang ba*), or "appearance(s) from (within) the ground" (*gzhi nas/las snang ba*). Elsewhere in Longchenpa's writings, the forms *gzhi'i snang ba* and *gzhir snang ba* are attested. For details on the nature of the ground manifestations and their relationship with the ground, see appendix 2B. In addition, as Germano (1992, 893) points out, Longchenpa explains the triad of ground manifestations, path manifestations (Tib. *lam snang*), and fruition manifestations (Tib. *'bras snang*). The ground manifestations appear as the ground's or awareness's own manifestations at its primordial level or in the intermediate state, when the ground is not yet recognized. The path manifestations represent the experiences, visions, and realizations that appear after basic awareness has been introduced by a guru. The fruition manifestations consist of the full-fledged appearance of the three kāyas.

39 That is, everything that appears as if it were something other than just the ground's very own self-appearances.

40 That is, the ground manifestations are immediately recognized for what they are—the ground's very own self-appearances or display—versus being misperceived as objects that are something other than the ground, which is the beginning of saṃsāric dualistic delusion. Gangteng Tulku Rinpoche (2003, 79) compares this to the situation when humans and dogs look into a mirror: humans immediately recognize themselves, whereas dogs do not. Rather, they perceive their own reflection as being another dog and act accordingly.

41 The three dharmas here are essence, nature, and compassionate responsiveness.

42 *Lamp*, fols. 9a.6–10a.4.

43 The Sanskrit (*vidhūtakalpanājālagambhīrodāramūrtaye / namaḥ samantabhadrāya samantaspharaṇatviṣe //*) and the Tibetan (*rtog pa'i dra ba rnam bsal cing / zab cing rgya che'i sku mnga' ba / kun tu bzang po'i 'od zer dag kun nas 'phro la phyag 'tshal lo //*) of this verse can be read in several ways. My translation primarily follows Śākyabuddhi's commentary, which has two ways of commenting on this verse, linking it to the four or three kāyas, respectively. In both cases, "pervasively radiating brilliance" stands for Samantabhadra's enlightened activity. Following the Tibetan, the verse would read something like:

I pay homage to the pervasively radiating
Brilliance of Samantabhadra
Who dispelled the web of thoughts
And possesses the profound and vast kāyas.

44 Besides "awareness," "self-arising wisdom" (Tib. *rang byung ye shes*) is arguably one of the most important Dzogchen terms for the ultimate nature of the mind. It is self-arising because it occurs effortlessly and naturally on its own without ever depending on anything else, such as being produced by other causes or contrivances. It is primordial (*ye*) because it has always been innately present since time without beginning. It is cognizant or knowing (*shes*) because it is the innate naturally lucid state of awareness that is empty of dichotomies such as subject and object, self and other, and lucid and nonlucid. It is self-awareness (Tib. *rang rig*) because it is devoid of any kind of awareness of anything that is other than itself (Tib. *gzhan rig*). Dzogchen texts usually distinguish between this primordial self-arising wisdom and the kinds of wisdoms that are not considered to be self-arising but expressions of the dynamic energy of primordial awareness. The latter include the sambhogakāya wisdom of apprehending characteristics, the nirmāṇakāya wisdom of pervading all objects, the two wisdoms of knowing suchness and variety, and the five wisdoms (such as mirror-like wisdom) that represent the fundamental change of the eight consciousnesses (or the five primary afflictions) and thus are impermanent and involve modulations through conditions and/or objects (for details on the classifications of these and other kinds of wisdom, see appendices 5B and 6).

45 I.28. For a number of comments on this famous verse, see Brunnhölzl 2014, 356–57, 560–62, and 855–99.

46 Anonymous 1973–77 (1:244–45) glosses these five aspects of Samantabhadra as follows:

> (1) The nature of our own awareness is light. Since the kāyas are included in the spaciousness of wisdom, the actuality of Samantabhadra's view is realized. This refers to awareness and the wisdom that arises from awareness. Awareness is free from the extremes of dualistic appearances and beyond being a plurality [but] not beyond being the essence of cognizing and being aware. Free from any extremes of entities, it is empty with a heart of wisdom. (2) Awareness is adorned by being empty, being empty is adorned by wisdom, wisdom is adorned by light, light is adorned by distinct lucidity, and lucidity is adorned by the inseparability of the three kāyas. It does not go beyond the essence of the three kāyas. (3) Having emanated kāyas in the manner of teachers in the realm Akaniṣṭha, these appear accordingly for the welfare of beings. The three kāyas are without emanating and not emanating, and they appear like that to sentient beings. (4) Awareness free from unawareness, buddhahood free from mind, dharmakāya free from mentation, wisdom free from breath, light's brilliance free from the elements: awareness has the character of the

kāyas—it is the unimpeded wisdom arising from the kāyas, has the character of prajñā, and is awareness free from thinking. (5) Awareness being unborn is realized as the dharmakāya. Awareness being luminous is realized as the sambhogakāya. Awareness's appearing as anything whatsoever is realized as the nirmāṇakāya. In awareness's essence of being the single sphere, it is realized as the inseparability of the three kāyas.

Dzogchen Ponlop Rinpoche (2002, 30–32) explains the five aspects as (1) the teacher (the three kāyas), (2) adornment (the teachings as the ornaments of the teacher Samantabhadra are just as pure as the primordially pure state of this teacher), (3) the path (taking the fruition as the path means that the path is not a cause that produces the fruition but is in itself the completely pure fruition), (4) awareness (the nature of our own mind—the primordial buddha within—that is to be realized on the path and is the same in Buddha Samantabhadra and any practitioner on the path), and (5) realization (the primordially pure realization of that awareness, which is nothing other than the primordial ground, is the fruition, which is thus nothing new).

47 As here, in the Great Perfection in general and the Mind Series in particular, (ultimate) bodhicitta is often used in its ultimate sense as an equivalent of primordial awareness, self-arising wisdom, the primordial ground, luminosity, awakening, and so on. *Buddhahood Without Meditation* revealed by Düjom Lingpa (Bdud 'joms gling pa 2004, 345) glosses "ultimate bodhicitta" (Tib. *don dam byang chub kyi sems*) as one of six synonyms of Dzogchen as follows: "It is the heart of the matter (*don*) because it is present as the final mode of being of all phenomena. It is genuine because it represents the highest to be realized (*dam*). It is the purity (*byang*) of all flaws and stains. It is the all-embracing consummation (*'ub chub*) of all the qualities of the kāyas, the wisdoms, the path, and the fruition. It is *citta* or the heart, that is, mind (*sems*) because it abides as the ground of the arising of everything as all kinds of displays of purity and equality—the sole life force of the three vajras."

48 "Container" and "contents" refer to the inanimate universe and its sentient inhabitants, respectively.

49 Tib. *sems nyid*. Especially in the Tibetan Mahāmudrā, Dzogchen, and *dohā* traditions, this term refers to mind's true ultimate nature (Tib. *sems kyi chos nyid* or *sems kyi de kho na nyid*), as opposed to the ordinary dualistic "mind" (Tib. *sems*); for details, see Higgins (2013, 79–86). As Higgins points out, "it is doubtful that *sems nyid* owes its origin or popularity to any Indian equivalent." Indeed, the most likely candidate, *cittatā*, is not attested anywhere (in the *Abhisamayālaṃkārālokā*, there is an instance of *nges 'byung sems nyid* rendering *naiṣkramyacittatvaṃ*, but this of course does not refer to mind's ultimate nature). Furthermore, Higgins presents

a number of cases in which *sems nyid* simply renders *citta* in the original Apabhraṃśa or Sanskrit. There is also a case of *sems nyid* rendering *caitanya* (a term for consciousness or spirit associated with Vaiṣṇavism and Sāṃkhya). Of course, the distinction between *sems* and *sems nyid* (or a potential one between *citta* and *cittatā*) closely parallels the one between *dharma* and *dharmatā*. However, as Higgins says, no evidence for the latter distinction serving as a model for the former has come to light so far.

50 Klong chen rab 'byams pa dri med 'od zer 1999a?, 216–19. The last quote is Anonymous 1973–77 (1:546–47); Longchenpa omits "by all" in the last line.

51 This is in contradistinction to depictions of sambhogakāya or nirmāṇakāya buddhas, who wear either the typical silken and golden ornaments of the sambhogakāya attire or the monastic attire of a nirmāṇakāya. The explanation for the fact that Vajradhara, the original buddha of the new translation schools of Tibetan Buddhism who also represents the dharmakāya, does wear the attire of a sambhogakāya buddha is that in his case this attire symbolizes that of a king, as opposed to the similar one of sambhogakāya buddhas, which stands for the attire of a prince or princess.

52 Compare Jigmé Lingpa's *Differentiating the Three Essential Points of Dzogchen* ('Jigs med gling pa mkhyen brtse 'od zer 1973, 3:118):

> Awareness is without support and all-pervasive.
> It is empty and provides room, just like the expanse of space.
> It is lucid and nonconceptual, similar to a polished clear crystal.

53 Along these lines, it is also sometimes said that Prajñāpāramitā—who embodies the ultimate realization of emptiness as the mother of the four kinds of noble ones (buddhas, bodhisattvas, śrāvaka arhats, and pratyekabuddha arhats) as well as the literature of the prajñāpāramitā sūtras—is the external emanation of Samantabhadrī. Likewise, Samantabhadrī is said to have emanated as Vajravārāhī and taught the mother tantras of the Vajrayāna.

54 It is common nowadays to speak of female buddhas in union with their male counterparts or both as "consorts." In the original texts, male and female buddhas in union are referred to as "Father" and "Mother": though they are obviously not physical parents, they are the parents of the birth of awakening in all its forms and levels. For details on the maṇḍala of the one hundred peaceful and wrathful deities, see *Ketaka* on the pertinent verses of the *Aspiration Prayer*.

55 Tib. Rig 'dzin rgod kyi ldem 'phru can dngos grub rgyal mtshan.

56 Tib. Zang zang lha brag ("Copper-Colored Divine Rock").

In contrast to the Northern Treasures (Tib. Byang gter), the Southern Treasures (Tib. Lho gter) refer to the treasures revealed by a number of persons, such as Nyangrel Nyima Öser (Tib. Nyang ral nyi ma 'od zer; 1136–1204), Guru Chöwang (Tib. Gu ru Chos kyi dbang phyug;

1212–70), Orgyen Pema Lingpa (Tib. O rgyan padma gling pa; 1450–1521), and Terdag Lingpa Gyurmé Dorjé (Tib. Gter bdag gling pa 'gyur med rdo rje; 1646–1714; first throneholder of Minling Monastery). Nyangrel Nyima Öser, Guru Chöwang, and Rigdzin Gödemchen are called "the three supreme nirmāṇakāyas" (Tib. *mchog gi sprul sku gsum*), that is, emanations of Padmasambhava's body, speech, and mind, respectively. In addition, Nyangrel Nyima Öser, Guru Chöwang, and Orgyen Pema Lingpa are three among "the five kingly treasure revealers" (Tib. *gter ston rgyal po lnga*). The remaining two are Dorjé Lingpa (Tib. Rdo rje gling pa; 1346–1405) and Jamyang Kyentsé Wangpo (Tib. 'Jam dbyangs mkhyen brtse dbang po; 1820–92), with all five being considered emanations of King Trisong Detsen (Tib. Khri srong lde btsan; 742–800).

As the colophon of *Lamp* indicates, another reason for calling this collection "Northern Treasures" is that the place of its revelation lies to the North of Samyé, Tibet's first monastery, which is a place of central importance for all Tibetans and the Nyingma School in particular.

57 Tib. Bkra bzang.

58 Tib. Sna nam rdo rje bdud 'joms.

59 Tib. Mang lam ri khrod pa bzang po grags pa.

60 Tib. Rgyang yon po lung (about 100 km southeast of Mount Trasang).

61 The full title of this collection of seven prayers that include many profound pith instructions is *The Vajra Speech of Oḍḍiyāna Guru Padmasambhava, The Supplications of Nondelusion in Seven Chapters* (Tib. *O rgyan gu ru padma 'byung gnas kyis rdo rje'i gsungs 'khrul pa med pa'i gsol 'debs le'u bdun ma;* in short *le'u bdun ma*). The seven prayers in it are (1) *The Supplication to the Three-Kāya Guru*; (2)–(6) the supplications requested by King Trisong Detsen, Yeshé Tsogyal (Tib. Ye shes mtsho rgyal), Namké Nyingpo (Tib. Nam mkha'i snying po), Nanam Dorjé Düjom, and Prince Mutri Tsenpo (Tib. Mu khri btsan po), respectively; and (7) *The Supplication that Effortlessly Fulfills All Intentions*. For English translations, see *The Seven Chapters of Prayer*, translated by Chhimed Rigdzin Rinpoche and James Low (Berlin: Wandel Verlag, 2010) and http://www.lotsawahouse.org/topics/leu-dunma/.

62 Tib. Ston pa bsod nams dbang phyug.

63 Tib. Gung thang.

64 This place was henceforth called "Windy Hollow" (Tib. Rlung gseng).

65 Tib. Zang zang lha brag brag ri dug sbrul spungs 'dra ba. This place is located about 200 km north of Mount Everest.

66 Tib. Byang la stod.

67 Tib. *phur ba*.

68 Tib. *Kun bzang dgongs pa zang thal*. The title of this tantra contains two Tibetan words with a wide range of meanings. *Dgongs pa* is an honorific term for "mind," "thinking," "realization," "wisdom," "consideration,"

"viewpoint," and "intention." The *Tantra that Teaches the Great Perfection as Samantabhadra's Unobstructed Awakened Mind*, in which *The Aspiration Prayer of Samantabhadra* appears, glosses *zang thal* as "a phenomenon that is directly visible" (Rgod kyi ldem 'phru can dngos grub rgyal mtshan 1973b, 90). Thus, the term's main meaning here appears to be "unobstructed" (or "unimpeded" or "unobscured"), while it may also be understood as "all-pervasive" (or "all-penetrating"). Still, the term is also variously translated as "transparent," "translucent," "pellucid," "totally open," "wide-open," "all-embracing," "free," "traversing freely," "openness," "clarity," and "substanceless," as well as combinations of these words. Thus, though I chose the rendering "unobstructed awakened mind" for *dgongs pa zang thal*, this Tibetan expression is impossible to translate in any single manner that includes all of the above meanings. In essence, "Samantabhadra's unobstructed awakened mind" is another expression for what was described above as Samantabhadra's freedom—awareness's unimpeded and all-pervasive self-recognition and innate natural state of being free in and of itself. For additional explanations on this in the root tantra of *Samantabhadra's Unobstructed Awakened Mind*, see chapter 6.

Besides the foremost root treasure of *Samantabhadra's Unobstructed Awakened Mind*, the Northern Treasures contain six more root treasures: (1) *The Fierce Self-Arising and Self-Appearing Eight Great Sādhana Teachings of the Northern Treasures* (Tib. *Byang gter sgrub chen bka' brgyad drag po rang byung rang shar*; the eight chief yidam deities of Mahāyoga), (2) *The Black Garuda of the Northern Treasures* (Tib. *Byang gter khyung nag*), (3) *The Three Cycles of Practice of the Northern Treasures* (Tib. *Byang gter sgrub skor rnam gsum*), (4) *The Heart Practice of the Northern Treasures* (Tib. *Byang gter thugs sgrub*), (5) *The Practice of the Lineage of Awareness Holders of the Northern Treasures* (Tib. *Byang gter rig 'dzin gdung sgrub*), and (6) *The Root Volume of Noble Great Compassionate Avalokiteśvara [in his Form Called] Freedom of all Beings of the Northern Treasures* (Tib. *Byang gter 'phags pa thugs rje chen po spyan ras gzigs 'gro ba kun grol gyi rtsa pod*). In addition, there is the one-volume cycle *Self-Arising Self-Emergent Alpha-Purity* (Tib. *Ka dag rang byung rang shar*), which together with the four volumes of *Samantabhadra's Unobstructed Awakened Mind* makes up the Dzogchen portion of the Northern Treasures (for more details on the cycles of this treasure collection, see Turpeinen 2016, 21ff. and Boord 1993 and 2013). As mentioned before, the Northern Treasures also contain the famous supplications to Padmasambhava in seven chapters (Tib. *gsol 'debs le'u bdun ma*).

Generally, the collection of the Northern Treasures is considered one of the, if not the, most important and profound among the old treasure collections (as opposed to the new treasures such as Chogling Tersar and Düjom Tersar). As Turpeinen (2016, 159) says:

> The transmission of the Dzokchen teachings of the anthology is highly sought-after, because it is regarded as a particularly sacred and potent system of practice that is usually practiced after studying other Great Perfection systems ... Even though the essence of the practices is considered to be the same, The Unimpeded Realization is ranked high in the Great Perfection context, and one reason for this is clearly the way the texts on contemplation are written: they are concise, to the point, and dynamic. Reading many of the texts evokes the ambiance of receiving a direct oral transmission at the feet of a master, and the dialogical format of the tantras and dialogue texts enhances the effect. Another reason for the anthology's reputation of profundity may be the integration of philosophy and contemplation, and the use of philosophical reflections on the nature of the mind, ground and dharmakāya as contemplations themselves in the practice of breakthrough [*khregs chod*].

In addition, it is said that the Northern Treasures were particularly designed to accomplish and preserve the happiness and well-being of the people of Tibet and to accomplish the original aspirations of King Trisong Detsen. Bdud 'joms 'jigs bral ye shes rdo rje 1991 (782) elaborates on this as follows:

> [T]his Northern Treasure ... contains ... everything that anyone might require for increasing the teaching, turning back invading armies, terminating infectious disease, the pacification of civil war, exorcism of Gongpo spirits, restoration of governmental authority, and the control of epidemics and plagues. It contains various ways to promote the happiness of Tibet ... and also the notices and keys for many sacred places and lands, foremost among which were seven great hidden lands. Therefore, this single treasure is universally known to resemble a minister who beneficially serves all Tibet and Kham.

69 Tib. Bla ma pad ma.
70 Tib. Rnam rgyal mgon po.
71 Tib. Rdo rje mgon po.
72 Tib. Thang stong rgyal po. His birth date is given as either 1361 or 1385, while the year of his death is variously presented as 1480, 1485, or 1486.
73 Tib. *sbas yul*.
74 For a detailed account of this, see Sardar-Afkhami 2001, 66–93.
75 Tib. Se bkra bzang.
76 Tib. Se ston bla ma.

77 Tib. Legs ldan rdo rje. His dates are as given by Valentine 2015 (BDRC has 1512–1625? and another source says 1452–1565).

78 Tib. Ngag gi dbang po.

79 Tib. Thub bstan rdo rje brag e wam lcog sgra. This monastery was located in the Lhoka (Tib. Lho ka) region of southern Central Tibet (about 50 km south of Lhasa) and completely destroyed during the Chinese invasion.

80 The second main Nyingma seat in Central Tibet is Mindröl Ling (Tib. Smin grol gling), while Dzogchen (Tib. Rdzogs chen), Shechen (Tib. Zhe chen), Katog (Tib. Kaḥ thog), and Béyül (Tib. Dpal yul) are all located in eastern Tibet. For more details on Rigdzin Gödemchen and his lineage, as well as the history and the contents of the Northern Treasures, see Bdud 'joms 'jigs bral ye shes rdo rje 1991 (780–83), Boord 1993 and 2013, Herweg 1994, Valentine 2013, 2015, and 2016, Turpeinen 2016, http://treasuryoflives.org/biographies/view/Rigdzin-Godemchen-Ngodrub-Gyeltsen/7767, and http://rywiki.tsadra.org/index.php/Jangter.

81 The current tenth Dorjé Tra Rigdzin, Tubten Jigmé Namdröl Gyatso (Tib. Thub bstan 'jigs med rnam grol rgya mtsho; born 1936), still lives in Tibet.

82 Tib. Stag lung rtse sprul rin po che.

83 Tib. Thub bstan rdo rje brag e vam lcog sgar chos 'khor rnam rgyal gling.

84 For a detailed discussion of the structure and contents of this cycle in its entirety, see Turpeinen 2016 (mainly chapters 2–5).

The Tibetan term for Cutting through Solidity, *khregs chod*, is usually explained in one of two ways. *Khregs* refers to something hard, solid, or rigid (all the delusions and habitual patterns of the dualistic mind), while *chod pa* is taken to mean "to (forcefully) cut through" or "to sever" (though it is actually an intransitive verb meaning "to be severed" or "to be interrupted"). The other interpretation refers to a bundle (*khregs*) that is untied or undone (*chod*), such as when the twine around a bale of hay is removed or cut through and the straws of hay just fall naturally wherever and however they may fall.

In the term *thod rgal*, or Direct Leap, *thod pa* means "skull" or "summit" and *rgal ba* "to cross." Thus, it is taken to mean "direct leap" or "direct crossing" (in the sense of directly leaping over a skull rather than walking around it or leaping to a distant destination in one bound rather than walking there step by step), "crossing the bridge that separates saṃsāra from nirvāṇa during the time one has a skull (i.e., is alive)," or "crossing the summit (of a mountain rather than walking around it)." Yet another interpretation is that *thod pa* means "forehead" and *rgal ba* "beyond," thus indicating the four visions of this practice as they appear in the space in front of one's eyes.

85 Tib. *Rdzogs pa chen po kun tu bzang po'i dgongs pa zang thal du bstan pa'i rgyud* (Rgod kyi ldem 'phru can dngos grub rgyal mtshan 1973b).

86 Tib. *Sems can la sangs rgyas kun tu bzang po'i dgongs pa zang thal du bstan pa'i rgyud* (Rgod kyi ldem 'phru can dngos grub rgyal mtshan 1973a).
87 Ibid., 410–11.
88 The term "conceit" (Tib. *snyems byed*) here specifically refers to apprehending and clinging to a self, which triggers all kinds of appearances of delusion, instead of recognizing the self-appearances of the ground as what they are.
89 Ibid., 411–12. As Higgins (2013, 205) points out, some may object that the single ground cannot serve as the support or cause of the two dissimilar appearances of saṃsāra and nirvāṇa because a singular cause cannot produce two opposite results. Longchenpa answers with the example of the Buddha's cousin Devadatta who appears as a friend to some and an enemy to others, while not being established in any way as either friend or enemy. Similarly, the ground can be perceived as saṃsāra or nirvāṇa while in itself not being established as either.
90 Rgod kyi ldem 'phru can dngos grub rgyal mtshan 1973a, 412–13.
91 Ibid., 419.
92 Ibid., 421–22.
93 Tib. *Rdzogs pa chen po kun tu bzang po'i dgongs pa zang thal gyi rgyud chen mthong ba dang thos pa dang btags pa dang smon lam btab pa tsam gyis sangs rgya ba'i rgyud.* As for "becoming a buddha merely through seeing, hearing, and wearing," see "the five (or six) methods that lead to freedom without the need for meditation" (a.k.a. "the six freedoms") in appendix 7.
94 Tib. *Rgyal ba thams cad kyi dgongs pa ye shes rang chas rig pa 'od du 'bar ba bstan pa'i rgyud.*
95 In that vein, the opening passage of the tantra says: "I pay homage to the primal one of all buddhas, glorious Samantabhadra, who teaches the heart of all Dharmas of the teaching as Samantabhadra's unobstructed awakened mind." Note that Samantabhadra is also referred to as "Buddha Changeless Light" (Tib. Sangs rgyas 'od mi 'gyur ba) in this text.
96 Tib. Smon lam stobs po che.
97 Actually, *aspirare* is the Italian word, while the French is *aspirer*, which means "to breathe in" (as well as "to aspire"), though this does not alter the basic meaning of what is said here.
98 http://www.buddhisma2z.com/content.php?id=15.
99 The Tibetan literally means "path of aspiration."
100 Krang dbyi sun et al. 1985, 2175. The definition of "aspiration" here matches the one in *Webster's Third New International Dictionary*: "a strong desire for realization." Other English renderings of *smon lam* by various translators include "aspiration," "aspiration vow," "prayer," "prayer vow," "wish-granting prayer," "supplication," "invocation," "wish," "resolve," "resolution," "commitment," and "vow." The Sanskrit equivalent *praṇidhāna* means "prayer" and "vow" but can also mean "application,"

"access," "entrance," "exertion," "endeavor," "respectful conduct," "attention," "profound religious meditation," "abstract contemplation," and "vehement desire."

101 XVIII.74–76 (Tibetan version 75–77).

102 D4034, fols. 128b.5–129b.5.

103 Asvabhāva's commentary (D4029, fol. 150b.3–4) says that aspiration prayers are impelled by wisdom because intention is transformed into, or dedicated for, wisdom.

104 According to Asvabhāva (ibid., fol. 150b.4), "immediate results" refers to desired goals that are accomplished immediately once bodhisattvas aspire for them.

105 These ten aspiration prayers that all bodhisattvas on the first bhūmi make are listed in the *Daśabhūmikasūtra* (H94, vol. ga, fols. 82b.4ff.) and explained in detail in Vasubandhu's commentary (D3993, fols. 137b.4ff.) as well as Abhayākaragupta's *Munimatālaṃkāra* (D3903, fols. 237a.4ff.). As Abhayākaragupta clarifies, since each of these ten aspiration prayers is very vast, all their details need to be accomplished gradually during the remaining nine bhūmis. In brief, he says, the first two aspiration prayers are for the sake of completing the accumulations of merit and wisdom, respectively. The following five are for the sake of maturing sentient beings. The last three are for the sake of realizing the distinctive features of one's own successively attained bhūmis, progressing to the final bhūmi of bodhisattvas, and reaching the consummation of everything. Furthermore, many sūtras and tantras, as well as a number of treatises in the Tengyur, contain other aspiration prayers of bodhisattvas, most famously the *Aspiration Prayer for Noble Excellent Conduct* (Tib. *'Phags pa bzang po spyod pa'i smon lam*) in the *Avataṃsakasūtra* (H94, vol. cha, fols. 336b.2–341a.4). There are also the ten pure aspiration prayers in the twenty-second chapter of the *Avataṃsakasūtra* (H94, vol. kha, fols. 48a.7–49b.4), the ten excellent aspiration prayers in the *Ratnameghasūtra* (H232, fols. 50b.7–53a.7), the ten kinds of aspiration prayers in the *Bodhisattvabhūmi* (D4037, fol. 145b.1–5), and many further brief and extensive aspiration prayers.

106 Brunnhölzl 2010, 609.

107 I.18ab.

108 Tib. *gsol 'debs*. This term can also mean "request," "invocation," "reverential petition," "appeal," "entreaty," "plea," and "imploration."

109 The remaining nine masteries are mastery over (1) life span (being able to live for infinite eons), (2) mind (firmly dwelling in samādhi through infinite wisdom), (3) necessities (displaying all worldly realms by blessing them with many embellishments), (4) karma (displaying karmic maturations just at the time when they can be blessed), (5) birth (displaying births everywhere in the worldly realms), (6) creative willpower (displaying all worldly realms as being completely filled with buddhas), (8) miraculous

powers (displaying all kinds of miraculous feats, such as going to all buddha realms), (9) Dharma (displaying the light of the Dharma doors without center and periphery), and (10) wisdom (displaying a buddha's powers, fearlessnesses, unique qualities, major and minor marks, and becoming completely perfectly awakened). Usually, it is said that these ten masteries are attained on the eighth bhūmi. However, even bodhisattvas on the lower bhūmis possess certain degrees of such masteries.

110 The first six pāramitās are generosity, discipline, patience, vigor, dhyāna, and prajñā. The last four pāramitās of means, aspiration prayers, power, and wisdom are considered to be branches or aids of the sixth pāramitā of prajñā and thus sometimes not taught separately.

111 These are eight types of inopportune birth in which one is not able to practice the Dharma: being born as a hell being, a hungry ghost, an animal, a long-lived god without discrimination in the fourth dhyāna level of the form realm, a human in a land without the Dharma, with incomplete faculties, with wrong views, or at a time when no buddhas have arrived and taught.

112 However, the tenth bhūmi is not actual completely perfect buddhahood yet. The display of the enlightened activity of tenth-bhūmi bodhisattvas appears to be equal to buddhas only from the perspective of ordinary beings as the recipients of this activity, but not from the perspective of those bodhisattvas as the performers of this activity. In fact, the difference between buddhas and bodhisattvas on the tenth bhūmi in terms of the extent and the power of their qualities (such as promoting the welfare of infinite sentient beings in infinite skillful ways) is said to be like the difference between the amounts of water held by the ocean and by the hoof print of an ox.

113 The fourfold discriminating awareness (Skt. *pratisaṃvid/-vedanā*, Tib. *so so yang dag par rig pa bzhi*) consists of the discriminating awareness of (1) dharmas (fully knowing the individual characteristics of all phenomena; or teaching the eighty-four thousand doors of Dharma as various remedial means in accordance with the different ways of thinking of sentient beings), (2) meanings (fully knowing the divisions and classifications of all phenomena, that is, knowing the meanings that are expressed by the words and statements about the general characteristics of phenomena—impermanence, suffering, emptiness, and identitylessness—and their ultimate characteristic—the lack of arising and ceasing), (3) semantics (knowing the languages, symbols, and terms of all the various kinds of sentient beings and being able to please them through this; being able to teach many meanings through a single word; and being free from words that are mistaken, rushed, or repetitive), and (4) self-confidence (being able to hear the Dharma from others and eliminate one's own doubts, explain the

Dharma to others and thus eliminate their doubts, and speak meaningfully, swiftly, without interruptions, and unimpededly).

114 Tib. *rdzogs smin sbyang.*

115 The Eighth Karmapa's commentary on the *Abhisamayālaṃkāra* (Brunnhölzl 2010, 557–59) elaborates on this as follows:

> (1) As for the full extent of the completion of aspiration prayers, what bodhisattvas actually aspire for is the permanent uninterrupted welfare of others by virtue of the two rūpakāyas for as long as there is no rising from dharmatā. However, this does not happen without having fully completed both accumulations. As for the reason for its happening once the two accumulations have been completed, the promotion of the welfare of those to be guided through the rūpakāyas without moving away from the dharmakāya takes place through the power of the fact of dwelling in dharmatā. Thus, in a mind stream of having thoroughly cultivated the two accumulations, it is feasible for the remedies of the obscurations to be produced. For the full completion of the remedies, one needs the full completion of the two accumulations, and in that case, the full completion of the remedies relinquishes the obscurations in a fully complete manner. Therefore, through the full completion of the two accumulations and the full completion of the remedies, the obscurations are completely relinquished. In this way, the relinquishment of everything that obscures this (that is, the rūpakāyas benefiting those to be guided without moving away from the dharmakāya, and thus the corresponding aspiration) is the full extent of having completed aspiration prayers. "If, once what obscures it is relinquished, the dharmakāya of engaging dharmatā promotes the welfare of others through the rūpakāyas not moving away from it, why is it not also doing the same at the time of the obscurations not having been relinquished?" Some say, "Through being obscured by the obscurations, any chance for the dharmakāya doing so is prevented." However, I do not think that the dharmakāya of engaging dharmatā does not perform the activities of the rūpakāyas even if the obscurations have not been relinquished. Since the dharmakāya that is dharmatā cannot be divided, no matter whether the obscurations have been relinquished or not, this principle is inconceivable. Others say, "But then it follows that sentient beings have completed the above aspiration prayers because the dharmakāya that is dharmatā in sentient beings performs the activities of having completed these aspiration prayers." There is no entailment—through the reason of the

dharmakāya that is dharmatā performing the activities of having completed these aspiration prayers, one is not able to prove that sentient beings (the bearers of dharmatā) perform the activities of having completed these aspiration prayers. Still, some may think, "In terms of those who complete these aspiration prayers that are taught here, completion refers to having been accomplished by some sentient beings because the accomplishment of these aspirations through the dharmakāya of engaging dharmatā does not qualify as the actual completion of aspiration prayers by someone who practices the path." Within the mind streams of bodhisattvas as those who practice the path, it is impossible for the completion of aspiration prayers through the dharmakāya, which is omnipresent dharmatā, to be completed through these bodhisattvas' own mind streams as something that is their own. Also, since bodhisattvas as the ones who practice the path cease after the end of the continuum of the ten bhūmis, how could it be possible for these bodhisattvas to complete these aspiration prayers? "But then it follows that the statement by others that bodhisattvas complete their aspiration prayers is nothing but words, while, ultimately, they are not able to complete their aspiration prayers." In terms of the definitive meaning, bodhisattvas themselves are not able to attain the completion of their aspiration prayers as something with which their own mind streams are endowed. However, as for those bodhisattvas who attained the power to eliminate all the many obscurations that obscure these very aspiration prayers which exist as being primordially complete through the dharmatākāya ["dharmakāya" is usually explained as being the abbreviation of "dharmatākāya"] of those bodhisattvas, they are able to free this completion of aspiration prayers through the dharmakāya from its obscurations. At that point, the termination of the obscurations (that from which this completion of aspiration prayers through the dharmakāya is to be freed) and the cessation of the bodhisattva (the one who frees it from its obscurations) are simultaneous. This is similar to fire arising from rubbing two sticks, in which case the burning of the sticks and the ceasing of the fire are simultaneous. It is this kind of activity that is referred to as "great bodhisattvas becoming truly complete buddhas through having completed their aspiration prayers," which is just stated in this way in terms of convenient worldly conventions. This approach here is the final position that is established through the fine examination of the definitive meaning, but for those with bad fortune, it remains an impenetrable secret. (2) As for the full extent of having matured sentient beings, this refers only to the kind of maturation that occurs under the influence of those beings to be guided for whom rūpakāyas are suitable to appear looking at these kāyas in any higher or lower sambhogakāya or nirmāṇakāya forms. It is these beings who appear as the retinues of these two kāyas, while any other beings do not appear as their retinues. (3) The full extent of having purified buddha realms refers to the buddha realms in which the three kāyas (the dharmatākāya and the two profound kāyas that are its natural outflow) dwell. These are not realms that consist of karma and afflictions, but represent the completely pure realms that are made of wisdom.

116 Dowman 2003, 113–14 (emphasis by Dowman).

117 Anonymous 1973–77 (2:460) glosses the second line as "through the arising of adventitious unawareness, sentient beings are as in the example of space obscured by clouds."

118 Klong chen rab 'byams pa dri med 'od zer 1999b?, 51.

That sentient beings or their skandhas are simply equated here with the cloud-like obscurations of the infinite sky of the dharmakāya or awareness may sound unusual and somewhat shocking, but it accords exactly with what is found in many other texts, such as the *Uttaratantra* and some of its commentaries, as well as the Eighth Karmapa's and the Fifth Shamarpa's commentaries on the *Abhisamayālaṃkāra*. For example, *Uttaratantra* I.52–63 explains that all the factors that make up a sentient being—improper mental engagement, afflictions, karma, skandhas, dhātus, and *āyatana*s (which resemble the material elements)—rest on the nature of the mind (which resembles space). Likewise, *Uttaratantra* II.4–6 describes buddhahood as being like the sunlit sky, while all obscurations are like clouds in that sky. One of the earliest Tibetan commentaries on the *Uttaratantra* says that all adventitious stains are nothing but thoughts, and through realizing the luminous nature of the mind and letting thoughts be as lucid wisdom in an uncontrived manner, their essence can be realized as lacking any root and that thus they are free in themselves. In other words, sentient beings are nothing but the adventitious flaws of thoughts, and therefore one familiarizes with them as being nonentities, and buddhahood is nothing but the luminosity of one's own mind having become free from these adventitious stains. Without thoughts and clinging, everything that appears and exists dawns as the essence of the three kāyas. This is the way to bring the naturally luminous tathāgata heart onto the path to buddhahood (Brunnhölzl 2014, 303).

This commentary also says, "through realizing one's own mind, there is not the slightest to be removed because there is no sentient being to be relinquished apart from [mind's] playing as thoughts without a basis" (ibid., 477). Gö Lotsāwa's commentary on the *Uttaratantra* states that sentient beings are just a continuous flow of afflictions and suffering (ibid., 100). Referring to the Third Karmapa, the Eighth Karmapa's commentary on the *Abhisamayālaṃkāra* (Brunnhölzl 2010, 439) explains,

> In his autocommentary on the *Profound Inner Reality*, he makes a twofold classification [of mind as such], saying, "what is pure is expressed as mind, and what is impure is [also] expressed as mind." By explaining that those who possess impure mental impulses are sentient beings, he elucidates that the dharmadhātu does not exist in such sentient beings. He presents these very sentient beings as being the adventitious stains that are produced by false imagination, which mistakenly strays from the dharmadhātu. By giving the pure mind names such as "ordinary mind," "original protector," and "original buddha," he says that it is exactly this [mind] that possesses the mode of being inseparable from the buddha qualities. This kind of [pure mind] is also the [buddha] heart that actually fulfills this function.

Based on *Uttaratantra* I.35–38, a similar distinction is found in the Eighth Karmapa's *Lamp That Excellently Elucidates the System of the Proponents of Shentong Madhyamaka*, which is a loose commentary on buddha nature as presented in the fourth vajra point of the *Uttaratantra* (Brunnhölzl 2014, 818 and 820):

> Unsurpassable completely perfect buddhas, through knowing the entirety of how all phenomena without exception actually are and how they appear, clearly realize the basic nature, ultimate reality, as being the pāramitās of supreme purity, permanence, bliss, and self. On the other hand, they clearly realize the ways in which [phenomena] appear—the adventitious elements of seeming sentient beings—as being impermanent, suffering, without self, and impure ... "But then, what is the meaning of the regent Maitreya's 'distinguishing between phenomena and their true nature' within the mind streams of ordinary beings?" After having explained phenomena just in general as being the adventitious stains that consist of cognitions and knowable objects [of ordinary beings], he explains their true nature as the sugata heart.

Following the Eighth Karmapa's commentary on the *Abhisamayālaṃkāra*, the Fifth Shamarpa equates sentient beings with the ālaya-consciousness, the impure dependent nature, nonafflicted ignorance, false imagination, and the consciousness that entails the dualistic appearances of apprehender and apprehended (ibid., 274–75). This accords with what both these authors say on the dharmadhātu as the disposition for buddhahood (the tathāgata heart).

Again relying on the Karmapa, the Shamarpa (ibid., 285) explains:

> The statement "Sentient beings have the [buddha] heart that fully qualifies as such" is not suitable ultimately, because sentient beings must be presented as the ālaya-consciousness, which is the aspect of being mistaken and has never been established right from the start. You may wonder, "So are sentient beings buddhas then?" That is not the case either because adventitious [stains] are certain to perish—it is impossible for them to be permanent. Nevertheless, from the perspective of convention, at the time of the ground, it is suitable to present merely the existence of one part of this Heart—its aspect of natural purity—in sentient beings, without it, however, being contained in, being mixed with, or being connected to the mind streams of these sentient beings.
>
> *Uttaratantra* [I.129] says:
>
> > ... the beginningless cocoons
> > Of the afflictions that are not connected to
> > The basic element of sentient beings ...
>
> In this context, the following statement applies: "Sentient beings are not the cause of buddhahood, but it is buddhahood itself that has become buddhahood."

Consequently, the Eighth Karmapa declares that it is impossible for sentient beings to become buddhas because they are the adventitious stains and thus have to disappear in order for the tathāgata heart to clearly manifest as buddhahood. The Shamarpa also states that "cloud-like adventitious stains obscure space-like suchness" (ibid., 275).

In sum, despite the many more conventional statements and examples in the *Uttaratantra* and elsewhere that buddha nature exists within sentient beings or the obscurations, as the above explanations show, in actual fact the obscurations or sentient beings exist within buddha nature. This is only logical since buddha nature is not something with physical or spatial dimensions and is certainly not limited to some place within the five skandhas. In other words, in being equivalent to the adventitious stains, sentient beings are nothing but the insubstantial clouds that float in and obscure the infinite sky of the dharmadhātu. Clinging to a personal self and the resultant notion of a sentient being is just like being stuck on the claustrophobic and gloomy outlook of fixating on the configuration of one of these clouds (which moreover keeps changing all the time) from within that cloud; on the other hand, being aware of the cloudless and sunlit expanse of the sky without any reference points is like the nonconceptual wisdom of the dharmadhātu of a buddha. For more details, see Brunnhölzl 2010 (284–85 and 428–46).

119 Klong chen rab 'byams pa dri med 'od zer 1999b?, 111.

120 Tib. *bskyur ba* emended to *bsgyur ba*.

121 Klong chen rab 'byams pa dri med 'od zer 1999d?, 6:1604–7.

122 Anonymous 1973–77, 1:258. For an extensive discussion of the "all-ground" and its classifications, see appendix 5A.

123 Klong chen rab 'byams pa dri med 'od zer 1999d?, 6:1044–46.

124 Kapstein 1995, 82.

125 Kapstein's reference: G. van der Leeuw, *Religion in Essence and Manifestation*, trans. J. E. Turner (Princeton, N.J.: Princeton University Press, 1986), Chapter 62. All uncited quotations in this and the following paragraphs may be found in this chapter.

126 Kapstein 1995, 87.

127 "Amnesis" and "mnemic engagement" are Kapstein's terms for "mindlessness" (Skt. *asmṛti*, Tib. *dran med*) and "mindfulness" (Skt. *smṛti*, Tib. *dran pa*), respectively. In the context of *The Aspiration Prayer*, this specifically refers to being versus not being aware or mindful of the ground or primordial awareness. See also chapter 8 for Kapstein's more detailed discussion of these two terms.

128 Kapstein 1992, 256–57.

129 Grammatically speaking, in English and other languages, transitive verbs are those that require a direct object (such as "to bring"), while intransitive verbs do not take direct objects (such as "to sleep" or "to go"). The distinction in Tibetan that in most cases is equivalent to the one between transitive and intransitive verbs is explained such that agent and object are or are not different (Tib. *bya byed tha dad* versus *bya byed tha mi dad*), respectively. However, for some intransitive verbs there is not only no object but not even any agent (though there may be a grammatical subject), as in verbs that express a state (for example, "to be sick," "to be drunk," or "to be free").

130 Of course, when Dzogchen texts speak of "I, Samantabhadra" or the like, this does not refer to the usual notion of an "I" or a self but to primordially free awareness—the self-arising wisdom that is the very heart of the matter.

131 Tib. *sgom pa* ("to familiarize," "to cultivate") is the transitive form of *goms pa* ("to be(come) familiar").

As for the use of the word "meditation" in Buddhism, in a general context, both the Sanskrit *bhāvanā* and the corresponding Tibetan *sgom pa* mostly mean "familiarizing with," "mentally cultivating," or "enhancing" something, either some certainty gained through prior reflection or a direct insight into true reality. Thus, this process can be either conceptual or nonconceptual. However, it should be noted that the original meaning of "meditation" is just "reflection" (Lat. *meditatio*, *meditare*), which is clearly conceptual, while the original meaning of the term "contemplation" (Lat. *contemplatio*, *contemplare*) is "viewing" or "looking" at something in a settled state of mind (possibly being either conceptual or nonconceptual).

Regarding meditation on compassion and other virtuous mental states, the point is not really to meditate *on* them as abstract objects or in a merely conceptual way, but to cultivate them and familiarize with them as integral constituents of one's mind. Of course, this is even more obvious in the case of mind's ultimate true nature, of which it is invariably said that it cannot be meditated on anyway, whereas familiarity with it can definitely be attained.

Likewise, the texts often speak about cultivating (or familiarizing with) a path, śamatha, and vipaśyanā, while it obviously makes no sense to say "meditating on a path," and even less to say "meditating on śamatha or vipaśyanā." Especially on the Sūtrayāna's path of familiarization, as well as in Mahāmudrā and Dzogchen, the point is not to "meditate on" mind's true nature (or anything else, for that matter) but simply to become used to how things actually are.

As for the Sanskrit term *bhāvanā*, it generally refers to an act of producing, manifesting, or promoting. Specifically, it means imagining, forming in the mind, occupying one's imagination with or directing one's thoughts to something. In this sense, the word *can* also refer to reflection, meditation, or contemplation (thus, depending on the context and to follow common consensus, I sometimes use the word "meditation" too). The term can also mean the application of perfumes and the like, or saturating or steeping any powder with fluid. Thus, "cultivation" or "familiarization" in this sense may be seen as "perfuming" the mind stream with virtuous imprints and liberating insights, just as a cloth might be so impregnated with a scent as to actually become inseparable from it.

132 Tib. Ban sgar 'jam dpal bzang po.

133 This is a version found in the Rangjung Yeshe Wiki—Dharma Dictionary (http://rywiki.tsadra.org/index.php/Dorje_Chang_Thungma).

134 This is the version by the Nālandā Translation Committee.

135 See Brunnhölzl 2007, 313.

136 The example refers to the famous French painter Monet having mispainted the church Notre Dame in Paris—he substituted Gothic (pointed) arches for the rounded ones that Notre Dame actually has, because that's how he expected them to be.

137 Forman 1989, 410–12 (emphasis by Forman).

138 In accordance with the lines above, Tib. *spyod pa* ("conduct") is emended to *dpyod pa*.

139 Klong chen rab 'byams pa dri med 'od zer 1999a?, 522–23.

140 The credit for the term "don'ting" goes to Harrison Moretz (director and founder of the Taoist Studies Institute in Seattle, WA).

141 Klong chen rab 'byams pa dri med 'od zer 1999a?, 527.

142 As here, the term "self-awareness" (Tib. *rang rig*) is widely used in Dzogchen literature as an equivalent of primordial awareness and self-arising wisdom (for further examples, see *Ketaka*, *Lamp*, and appendices 2–7). In that regard, it is closely related to terms such as "self-arising awareness" (Tib. *rang byung rig pa*), "self-arising wisdom" (Tib. *rang byung ye shes*), "self-aware wisdom" (Tib. *rang gi(s) rig pa'i ye shes*) and "personally experienced wisdom" (Tib. *so sor rang gi rig pa'i ye shes*), as well as luminosity and buddha nature. However, Longchenpa and other Dzogchen authors vehemently reject the notion of an ultimately real (reified) self-awareness free from the duality of apprehender and apprehended (as it is, according to the Tibetan tradition, proposed in both the Sākāravāda and the Nirākāravāda branches of the so-called Mind-Only School) and declare primordial self-awareness to be far superior.

143 Klong chen rab 'byams pa dri med 'od zer 1999a?, 529.

144 Somewhat of an exception is Tib. *mtha' grol*, which indeed means "being free from extremes" but this is still embedded in *rigpa*'s own primordial and intrinsic freedom.

145 The Padmakara Translation Group (Jigme Lingpa and Kangyur Rinpoche 2013, xxix) also dismisses expressions such as "the mind 'self-liberates'" as "an unfortunate piece of 'Buddhist Hybrid English'" and instead suggests "to subside." However, in my opinion, "to subside" is too bland and negative a word, which certainly does not convey the greatly positive and inspiring quality of *rigpa*'s innate freedom. Thus, it only emphasizes the negative aspect of something disappearing (which is conditioned) rather than the positive aspect of always being free already (which is unconditioned). Also, "subsiding" sounds as if first there is something and then it subsides (which is definitely not the case for *rigpa*). As the Padmakara Group itself admits, at least the expression "primordial subsiding" is "awkward ... since it is difficult to imagine a subsiding that occurs even before anything that has arisen!" Moreover, and most importantly, while "subsiding" may work to some extent in cases such as "thoughts are self-subsiding" (though the real point is here too that thoughts are already free in themselves), it does not work at all in relation to the natural state of *rigpa* because *rigpa* is the only thing that never subsides; rather, it is always self-arising and always remains naturally free in that. It makes no sense to say "*rigpa* self-subsides" or "*rigpa* subsides primordially."

146 "Being free *in* itself" (or "being free in and of itself" or "being free on its own") appears to be the most common meaning of *rang grol* because of rigpa being naturally free in itself as its very own intrinsic way of being.

However, sometimes, Dzogchen texts also speak of "being free *by* itself" (*rang gis grol ba*) or "being free *in* itself *by* itself" (*rang gis rang grol*).

147 For details on the different sets of three, four, five, or six kinds of "being free," see appendix 7.

148 Tib. *Sgra thal 'gyur gyi rgyud*. The obscure title of this tantra is notoriously difficult to translate. English renderings include "Consequence of Sound" (absurdly taking *thal 'gyur* to have the meaning of an [absurd] consequence as in the context of Madhyamaka reasoning, which is certainly not what the term refers to here), "Penetrating Sound," "the Penetration of Sound," and "Reverberating Sound."

As Smith (2016, 5–6) points out, the tantra and its commentary by Vimalamitra provide some explanations of what the two words *thal* and *'gyur* (taken separately) in this title mean. The beginning of the tantra (Anonymous 1973–77, 1:22) lists eight *thal ba'i gnas* ("locations of universes"; Smith "location of realms") and the commentary glosses *thal ba* as buddha realms that are strewn with powders of precious materials such as gold, sapphires, or rubies ("powder" is one of the meanings of *thal ba*). In addition, the tantra (Anonymous 1973–77, 1:22ff.) lists thirteen universes, all including the word *thal ba*. Since another meaning of *thal ba* is "dust," the term thus appears to be used in the sense of "clusters of dust or powder" in both the sense of actual universes or galaxies ("stardust," so to speak) and in a more abstract or figurative sense of "universe" (such as the universe of commitments). The term *'gyur ba* is explained in the tantra (Anonymous 1973–77, 1:28) as referring to the changes or transitions in terms of the material elements and time. Though these explanations are not explicitly said to be glosses of the title of this tantra, they seem to be significant enough to tentatively render its name accordingly.

149 Ibid., 1:124–25.

150 Ibid., 1:178–79.

151 The phrase "nothing to become free" (Tib. *grol rgyu*) here and in the next paragraph could also be read as "no cause to become free."

152 Klong chen rab 'byams pa dri med 'od zer. 1999d?, 6:1614–17.

153 Higgins 2013, 219–21 (emphasis by Higgins). For the distinction between "ground" and "all-ground," see appendix 5A.

154 Ibid., 262 (emphasis by Higgins).

155 Tib. Rong zom Chos kyi bzang po.

156 *Rong zom bka 'bum*, Thimpu edition, 276 (Tibetan translated as quoted in Higgins 2013, 262n621).

157 Rong zom chos kyi bzang po 1999, 507.

158 An asterisk preceding a Sanskrit word indicates its (tentative) back-translation from a Tibetan word.

159 Higgins 2013, 262–63 (emphasis by Higgins).

160 (1) "The unawareness that has the same identity as the cause" (often abbreviated as "the unawareness of same identity") means not recognizing that the cause of both unawareness and awareness (or delusion and nondelusion) is identical: it is nothing other than the nondual primordial ground before any bifurcation into delusion and nondelusion, or recognition and nonrecognition, occurs. (2) As for "connate unawareness," another rendering of "connate" would be "innate," which is indeed more appropriate in many other cases. Here, however, I chose "connate" because connate unawareness is explicitly explained as the unawareness that coexists or arises simultaneously with the most basic form of unawareness, the unawareness that has the same identity as the cause. That is, it is the simultaneous nonrecognition of the most fundamental nonrecognition itself. (3) The subsequent "imaginative unawareness" means that, based on the preceding twofold unawareness, the ground manifestations are mistaken for something other than the ground, thus straying into the full-blown duality of subject and object as well as self and other. In sum, the unawareness of same identity means not seeing things as they actually are, connate unawareness means not seeing this error, and imaginative unawareness means consequently seeing things as something other than they are.

Other sources sometimes present a correlation of these three kinds of unawareness with the ground's own triad of essence, nature, and compassionate responsiveness. That is, the unawareness of same identity derives from not recognizing the empty essence's dimension of nonconceptuality. Connate unawareness derives from not recognizing the luminous nature as awareness's self-nature. Imaginative unawareness derives from not recognizing compassionate responsiveness's intrinsic awareness. (See *Lamp*, fol. 13b and Smith 2016, 76–77: the essence is made the cause of delusion, the nature is made the condition of delusion, and compassionate responsiveness is made the result of delusion.) For more details, see Germano 1992n156 and Higgins 2013, 69ff.

161 Typically, desire is described as the primary affliction of the human realm, while avarice is the one that leads to rebirth as a hungry ghost. However, according to *The Aspiration Prayer*, desire results in being reborn as a hungry ghost, while the human realm and avarice are not mentioned. Since desire is generally held to be the main underlying affliction that triggers clinging to possessions or pleasant feelings, poverty mentality, and avarice (the inability to let go), it can be said to cause rebirth as a hungry ghost in an indirect manner.

As for the reason why Samantabhadra does not speak of the human realm in *The Aspiration Prayer*, Khenchen Palden Sherab Rinpoche and Khenpo Tsewang Dongyal Rinpoche (2010, 20) say this:

> Because the human realm is the intersection of the other five realms. Even though humans don't directly experience the

conditions of those other realms, whenever their negative emotions are raging humans are right at the threshold of those realms. The Buddhist teachings say that among all the realms the human realm is the realm of the causes and conditions for nirvana, as well as the other five realms of samsara, which collectively are known as the "realms of result." The three lower realms have tremendous burdens of suffering, which prevent beings there from doing anything but suffer. The two higher realms have such intense pleasure that beings there don't have time or interest in doing anything except enjoying their pleasures. The human realm, on the other hand, involves a variety of pain and pleasure, and in this way it is a training ground for how to best handle suffering and happiness. We have the opportunity to learn to use these experiences as a path of spiritual development. Although the human realm is not mentioned by name, principally this teaching is for humanity. It is a reminder to us of how special and rare this opportunity of a human life is.

Thus, as a practice text, *The Aspiration Prayer* is designed for us who have currently been born as humans. We are encouraged in our human existence to transcend the five primary afflictions of desire, hatred, pride, envy, and ignorance in order to avoid their results of being reborn in the other five realms of saṃsāra, in which practicing the Dharma is impossible or at least much more difficult. More importantly, we as humans are urged to gain immediate freedom from saṃsāra through recognizing our afflictions for what they truly are—the distorted expressions of the five wisdoms, which are in themselves the dynamic energy of primordial basic awareness.

162 Kapstein (1992, 246–47) distinguishes four primary categories of the use of "mindfulness" or its lack (Tib. *dran pa*) in Dzogchen texts: (1) "mnemic engagement" in the sense of mnemic acts (memory, recollection, recognition, and so on) that are determinations of the domain of mundane possibilities or saṃsāra (I render this as "minding"); (2) "mnemic engagement" in the sense of mindful attentiveness, which is directed to whatever contributes to advancement on the path; (3) "mnemic engagement" in the sense of the immediate recovery of the self-presenting awareness of the dharmakāya (I render both the second and third as "mindfulness"); and (4) "amnesis" (Tib. *dran med*) in the sense of negatively valued engagement in discursive thought, which represents oblivion with respect to primordial awareness (I render this as "mindlessness"). As the negation of the second and especially the third, this last refers to the discursive engagement that constitutes the unawareness and delusion of saṃsāra, so that in a sense the fourth is equivalent to the first. As *The Aspiration Prayer* makes clear, the fourth

marks a drifting away from the original ground of awareness on the part of sentient beings. However, as Kapstein says, in some contexts, *dran med* is used in the opposite sense of characterizing the advanced practice of the path of the Great Perfection, in such cases referring to the contemplative "oblivion" that is marked by complete freedom from discursive thought and reference points (I render this as "nonminding"). What is meant here in lines (123–30) of *The Aspiration Prayer* (as well as in most other instances throughout this volume) is mindfulness in the sense of the third of these categories.

163 Among the five editions of the *Tantra of Samantabhadra's Unobstructed Awakened Mind* under Rgod kyi ldem 'phru can dngos grub rgyal mtshan 1973b, the editions of 1973, 1979, and 2000 all contain identical copies of TV1, while the edition of 2015 contains TV2 (computer input). Unfortunately, pages 61–66 in the *dbu med* edition of 1978, which contain the nineteenth chapter of the tantra with *The Aspiration Prayer*, are completely blank.

164 Though there are many editions of CV, they do not show significant variants among each other and are therefore treated as one here.

165 Since TV2 is a computer input, some minor variant readings may also just be typos. However, it is not clear what original this input is based on.

166 The only exception appears to Kapstein's English rendering of *The Aspiration Prayer* (1992, 260–64 and 1995, 80–87), which is explicitly based on TV1.

167 Interestingly, all three commentaries on *The Aspiration Prayer* show elements of TV1, TV2, CV, and RTV, though with varying preferences (for details, see chapter 11).

168 Tib. *ngo sprod pa* (lit. "face-directing" or "face-joining") means "introducing," as in introducing a person. Despite the widespread use of the expression "pointing out (instruction)," "introducing" or "introduction" seems to be the more appropriate term here because it has a sense of making us re-recognize or realize what we truly are. It also works better for the form *ngo 'phrod pa* (lit. "face-meeting"), which means being identified or recognized in the sense of the own true face or essence of awareness being recognized or directly revealed (whether or not it is introduced by someone else). However, as discussed above, it is not that some "I" or person recognizes or meets its own true nature, since this entails duality and the true nature of the mind is completely beyond being an object of any ordinary state of consciousness, let alone being an object of a self or "me." All this is about the nature of the mind recognizing itself for what it is instead of being obscured by dualistic deluded sense perceptions, thoughts, emotions, and ego-clinging. In other words, all that we as a sentient being or practitioner can do is step back and allow nondual innate awareness to fully be what it always has been.

169 Dowman 2003, 114 (emphasis by Dowman).
170 Ibid., 114 (emphasis by Dowman).
171 Ibid., 116.
172 In addition, it is of course also beneficial to merely see its text or wear it on one's body, though such is not explicitly suggested anywhere; different from the case of specific diagrams (Skt. *yantra*, Tib. *srung 'khor*) that are designed for becoming free through seeing and wearing (see appendix 7).
173 Turpeinen 2016, 207.
174 Tib. 'Jigs med gling pa rang byung rdo rje mkhyen brtse 'od zer.
175 Tib. Dpal ri.
176 Tib. Thugs mchog rdo rje.
177 Tib. Bsam yas mchims phu.
178 Tib. Rtse le sna tshogs rang grol.
179 Tib. Phreng po gter chen shes rab 'od zer (a treasure revealer who was the founder of Palri Monastery).
180 Tib. Tshe ring ljongs padma 'od gsal theg mchog gling.
181 This biographical sketch is based on van Schaik 2004b (21–24). For longer biographies, see Goodman 1992 and Gyatso 1998.
182 The text contains one phrase that is unique to TV1 but also a few that clearly belong to TV2, CV, and even RTV (this could suggest that RTV existed already at Jigmé Lingpa's time before it was later incorporated in the *Treasury of Precious Treasures*). Throughout the translations of all three commentaries, I have retained their individual variant readings of *The Aspiration Prayer*.
183 Tib. Mkha' khyab rdo rje.
184 Tib. Pad ma dbang phyug rgyal po.
185 Tib. Mkhyen brtse 'od zer; a.k.a. Karsé Kongtrul (Tib. Kar sras kong sprul), "the Kongtrul who is a son of the Karmapa."
186 Tib. 'Jam mgon kong sprul blo gros mtha' yas.
187 Tib. Mchog gling gter gsar.
188 Tib. Bla ma bsam gtan rgya mtsho.
189 Tib. Mchog gyur gling pa.
190 Tib. Mkha' 'gro tshe ring dpal sgron rin po che.
191 Tib. Smin gling khri chen kun bzang dbang rgyal.
192 Tib. Grags pa rgya mtsho.
193 This brief sketch of the Fifteenth Karmapa's life is based on Lama Kunsang, Lama Pemo, and Marie Aubèle 2012, 191–202.
194 Despite being a shorter text than *Lamp*, *Ketaka* has a more-detailed outline and also often differs in content, but the basic division of the passages of *The Aspiration Prayer* is the same in both commentaries. For more details, see appendix 1.
195 Tib. Tshul khrims bzang po. According to Thondup 1996, Tsültrim Sangpo's birth year is 1884 and the Khordong Monastery website says that

he died when he was seventy-three. What is clear is that he wrote his secret biography of Tertön Sogyal in 1942. Tsültrim Sangpo is also known as Tulku Tsullo (Tib. Sprul sku tshul lo) or Tulku Tsurlo.

196 Tib. Bsod rgyal las rab gling pa.

197 Tib. Rdo grub 'jigs med bstan pa'i nyi ma.

198 Tib. A mye mkhan po dam chos 'od zer.

199 Tib. Shugs 'byung.

200 Tib. 'Khor gdong

201 Tib. 'Gyur med rdo rje.

202 Tib. 'Khor gdong gter sprul 'chi med rig 'dzin.

203 Tib. O rgyan bstan 'dzin (Sprul sku rgyan lo).

204 Tib. Gzhi chen 'on sprul rin po che.

205 The numbering of the Tibetan folios jumps from 21a to 22a (the latter also has "22b" in Arabic numerals on the right margin) and then continues with 23a and so on. Thus, without any content missing, the text skips the numbering of one entire folio (numbers 21b and 22a) and ends with folio 28b.

206 For more details, see appendix 1.

207 Contemporary published commentaries on *The Aspiration Prayer* include those by Chamgon Kenting Tai Situ Rinpoche, Dzogchen Ponlop Rinpoche, Khenchen Palden Sherab Rinpoche and Khenpo Tsewang Dongyal Rinpoche (all in English), and Gangteng Tulku (in German); see bibliography.

208 The tantra has *tsitta ā*.

The Sanskrit term *citta* (as here, often transliterated as *tsitta* in Dzogchen texts and otherwise usually translated into Tibetan as *sems*) has a very specific meaning in the Great Perfection. It refers to the principal seat of pure awareness within our body at the level of our physical heart but in the center of the body: the heart cakra. It is described as an octagonal small dome of five-colored light (also sometimes compared to a pitched tent). Primordial awareness is said to be present in this palace of *citta* as the innate three kāyas in the form of the mustard-sized maṇḍala of the forty-two peaceful deities. Moreover, this awareness's radiance is present as the mustard-sized maṇḍala of the fifty-eight wrathful deities in our skull, referred to by the Sanskrit word *bhanda* or "conch-shell mansion" (Tib. *dung khang*). Thus, in Dzogchen, the Sanskrit terms *citta*, *bhanda*, and also *cakṣu* are used to distinguish the subtle luminous loci of awareness in the body from the coarse material heart, skull/brain, and eyes.

The syllable "A" (pronounced "AH" in English but not to be confused with the Sanskrit "AḤ" or "ĀḤ") in Dzogchen symbolizes alpha-purity, the infinite primordial expanse, and the ultimate body of light. It is typically depicted in a round sphere or circle (Tib. *thig le*) of rainbow light, which symbolizes innate presence. Together, "A" and that circle stand for compassionate responsiveness as the unity of alpha-purity (essence) and innate presence (nature). This is related to the meaning of "A" in the Sūtrayāna in general and the prajñāpāramitā sūtras in particular, where "A" stands for being unborn (Skt. *anutpannatva*) and thus represents emptiness. Khenchen Palden Sherab Rinpoche and Khenpo Tsewang Dongyal Rinpoche 2010 (33) explain that

> we would say, "Gong pa zang thal ten pa'i tsitta AH." That means, "The unimpeded mind of Küntuzangpo is within the heart: AH." One could also say, "This moment is in awareness—it is beyond conception" ... The seed syllable AH is very important. It symbolizes the dharmadhatu, the true nature, and the great Mother Prajnaparamita. All of the many teachings on Prajnaparamita, from the One Hundred Thousand Stanza version through the series of progressively shorter and more condensed versions, all come finally to the Prajnaparamita in One Syllable. That single syllable is AH. This AH is said to be the primordial sound, source of every sound of nature and of the human voice. All other sounds of human speech, vowels and consonants, are produced using different parts of the mouth and throat, such as the palate, tongue and throat muscles. Only the AH comes without effort. For all these reasons it is the symbol of the absolute true nature.

209 TV1 TV2 CV *thams cad kyis* RTV *thams cad kun*.

210 TV1 TV2 *las* CV RTV *la* ("within").

211 TV1 *dri mas bral* CV *sgrib ma gos* ("untainted by the obscurations") TV2 RTV *dris ma gos* ("untainted by flaws").

212 TV1 RTV *kha dog* TV2 CV *dug lnga* ("the five poisons").

213 TV1 TV2 CV *las* RTV *la* ("within that").

214 TV1 CV RTV *nga yi* TV2 *nga yis*.

215 TV1 CV RTV *gnas* TV2 *lam* ("paths").

216 TV1 CV RTV *dang po* TV2 *dang po'i*.

217 I follow TV2 CV *las* against TV1 *la* ("within") and RTV *yis* ("through").

218 TV1 TV2 CV *de las* RTV *de la* ("within that" or "there").

219 TV1 *khams gsum sems can thams cad kyi / kun gyis rig pa rang shes shog* (the first line is definitely corrupt in connection with the second one and appears to be redundant) TV2 *kun gyis rig pa rang shes shog* CV *kun gyi rig pa rang shes shog* RTV *kun gyis rig pa ngo shes shog* ("may all recognize awareness's face"). I follow the second line of TV1 and TV2.

220 TV1 TV2 *thom me ba* CV RTV *g.yengs pa yin* ("distracted").

221 TV1 TV2 CV *thams cad kyi* RTV *thams cad kun*.

222 I follow TV2 CV RTV *yi dvags su* against TV1 *yi dvags lus* ("[as/in] a hungry ghost's body").

223 I follow TV2 CV RTV *brkam chags* against TV1 *skam chags*.

224 TV1 CV RTV *gdung ba* TV2 *gdung bas*.

225 TV1 CV RTV *zhen pa* TV2 *zhen pas.*

226 TV1 *dgrar 'dzin brdeg gsod rags pa* TV2 *dgra 'dzin brdeg gsod hrags pa* CV *dgrar 'dzin brdeg gsod hrag pa* ("… powerful beating …") RTV *dgrar 'dzin rtog pa rag pa* ("leads to coarse thoughts of fixating on enemies").

227 TV1 CV *thams cad kyi* TV2 RTV *thams cad kun.*

228 TV1 *rang sor bzhag* TV2 *rang sar klod* ("relax in its own place") CV *rang sor klod* RTV *rang sor glod* ("relax in its own state").

229 TV1 *las* TV2 *na* ("when") CV RTV *la* ("with").

230 TV1 CV RTV *drag po* TV2 *dregs pa* ("arrogant").

231 TV1 TV2 *spyod* CV RTV *myong.*

232 TV1 TV2 *mnyam nyid ye shes thob par shog* CV/RTV *mnyam pa nyid kyi don rtogs shog* ("and the actuality of equality thus be realized").

233 TV1 *skyes pa na* TV2 CV RTV *skyes pa rnams* ("the arisen").

234 TV1 TV2 CV *phrin las thogs med ye shes* RTV *phrin las ye shes thogs med* ("the unimpeded wisdom of enlightened activity").

235 TV1 CV RTV *gis* TV2 *gi.*

236 TV1 TV2 RTV end this line with *dang*, while most versions of CV have *yis* (some have *yi* and one has *las*).

237 TV1 TV2 RTV *nas* CV *bas.*

238 TV1 *thams cad kyang* TV2 CV RTV *thams cad kun.*

239 TV2 E MA HO.

240 TV1 *ngang* TV2 CV RTV *nas* ("from within").

241 TV1 TV2 end this line with *thams cad kyang*, RTV with *thams cad kun*, and CV with *thams cad la* (the latter would result in "Through the aspiration prayer of such yogic practitioners for all sentient beings of the three realms, they will gradually…").

242 TV1 *myur bar* TV2 CV *mtha ru* ("in the end," "finally") RTV *mthar thug* ("ultimately," "finally").

243 RTV here adds four more lines:

The supreme principal of these kings of aspiration prayers
Brings benefit to all limitless beings
And is established as a text adorned by Samantabhadra—
May the miserable realms be empty of [all] mind streams without exception.

244 TV1 TV2 *le'u ste bcu dgu pa'o* CV *le'u dgu pa khol du phyung(s) ba* ("Excerpted from *The Tantra* … this is the ninth chapter") RTV *le'u dgu pa nas khol du phyung ba* ("This is excerpted from the ninth chapter … in *The Tantra*"). All currently available English translations likewise say "ninth chapter."

245 TV1 TV2 *sems can* CV RTV *sems can thams cad* ("all sentient beings").

246 Following all other versions, CV *kun gyi* is emended to *kun gyis.*

247 As mentioned before, the prayer is an excerpt from the nineteenth chapter of the tantra, but all editions of CV say "ninth."

248 In this somewhat obscure title, "guide" (Tib. *'dren byed*) is a rendering of the Sanskrit word *nayana* or *netra*, which is one of the many expressions for the eye. Thus, the title uses the common Indian and Tibetan analogy of clearing or eliminating a physical obscuration of the eye (such as cataracts) with a surgical instrument, which means that this commentary (*ṭīkā*) resembles a lancet or a scalpel that skillfully removes whatever obscures our clear seeing of the meaning of *The Aspiration Prayer*.

249 These lines contain a play on Skt. *samanta* (Tib. *kun tu*; "universal") in the name Samantabhadra ("Universal Goodness"), emphasizing it further by repeating it (Tib. *kun tu kun nas*; "absolutely universal" or "in each and every respect"). "The heart of having gone to bliss" is a translation of *sugatagarbha* as the "basic element" (*dhātu*) in all sentient beings, while the three doors to liberation (a common template found in the prajñāpāramitā sūtras) are emptiness, signlessness, and wishlessness. In this way, Jigmé Lingpa equates *prajñāpāramitā* or emptiness (the second turning of the wheel of Dharma), buddha nature (the third turning of the wheel), and the primordial awareness of Dzogchen (the nature of Samantabhadra), highlighting the fact that ultimately, buddha nature, prajñāpāramitā, and basic awareness are all beyond being lost, obscured, attained, or realized. This is often emphasized in all three systems, such as in the famous verse found as both *Uttaratantra* I.28 and *Abhisamayālaṃkāra* V.21:

> There is nothing to be removed from this
> And not the slightest to be added.
> Actual reality is to be seen as it really is—
> Whoever sees actual reality is liberated.

250 "The indeterminate ground" and "the ground of alpha-purity" are two among the seven ways of asserting the ground. Interestingly, in the next paragraph, *Lancet* switches to employing the perspective of the ground of alpha-purity. For details on these seven ways of asserting the ground, the refutations of the first six, and the correct identification of the ground as alpha-purity, see *Lamp*'s comments on the line "The ground of all is unconditioned," appendix 2A (see also Germano 1992, 143ff.), and Smith 2016 (55–74).

251 Tib. *la* emended to *las*.

252 According to Longchenpa (see the beginning of appendix 3), when the ground dawns as the ground manifestations, the dynamic energy of compassionate responsiveness is self-arising as a lucid and aware cognizance that is able to discern objects. Based on not recognizing its own face, this cognizance dawns as being associated with threefold unawareness (the unawareness of same identity, connate unawareness, and imaginative unawareness). Thus, the term "cognizance" is normally used in Dzogchen texts in contradistinction to primordially pure and unchanging "awareness" as an expression for the subtle initial mental stir that, though

indeterminate in itself as either saṃsāra or nirvāṇa, turns into unawareness if unrecognized as an expression of awareness (this is sometimes referred to as "cognizance's stirring or moving away from the ground"). However, Jigmé Lingpa's commentary explains in the second to next paragraph that "nonconceptual, self-arising cognizance" refers to the great self-lucidity that is beyond mind and further equates it with awareness, thus obviously referring to this cognizance's having recognized its own face as being awareness in its essence—and thus being free. This means that this indeterminate cognizance is still very close to awareness as its source and thus is more easily recognizable as awareness than the ensuing dualistic eight consciousnesses, their objects, and the many layers of reifying those, including the clinging to a real self and real phenomena, which represent the further evolutions of delusion, when this initial cognizance is not immediately recognized for what it is.

253 According to the *Abhidharmakośabhāṣya* on III.100–102, in general, when the universe is destroyed by fire, everything below the second dhyāna level of the form realm is annihilated; when it is destroyed by water (rain), everything below the third dhyāna level is annihilated; and when it is destroyed by wind, everything below the fourth dhyāna level is annihilated. After such a destruction of the universe by fire has occurred seven times, it is destroyed once by water. After this entire cycle of seven destructions through fire and one through water has been repeated seven times, the universe is once again destroyed seven times by fire and then finally once by wind. Thus, all in all, there are sixty-four destructions (fifty-six by fire, seven by water, and one by wind), which continue to occur endlessly in that pattern. That the fourth dhyāna level is never destroyed by fire, water, or wind is because, unlike the lower dhyāna levels, it is free from the inner flaws that correspond to those three elements and thus is immovable and free from agitation. However, it is not permanent because its different celestial palaces arise and disappear together with the gods who live there. Obviously, since there are no physical phenomena in the formless realm, there is nothing to be destroyed by any physical elements; the mental skandhas of the gods there simply cease, and the gods are reborn somewhere else.

254 "The three seats' completeness" means that the skandhas, dhātus, and āyatanas of the body are in fact the maṇḍala in which the three seats of tathāgatas, bodhisattvas, and wrathful deities are complete; the skandhas and dhātus represent the seat of the male and female tathāgatas, the āyatanas the seat of the male and female bodhisattvas, and the limbs (the body with its sense faculties) the seat of the male and female wrathful deities.

255 Following TV1/TV2 and CV, *rgyu* is emended to *rnams*. With *rgyu*, the first two lines of this section would read:

The first cause of sentient beings' delusion
Is that awareness does not dawn in the ground.

In that sense, these and the following lines in this section describe even more explicitly the first one among the three kinds of unawareness—"the unawareness of same identity," though our text explicitly only speaks of "the twofold ground of delusion," which consists of the two remaining kinds of unawareness—connate and imaginative unawareness—that are discussed in the next section (for details on these three kinds of unawareness, see appendix 3A).

256 Tib. *bltas pa* emended to *brtas pa*.

257 This refers to the sequence of the twelve links in their progressive order.

258 Tib. *rgyu* emended to *rgyud*.

259 For more details on connate unawareness and imaginative unawareness, see the parallel passages of *Ketaka* and *Lamp*, as well as appendix 3A.

260 Tib. *tha mal gyi shes pa*. It is interesting that Jigmé Lingpa here uses this expression that is such a hallmark of Mahāmudrā.

261 As mentioned before, the Pith Instructions Series is commonly classified into four cycles: the Outer Cycle, the Inner Cycle, the Secret Cycle, and the Unsurpassed Secret Cycle, with the last cycle consisting of the Seventeen Tantras, beginning with the *Tantra of the Universes and Transformations of Sound*.

262 "Stainless light rays" (Tib. *dri med 'od zer*) is the personal name of Longchenpa, and the *Precious Treasury of the Supreme Yāna* (a commentary on the Seventeen Tantras of the Pith Instructions Series) is one of his seven treasuries.

263 This is the fifth incarnation of Rigdzin Gödemchen, the Fifth Dorjé Trag Rigdzin, Kelsang Pema Wangchug (Tib. Rdo rje brag rig 'dzin Skal bzang padma dbang phyug; 1719/20–1770s), who was one of Jigmé Lingpa's students.

264 This is one of the aliases of Jigmé Lingpa, which alludes to his close relationship with Longchenpa ("Great Expanse") through the latter's blessings of body, speech, mind, and teachings, as well as to his having received the mind terma of the *Longchen Nyingtig* in a vision; in this later case, "great expanse" refers to the text. The alias can also be understood to mean "the sky of this yogin's mind, which is a great expanse."

265 The Sanskrit word *ketaka* is an alternative spelling of *ketakī*, which refers to the fragrant screw pine (*Pandanus odorifer*; a.k.a. kewda, umbrella tree, or screw tree) as well as its flowers. According to Krang dbyi sun et al. 1985 (26), the Sanskrit *ketaka* refers to the fruit of the ketaka tree or to a precious stone that is able to purify muddy water. I could not find any Sanskrit references for this latter use of the term, but in Tibetan, *nor bu ke ta ka* (*nor bu* meaning "gem") is found in the titles of a number of texts,

such as Mipham Rinpoche's famous commentary on the ninth chapter of the *Bodhicaryāvatāra*.

266 "I pay homage to you, the guru, glorious supreme Lotus-Born" (*Ketaka* has *Uttārabhyaḥ*; ablative).

267 This appears to refer to three of the many epithets of Jamgön Kongtrul Lodrö Tayé, one of the two main gurus of the Fifteenth Karmapa. Jamgön Kongtrul's bodhisattva name was Pema Karwang Lodrö Tayé (Tib. Padma gar dbang blo gros mtha' yas) and his initiatory names were Pema Karwang Trinlé Drodül Dsal (Tib. Padma gar dbang phrin las 'gro 'dul rtsal) and Pema Kargyi Wangchug Dsal (Tib. Padma gar gyi dbang phyug rtsal).

268 According to Longchenpa's *Treasure Trove of Scriptures* (Klong chen rab 'byams pa dri med 'od zer 1999a?, 621), the three classes, or main scriptural divisions, of the Expanse Series are the white expanse, the black expanse, and the multicolored expanse. The white expanse is further divided into (1) the expanse of space, (2) the expanse of the ocean, and (3) the expanse of the mountain; the black expanse into (4) the black expanse of compassionate responsiveness, (5) the black expanse of enlightened activity, and (6) the black expanse series of emanation; and the multicolored expanse into (7) the multicolored expanse that accords with the Mind Series and speaks of existence, (8) the multicolored expanse that accords with its own series and speaks of nonexistence, and (9) the multicolored expanse that accords with the Pith Instructions Series and speaks of the unity of existence and nonexistence (in this triad, "existence" and "nonexistence" refer to mind's luminosity and emptiness, respectively).

In his *Precious Treasury of Philosophical Systems* (Klong chen rab 'byams pa dri med 'od zer 1999c?, 339–48), Longchenpa explains that the Expanse Series consist of (1) the black expanse of speaking in terms of the lack of causes, (2) the multicolored expanse of speaking in terms of diversity, (3) the white expanse of speaking in terms of mind, and (4) the infinite expanse of having passed beyond cause and result. He also gives detailed explanations of each one of these four categories and their subcategories, which match the above with the addition that the infinite expanse is divided into the outer, the inner, the secret, and the infinite expanse of suchness. All of this can be summarized as (1) the expanse of play, (2) the expanse of adornment, (3) the expanse of dharmatā, and (4) the expanse of being free from anything to be done.

Finally, Longchenpa says in the same text, the nine expanses of the Expanse Series consist of (1) the expanse of the view without any change or transition, (2) the expanse of meditation without any "is" or "isn't," (3) the expanse of the fruition without any hope or fear, (4) the expanse of the essence without any establishing or eliminating, (5) the expanse of the unceasing play within the nature, (6) the expanse of the freedom of appearances and mind within their characteristics, (7) the expanse of the basic space without any change or transition, (8) the expanse of self-arising unceasing play, and (9) the expanse of natural, equal, and primordially free letting be. These nine can be summarized as (1) the expanse of the great vastness of innate presence, (2) the expanse of effortless self-lucidity, and (3) the expanse of primordial accomplishment without having done anything (for more details, see Longchenpa Rabjam 2007, 316–24).

However, as Germano 1992 (285) and Anspal 2005a (38) point out, none of Longchenpa's divisions of the Expanse Series seem to be attested in the actual tantras categorized under this series in the currently available collections of Nyingma tantras. Thus, these divisions appear to be of a thematical nature indicating different styles of contemplation rather than being categories of actual literature. By contrast, according to the description of the Expanse Series in the *Blue Annals* ('Gos lo tsā ba gzhon nu dpal 1996, 172), the subject matter of the greater and lesser tantras called *Equal to the Limits of Space* consists of the following nine expanses: (1) the expanse of the view, (2) the expanse of conduct, (3) the expanse of the maṇḍala, (4) the expanse of empowerment, (5) the expanse of samaya, (6) the expanse of practice, (7) the expanse of enlightened activity, (8) the expanse of paths and bhūmis, and (9) the expanse of the fruition. According to Anspal 2005a (16–24 and 38), this represents the standard list of the nine expanses of the Expanse Series on its own (rather than being viewed from the perspective of the Pith Instructions Series), as there are several more tantras based on this list. The *Tantra Equal to the Limits of Space* makes it clear that these nine expanses are not separate realities but nine aspects of the single ground of mind's fundamental nature, which is the ultimate reality of all phenomena. This ground resembles a vast expanse, and the nine expanses represent specific ways in which the awareness of this expansive nature of mind is related and even surpasses different aspects of the Vajrayāna path. Finally, yet another classification of the Expanse Series is said to consist of (1) the expanse of the heart of the matter, (2) the expanse of primordial nonarising, (3) the expanse beyond bindu, (4) the expanse free from reference points, (5) the inexpressible expanse, (6) the expanse of true reality, (7) the expanse free from all extremes, and (8) the expanse of nonduality.

269 As mentioned before, this refers to the explanatory tantra called the *Tantra That Teaches the Great Perfection as Samantabhadra's Unobstructed Awakened Mind* in the Northern Treasures' cycle *Samantabhadra's Unobstructed Awakened Mind*.

270 Tib. Nyi ma'i 'od kyi seng ge (here abbreviated as Nyi 'od seng ge). According to the traditional accounts, this little-known Indian master flourished during the late eighth and early ninth centuries.

As van Schaik (2004a, 170) says, the earliest known commentary on the *Guhyagarbhatantra*, the *Rin po che spar khab* by an Indian author named

Vilāsavajra (there were several persons with that name), probably written in the 770s, does not give any special precedence to the term Dzogchen and does not employ it in any specific technical sense. By contrast, the only other known Indic commentary on the whole tantra, the longer commentary ascribed to Sūryaprabhāsasiṃha (*Śrīguhyagarbhatattvaviniścayavyākhyānaṭikā*, P4719), places far more weight on the term and uses it much more frequently. According to the *Blue Annals* ('Gos lo tsā ba gzhon nu dpal 1996, 108), Bdud 'joms 'jigs bral ye shes rdo rje 1991 (688), and other sources, this commentary was translated by Vairocana, one of the twenty-five main disciples of Padmasambhava. As mentioned before, Vairocana was a student of Śrī Siṃha and is considered the main person to bring the teachings of the Mind Series and Expanse Series to Tibet. However, as van Schaik (2004a, 193n81) points out, the colophons of the canonical editions of this commentary do not mention Vairocana as the translator but someone called Pema Rutsé (Tib. Padma ru tshe; according to BDRC, a translator of that name flourished in ca. the fourteenth or fifteenth century: https://www.tbrc.org/#!rid=P4CZ15601).

For more information on *Sūryaprabhāsasiṃha, his role in the early Dzogchen tradition, his commentary, and a summary of its first chapter, see Martin 1987 and van Schaik 2004a (193–95).

271 There are a great number of Tibetan works with this title, but given the context, this must be Longchenpa's commentary on the *Guhyagarbhatantra*, called *Eliminating the Darkness of the Ten Directions* (Tib. *Gsang snying 'grel pa phyogs bcu mun sel*).

272 One could also say that "HO!" is an expression of nondual speech, an inexpressible expression, or an expression of what is inexpressible. More specifically, it refers to the inexpressible amazement that occurs when suddenly experiencing naked awareness within ordinary states of mind, such as strong emotions. This experience includes the basic unconditioned satisfaction that transcends the fundamental dissatisfaction of the saṃsāric mindset.

273 Tib. *rnam par dgyes pa* emended to *rnam par gyes pa*.

274 Thus, "what appears" refers to the environment and "what is possible" to the sentient beings with their five skandhas that live therein. "The four names" refers to the four mental skandhas without the first skandha of form because beings in the formless realm have no physical bodies or environments.

275 Tib. *yi don gyi kun gzhi* emended to *ye don gyi kun gzhi*. There is an identical misprint of *yi* versus *ye* in *Ketaka*'s following paragraph and the text uses *ye don gyi kun gzhi* twice more in the same sense.

In later Dzogchen writings, especially those of Longchenpa, "the primordial ultimate all-ground" is the first one among four specific kinds of all-ground that indicate how basic unawareness stirs and solidifies as saṃsāric appearances. In this specific technical term, "ultimate" does not refer to "ultimate reality" but to the most basic and initial form of unawareness, which is the ultimate ground or source of saṃsāra. The remaining three classifications of the all-ground are "the ultimate all-ground of linking," "the all-ground of diverse latent tendencies," and "the all-ground of the bodies of latent tendencies" (the first two among these terms also appear right below in this paragraph of *Ketaka*).

However, as *Ketaka*'s explanation in the present sentence of "the primordial ultimate ground of all"—the actual dharmatā that is completely beyond any notion of saṃsāra or nirvāṇa and thus does not serve as the basis of either one—clearly shows, the text obviously understands this expression as referring to the actual primordial ground and not to the basis of unawareness and subsequent delusion that Longchenpa calls "primordial ultimate all-ground." It appears that *Lancet* and *Lamp* agree with *Ketaka*'s specific use of the term *kun gzhi* for the ultimate ground (as opposed to the ground of unawareness and delusion). This is also confirmed by *The Aspiration Prayer*'s eighth line "the ground of all is unconditioned," which clearly refers to the unconditioned primordial ground, as opposed to the conditioned all-ground (this is explicitly pointed out by the commentaries). Furthermore, toward its end, *The Aspiration Prayer* equates "the ground of all" with the original buddha, Samantabhadra, in the sense of the primordial ground before any unawareness and delusion have set in.

Therefore, in both *The Aspiration Prayer* and all three commentaries, I render the term *kun gzhi* not as "all-ground" (as I do in contexts when "ground" and "all-ground" are clearly distinguished) but as "ground of all" in order to highlight the different use of this term. What adds further complications in this context is that throughout the development of the literature of the Great Perfection, different authors used all the above terms in different and even opposite ways.

For an overview of the stages of differentiating between the primordial ground and the all-ground, see Higgins 2013 (183ff., especially table F on p. 198), who distinguishes three phases: (1) Particularly early Dzogchen texts (eighth to early tenth century) typically say that saṃsāra and nirvāṇa, or sentient beings and buddhas, share a common ground (referred to as "all-ground"), but differ in terms of whether or not this ground is directly realized. (2) This is followed by a period (910–1249) of indications of divergence between all-ground and primordial ground. (3) Finally, during the "classical period" (1249–1705), there is an increasing trend toward clearly differentiating the two. Over time, terms such as "primordial ultimate all-ground" (Tib. *ye don gyi kun gzhi*) and "the ultimate all-ground of linking" (Tib. *sbyor ba don gyi kun gzhi*) that were originally used to indicate the unconditioned primordial ground in writings oriented toward Mahāyoga and the Mind Series were reinterpreted in most texts based on the Pith Instruction Series as being nothing but conditioned expressions of unawareness, delusion, and karmic processes.

Thus, the use of many of these technical terms sometimes differs greatly between different authors at different times and sometimes even in different texts of the same author, which can be very confusing if the context, the development of these terms over time, and their scriptural basis are not accounted for. For example, some texts of Longchenpa that are more based on the Mind Series use even the term "the ultimate all-ground of linking" for the unconditioned ground, while his works that are based on the Seventeen Tantras of the Pith Instructions Series always present this term as one of the four kinds of the conditioned all-ground (for details on Longchenpa's distinction between the primordial ground and the all-ground as well as the fourfold classification of the latter, see appendix 5A).

In sum, just as in *Lancet*, *Ketaka*, and *Lamp*, certain Dzogchen texts use the term *kun gzhi* on its own or in the expression "primordial ultimate ground of all" as an expression for the pure ground in the more general sense of its potentially being "the ground of all" (that is, the indeterminate ground from which all determinate manifestations of saṃsāra and nirvāṇa are suitable to arise) as opposed to the term's more technical sense of "all-ground" as the most basic form of unawareness. In the case of *Lancet*, *Ketaka*, and *Lamp*, such a use of the term may seem surprising given its above-mentioned historical development; these three commentaries clearly post-date Longchenpa, who in his main works had so clearly and in such detail insisted on differentiating the ground from the all-ground and whom the Nyingma tradition considers as the most authoritative systematizer of the Dzogchen teachings. However, the reason why *Lancet*, *Ketaka*, and *Lamp* explain the term *kun gzhi* in the sense of the primordial ground as opposed to the ground of delusion must be that *The Aspiration Prayer* itself uses the term in this way. As a part of the Northern Treasures, *The Aspiration Prayer* was discovered only two years after Longchenpa's passing away and, as a treasure text, it is by definition considered to have been concealed by Padmasambhava, thus belonging to a much earlier stage of the differentiation of Dzogchen terminology. In addition, Tibetan authors in general seem to love playing around with this term (and others), shifting from one meaning to another, sometimes even in the same paragraph, without blinking an eye or preannouncing such a shift (as evidenced by *Ketaka* use, in one paragraph, of the expressions "the ultimate all-ground of linking" and "the all-ground of diverse latent tendencies" in the sense of the ground of delusion in the same way as Longchenpa does, while identifying "the primordial ultimate ground of all" as the pure ground).

Hence, while it is important to take the date of a text's provenence into consideration, it is solely the context in a given text that determines the exact meaning of the term *kun gzhi*. This appears to be similar to the often-ambiguous use of that term in the sense of ālaya in non-Dzogchen texts, where it can either refer to the ālaya-consciousness or the ālaya in the sense of buddha nature or ālaya-wisdom. Finally, my reason for rendering *kun gzhi* as "all-ground" instead of "ālaya" in a Dzogchen context is that Dzogchen usually clearly differentiates between *kun gzhi* (not described along the lines of the ālaya-consciousness) and *kun gzhi'i rnam shes* (the "all-ground consciousness," which is the actual ālaya-consciousness) and explains both in the sense of being the ground for everything that subsequently evolves from them (versus the classical Yogācāra explanations of the meaning of ālaya): from the all-ground as the most fundamental layer of unawareness, the all-ground consciousness evolves, which in turn gives rise to the remaining seven consciousnesses and the plethora of their objects.

276 Right from the start, when the ground manifestations arise from the ground, they are either recognized for what they are and thus are free as Samantabhadra (the dharmakāya), or they are not recognized and thus stray into delusion as all kinds of saṃsāric sentient beings. Thus, the all-ground as the basic unawareness or nonrecognition that is the source of delusion is present with the ground right from the start of saṃsāra though its presence never stains the essence of the primordial undifferentiated ground beyond saṃsāra and nirvāṇa or, in other words, the originally pure nature of Samantabhadra. For the notion of "depth-lucidity," see appendices 2A and 6IB.

277 *Ketaka* also marks "I" and "make" as being words of *The Aspiration Prayer*.

278 Tib. *yi* ("of") emended to *ye*.

279 In accordance with *The Aspiration Prayer* and the context, Tib. *gzhin* is emended to *gzhi ni*.

280 The meanings of the intransitive Tibetan verb *mngon du 'gyur ba* are "to be revealed," "to become manifest," "to be actualized," "to be realized," "to become directly perceptible," and "to become evident." The corresponding transitive verb *mngon du byed pa* means "to reveal," "to manifest," "to actualize," or "to realize," "to directly perceive," and "to make evident." Though I generally render these verbs with the first of their meanings, it should be understood that their other meanings are always implied.

281 This refers to the story, often found in Dzogchen texts, about a prince who was unaware of his royal descent and thus lived among common people until he eventually recognized his status and assumed the formal position of the rightful king. Similarly, sentient beings wander in saṃsāra until they realize what they have always been—completely perfect buddhas. Obviously, this is very similar to the many examples and descriptions of all buddha qualities' already being present in ordinary sentient beings, only to be revealed, that are found in the common Mahāyāna teachings on buddha nature.

282 Tib. *sprug pa* in the expression *'khor ba dong sprug* can mean "shaking," "exhausting," or "purifying." Thus, this expression means "shaking/stirring/dredging/emptying/purifying the pit or depths of saṃsāra."

283 "The six distinctive features of alpha-purity" obviously refer to the well-known "six distinctive features of Samantabhadra's freedom" found in a number of Dzogchen sources. For example, the eleventh chapter of Jigmé Lingpa's *Treasury of Precious Qualities* lists these six as follows: (1) In the instant that the ground manifestations appear, they are immediately recognized as the ground's own appearances. (2) Since these self-appearances thus never stray into delusion, Samantabhadra's freedom is superior to the ground itself. (3) In a single instant, prajñā perfectly differentiates the entire variety of the ground's many qualities. (4) As soon as these qualities are differentiated, that prajñā matures as the dharmakāya. (5) Samantabhadra's freedom does not depend on anything extraneous and (6) always remains in its very own place. Though *Ketaka*'s words in this section do not always explicitly correspond to Jigmé Lingpa's phrasing of these six features, the meaning of this section is close enough to warrant a matching numbering of the six. For commentaries on Jigmé Lingpa's description of these six features and alternative explanations, see note 482.

284 This refers to the second among the three doors to liberation, which are the door to liberation that is emptiness, the door to liberation that is signlessness, and the door to liberation that is wishlessness. That is, the very dharmatā is emptiness, causes lack any signs or defining characteristics, and the appearance of results is not bound to or by aspirations, expectations, or wishes. With these meanings, the remaining two doors to liberation are also mentioned in the next two paragraphs of *Ketaka*.

285 As mentioned before, the eight ground manifestations manifest from within the primordial ground and consist of the six modes of appearing as (1) compassion, (2) light, (3) kāyas, (4) wisdom, (5) nonduality, and (6) freedom from extremes, as well as the two gateways to (7) saṃsāra and (8) nirvāṇa. Thus, the two gateways represent the two possibilities to interpret the six modes of the ground's own manifestations, which hinge upon awareness's recognition or nonrecognition of its own self-appearances. If awareness recognizes this sixfold efflorescence as its own self-arising dynamic energy or display, the six manifestations pass through the gateway to nirvāṇa. If awareness fails to recognize this display as its own self-arising appearances, these manifestations pass through the gateway to saṃsāra, which means that the six manifestations of innate presence become mistaken, and increasingly solidified, as the six realms of saṃsāric beings. In the case of awareness's self-recognition, the eight gateways immediately reverse into a corresponding eightfold dissolution as the entire unfolding of outer luminosity returns to inner luminosity as the full awareness of awakening. This is what is referred to as "Samantabhadra's

mode of freedom" (see appendix 2C). In the case of nonrecognition, the five lights of innate presence become solidified and distorted as the corresponding five material elements and so on, which represents "the delusion of sentient beings" (see appendices 2A and B, 3A, and 4B). For the term "precious innate presence" as the sphere from or within which the ground manifestations arise, see appendix 3A ("2.2. Detailed explanation of the factors that consist of the conditions that are its aspects").

286 "The faculty of being endowed with perfect cognizance [or knowledge]" refers to the third among the three uncontaminated faculties that are primarily discussed in the Śrāvakayāna—(1) the faculty of causing perfect knowledge, (2) the faculty of perfect knowledge, and (3) the faculty of being endowed with perfect knowledge. (1) The faculty of causing perfect knowledge consists of a specific set of nine faculties in the mind stream of someone on the śrāvaka path of seeing. This set, which relinquishes the afflictions to be relinquished through seeing and makes one know everything one did not know before, consists of the five pure faculties (confidence, vigor, mindfulness, samādhi, and prajñā), and the "faculties" of pleasant physical sensations, pleasant mental feelings, equanimity, and the mental sense faculty. (2) The faculty of being endowed with perfect knowledge refers to the same set of faculties in the mind stream of someone on the śrāvaka path of familiarization, which relinquishes the afflictions to be relinquished through familiarization. This faculty knows everything through clearly differentiating between antagonistic factors and remedial factors. (3) The faculty of being endowed with perfect knowledge refers to the same set of faculties in the mind stream of an arhat on the path of nonlearning. That is, by virtue of having relinquished all afflictions to be relinquished through seeing and familiarization without exception, arhats are endowed with the wisdom of realizing that all afflictions and all suffering have been terminated and will never arise again. In the present context, this third faculty obviously does not refer to the realization of an arhat but to that of the completely perfect buddha Samantabhadra; what is perceived as its "object" is nothing but the nonconceptual, nondual, and luminous dharmadhātu.

287 The term *isolate* (Skt. *vyāvṛtti*; Tib. *ldog pa*) refers to conceptual objects by indicating the process through which they appear for the thinking mind. For example, impermanent phenomena and phenomena that arise from causes and conditions are not different in nature, since all impermanent phenomena arise from causes and conditions, and all phenomena that arise from causes and conditions are impermanent. However, when we think "impermanent phenomena," a different mental image or notion comes to mind than when we think "phenomena that arise from causes and conditions." It is said that we select the specific notion of "impermanent phenomena" through the conceptual exclusion of everything that is not

an impermanent phenomenon. In this way, a certain notion is isolated or distinguished from all other notions, and this is why it is called an isolate. In this case here, the following five wisdoms represent five such isolates with regard to the single essence of wisdom.

288 In other words, the five wisdoms are five facets of primordial awareness: dharmadhātu wisdom is its aspect of emptiness, mirror-like wisdom its aspect of luminosity, the wisdom of equality its aspect of lacking any distinctions or biases, discriminating wisdom its aspect of precisely perceiving every detail of relative appearances, and all-accomplishing wisdom its aspect of being able to unimpededly fulfill all wishes and skillfully achieve all goals.

289 More often, the last family is called "*buddha* family" but here it is named after the symbolic wheel (*cakra*) that Vairocana as the head of this buddha family holds in his hands.

290 *Tib. ta krī ta* is corrupt and most probably should be *daudārika* (Tib. *sgo ba*).

291 In terms of our body, the forty-two peaceful figures or deities are said to reside in the heart cakra and appear after death during the intermediate state of dharmatā (Tib. *chos nyid kyi bar do*). The five male buddhas and their female counterparts are Vairocana and Ākāśadhātvīśvarī, Akṣobhya and Buddhalocanā, Ratnasambhava and Māmakī, Amitābha and Pāṇḍaravāsinī, and Amoghasiddhi and Samayatārā (center, east, south, west, and north). The eight male bodhisattvas (in the order of their appearance in pairs as the retinues of the four buddhas other than Vairocana) are Kṣitigarbha, Maitreya, Ākāśagarbha, Samantabhadra, Avalokiteśvara, Mañjuśrī, Vajrapāṇi, and Sarvanivaraṇaviṣkambhin. The corresponding eight female bodhisattvas are Lāsyā, Puṣpā, Mālā, Dhūpā, Gītā, Alokā, Gandhā, and Naivedyā. The six sages are the buddhas of the six realms of sentient beings: Indra Kauṣika (gods), Vemacitra (asuras), Śākyamuni (humans), Dhruvasiṃha (animals), Jvālamukha, (hungry ghosts), and Dharmarāja (hell beings). The four male gatekeepers are Vijaya (Acala), Yamāntaka, Hayagrīva, and Amṛtakuṇḍalin. The four female gatekeepers are Aṅkuśā, Pāśā, Śṛṅkhalā, and Ghantā. In the center of or above these forty-two figures, Samantabhadra and Samantabhadrī appear in union. According to Gangteng Tulku Rinpoche (2003, 94), as long as wisdom or its dynamic energy is not recognized as such, the forty-two peaceful deities are nothing but forty-two coarse thoughts. They are only perceived as these deities once the ground's dynamic energy is recognized for what it is. The same obviously goes for the wrathful deities.

292 Tib. *drug* ("six") emended to *lnga*.

293 The fifty-eight wrathful figures or deities are said to reside in the crown chakra and appear in the intermediate state subsequent to the peaceful ones. The five herukas and their female counterparts are Buddhaheruka and Buddhakrodhīśvarī, Vajraheruka and Vajrakrodhīśvarī, Ratnaheruka and Ratnakrodhīśvarī, Padmaheruka and Padmakrodhīśvarī, and

Karmaheruka and Karmakrodhīśvarī (center, east, south, west, and north). The eight wrathful gaurīs are Gaurī, Caurī, Pramohā, Vetālī, Pukkasī, Ghasmarī, Caṇḍālī, and Śmaśānī (east, south, west, north, southeast, southwest, northwest, and northeast). The eight piśācīs are Siṃhamukhā, Vyāghrīmukhā, Śṛgālamukhā, Śvānamukhā, Gṛdhramukhā, Kaṅkamukhā, Kākamukhā, and Ūlumukhā (east, south, west, north, southeast, southwest, northwest, and northeast). The four female gatekeepers are Aṅkuśā, Pāśā, Śṛṅkhalā, and Ghantā (east, south, west, and north). The twenty-eight īśvarīs are the six yoginīs of peaceful activity (Rākṣasī, Brāhmī, Mahādevī, Lobhā, Kumārī, and Indrānī; east), the six yoginīs of enriching activity (Vajrā, Śāntī, Amṛtā, Candrā, Daṇḍā, and Rākṣasī; south), the six yoginīs of magnetizing activity (Bhakṣinī, Ratī, Mahābalā, Rākṣasī, Kāmā, and Vasurakṣā; west), the six yoginīs of wrathful activity (Vāyudevī, Nārī, Vārāhī, Vajrā, Mahāhastinī, and Varuṇadevī; north), and the four yoginīs of the gates (white Vajrā, yellow Vajrā, red Vajrā, and green Vajrā; east, south, west, and north). In the center of or above these fifty-eight deities, there appear Mahāparamaheruka and Krodhīśvarī in union (the wrathful forms of Samantabhadra and Samantabhadrī), thus making sixty.

294 As in most cases below, *Ketaka* here pulls apart the two components of Tib. *smon lam* (lit. "path of aspiration"), taking "path" as a separate word of the root text.

295 *Ketaka* pulls apart the two components of Tib. *mtha' rgyas* ("fully unfold"), making *mtha'* a part of *mtha' grol* ("freedom from extremes"). This and the preceding paragraph mention the classical Dzogchen notions of "primordial freedom," "complete freedom," and "freedom from extremes," while "freedom in itself" is mentioned at the end of the following section, "The aspiration prayer in terms of the manner in which emanations unfold as other-appearances." For details on these four modes of freedom and others, see appendix 7.

296 *Ketaka* here retains the Sanskrit word *duḥkha*. Originally, this term referred to an axle not fitting properly into the hub of a wheel or that hub being off-center so that, in either case, the wheel would not roll smoothly (with *sukha* indicating the opposite). In this sense, *duḥkha* refers to saṃsāric existence as fundamentally "mis-fitting" and always being "off-center," even if it subjectively seems to roll along smoothly (*sukha*) for a while. Thus, the term includes all manifest and latent kinds of uneasiness, unpleasantness, difficulties, problems, sorrows, and pain that sentient beings experience in the three realms of saṃsāra. Obviously, this goes way beyond and far deeper than the usual meaning of the word "suffering," so renderings such as "(basic) dissatisfactoriness" or the like seem to be more appropriate.

This is especially true when one considers the three kinds of such dissatisfactoriness in the Buddhist teachings: (1) the all-pervasive dissatisfactoriness of the conditioned formations of saṃsāra, (2) the dissatisfactoriness of change, and (3) the dissatisfactoriness of pain or manifest suffering. The first refers to the fact that any birth in saṃsāra, even in the highest god realms, inevitably and intrinsically bears the seed for manifest suffering and pain, for it was caused by mental afflictions and conditioned karmic actions, all of which are based on the fundamental delusion of clinging to a seemingly real identity of oneself and all other phenomena. The second is what ordinary beings experience as happiness; the problem is that happiness will inevitably cease and turn into manifest suffering. The third is what could be properly translated as "suffering"—all obvious and manifest troubles, conflicts, calamities, mental or physical pains, diseases, and so on. Obviously, the first and second would never be called suffering in the usual sense, because the first one is not perceived at all by ordinary beings and the second one is seen as the exact opposite of suffering. Nevertheless, since there seems to be a quite pervasive and strong habituation to the term "suffering" in Western Buddhist audiences and literature (though, ironically, nobody really wants to hear about suffering), I follow that consensus.

297 "Great Glacial Lake of Wisdom" (Tib. *ye shes gang chen mtsho* for Skt. *mahāsagara* ["Great Ocean"]) is another name of Vairocana Mahāsagara, who resides in the sambhogakāya realm Richly Adorned Akaniṣṭha in the aspects of the five buddha families (Vairocana-Vairocana, Vairocana-Akṣobhya, Vairocana-Ratnasambhava, Vairocana-Amitābha, and Vairocana-Amoghasiddhi).

The "Realm Whose Ground and Center Are Adorned with Flowers" is the central world system in a vast universe of world systems that is located in the single minute particle in the center of Vairocana's palm. This realm represents the sphere of a single supreme nirmāṇakāya (such as Buddha Śākyamuni). In the outer rim of that realm, we find our larger world system Endurance (Skt. Sahā), in whose center there is our own particular four-continent world. (All of this is also described in the *Avataṃsakasūtra*.) In the teachings of the Great Perfection, Samantabhadra's realm of the dharmakāya is called "The Vajra Heart of Luminosity," the sambhogakāya realm of Vairocana in his five aspects "The Sound of Brahmā's Drum," and the realm of all nirmāṇakāyas "Eon of Mahābrahmā."

The "twelve fully perfected teachers" in the Dzogchen tradition are all nirmāṇakāya buddhas who gradually appear in twelve different reams at twelve different times, from the Youth Genuine Illumination (Tib. Khye'u snang ba dam pa), said to be an emanation of Vajradhara who taught the *Tantra of the Universes and Transformations of Sound* to the 1,002 buddhas of this eon, up to Buddha Śākyamuni (for details, see Kongtrul Lodrö Tayé 1995, 98–105 and Bdud 'joms 'jigs bral ye shes rdo rje 1991, 115–19, 123–38, and 409).

298 There are three kinds of nirmāṇakāyas: (1) natural nirmāṇakāyas, that is, Vairocana, Akṣobhya, Ratnasambhava, Amitābha, and Amoghasiddhi in their respective realms of Akaniṣṭha, Abhirati, Śrīmat, Padmakūṭa, and Karmaprasiddhi; (2) nirmāṇakāyas who guide beings, that is, emanations of the natural nirmāṇakāyas who manifest as teachers of the six classes of beings (such as Buddha Śākyamuni in the past or Maitreya in the future in this world); and (3) diversified nirmāṇakāyas, who appear in all kinds of ways to benefit beings, such as artists, scientists, healers, animals, and even inanimate phenomena. For more details on these three kinds of nirmāṇakāyas, see appendix 6IIE, Bdud 'joms 'jigs bral ye shes rdo rje 1991 (128–34), and Jigme Lingpa and Kangyur Rinpoche 2013 (300–314).

299 Here, Tib. *lhun grub* may also be understood as "effortlessly accomplished."

300 *Tib. rgyu drug* ("six causes") emended to *rgyud drug*.

301 As for the somewhat obscure reference to the shortcomings of the Peak of Existence (the highest realm of the formless realm) in the above heading "The aspiration prayer for awareness to be free as wisdom through teaching that the shortcomings of the Peak of Existence arise from unawareness," the Peak of Existence is not mentioned in what follows. It is only in the first paragraph of *Ketaka*'s comments on the end of *The Aspiration Prayer* ("2.1.2.2.2.2. The aspiration through a summary of the topic at hand") that the text explicitly refers to the Peak of Existence. This paragraph somewhat parallels the one at hand here, concluding that, as progressively coarser conceptions of apprehender and apprehended evolve, the formless realm, the form realm, and the desire realm manifest within the one-pointed all-ground that represents the meditative absorption of the Peak of Existence. Thus, it appears that *Ketaka* identifies the state of the Peak of Existence (which is often described as being similar to being unconscious and completely without any object) as representing the most subtle and at the same time most basic form of saṃsāric existence in that it consists of undistractedly remaining in the indeterminate state of the all-ground that is the most basic form of unawareness: as *Ketaka* here says, "the unclear cognizance of being absolutely mindless about apprehender and apprehended that is as oblivious as deep sleep." In other words, *Ketaka* seems to equate the Peak of Existence with "the unawareness that has the same identity as the cause," from which the subsequent connate and imaginative unawarenesses as well as all other coarser forms of saṃsāric existence derive.

302 In accordance with the context and a parallel phrase at the beginning of 2.1.2.2.2.1.2.5. "The aspiration prayer in terms of introducing nescience as being the dharmadhātu of nonconceptual wisdom," the nonsensical Tib. *shes g.yul* is emended to *shes pa yul*.

303 Tib. *'gyur* ("becomes") emended to *'gyus*.

304 In Dzogchen texts, this refers either to five distinct appearances of white, blue, yellow, red, and green lights or an appearance of five-colored light as in a rainbow.

305 *Ketaka* marks both occurrences of *'khor* in this sentence ("saṃsāra" on its own above and as a part of *'khrul 'khor* here) as being part of *The Aspiration Prayer*. "Whirl of delusion" (*'khrul 'khor*) can also be rendered as "wheel of delusion," "deceptive round," "vicious circle," "magical wheel," "machinations," "mechanism," and "machinery," all of which characterize the process of unawareness's triggering and sustaining the plethora of delusion in its many forms.

306 For more details on the unawareness of same identity, connate unawareness, and imaginative unawareness, see the parallel passages of *Lamp* and appendix 3A.

307 Here, *Ketaka* takes *'khor ba* (which can mean "saṃsāra" or "to cycle") as a verb.

308 Tib. *las tsam ste* emended to *las rtsom ste*.

309 Tib. *sdang ba* ("hatred") emended to *ldang ba*.

310 Lines 341–42 (a.k.a. "People Doha"). *Ketaka*'s phrasing *lha dang bung ba glang chen bye sleb dang / 'dir ni de dag bzhin du blta bar byos/* is quite corrupt. The full verse (lines 339–42) reads:

Kyeho, fools, Saraha says this:
Do not fetter yourself through clinging to objects!
Regard this as in the case of fish,
Butterflies, elephants, bees, and deer.

Advayavajra's *Dohakoṣapañjikā* (D2256, fols. 199b.7–200a.1) comments as follows:

> Saraha says this: "Do not fetter yourself by way of enjoying the five kinds of sense pleasures through clinging to objects!" For, if you do, [you end up] like fish attached to taste desiring foam and thus swimming elsewhere and getting killed by others, butterflies attached to visible form dying in a lamp, elephants dying through being attached to tangible objects, bees [dying] through being attached to smells, and deer [dying] through being attached to sounds, all of which are preceded by attachment.

Avadhūtipa's *Dohakoṣahṛdaya arthagītiṭīkā* (D2268, fol. 91a.4–91b.1) says that the examples of the common five sense pleasures for those who do not trust in what Saraha says are easy to understand. The uncommon sense pleasures of yogic practitioners are as follows:

> To be attached to the taste of bliss is like being a fish. To be attached to the maṇḍala of male and female deities is like being a butterfly. To take the experiences of [the practice of] the prajñā-jñāna [empowerment], which are the example, to

> be the actual thing is like being an elephant. To be attached to the smell of emptiness is like being a bee. These four are taught with regard to [such] experiences. By virtue of the instructions of genuine gurus with regard to [these experiences that are similar to those of] fish, butterflies, elephants, and bees, [there are] means for not being fettered even when enjoying objects. The instructions are like the sun, objects are like scattered flowers, and mindfulness is like a bee—it enjoys the objects and takes flight into the dharmadhātu. As for delighting in [the conventional expressions for these] bee[-like experiences] and the conventional expressions of many terms, valid cognitions, scriptures, and treatises, these many conventional expressions do not bestow the experience of the true intention of the Buddha-like secret utterances of instructions in three words, which is similar to a young woman's secret utterances being spoiled. This is to be regarded like a deer [chasing after sounds].

The *Dohanidhikoṣaparipūrṇagītināmanijatattvaprakāśaṭīkā* (D2257, fol. 249a.1–6) comments:

> Yogic practitioners should not fetter themselves through clinging to the objects that are sense pleasures and to thoughts of their being different. Therefore, with a sense of amazement, [Saraha] exclaims "Kyeho, fools!" toward all saṃsāric sentient beings. What is the point of doing so? It means "Listen to what Saraha says!" What is it [that he says]? Regard this as in the case of fish being attached to taste, butterflies being attached to tangible objects, elephants being attached to the smell of black fragrant aloe wood, bees being attached to the colors of flowers, and antelopes being attached to sweet songs. You may say, "These [sense pleasures] are flawed: they serve as the causes of saṃsāra because attachment increases [through them]." No, it is fitting [for yogic practitioners to engage them as follows]. Similar to fish being attached to the taste of foam [on the water], yogic practitioners taste suchness. Butterflies being attached to the pleasure of tangible objects resembles the way in which yogic practitioners dwell in bliss, first in the body and then in the mind. Similar to elephants being attached to smell, yogic practitioners are not attached to bliss but pervaded by the smell of emptiness. Similar to bees being attached to colors, yogic practitioners know [all] that appears and is possible to be the dharmakāya—utterly pellucid Mahāmudrā. Similar to deer chasing after songs, yogic

practitioners swiftly run after the song of the inseparability of bliss and emptiness.

311 The definition of a result of concordant outflow is "a phenomenon that is either the same as its specific cause or accords with it in its aspect of appearance." There are two types of such results: (1) results of concordant outflow that are actions and (2) results of concordant outflow that are experiences. An example for the first is the wish to engage in virtue in this life by virtue of having committed virtuous actions in former lives. An example for the second is the experience of abundant wealth as a result in later lives by virtue of having performed generosity in the present life. The definition of a result of maturation is "an unobscured and neutral phenomenon that has arisen from either contaminated virtuous actions or nonvirtuous actions," such as the five skandhas at birth. The definition of a dominated result is "that which is produced by its specific causes by their own power" and the most common instance of this is the environment in which a given being is born and lives (see also *Abhidharmakośa* II.57abc and 58cd).

312 "Time" refers to those hungry ghosts who suffer from extreme hunger and thirst due to not finding any food or drink for centuries. Sometimes, even if they see a little bit of food or drink from a distance and crawl there under great pain, once they arrive there, it has disappeared, became spoiled, or is guarded by large numbers of people with weapons who beat them and chase them away.

"Being burned" indicates those hungry ghosts whose mouths and throats are no wider than the eye of a needle and a hair, respectively, while their stomachs are as big as a whole country or Mount Meru. Even if they are sometimes able to swallow enough to satisfy them, it will burst into flames and burn their inner organs from within.

"Being distorted" refers to those hungry ghosts who have all kinds of different individual predicaments, such as eating their own flesh and blood, food given to them turning into inedible things (such as pus, stone, or iron), getting into fights over food and drink with other hungry ghosts and becoming terribly wounded in the process, or many creatures living in or on their bodies and devouring them.

These three classes of hungry ghosts are usually referred to as those who have outer, inner, and specific obscurations, respectively (see the parallel comments in *Lamp*).

313 The Avīci hell is the lowest and worst of all the eight hot hells. According to the *Abhidharmakośabhāṣya* on III.58, two reasons are given for its name: unlike in other hells, there is never any interruption (*vīci*) of suffering, or there is no agreeable state (*vīci*) there at all (in other hells, there are also no pleasant feelings that are results of maturation but there may be pleasant feelings that are results of concordant outflow).

314 Tib. *rtogs* emended to *rtog*.

315 It is said that the outwardly radiating luminosity of wisdom is withdrawn or absorbed into the ultimate expanse, but this does not mean that this wisdom is dull or obscure because its capacity of knowing is not lost: there remains the wisdom of extremely subtle inner luminosity. In other words, the self-arising manifestations of the ground sink back into the ground itself, while the wisdom of luminosity never stirs from the ultimate inner expanse free from all reference points. For more details, see appendix 6.

316 Compare also the two allegorical descriptions according to the lower yānas (all those below Atiyoga) and the higher yāna (Atiyoga) of how the basic awareness of sentient beings strays into unawareness, delusion, and the five mental afflictions and how it becomes free again in the *Tantra of the Eradication of Delusion at Its Root* (Tib. *'Khrul pa rtsad gcod kyi rgyud*; see Kapstein 1992, 251–54).

317 Tib. *snyongs* ("rub," "anoint") emended to *myongs*.

318 *Ketaka* here separates the two syllables of the Tibetan *sangs rgyas* for "awakening" (or "buddhahood"): *sangs* means "purified" or "awakened" and *rgyas* "unfolded."

319 Similar to "HO" at the beginning of *The Aspiration Prayer*, "A HO" (and similar utterances such as "E MA HO" and "A LA LA HO") have the meaning of delight, joy, satisfaction, and amazement. That is, "A HO" here is an expression for how wonderful, joyful, and deeply satisfying the natural state of open, spacious, and relaxed awareness is—there is no greater happiness and joy. In more technical terms, "A" stands for primordially pure emptiness and "HO" for bliss or awareness; thus "A HO" refers to the unity of bliss and emptiness, or of awareness and emptiness. In the Great Perfection in particular, "A" symbolizes alpha-purity and the meditative approach of Cutting through Solidity, while "HO" refers to innate presence and the approach of Direct Leap; thus "A HO" refers to the unity of alpha-purity and innate presence or of Cutting through Solidity and Direct Leap.

320 Tib. *rgun* ("grape") emended to *dgun*.

321 According to Gangteng Tulku Rinpoche (2003, 116–17), "loud noises" does not so much refer to thunder but primarily to natural sounds that arise through imbalances in the elements.

Further favorable times to recite the prayer include the tenth days of the waxing and the waning moon, as well as the day of the full moon. Similar to reading the *Tibetan Book of the Dead*, it is helpful to read *The Aspiration Prayer* to people while they are in the process of dying, as well as once they have passed away and at their funeral. There are also a number of places that are conducive to reciting this aspiration prayer, such as high up on a mountain, at the ocean, or at a great river. It is also beneficial to recite it together with the winds that occur during great storms.

322 As mentioned before, the source of *The Aspiration Prayer*—the *Great Dzogchen Tantra of Samantabhadra's Unobstructed Awakened Mind, the Tantra of Becoming a Buddha Merely Through Seeing, Hearing, Wearing, and Making Aspiration Prayers*—contains instructions on freedom through wearing in its eighteenth "chapter that teaches the means of drawing and placing freedom through wearing." There are also the six tantras of the Essence of Freedom through Wearing (Tib. Btags grol snying po'i rgyud drug), the primary tantras of the *Khandro Nyingtig* revealed by Pema Ledreltsal. For an English translation of the root tantra and its commentary, see http://www.buddhavisions.com/wp-content/uploads/2015/11/Liberation-by-Wearing-Essence-Tantra-and-Commentary.pdf.

323 This refers to the three lineages of the Great Perfection—the lineage of the awakened mind of the victors, the symbolic lineage of awareness holders, and the ear-whispered lineage of persons.

324 The lesser awareness-holders are the awareness-holders of the eight common siddhis, the middling are the common awareness-holders of the desire realm, and the greater are the awareness-holders of the realms of desire and form.

325 Tib. *lho 'phye* emended to *lto 'phye*. This refers to Sangsang Lhatra (Tib. Zang zang lha brag brag ri dug sbrul spungs 'dra ba), the place where the Northern Treasures were discovered, which resembles a cluster of poisonous snakes.

326 This refers to Rigdzin Gödemchen, the revealer of the Northern Treasures.

327 *Buddhahood Without Meditation*, revealed by Düjom Lingpa (Bdud 'joms gling pa 2004, 346), glosses "the single sphere" (Tib. *thig le nyag gcig*) and "the all-embracing consummation of saṃsāra and nirvāṇa" (Tib. *'khor 'das 'ub chub pa*) as two of six synonyms of Dzogchen as follows: "It is a sphere (*thig le*) because it is beyond all the [hard] edges of thoughts. It is single (*nyag gcig*) because saṃsāra and nirvāṇa are of one taste as bodhicitta ... It is the all-embracing consummation of saṃsāra and nirvāṇa because all phenomena of saṃsāra and nirvāṇa are contained within the embrace (*'ub*) of the sugata heart and completely consummate (*chub*) therein."

328 Tib. *'di na* ("in this") emended to *'di ni* ("this"). If read as it stands, "in this" might refer back to the single sphere in the previous line.

329 Tib. Zil gnon nam mkha'i rdo rje, a Nyingma master born in the nineteenth century.

330 Tib. Mkha' khyab rang byung bde ba'i rdo rje.

331 This refers to the line of the Karmapas as successive incarnations of Avalokiteśvara.

332 This is a poetic reference to Tsurphu Monastery (Tib. Mtshur phu), the principal seat of the Karmapas. It is one among the three main monastic seats of the Karma Kagyü lineage in Tibet, all established by the First Karmapa: Gambo Kangra (Tib. Kam po gang rva)—a.k.a. Gambo Nenang (Tib. Kam po gnas nang)—in 1164, Karma Gön (Tib. Ka rma dgon) in 1185, and Tsurphu in 1189. In due order, these three seats are said to

correspond to the maṇḍalas of the enlightened body, speech, and mind of Cakrasaṃvara.

The expression "the supreme bliss of the ḍākinīs's web" (Skt. *ḍākinījālasaṃvara*, Tib. *mkha' 'gro ma drva ba sdom pa*) appears to be a common notion in the Buddhist tantras; for example, the *Hevajratantra* is also called *Śrīhevajraḍākinījālasaṃvaratantrarāja* (for the several meanings of this expression, see Tsuda 1970, 58–64). Moreover, Skt. *saṃvara* is an abbreviation of Cakrasaṃvara (Tib. 'Khor lo bde mchog or 'khor lo sdom pa), so *Ketaka*'s phrase "the wheel of the enlightened mind of the supreme bliss of the ḍākinīs' web" (Tib. *mkha' 'gro drva ba sdom pa'i thugs kyi 'khor lo*) is also a play on the name and the meaning of Cakrasaṃvara. When reading this phrase solely from the Tibetan, it could even mean "the cakra of the enlightened mind where the ḍākinīs weave their web," possibly as a reference to the Karmapa's black crown, whose original was woven by the ḍākinīs from their hair, and offered to him as a token of his realization.

333 Tib. Ka rma thub bstan 'jam dpal tshul khrims grags pa.

334 The second verb here is an honorific one in Tibetan, thus already indicating the contrast between the path of delusion that leads to the appearances of saṃsāra and the exalted path of the Dharma that leads to the realization of nirvāṇa.

335 As in most other cases below, *Lamp* here pulls apart the two components of Tib. *smon lam* (lit. "path of aspiration") and takes "path" as a separate word of the root text.

336 According to Longchenpa (see appendix 2A, 2.3. "Concluding summary through their aspects"), "the locus of freedom" refers to the primordial ground that is always unstained and free in and of itself. By contrast, the ground manifestations as "the ground of freedom" are not manifestly free yet but function as the condition for freedom when recognized as the self-appearances of the primordial ground. Thus, the approaching of freedom occurs via the "exteriorization" of the ground—the ground manifestations—while the actual already present freedom lies within the ground's original purity. In other words, the ground manifestations as the ground of freedom serve as the path to freedom, while the ground is the destination that in itself is freedom or freedom's very own natural state.

337 The qualities of freedom consist of the thirty-two qualities of the dharmakāya (the ten powers, the four fearlessnesses, and the eighteen unique qualities), while the qualities of maturation consist of the thirty-two major marks of the rūpakāyas.

338 Anonymous 1973–77, 1:102. The first and third lines of this quote in *Lamp* read: "What is this primal foundation of saṃsāra? ... What is the basic nature of one's own wisdom?" In general, when *Lamp* exhibits variant readings of the eighteen tantras of the Pith Instructions Series, it seems

that the text copies the versions as they appear in Longchenpa's works because the latter often show the same variants.

339 Tib. *kun gzhi ma.*

340 Tib. *thog* emended to *thob.*

341 Following Anonymous 1973–77 (2:532), *lags* ("are") is emended to *bshad* ("are explained as").

342 As *Lamp* (based on Longchenpa) explains at the end of its discussion of the six flawed views, they all represent only partial characteristics of the ground; they mistake a single one of its innately present and alpha-pure qualities as the actual defining characteristic of the ground. As the text says, "This resembles the example of seven blind people [each] mistaking certain parts or limbs of the body of an elephant for its body, which possesses [all these] parts." Furthermore, the six mistaken views, as well as other views about the ground that are held on the basis of different theorizing philosophical or metaphysical positions, are sometimes categorized as "the ground as a knowable object" (Tib. *shes bya'i gzhi*). By contrast, the true ground that is the basic nature (Tib. *gnas lugs kyi gzhi*) is a matter of the direct experience and realization of those who actually practice the path of Dzogchen.

343 Anonymous 1973–77 (2:172) inserts "if results were innately present" after "yet again." The last two lines are glossed as "As soon as results are innately present, there would be no need to attain any results through effort. Since results are innately present, one is not able to eliminate the flaw that causes and results come to an end on their own."

344 Following Anonymous 1973–77 (2:173), *rtog bcas* ("conceptual") in the second line is emended to *ldog bcas* ("opposite"). In the tantra, the fourth line is an almost literal repetition of the third, but just as in *Lamp*, the fourth line as quoted in Longchenpa's *Precious Treasury of Words and Their Meanings* has the correct reverse order of "determinate" and "indeterminate." The text of the tantra glosses the first line as "due to vacillating similar to sometimes being a horse and sometimes an elephant, it would sometimes be the ground and sometimes the path," the second line as "like asserting that water is fire," and the last two lines as "How could indeterminate water have the nature of water?"

345 Anonymous 1973–77 (2:174) glosses "the true actuality" as "among knowable objects" and the second line as "being determinate as a cause, the result would absolutely not arise; thus, what would be the difference if the result arose from the cause or the cause arose from the result?"

346 Following Anonymous 1973–77 (2:174), *grol ba* ("being free as") in the last line is emended to *'gro ba* ("turning into"). In the fifth line, I follow *Lamp*'s *dgos med do* ("would be unnecessary") against *dgos med par.* The text of the tantra glosses the second line as "if the basic nature were capable of transforming, the flaw of the result being endless would have to be eliminated," "the cause" in the third line as "the cause of sentient

beings," and the last two lines as "for example, if the ground were to change, material phenomena would transform right now into something that has self-awareness."

347 Following Anonymous 1973–77 (2:175), *ngo bor* ("as having the nature of") in the first line is emended to *yin ngor* ("as having the essence of being"). The text of the tantra glosses the first line as "it is not determined as being searchable as purity, nor is it found as impurity because purity and impurity are mixed."

348 Following Anonymous 1973–77 (2:175), *rgyu dang 'bras bu* ("cause and result") in the first line is emended to *rgyu gcig 'bras bu* ("a single cause ... results") and the difficult second line *gang gi ngo bos de snang ba* to *gang gis ngo bo 'di snang bas*. These three lines are particularly obscure but are explained by a commentary on this tantra by Vimalamitra (see Germano 1992n57) as follows. If the ground were diversity, it would either have to be diverse in terms of its changing or diverse despite its being unchanging and unfabricated. The first possibility refers to the first line and the second to the remaining two lines. "Changing" would mean that the ground somehow kept shifting between being or resulting in different things or appearances, while "unchanging" would entail that it from the start consists of different distinct parts that constitute its diversity. However, since its essence would then appear in accordance with whatever descriptions of these different parts are given (such as "it is also white" or "it is also black"), freedom within a single dimension that is the true basic nature would be impossible, because the results of a ground that is intrinsically diverse would also have to be different.

349 Anonymous 1973–77, 1:127.

350 Ibid., 1:529. *Lamp* has this as two lines of verse:

> The ground of great alpha-purity
> Is endowed with essence, nature, and compassionate
> responsiveness.

351 "The youthful vase body" is a Dzogchen expression that is used for (1) the ground (tathāgatagarbha) and also (2) the fruition that is the dharmakāya.

(1) Regarding its meaning as the ground, inner luminosity's qualities—kāyas, wisdoms, and compassionate responsiveness—are not directly manifest but exist internally like a body within a vase. That is, the innately present self-radiance of awareness's nature is present in the form of the dynamic energy of inner luminosity for as long as this inner luminosity does not encounter any conditions for the appearances of innate presence to spread to the outside. Therefore, this is referred to as "the youthful vase body," which does not manifest externally since its seal is not yet broken. This body of awareness's luminosity is described as "youthful" because its qualities are pristinely pure (never tainted by saṃsāra) and completely beyond birth and death. That is, in its timelessness, primordial awareness

is ever youthful even when sentient beings appear to age, decay, and die. Another explanation is that it is youthful because its capacity of knowing is unceasing and unchanging. Once the seal of the vase is broken, the light sphere of wisdom or the ground manifestations dawn as outer luminosity while not moving away from the original alpha-pure ground or inner luminosity. This is called "the appearance of the nature that is innate presence."

According to Yönten Gyatso's commentary on Jigmé Lingpa's *Treasury of Precious Qualities* (Yon tan rgya mtsho 1982–87, 542–44), "youthful" means that since the nature of awareness is unconditioned, it does not decay or disintegrate like conditioned phenomena. "Vase body" means that inner luminosity or awareness is the unceasing ground of the arising of the three kāyas within the ultimate expanse.

During the state of the youthful vase body, it is not that the qualities of the three kāyas in their entirety are something nonexistent; the ground manifestations exist in such a way that they are suitable to arise from them, and when they arise, all kinds of pure and impure manifestations become directly apparent without being mixed. Thus, unlike the horns of a rabbit, it is not impossible for the qualities of the three kāyas to appear. Nor are these qualities something existent because they are not at all established as any characteristics whatsoever. Having just these reasons in mind, those qualities are labeled with the conventional expression "youthful vase body."

For example, when a statue complete with its face, arms, and so on exists within a vase, though all its parts are complete, they are obscured by the vase and thus not visible from outside. Likewise, the wisdom of inner luminosity is endowed with all aspects of its qualities, but they are not manifest as external luminosity. Still, the example does not apply in all respects because inner luminosity does not have to have physical characteristics such as color and shape or a face and arms; rather, what is referred to here is the sheer unimpeded inner radiance that is suitable to appear as such characteristics.

Similarly, the sūtras of definitive meaning and the commentaries on their intention that accord with this use the same or similar examples for the existence of the sugata heart within the cocoon of the obscurations. The *Kuśalamūlasaṃparigrahasūtra* (D101) says: "The tathāgata heart is like a lamp within a vase. When the vase breaks, it becomes lucidly visible" (I could not locate this quote in that sūtra but the same example is used in the *Mahābherīsūtra* [D223, fol. 182a.4–182b.1] and the *Aṅgulimālīyasūtra* [D214, fol. 294a.5]). Likewise, Nāgārjuna's *Dharmadhātustava* 5–7 says:

> Just as a lamp that's sitting in a vase
> does not illuminate at all,
> while dwelling in the vase of the afflictions,
> the dharmadhātu is not seen.
> From whichever of its sides
> you punch some holes into this vase,

from just these various places then,
its light rays will beam forth.
Once the vajra of samādhi
has completely smashed this vase,
to the very limits of all space,
it will shine just everywhere.

The *Uttaratantra* teaches this through nine examples, beginning with the one of a buddha sitting within a lotus, and Saraha's *Dohākośagīti* ("People Dohā"; lines 166–69) declares this:

Mind as such alone is the seed of everything,
From which existence and nirvāṇa bloom.
I pay homage to mind, which grants the fruitions we wish for,
Just like a wish-fulfilling jewel.

(2) When the term "youthful vase body" is used for the dharmakāya, it is in the sense that the dharmakāya's wisdom remains inwardly radiant within it, even when it radiates out as the rūpakāyas, similar to light within a crystal or prism. That is, the dharmakāya's own qualities are always only present as its own unceasing internal luminosity, but do not manifest as the sambhogakāya of outer luminosity. Therefore, Jigmé Lingpa refers to it as "the beautiful interior of the mansion of the vase." *Buddhahood Without Meditation* revealed by Düjom Lingpa (Bdud 'joms gling pa 2004, 346) glosses this expression as one of six synonyms of Dzogchen as follows: "It is youthful (*gzhon nu*) because it is free fom all birth, death, aging, and decay. It is a vase (*bum pa*) because the outer seal of innate presence has not been rent open. It is a body (*sku*) because it resembles a collection through the gathering of all qualities of wisdom." See also appendix 6.

352 Anonymous 1973–77, 1:152. *Lamp* says:

Within the wisdom of the alpha-pure essence,
What is called "unawareness" is not possible.
Within dharmatā not differentiated as anything,
It is not [even] established as mere wisdom.

353 Anonymous 1973–77, 1:152–53. The last two lines of *Lamp* say:

Within the appearance of infinite dynamic energy
And qualities as a sheer play.

354 Following Anonymous 1973–77 (1:153), *mi bzad* ("unbearable") in the first line is emended to *mdzad* ("nonactivity") and *la* (within") in the fourth line to *las* ("from within").

355 The expression "the Madhyamaka free from extremes" (Tib. *mtha' bral dbu ma*) is a name for the Madhyamaka view of those in Tibet who are called "the earlier Mādhyamikas." This view was proclaimed by Patsab Lotsāwa (born 1055) and his four main disciples (especially Shang Tangsagba); the

Sakya masters Rendawa (1349–1412), Dagtsang Lotsāwa (born 1405), and Gorampa Sönam Senge (1429–89); the Eighth Karmapa Mikyö Dorjé (1507–54) and his student Pawo Rinpoche (1504–66); and others. This view uses Madhyamaka analysis that results in an unqualified negation of all four positions of the typical Madhyamaka tetralemmas without asserting anything instead in order to completely overcome all conceptualizations. In this way, it is certainly an accurate characterization of the Indian *Prāsaṅgika Madhyamaka approach. This is also what is understood by "the view of neither existence nor nonexistence" when this expression is used by its advocates as solely pertaining to ultimate reality—that is, that "the middle" in the sense of ultimate reality is "neither the existence of a nature nor the nonexistence of a nature."

Starting with Tsongkhapa (1357–1419), "the later Mādhyamikas" in Tibet—the Gelugpa School—criticized this view by saying that "nonexistence of a nature" is the correct Madhyamaka view and thus not to be negated. In addition, in order to discredit the above understanding of Madhyamaka, its critics linked "the view of neither existence nor nonexistence" with the notorious stereotype of Hvashang Mahāyāna, through which this understanding, in their eyes, assumed a pejorative meaning. Mipham Rinpoche's *Lamp of Certainty* says that "the view of neither existence nor nonexistence" is also used as a pejorative for the system of Dzogchen (see Pettit 1999, 297). Given this background, it seems not just coincidental that *Lamp* uses the expression "Madhyamaka free from extremes."

356 Anonymous 1973–77, 3:40.

357 Ibid., 2:535.

358 Following Anonymous 1973–77 (2:178), *gsum* ("three") in the last line is emended to *tshig* ("words").

359 TOK (3:293) elaborates on the triad of identifying the ground's own true face (or its essence) on the basis of itself, firmly deciding on this one thing, and gaining confidence in being free (which make up Garab Dorjé's famous *Three Words That Strike the Vital Point*) as follows. Samantabhadra—the awakened perspective of unobstructed wisdom, the basic nature of primordial original alpha-purity just as it is—is identified on the basis of itself right now. Therefore, this means identifying the true face on the basis of itself. This very awareness just as it is, which is not altered by any objects, not impaired by any clinging, and not engaged in anything to be relinquished or remedies, does not go beyond the dharmakāya—self-arising wisdom. Therefore, this means firmly deciding on this one thing. Whatever appears and whatever arises, all of it first originates as the dynamic energy of dharmatā, which at present abides within the natural state of dharmatā, and at the end dissolves on its own within the natural state of dharmatā. Therefore, this means gaining confidence in being free

(note that "confidence in being free" refers to both having confidence in the fact of being free and the arising of confidence within the state of being free). Compare also the parallel passage in *Lamp* below (fol. 17a–b).

360 II.224ab.

361 Compare the presentations of the same six flawed positions and the one correct one on the nature of the ground in appendix 2A (see also Germano 1992, 143ff.) and Smith 2016 (55–74; similar to *Lamp* but more detailed).

362 Though *The Aspiration Prayer* does not contain any clearly identifiable four-line verses, throughout, *Lamp* uses the term "stanza" for a unit of four lines merely as a way of counting the lines of the prayer.

363 I switched *Lamp*'s reversed positions of "over there" and "over here" in this sentence, which are hard to make sense of, especially in connection with the parallel "inside" and "outside," respectively, and the following phrase "I am here and that is over there."

364 Anonymous 1973–77, 1:107.

365 This is another Atiyoga tantra, contained in Anonymous 1982 (vol. cha, 464–520).

366 Tib. *yi* emended to *yis*.

367 I could not locate this quote in this or any other one of the Seventeen Tantras.

368 That is, everything that appears as if it were something other than just the ground's very own self-appearances.

369 In this and the preceding paragraph, *Lamp* marks *grol* ("free"), *bye brag phyes te* ("through differentiating"), and *gzhan las ma byung* ("does not arise from anything other") as being words of *The Aspiration Prayer*. This is probably just a mistake because these words (making up a possible line "being free through differentiating does not arise from anything other") are not found in any known version of *The Aspiration Prayer*.

370 Following Anonymous 1973–77 (2:500), *gnas lugs* ("the basic nature") in the first line is emended to *gnas su* ("as the abode"). The tantra glosses "free" as "primordially."

371 Following Anonymous 1973–77 (2:536), *grol ba* ("freedom") is emended to *grol sa* ("locus of freedom"). The tantra glosses "the beginning" as "the alpha-purity of the ground."

372 These three lines are actually from the *Universes and Transformations of Sound*. Following Anonymous 1973–77 (1:155), *shes bya* ("what is to be known") in the first line is emended to *shes pas* ("through cognizance"), *chos nyid* ("dharmatā") in the second line to *don nyid* ("the heart of the matter itself"), and *mthar phyin pa'o* ("is the completion") to *sar phyin pa'o* ("has arrived at the locus").

373 *Lamp* marks *rang sar gnas pa'i* ("that rests in its very own place") as being words of *The Aspiration Prayer*.

374 This could also be read as "Through thoughts' not creating any opportunities within [natural] distinctness" or "Through thoughts' not providing any opportunity for distinctness."

375 Following Anonymous 1973–77 (2:223), *mthong ba* ("seeing") in the last line is emended to *rtog pa* ("thoughts"). Adding the two lines before and in between the two lines cited, the tantra says:

> Through the self-arising of the appearances of emptiness,
> they have gone beyond to the place without going.
> Through the self-lucidity of the sphere of great emptiness,
> the single buddha without thoughts is seen.

376 The three dharmas here are essence, nature, and compassionate responsiveness.

377 For more details on Samantabhadra's mode of freedom, see appendix 2C.

378 This quote is actually from the *Universes and Transformations of Sound* (Anonymous 1973–77, 1:199–200).

379 "The three distinctive features" are essence, nature, and compassionate responsiveness.

380 Anonymous 1973–77, 1:125. For more details on all these wisdoms, see Longchenpa's explanation of wisdom as understood in the Great Perfection in appendix 6IB and at the end of appendix 5B.

381 Anonymous 1973–77, 1:126.

382 Ibid., 2:63.

383 VIII.33.

384 IX.16ab.

385 X.5cd.

386 As before, *Lamp* here pulls apart the two components of Tib. *smon lam* (lit. "path of aspiration"), taking "path" as a separate word of the root text.

387 "The state of the previous time" refers to a lifetime from right after birth until right before dying.

388 Anonymous 1973–77 (2:473) glosses the first line as "the very essence," "existents" as "phenomena that are entities," "nonexistents" as "phenomena that are empty," "the general ground" as "innate presence," "unawareness" as "the three such as connate unawareness," "what is to be known" as "[to be known] as the mother-ground that is the very essence," and the rest of the last line as "the dimension of wishing for objects stirs."

389 Following Anonymous 1973–77 (2:460), the fourth line *blo la 'khrul pa'i tshul du snang* ("appears to the mind as the mode of delusion") is emended to *glo bur 'khrul pa'i tshul dang ldan*. The tantra glosses the second line as "since adventitious unawareness has arisen, it is obscured by sentient beings [who correspond to] the example of clouds in the sky," the third line as "though delusion is primordially pure," "the mode of adventitious delusion" as "in the minds of sentient beings, what is nonexistent is taken

to be existent," and "causes and conditions" as "fourfold unawareness and its focal objects."

390 Anonymous 1973–77 (1:140–41).

391 As mentioned before, this means that the unawareness of same identity derives from not recognizing the empty essence's dimension of nonconceptuality, connate unawareness from not recognizing the luminous nature as awareness's self-nature, and imaginative unawareness from not recognizing compassionate responsiveness's intrinsic awareness.

392 Among the twelve links of dependent origination, "the three paths of dependent origination" refer to (1) the afflictiveness of afflictions (the links of ignorance, craving, and grasping), (2) the afflictiveness of karma (the links of formations and becoming), and (3) the afflictiveness of birth (the remaining seven links).

Mipham Rinpoche's commentary on the *Madhyāntavibhāga* ('Ju mi pham rgya mtsho 1984, 769–70) explains thusly: (1) The afflictiveness of afflictions consists of (a) the causes of wrong views, (b) the causes of the three poisons (passion, aggression, and ignorance), and (c) the striving for rebirth. The remedies for (a)–(c) are the realizations of the three doors to liberation—emptiness, signlessness, and wishlessness, respectively. (2) The afflictiveness of karma consists of the formation of virtuous and nonvirtuous actions. Its remedy is the realization of the door to liberation that is nonformation. (3) The afflictiveness of birth consists of (a) being born in a new existence, (b) the minds and mental factors that occur in each moment after having been born in that existence up through dying, and (c) the continuum of rebirth (the state of dying, the state of birth, and the intermediate state). The remedies for (a)–(c) are the realizations of the lack of birth, the lack of occurrence, and the lack of nature, respectively.

393 Tib. *bral ba* ("free from") emended to *'brel ba*.

394 The two words "arising" (*skyes pa*) and "simultaneously" (*lhan cig*) here represent the two elements of a more literal rendering of "connate."

395 For more details on the three kinds of unawareness and the four conditions, see appendix 3A.

396 As before, *Lamp* here pulls apart the two components of Tib. *smon lam* (lit. "path of aspiration"), taking "path" as a separate word of the root text.

397 *Lamp* has *su dengs pa* ("have vanished in"), with *dengs* being marked as a word of *The Aspiration Prayer*, instead of *su dvangs pa* ("are transparent in/as"). This could be a deliberate variation or a typo.

398 The basis of all vows is to avoid the three nonvirtuous states of mind: covetousness, hatred, and ignorance.

399 Anonymous 1973–77 (2:517) glosses "the distinction" as "the meaning of."

400 Ibid., 2:164.

401 Ibid., 1:128.

402 Ibid., 2:518.

403 Following Anonymous 1973–77 (2:517), both *yul* ("object") and *sems* ("mind") are emended to *yin* ("being"). *Lamp*'s version of the third line reads: "the apprehended object and the apprehending mind."

404 Anonymous 1973–77 (2:518) glosses this line as "because it lacks the clinging of thoughts." The immediately preceding line says, "Since minding (*dran pa*) itself is nonminding," and "nonminding" is glossed as "beyond mentation."

405 Compare the parallel passage in *Lamp* above (fol. 7b).

406 Tib. *yid du 'ong ngam mi 'ong / yid 'ong yin nam* emended to *yid du 'ong ngam mi 'ong yin nam*.

407 Tib. *la* emended to *las*.

408 According to the Vaibhāṣikas, "volitional karma" (Skt. *cetanākarma*, Tib. *sems pa'i las*) refers to mental actions and "volitioned karma" (Skt. *cetayitvā karma*, Tib. *bsam pa'i las*; more literally "karma subsequent to volition") to the physical and verbal actions motivated and triggered by the former. According to the other Buddhist schools, both volitional and volitioned karmas consist of the mental factor impulse (Skt. *cetanā*, Tib. *sems pa*), with the former referring to the impulse that serves as the causal motivation, and the latter to the impulse that serves as the motivation at the time of actually engaging in an action (see *Abhidharmakośa* IV.1bd and its *Bhāṣya*, as well as the comparison of the Vaibhāṣika and Sautrāntika positions in the *Bhāṣya* on IV.3c).

409 On these three obscurations, see note 312 on the corresponding passage in *Ketaka*.

410 As before, *Lamp* here pulls apart the two components of Tib. *smon lam* (lit. "path of aspiration"), taking "path" as a separate word of the root text.

411 Following Anonymous 1973–77 (2:490), *las kyis bcings* ("bound through the activity of") in the second line is emended to *gis bcings kyang* ("though bound through") and *cing* ("and") in the third line to *pas* ("due to"). The tantra glosses "bound" as "themselves," "lack of nature" as "primordial," and "freedom is certain" as "if [this lack] is realized."

412 Anonymous 1973–77 (3:183–84) glosses "body and its shadow" as "the pair of connate unawareness and awareness" and "purification" as "of the ground."

413 These three ways of thoughts' being free represent "the three modes of freedom" of being free upon arising (Tib. *shar grol*), being free in itself (Tib. *rang grol*), and being free without benefit or harm (Tib. *phan med gnod med du grol ba*). See also the beginning of appendix 7.

414 The text of *The Aspiration Prayer* here already uses each of the three equivalent or closely related words "desire," "attachment," and "clinging" twice, but *Lamp* obviously tries to drive home the point even further through repeating these words and adding "craving" as yet another equivalent of desire several times, thus highlighting the intense, pervasive,

and ongoing arising of the plethora of afflictions such as desire in the mind streams of ordinary beings.

415 "Knowing one, all is free" (Tib. *gcig shes yongs grol*) could also be read as "knowing one, being completely free"; as one of the Great Perfection's five modes of freedom that are discussed here, *yongs grol* means "being completely free." However, in terms of the meaning, there is no difference because "being completely free" is explained as not just a partial or isolated kind of freedom but in the sense that the entirety of all possible thoughts, emotions, perceptions, and obscurations in any possible situation is free.

416 Anonymous 1973–77, 1:125. "Completely free" is the most natural reading of Tib. *yongs su grol ba*. However, in light of *Lamp*'s above comments on "knowing one, all is free" (which use the same expression), one could also read this as "Since it is free in/as everything."

417 These five are being primordially free, free in itself, nakedly free, completely free, and free from extremes as described just above. For more details and different explanations of these five, see appendix 7.

418 The remaining six attitudes are the following: "This person has helped those who harmed me in the past," "This person helps those who harm me in the present," "This person will help those who harm me in the future," "This person has harmed my relatives or friends in the past," "This person harms my relatives or friends in the present," "This person will harm my relatives or friends in the future."

419 As mentioned before, the numbering of the Tibetan folios here jumps from 21a to 22a (the latter also has "22b" in Arabic numerals on the right margin) and then continues with 23a and so on. For the sake of easier reference to the Tibetan, I retain this numbering.

420 *Lamp* marks *dregs pa* ("arrogant") instead of *drag po* ("intense") at the end of this sentence as being a word of *The Aspiration Prayer*.

421 As before, *Lamp* here pulls apart the two components of Tib. *smon lam* (lit. "path of aspiration"), taking "path" as a separate word of the root text.

422 The eight worldly dharmas are gain, loss, fame, disgrace, praise, blame, happiness, and suffering.

423 The definition of a result produced by persons is "a phenomenon that has arisen due to the force of its specific causes," such as a harvest brought about by the efforts of a farmer or wealth obtained through business. Just as all harvests are produced through the activity of persons, all entities are said to be "results produced by persons" in the sense of being something that has arisen through the force of its specific causes.

424 As before, *Lamp* here pulls apart the two components of Tib. *smon lam* (lit. "path of aspiration"), taking "path" as a separate word of the root text.

425 *Lamp* has *brtas pa* ("flourish") instead of *skyes pa* ("arise") and marks it as a word of *The Aspiration Prayer*.

426 As before, *Lamp* here pulls apart the two components of Tib. *smon lam* (lit. "path of aspiration"), taking "path" as a separate word of the root text.

427 As for the five afflictions being recognized as the five wisdoms, compare also Patrul Rinpoche's text translated in appendix 10.

428 That is, the essential meaning and principal purpose of the Great Perfection—recognizing the primordially free nature of the ground of basic awareness.

429 *Lamp* marks *byung* ("there arises") as being a word of *The Aspiration Prayer.*

430 *Lamp* marks *thog med* ("without origin") instead of *thog ma* ("original") as being words of *The Aspiration Prayer.*

431 The phrase "which represents the bodhicitta" (Tib. *thugs bskyed*) could also be rendered as "which are generated in the mind."

432 The last syllables of the first line of page 27 are illegible (*skal dm* ...). Thus, the phrase "those of inferior" is tentative but, given the context, the most probable.

433 *Lamp* marks "may" as being a word of *The Aspiration Prayer.*

434 "Separating the pure essence (Tib. *dvangs ma*) from the dregs (Tib. *snyigs ma*)" is a typical Vajrayāna presentation, which refers to distinguishing between the pure essence (or quintessence) and the dregs of mind, winds (*vāyu*), and bindus. According to the Third Karmapa's *Profound Inner Reality* (Tib. *Zab mo nang don*), the pure essence of the mind consists of ālaya-wisdom and stainless mentation, while the dregs are the eight consciousnesses. The pure essence of the winds consists of the wisdom winds, while the dregs are the karmic winds. The most refined and pure essence of the material bindus consists of the white and red bindus, while the dregs are the coarse material bindus (semen and ovum). Jamgön Kongtrul Lodrö Tayé's commentary on the Karmapa's text (Kong sprul blo gros mtha' yas 2005, 34) reports the following explanation by Tagpo Rabjampa (1449–1524; Tib. Dvags po rab 'byams pa): "In each one of all phenomena (skandhas, āyatanas, and dhātus), there is the pure essence (the aspect of wisdom) and the dross (the aspect of [mistaken] consciousness). By taking the collection of both the pure essence and the dross as the basis for purification, with the dross as that which is to be purified, through the two means for purification (maturation and liberation) according with the progressive [purification] of the basis of purification, the result of purification (the three kāyas) is revealed." The Second Pawo Rinpoche's commentary on the *Bodhicaryāvatāra* (Dpa' bo gtsug lag phreng ba n.d., 887–88) warns that when misinterpreting this, one may falsely cling to the utter nonexistence of ordinary mistaken consciousness and to the real existence of nonconceptual wisdom.

435 Tib. Rdo grub.

436 This refers to Sogyal Lerab Lingpa (1856–1926), another guru of the author.

437 Tib. Gsang 'dzin mgon po dbang rgyal. According to a biography of this master in Tsültrim Sangpo's collected works, his full names are Mgon po dbang gi rgyal po or Gsang 'dzin dpa' bo dgyes rab rdo rje rtsal (1845–1915). He was the then abbot of Kordong Monastery and another one of Tsültrim Sangpo's gurus.

438 Tib. Lha brag bla ma phrin las mthu stobs.

439 Tib. Rdo rje rgyal mtshan.

440 The year of the "wrathful" Wood Ox is always the fifty-ninth in the successive sexagenary cycles of the Tibetan calendar. Given the author's birth in 1884 CE, the year in question here can only be 1925 CE.

441 Tib. Brag ri dkar po lha'i mchod rten'dra ba.

442 Tib. Gnyan yul zang zang.

443 Tib. Dpal bsam yas.

444 Jigmé Lingpa's text contains no explicit outline, so the following one is compiled based on some of its central comments.

445 Certain parts of Longchenpa's text have not been included in the excerpts from it in appendices 2 to 7 due to lack of relevance. Such elisions are marked with ellipses.

I have supplemented certain parts of those excerpts in appendices 2 and 3 with parallel excerpts from two commentaries on Jigmé Lingpa's *Treasury of Precious Qualities* by Yönten Gyatso (nineteenth century; Yon tan rgya mtsho 1982–87) and the late Kangyur Rinpoche, Longchen Yeshé Dorjé (1897–1975; Klong chen ye shes rdo rje 1991), which largely follow the structure of the first two chapters of Longchenpa's work.

As Malcolm Smith (http://www.atikosha.org/2012/09/a-preliminary-note-on-vimalamitras.html and 2016, 8ff.) and Turpeinen (2016, 194ff.) point out, the titles, structure, and even entire passages of the eleven chapters of Longchenpa's *Precious Treasury of Words and Their Meanings* are paralleled by the early *Great Perfection's Eleven Words and Their Meanings* by Kepa Nyima Bum (Tib. Mkhas pa nyi ma 'bum; 1158–1213) as well as by the largely identical *Great Ear-Whispered Lineage of Vimalamitra* in the Northern Treasures' cycle *Samantabhadra's Unobstructed Awakened Mind*. The model for this elevenfold template appears to be a passage at the end of the eighth and last chapter of the *Garland of Pearls* (Anonymous 1973–77, 2:535–36; for a translation, see Smith 2016, 8–9).

446 As evidenced below, among the Seventeen Tantras, it is the *Sixfold Expanse* (Anonymous 1973–77, 2:169ff.) that discusses these seven positions in some detail and critiques the first six (some parts of these critiques are also quoted in *Lamp*). These seven also appear briefly in the *Universes and Transformations of Sound* (Anonymous 1973–77, 1:181) as follows:

> The basic nature as it is established in its own way,

in terms of the modes of its sevenfold abiding,
is held to be (1) innate presence from the perspective of its diversity,
(2) indeterminate from the point of view of its scope of changeability,
(3) determinate due to its being unchanging,
(4) the dynamic energy of manifesting, which transforms into anything whatsoever,
(5) assertable [as anything] because it [is able to] arise as everything,
(6) alpha-purity because delusion is pure,
and (7) variegated [in terms of] its different modes of appearing.

As mentioned before, *Lamp* explains that the six flawed views represent only partial characteristics of the ground. Furthermore, the six mistaken views and others about the ground that are held on the basis of different theorizing philosophical or metaphysical positions are sometimes categorized as "the ground as a knowable object," while the true ground that is the basic nature is a matter of the direct experience and realization of those who actually practice the path of Dzogchen.

Vimalamitra (Smith 2016, 57) compares those who adhere to philosophical systems to people who tell stories about Vajrāsana (the place under the bodhi tree in Bodhgāya where Buddha Śākyamuni became awakened) without ever having been there, and compares those who adhere to the path to people who saw this place with their own eyes.

As Higgins (2013, 209ff.) points out, there have been different opinions on whether all seven of these views are to be considered mistaken or only the six apart from alpha-purity. The tantras the *Universes and Transformations of Sound* and the *Sixfold Expanse* explicitly consider all seven to be flawed because they only represent one-sided partial perspectives. The commentary on the *Universes and Transformations of Sound* agrees with this, while the one on the *Sixfold Expanse* adds another flawed view of the ground (doubling the fifth one) in order to exclude alpha-purity from the set of seven flawed views. Both Kepa Nyima Bum's *Eleven Words and Their Meanings* and Longchenpa's *Precious Treasury of Words and Their Meanings* assert alpha-purity as the only flawless view, which is also the stance of the treasure cycles *Embodiment of the Guru's Awakened Mind* (Tib. *Bla ma dgongs 'dus*) and *Samantabhadra's Unobstructed Awakened Mind*, as well as the *Heart of the Sun* (Tib. *Nyi ma'i snying po*) by Dsélé Natso Rangdröl (Tib. Rtse le sna tshogs rang grol; born 1608).

Interestingly, Longchenpa's later work the *Precious Treasury of the Supreme Yāna* refutes the position of the ground as alpha-purity if this is wrongly understood as an utter emptiness devoid of the dynamic energy of its own internal glow and hence incapable of being the source of any kind of awareness, appearance, and in particular the pure wisdom of a buddha. Instead, here, Longchenpa identifies the ultimately correct understanding of the ground as "the inseparability of alpha-purity and innate presence" (see also Germano 1992n14 and n59). Jigmé Lingpa's and Yönten Gyatso's works follow this position. However, it should be noted that, as the following shows, Longchenpa's explanation in his *Precious Treasury of Words and Their Meanings* likewise identifies the alpha-purity of the original ground as the pure dharmatā that is both luminous and empty, whose essence is alpha-purity, and whose nature is innate presence. Compare also the presentations and refutations of those seven positions on the ground in *Lamp* (fols. 4aff.), Germano 1992 (143ff.), and Smith 2016 (55–74).

447 Anonymous 1973–77 (2:171–72) glosses "awareness" in the seventh line as "the innately present cause," "double" in the eighth line as "simultaneously," and the last line as "if the result is not innately present."

448 Following Anonymous 1973–77 (2:173), *rtog bcas* ("conceptual") in the fifth line is emended to *ldog bcas* ("reverse"). In the tantra, the seventh line is an almost literal repetition of the sixth, but *Lamp* and Longchenpa's *Precious Treasury of Words and Their Meanings* have the correct reverse order of "determinate" and "indeterminate." The text of the tantra glosses the fourth line as "due to vacillating [similar to] sometimes being a horse and sometimes an elephant, it would sometimes be the ground and sometimes the path," the fifth line as "like asserting that water is fire," the sixth and seventh lines as "How could indeterminate water have the nature of water?", the eighth line as "If [the ground] itself were indeterminate, there would be an infinite regress [of indeterminacy]," and "it would be determinate" in the ninth line as "Therefore, it would become determinate." In other words, if the ground were indeterminate, even its indeterminacy would be indeterminate and thus it could (also) be determinate, similar to the determinacy of karmic causes and their results. But then it would just be something on the level of seeming reality.

449 One is tempted to read "unlike" instead of "just like" here, since water and fire can of course appear in many different ways. However, what is probably meant here is that the ways in which the ground intrinsically appears or manifests can never be altered or transformed, just as the ways that water appears can never be changed into the ways that fire appears and vice versa.

450 Anonymous 1973–77 (2:173–74) glosses "conch shell" in the third line as "white"; the fourth line as "due to being affected by disease"; in the fifth line, "its own status's becoming inverted" as "If the conch shell itself were yellow, through what would it be realized that the conch shell's dharmatā lacks any yellow?"; in the sixth line, "it lacks both self and other" as "just as both one's own perspective and the perspectives of others fail"; in the

seventh line, "the true actuality" as "among knowable objects"; and the eighth line as "being determinate as a cause, the result would absolutely not arise; thus, what would be the difference if the result arose from the cause or the cause arose from the result?" As for the third through sixth lines, just as a conch shell is ascertained as white by one person and as yellow by another, without what one person sees being true for the other, any uniformity of perception of the ground is obviously not the case, because it is perceived as what it is by some (such as Samantabhadra) and as all kinds of saṃsāric delusion by others (called "sentient beings"). Therefore, the ground's own reality is beyond the limitations of being determined in one way or another, whether it is in terms of one's own perspective or that of others.

451 More literally "its nature does not exist as two," that is, it does not have two natures but just a single one that never changes.

452 In other words, from one moment to the other and without any cause, deluded sentient beings without any experience of the path could transform into fully awakened buddhas without any need to have progressed through the stages of the path of transcending delusion.

453 Following Anonymous 1973–77 (2:174), *grol ba* ("being free as") in the last line is emended to *'gro ba* ("turning into"). In the fifth line, I follow Longchenpa's *dgos med 'gyur* ("would be unnecessary") against *dgos med par*. The text of the tantra glosses the third line as "if the basic nature were capable of transforming, the flaw of the result being endless would have to be eliminated," "the cause" in the fourth line as "the cause of sentient beings," and the last two lines as "for example, if the ground were to change, material phenomena would transform right now into something that has self-awareness."

454 Anonymous 1973–77 (2:175) glosses the second line as "when it is held to be assertable as anything whatsoever" and the fourth line as "it is not determined as being searchable as purity, nor is it found as impurity because purity and impurity are mixed."

455 Longchenpa omits this line.

456 Following Anonymous 1973–77 (2:174–75), *gang gi* is emended to *gang gis*. The tantra glosses the first line as "This [assertion] is not able to relinquish the flaw of a single ground's own mode of appearance assuming different [forms]. This resembles the example of saying that something is both a pillar and a blanket. [However,] whatever is a pillar is [necessarily] not a blanket."

As mentioned before, the third through sixth lines are particularly obscure but are explained by a commentary on this tantra by Vimalamitra (see Germano 1992n57) as follows. If the ground were diversity, it would either have to be diverse in terms of its changing or diverse despite its being unchanging and unfabricated. The first possibility refers to the third line and the second to the following two lines. "Changing" would mean that the ground somehow kept shifting between being or resulting in different things or appearances, while "unchanging" would entail that it from the start consists of different distinct parts, which constitute its diversity. However, since its essence would then appear in accordance with whatever descriptions of these different parts are given (such as "it is also white" or "it is also black"), freedom within a single dimension that is the true basic nature would be impossible, because the results of a ground that is intrinsically diverse would also have to be different. Since the plurality of assertions about such a ground will invalidate each other, this view is not tenable.

457 Compare the opening lines of Jigmé Lingpa's *Aspiration Prayer For Ground, Path, and Fruition* (appendix 8): "The original basic nature is naturally free from reference points ... May the basic nature of the ground of the Great Perfection be realized."

458 This second triad is basically another way of phrasing the first triad. In other sources, including the explanatory quote that follows this paragraph, the members of the second triad are correlated with the three kāyas and respectively explained as the ground's emptiness, its luminosity, and the unceasing play of this empty luminosity as diverse structures of cognitions and appearances (Germano 1992n67).

459 In brief, while the ground itself is entirely beyond both saṃsāra and nirvāṇa, the ground manifestations ("the general ground") can be classified in a general way as the dimension of nirvāṇa, though their essence remains beyond any polarized classifications such as saṃsāra and nirvāṇa. The ground manifestations dawn from the primordial ground before there is any straying into mistaking them as saṃsāra or recognizing their true nature. Though the essence of the ground manifestations is like that, they still act as the condition of both freedom and delusion in that their essence can either be recognized or not recognized as the self-appearances of the ground. For example, when we meet a long-lost sister whom we do not recognize as such, our not recognizing her does not change the fact that she is our sister or the fact of her presence right before our eyes. However, once we recognize her, our attitude and our relationship with her will fundamentally change. Likewise, when our own basic awareness manifests as the outer luminosity of the ground manifestations, it does not change in any way despite our failing to recognize it for what it truly is and our being deluded about it by mistaking it for something other. Once the ground manifestations are recognized as primordial awareness's very own dynamic play, there is no more dualistic split into apprehender and apprehended or self and other with all the ensuing afflictions, karma, and suffering; instead, the infinite qualities and enlightened activities of awakening are revealed.

460 Anonymous 1973–77 (2:513–14) glosses "alpha-purity" as "stainless," "innate presence" as "endowed with the eight gateways of the arising [of innate presence]," and "self-arising" as "for sentient beings."

"Spontaneously arising" is glossed as "uncreated," "universal appearance" as "primordial," "all-encompassing" as "with regard to all objects," and "inclusiveness" as "within the essence." "Self-purity of stains" is glossed as "free from awareness," and "the arising of diversity" as "buddhas and sentient beings." The line "the general ground appears to be established" reads here "the ground that is the general sphere appears as delusion" (Tib. *spyi sa'i gzhi ni 'khrul par snang*), which is glossed as "[through] the threefold unawareness and the four conditions [for the arising of delusion]" (on these, see appendix 3A).

461 Anonymous 1973–77 (1:529). Longchenpa omits *rnam* ("aspects").

462 As mentioned before, the Pith Instructions Series is commonly classified into four cycles: the Outer Cycle, the Inner Cycle, the Secret Cycle, and the Unsurpassed Secret Cycle (the latter consists of the Seventeen Tantras, for instance, the *Universes and Transformations of Sound*).

463 The threefold radiance consists of primordial radiance (Tib. *ye gdangs*), self-radiance (Tib. *rang gdangs*), and radiant radiance (Tib. *zer gdangs*). This means that the primordial ground is not a sheer emptiness but inherently and dynamically luminous and radiant. For more details, see Germano 1992n85.

464 That is, the four levels of the formless realm.

465 Following Anonymous 1973–77 (1:729), *chen po* ("great") in the first line is emended to *ye shes* ("wisdom").

466 Tib. *yod* emended to *med* (for the reasons, see the next note).

467 Elsewhere, Longchenpa explicitly compares the dissolution of the sambhogakāya and nirmāṇakāya into the dharmakāya during awakening to a crystal being separated from the condition of the sun's light rays. Thus, the crystal's not being in the sun at all must correspond to the time of the ground before any ground manifestations appear, which also matches the order of the primordial undifferentiated ground ("the alpha-purity of the expanse") and buddhahood ("the alpha-purity of the final state of freedom") two sentences earlier.

However, there are also possible interpretations of this passage without emending "a crystal ball at the time of its being in the sun" to "a crystal ball at the time of its not being in the sun [at all]." That is, buddhahood would then correspond to a crystal being within the sun and thus not radiating any comparatively weak five-colored lights with limited reach, because everything would already be flooded with intense and infinite sunlight. The crystal in the shadow would then correspond to the time of the primordial ground (for a detailed discussion of all these possible interpretations, see Germano 1992n112).

In any case, as explained in the following paragraph, both at the time of the primordial ground (before the appearance of any ground manifestations) and at the time of buddhahood (after every aspect of the ground manifestations has returned to its source), awareness does not radiate outward, whereas it radiates as the ground manifestations during all states in between.

468 "The ground in its temporary state" (Tib. *gnas skabs kyi gzhi*) contrasts with "the ground that is the expanse" (Tib. *dbyings kyi gzhi*) or "the primordial ground" (Tib. *ye gzhi*), which refers to the original state of the ground beyond all seeming temporal and spatial transitions that appear as the ground manifestations.

469 The four visions in the context of Direct Leap are "perception of dharmatā" (Tib. *chos nyid mngon sum*), "increase of experience" (Tib. *nyams snang gong 'phel*), "awareness reaching fullness" (Tib. *rig pa tshad phebs*), and "exhaustion in dharmatā" (Tib. *chos nyid zad pa*).

470 "Awareness in an immature form" basically means that awareness is not yet fully self-aware of its own nature. It is "matured" through the path until it fully manifests as the awakening of buddhahood. Just as a peacock's egg is said to glow with the vibrant colors of the fledgling within, awareness glows with its five-colored vibrancy, which is present within our hearts but not manifest and is ultimately born as the three kāyas.

Bdud 'joms 'jigs bral ye shes rdo rje 1999 (564–65) explains in the context of Direct Leap that the instantaneous awareness that observes directly perceptible luminosity puts an end to or turns away from all minds and mental factors of the three realms including the all-ground. Through looking at this directly perceptible luminosity, there is no proliferation or withdrawal of internal imagination. Therefore, it turns away from the desire realm. Since there is no remedy that establishes the natural state of lucidity as being lucid, it turns away from the realm of form. Since there is no mind of clinging to one-pointed nonconceptuality within the natural state of dharmatā, it turns away from the formless realm. Since it is clearly transparent yet aware, it turns away from the all-ground. Since it is determined to be self-arising wisdom, it turns away from the all-ground consciousness. Since there are only appearances that are objects of luminosity but no ordinary appearances, it turns away from the five sense consciousnesses. Since there are no discerning thoughts and no imaginations of desire and hatred at that time, it turns away from the mental consciousness and the afflicted mind. In brief, this buddha wisdom that is free from all minds and mental factors of the three realms is the consummate ultimate state that is nothing other than peace, that is, nirvāṇa (compare Bdud 'joms 'jigs bral ye shes rdo rje 1991, 340).

471 Following Anonymous 1973–77 (2:372), *ldan* ("possessing") in the third line is emended to *bstan* ("displaying"). In the eighth line, *rnams* (plural) is emended to *nas* ("from") and *dper na* ("example") is added.

472 Klong chen rab 'byams pa dri med 'od zer. 1999b?, 6–29.

Longchen Yeshé Dorjé's commentary on Jigmé Lingpa's *Treasury of Precious Qualities* (Klong chen ye shes rdo rje 1991, 487–91) explains the ground as follows. Within the essence of awareness that is alpha-purity free from reference points, the dimension of qualities that consists of the self-lucid unceasing self-radiance that has the character of the kāyas and wisdoms and is like the sun and its rays is primordially and innately present. However, since alpha-purity and innate presence differ in their isolates of emptiness and appearance, respectively, they are not identical. Still, since their essence is the same, just as a vase and its emptiness are inseparable, they are not different substances, similar to water and its moisture.

From the perspective of emptiness, awareness is free from all reference points of entities and characteristics that can be identified as having a certain nature, such as shape and color. Therefore, apart from cutting through all reference points by way of the via negativa (apophasis), awareness's own essence is inexpressible as being such and such by way of any via positiva (kataphasis). Therefore, it is expressed as "alpha-purity." However, it is not that awareness is simply nothing whatsoever, just like empty space. Rather, from the perspective of appearance, awareness's dimension of depth-lucidity—unceasing self-radiance—exists as the dynamic energy of compassionate responsiveness that is suitable to appear as anything whatsoever. Therefore, it is expressed as "innate presence."

Thus, the extremes of permanence and extinction are relinquished as a matter of course. You may wonder, "If either of the states of alpha-purity and innate presence on their own are rejected as correctly characterizing the ground, is it not equally flawed to explain that the ground is both?" Here, the single essence of the ground—mind's true nature—is merely differentiated as two isolates, that is, existence and nonexistence, or innate presence from the perspective of appearance and alpha-purity from the perspective of emptiness, but these are not two different substances. Therefore, it is not the case that two mutually exclusive phenomena are combined into one. For example, without moving away from the single essence of sleep, there occur both dreamless deep sleep without any thinking activity and dreams due to the unfolding of mind's radiance through being carried away by the winds. Likewise, in the dimension of the essence that is alpha-purity, delusion is not established within the ground. Therefore, there was never any circling in saṃsāra in the past, nor is there any at present, nor will there be any in the future. Still, by virtue of the unceasing dynamic energy or radiance of the nature that is innate presence, all kinds of natural displays unfold that are suitable to appear as anything whatsoever in saṃsāra or nirvāṇa.

For example, though the natural brilliance of a blue beryl or a clean crystal that is able to produce rainbows dwells within these gems as their natural depth-lucidity, without being prompted by conditions such as sunlight, this natural brilliance does not appear on the outside. In accordance with this example for the ground and the ground manifestations, when dwelling in ground luminosity, such as when dying, alpha-pure awareness lacks any conditions, just like the autumn sky pure of contaminations. At that time, there is nothing that appears as any entities or characteristics, be it impure appearances (such as objects and the six consciousnesses that apprehend them) or pure appearances (such as kāyas and light rays). Still, the innately present self-radiance of awareness's nature is present in the form of the dynamic energy of inner luminosity for as long as this inner luminosity does not encounter any conditions for the appearances of innate presence to spread to the outside. Therefore, this is referred to as "the youthful vase body" that does not manifest externally since its seal is not broken.

Since the essence of the ground is free from any thinking and expression through any coarse or subtle thoughts, it is empty in that it is unarisen. Still, by virtue of its dimension of innately present self-radiance, the appearances of the three kāyas can arise unimpededly. Therefore, the awareness that is the ground abides as the ground of the arising of all appearances of saṃsāra and nirvāṇa. However, since alpha-purity and innate presence have the same nature, the ground manifestations do not actually stir away from the ground that is empty luminosity. Since this basic nature has never been tainted by the stains of the five skandhas, the ground manifestations are primordially pure. Hence, this basic nature is called "purity" (*byang*). Since it is inherently endowed with the qualities of the three kāyas, it is called "realization" (*chub*). Since its manner of appearing is unceasing in its appearing as anything whatsoever, it is called "mind" (*sems*).

When this (ultimate) bodhicitta ("pure and realized mind") that is subtle wisdom is present in the form of inner luminosity, it does not manifest outwardly as any biased appearances in terms of saṃsāric delusion or nirvāṇic freedom that consist of impure or pure characteristics such as colors, self, and other. From the perspective of alpha-purity, this general ground of saṃsāra and nirvāṇa that is the basic nature is not established as any nature of kāyas and wisdoms and therefore is not a buddha. Since it does not exist as the skandhas, dhātus, āyatanas, and so on either, it is not a sentient being. Though it is expressed as "the one and only bindu," it does not exist as an entity that is a single cause. Though it is designated as the three kāyas and so on, the single expanse is not established as involving any difference. Since it is free from reference points, it cannot be posited as a middle or an extreme.

On the other hand, if evaluated from the perspective of the ground's nature that is innate presence, it is not an utterly blank emptiness but the ground of the arising of the kāyas and wisdoms. However, it is not established as a material entity.

As for this state of the ground that is without any conditions for delusion or freedom, the dharmatā of the essence's freedom from all extremes of reference points is the ground's alpha-purity that is not established or differentiated as anything whatsoever. Since its nature is unceasing, it is the innate presence that is inseparable from the kāyas and wisdoms. Since its compassionate responsiveness is unimpeded, its enlightened activity pervades the entire sphere of saṃsāra and nirvāṇa. Thus, this sheer ground is presented as what is present as having the character of being inseparable from the nature of these three appearances of essence, nature, and compassionate responsiveness being one.

Higgins (2013, 207) makes the following remarks on the nature of the ground:

> As tempting as it may be to view this affirmation of a primordial ground as a foundationalist enterprise, its portrayal in rDzogs chen sNying thig sources suggests the opposite. There the ground is presented not as an object of metaphysical speculation or even rational inference but as an implicit, if generally obscured, mode of being that is nonetheless accessible to personal experience. To directly recognize open awareness (*rig pa rang ngo shes*) is to ascertain the ground (*gzhi gtan la dbab pa*). Here, one ought not disregard the context of living praxis and pedagogy within which this attestation of the ground is traditionally situated. To do so would be to underplay the testimonial tenor of rDzogs chen ground presentations which owe their evidential force less to abstract reasoning and deductive inference than to first-hand accounts of personal experience. Indeed, writings on rDzogs chen praxis customarily specify a number of indications (*rtags*) and measures (*tshad*) of attainment that are said to accompany the ascertainment of the ground. Later exegetes such as Klong chen pa further explained that the ground is so-named precisely because it is *groundless*, having no further foundation from which it originates or root from which it develops (*gzhi med rtsa bral*). This original "groundless" ground is precisely what remains when reifying abstractions have ceased, the most pernicious of which is [sic] the beliefs in real entities and their having real characteristics" (emphasis by Higgins).

473 For details on "the natural nirmāṇakāya," see appendix 6IIE.

474 "The amulet-box of precious innate presence" is a poetic term for the ground's innate presence as the immediate source of the ground manifestations in their eightfold dynamic appearance, similar to an amulet-box's containing or hiding precious substances within.

475 In this tantra, the speaker here is a buddha called "Self-Appearing Awareness." In the first two sentences in Anonymous 1973–77 (1:213–15), "I" is glossed as "alpha-purity," "delusion" as "emerging as sheer innate presence," and "the unchanging ground" as "alpha-purity." "The eightfold mode of arising" is glossed as "compassionate responsiveness, light, kāyas, wisdom, nonduality, freedom from extremes, purity, and impurity." Following Anonymous 1973–77, *lngar* ("as five") in sentence (2) is emended to *ltar* ("as if"), *ma 'gags pa* ("unimpeded") in (5) to *ma nges pa* ("indeterminate"), and (8) *ma dag pa'i thugs rje ma 'gags pa* ("The compassionate responsiveness that is impurity is unimpeded") to *ma dag pa ltar 'char ba'i sgo thugs rje ma 'gags pa*.

476 Tib. *de nyid* could also be read as "true reality."

477 In the first line, Anonymous 1973–77 (3:90–91) has *mi mjed* ("fearless") instead of *mi 'byed* ("undifferentiated"), but the latter seems to make more sense here. Following Anonymous 1973–77, *gdags pa* ("imputed, designated") in the second line of this quote is emended to *dag la* ("pure yet"), *mkhyen cha'i snang ba* ("appearance of its knowing dimension") in the first line of (3) to *mkhyen pa'i snang cha* ("its appearance dimension of knowing"), and *snang* ("manifest") in the third-to-last line of the quote to *'byung* ("come about"). On the other hand, in the first two lines of (6), I follow *gnas med pas* and *snang bar* against *gnas pa med* and *snang ba* in Anonymous 1973–77 because this matches the pattern of the other lines. In the second and fourth lines of (8), I follow *kun* ("all") against *rnams* (plural) and *las* ("from") against *la* ("within").

478 Longchenpa's *Treasure Trove of Scriptures* (Klong chen rab 'byams pa dri med 'od zer 1999a?, 274–78) explains that even the statement that the appearances of saṃsāra and nirvāṇa arise from the dynamic energy of awareness is just a conventional expression, while in fact all such appearances never really existed in the first place and thus lack any arising and ceasing. In fact, the essence of awareness is not established as anything whatsoever but can appear in any way whatsoever. Therefore, all phenomena of saṃsāra and nirvāṇa arise ceaselessly from within the state of nonarising. For example, though a crystal ball does not exist as anything other than having the essence of being transparent and stainless, due to its encountering the condition of sun rays, an effulgence of five-colored light arises. Similarly, since the essence of awareness is not established as anything whatsoever, it is present as the empty yet lucid pure dharmakāya. However, due to the condition of realizing or not realizing this, this essence appears as all kinds of displays from the dynamic energy that manifests as either saṃsāra or nirvāṇa.

Within the great complete purity of mind as such, just as it is, which has the nature of space without any specific aspect at all, all aspects of the entire diversity of appearances are perfect in the manner of being innately present. This is called "the great emptiness that is endowed with all supreme aspects." The mind that attempts to own the six objects that appear within this emptiness creates all kinds of karmas (pleasant, unpleasant, and so on), latent tendencies, surroundings, and their contents, all of which are perfect within awareness's own essence. Since this essence is not established as anything whatsoever, it is beyond appearing and being empty. By virtue of the essential point that it is not an object that can be pointed to or expressed, whatever appears within its natural state consists solely of delusive appearances that have never existed in the first place. From the very time of their appearing to arise, they lack any arising. From the very time of their appearing to abide, they lack any abiding. From the very time of their appearing to cease, they lack any ceasing. From the very time of their appearing to come or go, they lack any coming and going. Thus, no matter how something may appear, it lacks any such nature.

To summarize this, the statement that phenomena arise as saṃsāra or nirvāṇa from the dynamic energy of awareness is also nothing but a conventional expression. In the essence of awareness, neither the slightest thing that arises as saṃsāra or nirvāṇa nor the slightest thing that makes it arise are established as being something different. Thus, nothing ever moves away from the natural state of the equality of the dharmatā of phenomena. For example, though it appears as if reflections of stars and planets arise in the clear ocean, they are ultimately without any arising. The locus of their seeming arising is simply the expanse of the ocean—nothing but clear water. What makes these reflections arise are the stars and planets themselves, which however do not move away from the sky. That is, these reflections do not exist as any phenomenon such that the ocean water and the stars and planets actually come together anywhere. Therefore, they are mere reflections that appear yet are empty. Likewise, it is to be understood that all phenomena are without arising, ceasing, coming, going, permanence, extinction, sameness, and difference and yet appear—they are mere dependently originating illusions.

479 Anonymous 1973–77 (2:460–61) glosses "unawareness" as "the cause [of delusion] that is not different from awareness." "Since awareness itself primordially lacks any cause of delusion," "it is not established as delusion." "It even lacks the names 'stains' and 'delusion'" means that "it cannot even be labeled as the mere words 'purity of stains,' 'afflictive [obscurations],' 'cognitive [obscurations],' or 'obscurations of wrong ideas.'" "No collections of names and letters" means that "it cannot be expressed in terms of being and not being." "The name 'dharma'" refers to "books and volumes." "There is not even the name 'mentally imputed delusion' as a conventional designation." "It naturally lacks any delusion that causes movement" means "it is naturally empty of what causes the breath to move." "Subtle and coarse stains" are "those that are established as the forms of particles." "Agent" and "what is acted upon" are glossed as

"body" and "mind," respectively (though the reverse would seem to make more sense), and "apprehending objects" as "apprehending the objects of the five sense gates."

480 As mentioned before, "the locus of freedom" refers to the primordial ground that is always unstained and free in and of itself. By contrast, the ground manifestations as "the ground of freedom" are not manifestly free yet; they function as the condition for freedom only when recognized as the self-appearances of the primordial ground. Thus, freedom is approached via the "exteriorization" of the ground—the ground manifestations—while the actual freedom takes place within the ground's original purity. In other words, the ground manifestations as the ground of freedom serve as the path to freedom, while the ground itself *is* the destination that is freedom or freedom's very home.

481 Klong chen rab 'byams pa dri med 'od zer, 1999b?, 29–34.

Longchen Yeshé Dorjé's commentary on Jigmé Lingpa's *Treasury of Precious Qualities* (Klong chen ye shes rdo rje 1991, 491–93) says the following on how the ground manifestations arise from the ground. From within the state of the self-radiance of the basic nature that is the ground (the vase body), the ground manifestations—the entire dimension of innate presence—emerge. The ground luminosity that is the unity of alpha-purity and innate presence is referred to as empty luminosity. Within that state, there abides the unbiased wisdom of being aware of the unity of appearance and emptiness that has the character of the life-force wind or essential wind. In it, there exist the other four winds as its branches: the upward-moving wind (the horse of the prajñā of self-recognition), the downward-expelling wind (the radiant light rays of the prajñā of waking up objective appearances), the fire-accompanying wind (which has the power of maturing or burning), and the pervading wind (which has the power of accomplishing or perfecting). The nature of these five winds is such that the ground's unceasing radiance, which is the ground or heart from which all appearances of innate presence dawn, begins to rise outward from the ground through the power of these five winds. Inner luminosity's kāyas, wisdoms, and compassionate responsiveness are inseparable from the five winds as being of one taste; they are not directly manifest but exist in the manner of the youthful vase body. Once its outer seal is broken, at the same time, the light sphere of wisdom or the ground manifestations dawn as outer luminosity while not moving away from the original alpha-pure ground. This is called "the appearance of the nature that is innate presence." When the appearances of innate presence dawn, similar to space, the radiance of the essence of the ground provides the spaciousness for the radiance of its nature to emerge in the form of the five lights. When that happens, the radiance of compassionate responsiveness emerges as the cognizance that discerns this very object that consists of these five forms of light. At that point, the essence that is alpha-purity resembles a cloudless sky: what is called "ignorance" is not established in the ground itself.

However, in contrast to the radiance of compassionate responsiveness appearing as awareness, that cognizance takes on the dimension of the unawareness of not recognizing these self-appearances of awareness. Therefore, from the alpha-purity that is as clearly transparent as a cloudless sky, the appearances of innate presence stir as outer luminosity. They dawn in eight ways: the six modes of arising and the two gateways. (1) Through their dawning as if they were innate presence, their dawning as if compassion leads to the welfare of sentient beings. Or, if dawning as innate presence is not counted (as in certain texts), (2) through their dawning as if light, all-pervasive light rays appear. (3) Through the unimpeded enjoyment of their dawning as if wisdom, wisdom's own light directly shines in pure buddha realms. (4) Through the unimpeded essence of their dawning as if the kāyas of deities, awareness matures as the kāyas and thus all appearances manifest as clusters of the five buddha families. (5) The undetermined view of their dawning as if nonduality, free from all clinging to dualistic phenomena, is to dwell in the nonconceptual samādhi of being free from singularity and plurality. (6) Through the unimpeded means of their dawning as if being free from extremes, they are not present as appearances of delusion but are present for a moment within dharmatā. As for the two gateways: (7) If there is the awareness that what appears in these ways as the wisdom that is awareness's self-appearance is indeed such a self-appearance, this is the gateway to the original ground's awakening as Samantabhadra. (8) If there is no such awareness, this is the gateway to deluded sentient beings.

During the phase of the ground, all ground manifestations dissolve through the power of delusion and thus are only present as inner luminosity. Since this radiance is suitable to arise as the appearances of both saṃsāra and nirvāṇa, it is called "the sphere of the precious innate presence of the ground." During the phase of the path, the ground manifestations appear as the four visions and so on, thus representing the blend of both delusion and freedom. This is the sphere of the precious innate presence of the path. During the phase of the fruition, the ground manifestations dissolve through the power of being free as the self-appearances of awareness. This is the ground of the arising of ocean-like buddha qualities. Thus, these are the three kinds of innate presence during ground, path, and fruition. These eight modes of arising or the three spheres of innate presence represent the juncture where saṃsāra and nirvāṇa are joined without any distinction. (For yet another presentation of the eight gateways, see Longchen Rabjam 1989, 53).

According to Yönten Gyatso's commentary on Jigmé Lingpa's *Treasury of Precious Qualities* (Yon tan rgya mtsho 1982–87, 558–59), camphor is an asset in the case of heat diseases, but it is a problem in the case of cold diseases. However, in the essence of camphor, neither being an asset nor being a problem are established. Likewise, for those who lack realization, the ground's innate presence appears as defects, but it appears as excellent qualities for those with realization. Therefore, the gateway of both delusion and freedom is innate presence.

Furthermore, if one does not understand the basic mode of being of the ground, one does not understand the philosophical system of Dzogchen. The essential point of this is as follows. From the perspective of the primordial ground's alpha-purity, neither saṃsāra nor nirvāṇa are established. However, these three spheres of innate presence resemble the juncture at which saṃsāra and nirvāṇa are joined without any distinction. (1) In the sphere of the precious innate presence of the ground, there is the unceasing radiance that is suitable to dawn as the appearances of either saṃsāra or nirvāṇa. Therefore, they are joined within this single ground. (2) The emergence of the ground manifestations from that ground is the sphere of the precious innate presence of the path. Since this is the condition of both delusion and freedom, they are joined in it as the unity of saṃsāra and nirvāṇa. Even when this innate presence of the path has become delusion, it is by virtue of the individual qualities of the eight gateways of innate presence, explained above, that it is suitable to be the object of a buddha's enlightened activity and suitable to become a buddha. (3) In the sphere of the precious innate presence of the fruition, there are kāyas, buddha realms, and so on that are suitable to appear. Having appeared from this sphere, they are able to display activities for those to be guided. This is the essential point of it being possible for those who guide and those to be guided to be connected.

482 Klong chen rab 'byams pa dri med 'od zer 1999b?, 35–36.

The first chapter of this text ends with a lengthy quote from *Mound of Jewels* about the eight ways in which innate presence dissolves back into the ground, which is the reversal of the eight gateways of innate presence that make up the ground manifestations. In brief, compassionate responsiveness, the five lights, wisdom, the kāyas, nonduality, and the freedom from extremes each dissolve back into their own essence on their own. The gateway of saṃsāra dissolves within the gateway of the essence's purity in a manner that is without saṃsāra having gone to this purity. The gateway of pure wisdom dissolves on its own within the essence, and thus the kāyas and wisdoms pass into nirvāṇa.

As mentioned before, the eleventh chapter of Jigmé Lingpa's *Treasury of Precious Qualities* lists the six distinctive features of Samantabhadra's freedom as follows. (1) In the instant that the ground manifestations appear, they are immediately recognized as the ground's own appearances. (2) Since these self-appearances thus never stray into delusion,

Samantabhadra's freedom is superior to the ground itself. (3) In a single instant, prajñā perfectly differentiates the entire variety of the ground's many qualities. (4) As soon as these qualities are differentiated, that prajñā matures as the dharmakāya. (5) Samantabhadra's freedom does not depend on anything extraneous and (6) always remains in its very own place.

Longchen Yeshé Dorjé's commentary on Jigmé Lingpa's text (Klong chen ye shes rdo rje 1991, 494–97) comments as follows on Samantabhadra's freedom. When the self-radiance of alpha-pure ground luminosity dawns, in the instant of seeing the ground manifestations' own essence, freedom manifests in the manner of six distinctive features. Thus, the recognition of one's own mind as such—self-arising wisdom—from the very outset, which is present prior to all buddhas, is what represents the original buddha, Samantabhadra, free from all flaws of clinging to any real existence of apprehender and apprehended, whose sphere of experience is utterly pure. The six distinctive features of Samantabhadra's seeing and freedom are as follows. (1) The ground manifestations appear as Samantabhadra's very own face; there is no unfolding of a continuum of delusion through an outwardly oriented cognizance's clinging to the ground manifestations—they are recognized as self-appearances within the perspective of self-awareness. (2) Samantabhadra's freedom is superior to the ground; through being aware that the ground manifestations are the self-appearances of awareness, they are superior to both the ground, whose nature is indeterminate as either saṃsāra or nirvāṇa, and the innately present ground manifestations. Since these very ground manifestations have thus become the ground of freedom, they will not function as the ground of delusion at any later point. (3) Freedom is differentiation: since the awareness of the ground manifestations is not something previously nonexistent that arises newly, it is through recognizing its own face that this awareness matures as the fruition that is wisdom. That is, by virtue of the realization of the essence of awareness through the prajñā or wisdom free from obscuring stains, in this single instant, the qualities with which the expanse is inherently endowed are differentiated as being greatly superior to the ground of saṃsāra in that they are this expanse's self-appearances. In essence, this differentiation happens through this expanse's already being primordially pure of the obscurations that consist of the all-ground of diverse latent tendencies, similar to the primordial brilliance of the sun becoming free from clouds. (4) This is freedom directly within such differentiation; right upon differentiating these qualities, that very prajñā matures as the svābhāvikakāya and thus, becoming inseparable from the wisdom dharmakāya, seizes the original alpha-pure ground as its stronghold and remains there forever without change or transition. (5) This freedom does not occur by virtue of anything else; such a direct perception of self-awareness constitutes buddhahood by way of being aware of its own essence through its own power, without depending on any other conditions for its arising, such as instructions by others. (6) This freedom always remains in its very own place; the ground of freedom remains in its own place within its own original state because there is no more operating of any conditions for delusion. (The same six features are also briefly mentioned in 'Gyur med tshe dbang mchog grub 2001, 58; see appendix 8.) Thus, by virtue of these six distinctive features, Samantabhadra sees the ground manifestations as the fruition that consists of the ocean of inconceivable kāyas and wisdoms and that has the character of the vase body. In this seeing, all accumulations are primordially complete and all obscurations are primordially pure. Thereby, Samantabhadra fully awakens in a single instant—this is the original buddha. While not moving away from the expanse of boundless purity and equality without any reference points (the alpha-pure original ground, the expanse of the dharmakāya), the qualities of the expanse that is free from all obscuring latent tendencies are self-arising from the gateways of innate presence that unfold as inner luminosity. These self-appearances dawn as the sambhogakāya's realms and kāyas of the five buddha families. By virtue of the individual dynamic energy of each of the five buddha families, the infinite inconceivable buddha realms that are based on the inexhaustible adornment wheel of the body, speech, and mind of Mahāsagara (the sambhogakāya buddha Great Glacial Lake Vairocana) in his five families are arranged as the Eon of Mahābrahmā, equal in extent to space (according to Bdud 'joms 'jigs bral ye shes rdo rje 1991, 118, the Eon of Mahābrahmā designates the entirety of nirmāṇakāya buddha realms).

For bodhisattvas on the bhūmis, whose obscurations are for the most part purified, this appears as the realms and teachers of the natural nirmāṇakāya. For sentient beings, who emerge from the impure gateway of saṃsāra, this is displayed in accordance with their individual appearances based on all their different kinds of constitutions and inclinations, ranging from the supreme nirmāṇakāya down to all kinds of emanations. The nirmāṇakāya's enlightened activities that render all appearances of saṃsāric delusion empty appear in an inexhaustible manner for as long as the boundless reaches of space exist. Through the power of the primordially and naturally pure dharmadhātu, uncontaminated wisdom, or the sugata heart's recognizing its own face, the adventitious obscurations including their latent tendencies become pure, whereby the fruition that is endowed with twofold purity becomes manifest. Though not having accomplished them through effort, the sambhogakāya perfectly masters the qualities of the two accumulations: the accumulation of wisdom through the prajñā of realizing the nature in its entirety and the accumulation of merit through the manifestation of all the qualities that already exist in an innately present manner within the expanse. Since all latent tendencies of mind and mental factors have become exhausted in buddhas, they lack any clinging to duality. Therefore, they do not think that they will display in the form of certain bodies or activities for certain sentient beings to be guided. However, similar to a wish-fulfilling jewel or a wish-fulfilling tree that satisfies all needs and desires, from within the natural state of the dharmakāya free from reference points, their effortless enlightened activity appears from the perspective of others as the unceasing radiance of great compassion.

According to Yönten Gyatso's commentary on Jigmé Lingpa's text (Yon tan rgya mtsho 1982–87, 563), yogic practitioners who attain the awakening with these six distinctive features by virtue of having cultivated the path are also referred to as the original buddha, Samantabhadra, because their awakening represents primordial awakening. The six distinctive features of Samantabhadra's freedom are as follows. (1) When the ground manifestations arise first, they are innately present appearances. (2) These innately present appearances are the self-appearances of innate presence. (3) These self-appearances are wisdom. (4) This wisdom is primordially free. (5) This primordial freedom is self-awareness. (6) This self-awareness is the dharmakāya. As the awareness of compassionate responsiveness slightly dawns outwardly, yogic practitioners instantly realize these six features and attain awakening.

Yet another explanation of these six distinctive features (Germano 1992n133) is that they consist of realizing (1) the instructions that do not emerge from precepts (awakening as a glorious self-arising buddha without needing a guru to teach or show the way), (2) the buddhahood that does not arise from any ordinary state of mind (wisdom itself awakens within its own natural radiance), (3) the fruition that does not arise from any cause (what is aware is awakened within its own natural state of being free all by itself), (4) self-appearance (the expanse's radiant mind as such appears as its own self-essence; here, "mind as such" refers to the pure ground of awareness itself, which is the locus of mind's exhaustion), (5) self-manifestation (awareness manifests itself as itself), and (6) being free in itself (when aware, awareness recognizes itself, which is in itself the great primordial state without any delusion). In sum, this self-awakening of Samantabhadra takes place right at the transition from the ground to the ground manifestations or at the very first stirring of the ground manifestations, without any intermediary nonrecognition of the ground manifestations and the ensuing illusion of delusion in saṃsāra. Thus, unlike historical buddhas who are typically portrayed as first straying into saṃsāra and then gradually returning to their primordial awakening, Samantabhadra is awakened from the start before any lack of recognition and delusion may even stir.

483 The ground is not only empty and luminous (its essence and its nature, respectively) but also inherently aware, knowing, and dynamic on its own accord. This latter feature is the compassionate responsiveness

of the ground, its dynamic cognitive vibrancy, which manifests as a proto-consciousness or cognitive capacity that is a part of the ground manifestations and can be either very sharp and lucid (thus immediately recognizing the ground manifestations for what they are and being free as Samantabhadra) or completely unaware of what the ground manifestations are (thus not recognizing them for what they are and straying into the delusion of saṃsāra). What follows in the text is all from the perspective of not recognizing the ground manifestations. Elsewhere, Longchenpa explicitly equates the cognizance mentioned here with the neutral or indeterminate all-ground that is described in appendix 5A and evolves into the eight consciousnesses (see Germano 1992n144).

484 Elsewhere, Longchenpa makes it explicit that "connate unawareness" refers to cognizance's nonrecognition of its own face, which implies that this nonrecognition now arises simultaneously with this cognizance's perceptions, unfolding in such a way that the dichotomous appearances of impure saṃsāra and pure nirvāṇa become manifestly present to it as discrete opposed appearances. In contrast, the unawareness of same identity refers only to cognizance's sheer nonrecognition of the ground manifestations (see Germano 1992n157).

485 As Higgins (2013, 71n162) points out, Longchenpa's *Precious Treasury of the Supreme Yāna* elaborates on this passage in terms of the onset and development of reifying cognizance:

> (1) Since a multitude of apprehender and apprehended arises from the sheer factor of [cognizance's] being unaware of its own face, what is called "ultimate nondelusion" has become delusion, just as when what is nameless has become a name. This is the unawareness that has the same identity as the cause. (2) The isolate of the sheer nonrecognition of just that [unawareness of same identity] is connate unawareness, which arises as the appearance dimension of both saṃsāra and nirvāṇa. (3) From the point of view of the appearance of light (the object) thus being split by mind into mere dualistic appearances, it has become the factor being conceived as names, referents, and a self. Therefore, this is called "imaginative unawareness." (Klong chen rab 'byams pa dri med 'od zer 1999d?, 5:743)

The same author's *Treasure Trove of Scriptures* (Klong chen rab 'byams pa dri med 'od zer, 1999a?, 234–35) describes connate and imaginative unawareness as follows:

> One's own self-awareness—the empty yet lucid essence of the innately present dharmakāya—lacks any entity and characteristics, similar to space. However, simultaneously with it, there

> occur two [kinds of unawareness]—the connate unawareness of not recognizing its own face and the imaginative unawareness of [mistakenly] apprehending it as something that it is not. Thereby, it becomes the dimension of the delusion of apprehender and apprehended, and arises as all kinds of saṃsāric appearances of delusion. Similar to apprehending dream objects and appearances as having a [real] identity, those who cling to the delusion of what appears and is possible—saṃsāra and nirvāṇa—apprehend nonexistent yet clearly appearing phenomena as [actual] referents. Therefore, this resembles clinging to the appearances in an illusion as being real, which should be understood to be very amazing.

Higgins (2013, 69) also says that these two kinds of unawareness may have developed from the notions of the innate and imaginative views about a real personality (*sahajasatkāyadṛṣṭi* and *parikalpitasatkāyadṛṣṭi*) that are distinguished in the *Yogācārabhūmi* and the *Abhidharmakośabhāṣya* (as well as in other texts). Similarly, the commentaries on the *Abhisamayālaṃkāra* as well as other Mahāyāna works on the paths and bhūmis extensively discuss the innate and imaginative kinds of clinging to a personal and phenomenal identity, innate and imaginative afflictions, and innate and imaginative conceptions about apprehender and apprehended.

486 For a description of the four conditions, see the detailed explanation of this topic below.

487 In brief, relative to the three unawarenesses: (1) The unawareness that has the same identity as the cause is the primordial mere nonrecognition of the single undifferentiated ground of awareness and unawareness (and the ensuing delusion). (2) Connate unawareness consists of the simultaneous arising or coexistence of that nonrecognition and cognizance. (3) Imaginative unawareness refers to subsequently mistaking the ground's self-appearances as the dualistic appearances of subject and object. Thus, the unawareness of same identity as the initial and most basic form of unawareness or nonrecognition that causes and eventually manifests as the entire plethora of delusion (saṃsāra with its six realms) does not recognize that ground and ground manifestations, cognizance and primordial basic awareness, or unawareness and awareness always have the same character or nature (which, however, does not mean that they are identical in appearance or manifestation). This basic and more passive form of nonrecognition occurs simultaneously with said cognizance as "connate unawareness" and thus becomes more active (observing the appearances of the ground manifestations without realizing that they are self-appearances of the ground). Consequently, this cognizance becomes directly isolated from the ground manifestations as a kind of proto-self or apprehender and—indirectly—from the ground itself. In the form of

imaginative unawareness, this isolation then gives rise to the notion that the appearances of the ground manifestations are something other than the ground: that is, the dualistic structures of self and other and apprehender and apprehended. Elsewhere, Longchenpa says that the radiance of awareness that stems from the ground's compassionate responsiveness manifests as the cognizance that is able to discern the observable aspects of the appearing lights and, due to the mere nonrecognition of those lights as its own nature, it is present as the "unawareness that is contingent on awareness" (see Germano 1992n142). Compare also the more detailed explanation of the three kinds of unawareness in this appendix below ("2.2. Detailed explanation of the factors that consist of the conditions that are its aspects").

488 For a description of the six mentations, see right below in this section.

489 Elsewhere, Longchenpa glosses "the ground" as "the essence that is alpha-purity" and "the appearance dimension" as "innate presence" (see Germano 1992n145).

490 Elsewhere, Longchenpa glosses "cognizance of the ground" as "not understanding the nature of the ground and the ground manifestations" and "distinction" as "grasping at the ground manifestations as being something other" (see Germano 1992n145). The ground itself always remains primordially pure and undivided into recognition and nonrecognition, or freedom and delusion, which is distinct from the cognizance that stirs from the ground within the ground manifestations and has the capacity for recognizing or not recognizing these ground manifestations as the self-appearances of the ground, thus leading to being free by itself or being deluded by itself, respectively.

491 That is, under the influence of the four conditions described in detail below, this originally highly lucid and aware cognizance becomes dimmed and obscured through focusing on the mistakenly objectified and solidified ground manifestations in accordance with the dimming of the originally brilliant five lights into the dense material world of the five elements and so on. Thus, the originally free flow of radiant open luminosity that characterized the ground manifestations becomes more and more constricted and limited as independently existing entities that are mistakenly perceived as "other."

492 While both the Tibetan terms for "unawareness" (*ma rig pa*) and "nescience" (*gti mug*) can be rendered as "ignorance" in a general sense, in this list here, "unawareness" represents the basic mental factor that underlies the very possibility of any other afflictions because it marks the onset of delusion, while "nescience" is merely one of the many subsequent mental factors that stem from that basic unawareness.

493 Anonymous 1973–77, 1:676.

494 Ibid., 1:678.

The tantra (ibid., 1:676–80) also provides explanations of each of the six kinds of unawareness and the six mentations (the latter are said to make up the fourth unawareness, that of thoughts, which is clinging):

> (1) The fundamental unawareness of mind is the actual connate unawareness. It is the delusion due to not recognizing the wisdom of awareness, that is, the arising of the cognizance that thinks, "Do these appearances of wisdom arise from me or are they not my appearances?" The arising of such thinking is the connate root unawareness. There is delusion by virtue of the arising of a mental state of conceiving of a self, which is what obscures the appearances of the wisdom of awareness. This is called "the fundamental unawareness of mind."
>
> (2) Now, the unawareness of objects, which is delusion, is taught. Delusion refers to that through which [mind] is deluded [Tib. *gong gis* emended to *gang gis*]. As for objects, previously, just when the world had not yet formed, there was the tree that arose from the blessings of the youthful vase body of buddhahood, called "the vast wish-fulfilling tree," as well as a birth from the heat and moisture arising from an egg. Thus, due to mentation's stirring up "self-arising wisdom," [our] worldly realm Endurance was formed. This is called "the unawareness of objects, which is delusion." [As for the poetic metaphors here, "the youthful vase body" obviously refers to the ground, while "the wish-fulfilling tree" appears to refer to the ground manifestations when they seem to be external appearances, and "a birth from the heat and moisture arising from an egg" to the initial cognizance or mentation that observes these appearances as eternal proto-objects.]
>
> (3) The unawareness of the ground, which is the basis of delusion, arises from its own being impure through itself. First, what is called "the causal condition" is the arising of actual unawareness—the unawareness of not recognizing the ground. From that, what is called "the object condition" arises, which is referred to as "the unawareness of objects, which is delusion." From that, what is called "the dominant condition"—the clinging to that tree as being "me"—arises. From that, what is called "the immediate condition" arises; once cognizance has become coarse, it apprehends objects through clinging. Due to that, it turns into coarse afflictions. This is called "the unawareness of the ground, which is the basis of delusion."
>
> (4) The unawareness of thoughts, which is clinging, is the one from which immeasurably many hosts of afflictions arise.

This is as follows. The six clinging mentations emerge ... (a) The mentation associated with unawareness is as follows: It is the actual fundamental unawareness, which involves the stirring of mentation. This is the mentation associated with unawareness. (b) As for [the mentation of] the mental consciousness, the cognizance that thinks that objects are what is "mine" apprehends a me and a self, thus coming to be under the sway of the afflictions. Therefore, this is called "[the mentation of] the mental consciousness." (c) As for the mentation of searching, through [cognizance's] having come under the sway of objects, it gathers all subtle afflictions as its companions. Therefore, it is called "the mentation of searching." (d) As for the mentation of ascertainment, since objects are apprehended by the cognizance that thinks of them as what is "mine," attachment for them arises and thus this is called "ascertainment." [Here, the tantra as well as Longchenpa's comments in his *Precious Treasury of the Supreme Yāna* reverse the order of (c) and (d), but I follow the above usual order.] (e) The mentations whose aspect is coarse refer to killing, committing many actions of letting samaya deteriorate [and so on] by virtue of coarse afflictions. (f) The mentation of determination refers to thinking about [certain among] these appearances as being "mine" [Tib. *lang* emended to *la nga yi*] and thinking [about certain others] as being those of others. This is the mentation of determination. [The tantra mistakenly adds here: "This is called 'the unawareness of thoughts, which is clinging.'"] (5) The unawareness of the path, which is fabrication, obscures the path of wisdom through the coming together of the six mentations. Mentation does not see wisdom, nor does it bestow it in a clear manner. Since wisdom lacks any thoughts, while mentation involves what causes stirring, the latter is what obscures the path to buddhahood. This is called "the unawareness of the path, which is fabrication."

(6) The unawareness of oblivion, which is nonrecognition, refers to cycling in saṃsāra again and again through not recognizing that [the ground's] self-appearances exist as light. This is called "the unawareness of oblivion, which is nonrecognition."

Thus, if these six kinds of unawareness arise, the appearances of wisdom are not recognized. This is as follows. In the appearances of the actuality that is alpha-purity, there is no unawareness, there is no mind, and there is no mentation either. It is within the dynamic energy of innate presence

> that unawareness arises. From the play of unawareness, mind arises. From the ornaments of mind, mentation arises. From the objects of mentation, the five poisons arise. From the five poisons, the sixteen afflictions arise.

This is followed by a list of these sixteen afflictions and further mention of twenty-five, fifty-one, and eighty-thousand afflictions.

In his explanation of this extended quote in his *Precious Treasury of the Supreme Yāna*, Longchenpa glosses (1) the unawareness of mind as "the ignorance of mistaking what is 'self' for 'something other,' which stems from original awareness's not recognizing its own essence." (2) The unawareness of objects is "the ignorance of not recognizing that the objects that appear are devoid of any independent existence." (3) The unawareness of the ground is "the ignorance of being deluded by virtue of conditions, such as when mistaking a cairn for a person." (4) The unawareness of thoughts is "the ignorance of clinging to identities in various aspects even while there are no such identities within awareness's essence." (5) The unawareness of the path is "the ignorance that transforms the antidote into poison, such that it can no longer grant freedom." (6) The unawareness of oblivion is "the ignorance of perpetually circling through saṃsāra through the power of not recognizing the presence of natural radiant light." Thus, through the power of this sixfold unawareness, the ground manifestations are not recognized.

As for the six mentations, (a) the mentation associated with unawareness refers to unawareness as the root of delusion in that it involves the flickering or stirring of the mind. (b) The mentation of the mental consciousness refers to that which experiences its own individual awareness and not just objects other than it (thus, the initial cognizance becomes aware of its own presence and knowing). In addition, this also refers to the mental consciousness's cognizing and relating to objects by thinking, "This is me." (c) Through the mentation of searching, a variety of objects emerge that are then apprehended from the perspective of "me." (d) The mentation of ascertainment determines these objects both in terms of what they are and how to relate to them. (e) The mentations whose manner of appearing is coarse consist of mind's being distracted toward objects as well as all coarse states of mental afflictions. (f) The mentation of determination refers to subjectively deciding or judging that certain appearances are "mine," while certain others are "those of others," and then fixating on them in these ways. (For more details, see Germano 1992nn147 and 148.)

495 In Dzogchen, similar to the distinction between mind (Tib. *sems*) and wisdom (Tib. *ye shes*; see appendix 5B), "mentation" (Tib. *yid*) as distorted cognition is distinguished from prajñā (Tib. *shes rab*) as properly differentiating insight. Both mentation and prajñā deal with the perception of objects but prajñā lacks mentation's characteristic conceptuality

(conceptuality in its most general sense of mental constructs or projections). Thus, it is also different from the indeterminate cognizance in the context of the ground manifestations mentioned before.

496 "The general ground" was explained before as the ground manifestations when they are still indeterminate as either delusion or freedom but can serve as the basis of either. What is discussed here is this very general ground now having strayed into delusion and thus becoming "the ground of delusion." That is, all appearances and experiences of saṃsāra are indirect derivatives of the ground via the failure to recognize the ground manifestations as the ground.

At the same time, however, delusion's appearances and experiences have no bearing on the essence of the ground itself. Longchenpa's *Treasure Trove of Scriptures* (Klong chen rab 'byams pa dri med 'od zer 1999a?, 583–84) explains that the unawareness that causes delusion is nothing other than an expression of awareness that adventitiously obscures awareness itself. For example, the sun's rays (its dynamic energy) cause warmth in soil and water, resulting in vapor, which in turn manifests as the play of clouds that then obscure both the sun and its rays from our point of view (not from the point of view of the sun itself, which always remains completely unaffected by clouds). Thus, it is the sun's own rays that bring about the clouds that then obscure its own display of light, all against the backdrop of the sky's original purity and vast openness. Likewise, when primordial awareness's own dynamic energy of innate presence within the infinite expanse of alpha-purity is not recognized as the self-appearance of that awareness, this results in all kinds of delusions that manifest as subjects and objects as well as self and others, which then in turn obscure the essential luminosity of this awareness.

Germano (1992, 463–64) adds that in this way, a part of the play (*rol pa*) of awareness obscures both awareness's essence and its natural dynamic energy (*rtsal*). That is, awareness's own dynamic energy comes to obscure itself indirectly through its own play ("play" thus has both pure and impure dimensions, with the latter being what obscures its source). In other words, the enlightened body, speech, and mind of a buddha are obscured by their corresponding deluded states of ordinary body, speech, and mind; the natural state of buddhahood is not manifest, while what is experienced are the saṃsāric appearances of delusion. Thus, the sun (our own inner core of indestructible and luminous awareness) remains unobscured in itself, though it may be obscured from a certain vantage point. When the obscurations of that vantage point are cleared away, the primordially present radiance is finally seen directly, just as the sun is recognized as shining forth freely throughout the entire sky once the clouds have disappeared. This is also highlighted in Longchenpa's *Treasure Trove of Scriptures* (Klong chen rab 'byams pa dri med 'od zer 1999a?, 295–96 and 306–7):

> The essence of the sun is its natural luminosity within the expanse of space. This essence of the sun cannot be obscured by clouds, nor can its luminosity be created in an adventitious manner through [a process of] causes and results. Likewise, it is impossible for causes and results or obscurations to exist in awareness's own essence. [Still,] when the humans on the four continents look, the sun sometimes appears to be obscured and so on. Though it seems [to them] that the sun is obscured, it is [in fact] their own eyes that are obscured by clouds and yet they still cling to this by thinking, "The sun is obscured." This is called "delusion." Similarly, though there is no straying or obscuration in awareness due to adventitious afflictions and so on, from the perspective of deluded thoughts, it appears to be obscured. Thus, people think, "Awareness possesses obscurations, so I should purify it and develop qualities." This is referred to as "delusion plain and simple" ... This essence of awareness, which is already primordially accomplished as buddhahood, is as if the sun is manifestly present [right now]. Others, similarly to holding [the belief] that the sun is seen later by virtue of the causes and conditions that dispel clouds and darkness, assert that buddhahood will be accomplished at the end of having made efforts that involve causes and conditions. Thus, since they engage in ways that are contradictory to innate presence, the texts of [all] the yānas [below Atiyoga] are internally contradictory. Therefore, they are distinguished [from Atiyoga] by way of the distinctive feature of whether or not this very awareness—self-arising wisdom—exists as buddhahood in a naturally present manner right now.

Compare also the stance of the *Uttaratantra* that all saṃsāric factors are contingent on buddha nature, while buddha nature is not contingent on any of them. (This is similar to the idea that the elements of the universe arise in and are supported by space, while space does not arise and is not supported by any of those elements; see particularly I.52–63.) However, the classical tathāgatagarbha teachings always greatly emphasize the separateness of buddha nature and its obscurations (which are not a derivative of buddha nature, just unreal illusory phenomena).

497 Tib. *spags pa* means "shift into" or "mix with," both of which would also make sense here. However, in accordance with similar prior instances and the context here of stainless awareness's becoming stained, *spags pa* is emended to *sbags pa*.

498 Elsewhere, Longchenpa identifies the causal condition as the three kinds of unawareness and the dominant condition as awareness. Alternatively, he describes the dominant condition as awareness itself in that it is the foundation for being deluded in the form of mind. In this regard it resembles camphor, which can act as a remedy for either hot or cold diseases depending on the present condition of the body. Similarly, if awareness is recognized, it acts as the condition for freedom; when not recognized, it serves as the condition for delusion. The object condition consists of the ground manifestations itself, which however are mistaken for being something other, similar to mistaking a rope for a snake. In this way, the ground manifestations are just a potential condition for delusion and only turn into an actual such condition through their being misperceived as something else.

The immediate condition consists of the temporary encounter between "awareness stained by unawareness" and the ground manifestations, which represent a kind of proto-apprehender and proto-apprehended, respectively. This is similar to the pain of being wounded ensuing from a weapon's making contact with a body (see Germano 1992n144). Yet another explanation is that the causal condition is the nonrecognition of the ground manifestations as the lucidity dimension of the naked nature of the mind. The object condition is the condition through which delusion arises, that is, mistaking luminosity for objects of saṃsāric perception. The dominant condition is the clinging to a self. The immediate condition is the simultaneous arising of the previous three conditions together (Dzogchen Ponlop Rinpoche 2002, 102–3 and 164).

499 Later, the text clarifies that, strictly speaking, awareness is not to be equated with the cognizance that stirs from it as a part of the ground manifestations, because this cognizance is awareness's dynamic energy or derivative. Thus, it is this subsequent cognizance of the ground—as distinct from primordial basic awareness itself—that is to be identified as the actual "agent of delusion" (see Germano 1992n152).

500 What is nonexistent consists of the duality of self and other, the duality of apprehender and apprehended, and the superimposed real and independent identities of persons and phenomena.

501 As mentioned before, other sources sometimes present a correlation of this triad of unawareness with the ground's own triad of essence, nature, and compassionate responsiveness. That is, the unawareness that is contingent on or is a derivative of awareness (whereas awareness is neither contingent on nor a derivative of unawareness) is threefold as follows: The unawareness of same identity derives from not recognizing the empty essence's dimension of nonconceptuality. Connate unawareness derives from not recognizing the luminous nature as awareness's self-nature. Imaginative unawareness derives from not recognizing compassionate responsiveness's intrinsic awareness (for details, see Germano 1992n156).

502 Tib. *byad* can mean "face," "physical shape," or "physical appearance." The latter two meanings would also make sense here but since the example continues below with "face" (and also begins with "face" in the versions of this example in other texts), I chose that term here as well.

503 In other words, delusion would not exist without threefold unawareness, just as a person's face would not exist without that person's body. Though not explicitly mentioned here, "the agent of delusion"—the cognizance that is a distorted form of basic awareness as "the cognizance of the ground" and is tainted by threefold unawareness—resembles the person whose body possesses that face.

504 Elsewhere, Longchenpa identifies the mirror as "stainless awareness" and the reflected condition as "whatever displays itself" in that mirror (see Germano 1992n158). Thus, the face of the five lights of the ground manifestations (ultimately, the ground manifestations are themselves just a reflection of awareness's own face or essence), when appearing as if an external object, is reflected within the mirror of awareness itself. Compare this to Vimalamitra saying, "The 'object condition' ... is like the surface of a mirror because each individually perceived object arises" (Smith 2016, 77).

505 The two sentences here under the third item in this list are somewhat problematic in both phrasing and contents. First, the phrase *bdag dngos sum du gzung ba* in the first sentence is corrupt; it could be read as *bdag dngos su gzung ba*, *bdag mngon sum du gzung ba*, or *bdag dngos mngon sum du gzung ba* (which is what I have translated here because the sentence appears to speak about the direct perception of a mirror, a face, and the actual person who sees their face in the mirror, which is then followed by thoughts about these three perceived elements).

Second, the exact meaning of *bdag* or *bdag dngos* (the latter in all probability renders Skt. ātmabhāva—"individual or personal existence," an expression for the sum of the five skandhas taken to be a person) in this phrase is not clear. However, given the obviously parallel triad of light, awareness, and dharmatā in the second sentence, *bdag* (*dngos*) appears to refer to the person who sees both the mirror and the reflection of their face in it thereby identifying themselves in their entire personal existence by thinking "This is me." At least that is what Vimalamitra says in this context: "since one's likeness arises within the mirror, when considering them both—'this is the surface of the mirror' and 'inside of this my likeness arises'—the thought that 'this likeness arising in the mirror is my face' is the dominant condition" (Smith 2016, 77).

Third, the exact correlations between mirror, face, and the looker's personal existence (or self) on the one hand and the five lights, awareness, and their dharmatā on the other hand are not clear either. In line with what Longchenpa said in the preceding note, the mirror would correspond to awareness, the reflection of the face in it to the five lights, and the looker's personal existence (or self) to the (unrecognized) dharmatā of this reflection (that is, the reflected ground). Or the actual face that is reflected corresponds to awareness (either in itself, as its expression as the nonexteriorized ground manifestations, or as the cognizance that mistakenly regards the seemingly externally appearing ground manifestations as something different from awareness), the face's reflection corresponds to the seemingly exteriorized ground manifestations (the five lights), and the dharmatā of those two to the underlying identical nature of awareness and ground manifestations despite the latter's appearing as if external to awareness. What is curious here though is that Longchenpa only mentions thoughts about the mirror and the face reflected in it (and not thoughts about the looker's personal existence or self), whereas the correlated next sentence speaks about thoughts about all three elements (lights, awareness, and their dharmatā). Note also that Longchen Yeshé Dorjé's commentary on Jigmé Lingpa's *Treasury of Precious Qualities* (Klong chen ye shes rdo rje 1991, 499) appears to switch the examples of the second and third items, saying that the object condition resembles apprehending a mirror and a reflection as being different while they are not so, whereas the dominant condition resembles apprehending a face in a mirror.

In any case, the gist of this is that the seemingly external reflection of the ground manifestations is in turn subjectively reflected in the cognizance that perceives this seemingly external object and mistakes it for something other than the expression of its very own innate luminosity or the ground of pristine awareness.

506 In sum, the structure of the four conditions for delusion and how they cooperate in the arising of delusion seems to be clear; what is unclear is how this matches the above-mentioned details of the third part of the example.

Germano (1992n158) discusses this paragraph at length but variously equates the "mirror" in the example with awareness, the ground manifestations themselves (or the five lights), or the reflection of the ground manifestations, and the "face" with awareness itself, the ground manifestations, or the latter's seemingly external reflection. He also speaks of three distinct examples here, while it seems to make more sense to understand this as three consecutive parts of a single example: by virtue of its physical existence, a person's body is suitable to appear as a visual shape, this shape (or here just the face) appears as a reflection when a mirror is present, and then that person mistakenly entertains thoughts about their actual face and its reflection being the same ("me").

Elsewhere, Longchenpa explains that the causal condition consists of the arising of the threefold unawareness as the subject, the object condition refers to the objects that are apprehended as something other than the self (similar to a person's shape appearing in a mirror), the dominant condition is the cognizance of dualistic clinging, and the immediate condition consists of the temporal conjunction of these three. Thus, in brief, the cognizing subject arises (unawareness), then objects (the five lights) are mirrored within awareness, then the subject takes the mirrored objects and itself as real and disparate, and thus all three elements coexist as an ongoing process. In this way, the lights (that is, the ground manifestations) are the ground of delusion in terms of objects, awareness is the ground of delusion in terms of mind (as the subject), and dharmatā represents the space for this delusion to take place.

Elsewhere, Longchenpa also says that dharmatā ("empty awareness") is the ground of delusion in terms of objects, awareness ("unceasing stirring") is the ground of delusion in terms of mind, and the five lights ("the radiance within the space of awareness") are the ground of delusion in terms of ordinary bodies (see Germano 1992, end of n158). In another translation of Longchenpa's *Precious Treasury of Words and Their Meaning* (Longchen Rabjam 2015, 79), the paragraph in question here is rendered as follows:

> The causal condition is the emergence of confusion by means of the combination of the three types of ignorance. This is analogous to a person whose complete physical appearance comes about as a matter of course. Then, the objective condition resembling a mirror arises objectively like a face reflected based upon the circumstance of a mirror. The controlling condition occurs from the arising of the light [of the ground], which appears as the external objective sphere. By holding the mirror, the reflection of the face and the self-image are held as true, and it is assumed that the face in the mirror actually exists there. Likewise, when light, awareness, and the dharmatā are conceptualized, that is referred to as the controlling condition. In this way, through the three causal states of ignorance and the three contributing circumstances coinciding, the immediate conjunction occurs and actual confusion comes about.

Compare also the parallel presentation of the same example for the four conditions in *Lamp* ("2.1.3.2. The particular distinct instruction on the [mode of delusion]"), which appears to be somewhat simpler and clearer.

507 As mentioned in appendix 2, the imagery of the ground as being surrounded by a "luminous mansion" or "dome of light" refers to its appearance as the ground manifestations in that awareness rises out of its state of self-contained pure potential (similar to a lamp radiating only within the confines of a vase) into actualization (similar to that lamp's radiating everywhere once it is out of the vase) and thus is surrounded by its own natural radiance. With this manifestation of awareness, both its recognition and nonrecognition become possible (while that issue was irrelevant in the state of the undivided ground itself). The "dim cognizance" mentioned in

the preceding paragraph corresponds to cognizance's lack of recognition of the light dome as its own natural radiance. Elsewhere, Longchenpa also says that although primordial awareness is devoid of delusion, delusion emerges via the three causes and the four conditions. This resembles the sun's lacking any darkness and obscuration in itself and yet becoming progressively darkened or dimmed down from our perspective by virtue of clouds obscuring its presence from us: once awareness's sun-like radiance in the ground manifestations' initial emergence has subsided, beings wander through the darkness of saṃsāra (see Germano 1992n161).

508 This could also be read as "There is delusion in that the ground itself does not recognize that it is itself the ground." However, it is usually stressed in Dzogchen that the ground itself is never deluded about itself, nor does it possess any delusion or cause of delusion. As Higgins (2013, 198ff.) shows, authors such as Longchenpa also make the point that delusion neither exists nor does not exist in the ground. That is, there is no delusion or cause of delusion in the ground, because otherwise the ground would not be the ultimate primordial nature of mind that is by definition free from delusion and can serve as the ground for awakening and nondelusion. On the other hand, if delusion did not exist at all in the ground in some way, there would be no cause of delusion whatsoever because there can be no other source of delusion outside of this most fundamental ground of all appearances and experiences. Thus, delusion occurs because the ground always serves as the ground of arising of everything (in the form of the eight ground manifestations). Just as reflections appear in a mirror or rainbows in a crystal without the mirror or the crystal being altered by that in any way, delusion arises without altering the ground. Thus, delusion arises by virtue of certain conditions due to ignorance (a.k.a. the illusory "all-ground" as the basis for all obscurations, karmas, and latent tendencies) without having any real basis. Examples for this include the appearance of dreams, mistaking a rope for a snake, and misperceiving a white conch as yellow under the influence of jaundice.

Some may object that the single ground cannot serve as the support or cause of the two dissimilar appearances of saṃsāra and nirvāṇa, because a singular cause cannot produce two opposite results. Longchenpa answers with the example of the Buddha's cousin Devadatta who appears as a friend to some and an enemy to others, while not being established in any way as either friend or enemy. Similarly, the ground can be perceived as saṃsāra or nirvāṇa while in itself not being established as either. In brief, though delusion does not exist in the ground itself, it can occur due to the indeterminacy of the ground's own manifestations, which may appear as if saṃsāra when not recognized for what they are and as if nirvāṇa when recognized. Since delusion is considered to be a part of the ground manifestations, which are self-appearances that lack any extrinsic foundation or basis, delusion can, as Higgins (ibid., 205–6) puts it, "be regarded as a kind of boot-strapping process that unfolds of its own accord under the appropriate conditions and also ceases of its own accord when the conditions for its functioning are no longer operative." Compare also Rog Bandé Sherab Ö's (1166–1244) *Lamp of the Teachings* (Rog bandhe shes rab 'od 1999, 295–96):

> If there were delusion by virtue of its existing within the ground, delusion would not be relinquished through [an attempt at] relinquishing it because it exists in the [changeless] ground. If there were delusion despite delusion's not existing within the ground, it would follow that even buddhas with a pure mind stream could be deluded [since delusion comes from outside of the pure ground]. So how is it then? Though delusion does not exist within the ground, the ground exists within delusion, just as in the case of a rope being mistaken for a snake. Though the rope lacks any aspect of a snake, it is the rope that functions as the basis for its being mistaken for a snake. Just as in this example, though no basis for delusion whatsoever is established within the fundamental ground to be known, delusion is created through not realizing this fundamental ground to be known. How does delusion occur? Within the ground, the uncontrived innately present dharmatā that is not established as any essence of its own whatsoever, its dynamic energy arises as anything whatsoever: it arises as the dynamic energy of the thought process (*dran pa*). Through this thought process itself not knowing its own essence, connate unawareness functions as the cause [of delusion]. Through that, the unawareness that imagines all objects in a wrong way functions as the condition [of delusion]. In that way, these objects are apprehended as being independently existent (*rang rgyud*). Thus, it is the ground's own reflection that is taken to be real (similar to a mirror and a face [that is reflected in it]) and what is not the case is taken to be the case (similar to mistaking a cairn for a human). This is self-bondage by itself, just as in the case of a silk worm's [becoming ensheathed in the threads made from its own] spittle.

509 Anonymous 1973–77, 1:332–33. Longchenpa has "from such an impure ground" (*gzhi de lta bu ma dag pa*).

510 This appears to mean that basic awareness as the very cause or source of all appearances is mistaken for something that involves dependence on a result, which is different from this cause, rather than recognizing that all appearances of awareness are its own self-arising and self-ceasing dynamics and thus never stray from or are something other than this basic awareness.

511 Klong chen rab 'byams pa dri med 'od zer 1999b?, 40–46. The last quote is Anonymous 1973–77, 1:216–17 (in the last sentence of its first paragraph; I however follow Longchenpa's *rang rkyen gyi gzhi la ldog pa* against *rang rkyen gyis gzhi las ldog pa*; see also Germano 1992n160). The last sentence of the quote's second paragraph means that cognizance apprehends and fixates on the pure energy of the five lights as precisely what they are not—reified objects perceived by an equally reified cognitive subject that is separate from these objects. Thus, the five lights mistakenly appear as dualistically perceived objects, such as the five elements. Similarly, there is clinging to what is not a self at all as being such a self. The tantra here adds the following gloss to the concluding line of its second chapter that states its name: "This is the second chapter in the *Tantra of Great Auspicious Beauty*, which teaches the manner in which delusion arises within the ground 'through this causal condition, dominant condition, object condition, and immediate condition representing the unawareness about nonconceptual awareness.'"

512 Longchen Yeshé Dorjé's commentary on Jigmé Lingpa's *Treasury of Precious Qualities* (Klong chen ye shes rdo rje 1991, 498–503) says the following on how delusion arises. Through being unaware that the very dawning of the ground manifestations—the sphere of precious innate presence—represents the self-appearances of awareness, the ground manifestations appear as the sentient beings of the three realms: those in the formless realm whose minds of one-pointed calm abiding are supported by the four name-skandhas, those in the form realm whose minds of dhyāna free from correct superior insight are supported by a lucid body of light, and those in the desire realm whose minds of coarse thoughts that appear and move around as all kinds of things are supported by a material body of flesh and blood. Within the essence of the alpha-purity and innate presence that constitute the original ground, there are no appearances of delusion including their causes, which means that, lacking its causes, there is no unawareness within the ground. However, it is not the case that there is no sheer radiance in the ground that is suitable to dawn as the ground manifestations. Thus, the ground of delusion arises from the factor of being ignorant or unaware that the radiance of the ground dawns in the form of the eight gateways as the self-appearances of awareness.

This unawareness exists neither within the ground nor later at the time when freedom manifests within the ground. Therefore, this unawareness is an adventitious condition (which is of three kinds): (1) Since awareness's own dynamic energy has become what obscures awareness itself, it is called "the unawareness whose character is identical to awareness." (Tib. *ma rig pa* is emended to *rig pa*. According to Yon tan rgya mtsho 1982–87 [569], the unawareness whose character is identical to awareness is actually the opposite of awareness; it is the failure to recognize awareness's own nature.

As such, it becomes the cause of the other two forms of unawareness.) (2) Through this unawareness's increase in power, a subtle capacity of a discerning cognizance wells up, which is connate unawareness. (3) Through not knowing that this cognizance is awareness's self-radiance, even when coarse thoughts about names, referents, and identities (of persons and phenomena) do not emerge, they constitute latent isolates that are always suitable to emerge. This is imaginative unawareness.

From these three kinds of unawareness, the four conditions of delusion unfold as follows. (1) The ground has the three aspects of essence, nature, and compassionate responsiveness. By virtue of that, within the radiance of alpha-purity that serves as the dimension of providing room like space, the very radiance of the nature dawns and remains like a mansion of light. This is the causal condition of giving rise to the subject that is deluded, which resembles a person's naturally possessing a form and limbs. (2) Within what appears thus as the causal condition, a subtle aspect of examination and discernment (which is in fact the radiance of compassionate responsiveness's awareness) dawns, and all subsequent delusions arise through its power. This is the dominant condition, which resembles apprehending a face in a mirror. (3) By virtue of the coming together of these two conditions, while an outer object and an inner subject do in fact not exist, they have become objects that are perceived as being different. This is the object condition that consists of the duality of apprehender and apprehended, which resembles apprehending a mirror and a reflection as being different while they are not so. (4) By virtue of the simultaneous existence of these three conditions, this functions as the condition for the uninterrupted arising of delusion. Therefore, this is the immediate condition.

From these four conditions, delusions in the form of all kinds of causes, results, names, and appearances arise. As for the manner in which this happens, *Auspicious Beauty* says:

> Delusion occurs through the four conditions, and its end [also] lies in these four conditions. By virtue of the causal condition of apprehending the ground manifestations as being something observable, there is delusion in the form of a cause with all kinds of results. By virtue of the dominant condition of apprehending the ground manifestations as a subject, there is delusion in the form of all kinds of names. By virtue of the object condition of apprehending the ground manifestations as involving a mind [with an object], there is delusion in the form of infinite results. By virtue of the immediate condition of apprehending [the preceding three conditions], there is delusion in the form of all kinds of appearances.

This is how delusion operates, but if these conditions are identified as what they actually are, freedom manifests within these very conditions themselves. For those who are not free in that way, due to the coming together of causes and conditions, the habituation to the appearances of delusion and the deluded apprehender gradually strengthens. Thus, thoughts of improper mental engagement, the hosts of afflictions, and the latent tendencies of places, referents, and bodies proliferate. Under their influence, higher and lower states in saṃsāra and all kinds of sentient beings appear as if they were established as such.

In this situation of saṃsāra, the twelve links of dependent origination beginning with ignorance constantly revolve like the wheels of a chariot. (1) Ignorance consists of the three kinds of unawareness of not recognizing compassionate responsiveness's own light. (2) By virtue of that, the four conditions constitute the formations of saṃsāra. (3) By virtue of that, coarse cognizance proliferates and thus discerns aspects that look like objects: this is consciousness. (4) By virtue of that, consciousness arises as different names and forms: this is name-and-form. (5) The āyatanas are the arising of the distinctive features of name-and-form as their individual parts and colors. (6) Contact is the experience of objects by virtue of that. (7) By virtue of that, feelings arise as the triad of pleasure, pain, and what is neither. (8) Craving is the craving for pleasure and the dislike of suffering by virtue of that. (9) Grasping is to eagerly seize objects by virtue of that. (10) By virtue of that, karma and afflictions expand and thus propel into the next rebirth: this is becoming. (11) Birth refers to being born in different forms of existence by virtue of that. (12) By virtue of that, after having experienced childhood and youth, aging and death occur. To illustrate this process based on this life, unrecognized, the ground luminosity of the previous life has subsided during the intermediate state of dying. Ignorance is the nonrecognition of the first instant that makes it possible for the intermediate state of becoming to appear. The period beginning with ignorance up through the cessation of the outer breath at death in the present life represents the twelve links in their progressive order. After the subsequent phases of inner dissolution have been completed, one arrives once again at ground luminosity: this makes up the reverse order of the twelve links.

If the fact that there is no unawareness within the ground and the ground manifestations is not recognized, this is saṃsāra. If that is recognized, it is freedom. Therefore, it is said that saṃsāra is free as nirvāṇa. If all the immeasurable phenomena of saṃsāric containers and contents that arise under the influence of the proliferating clinging to the ground manifestations as having real identities are summarized, they consist of the six forms of existence (the three higher realms and the three miserable realms) and the four ways of taking birth. While nonexistent, they appear like strands of hair under the influence of floaters. Just like an illusion, in their own essence, there is not even a single atom that is established; from the very moment they appear, they lack any nature of their own.

Thus, what stands at the beginning of the present state of delusion that is solely based on empty forms that never existed is unawareness. From the play of unawareness, mind arises; from the ornament of mind (interlinear gloss: clinging), discerning mentation; and from mentation, afflictions. Therefore, there is delusion. The six discerning mentations are (1) the mentation associated with unawareness (interlinear gloss: the connate self, thinking, "This is me"), (2) the mentation of the mental consciousness (interlinear gloss: the imaginary self and so on), (3) the mentation of ascertaining (interlinear gloss: good and bad), (4) the mentation of searching (interlinear gloss: pleasure and suffering), (5) mentations whose aspect is coarse (interlinear gloss: eagerly taking up killing and so on), and (6) the mentation of definite settling (interlinear gloss: the nonforgetfulness of repeatedly ascertaining something in the mind). Then the very coarse thoughts of the six collections of consciousness arise. Under the influence of such conceptions of clinging to what does not exist as being existent, the tight fetters of clinging to imaginary phenomena as having real identities is very powerful. This mind as such is like the element of space: it lacks any essence, is free from any reference points, and is devoid of any bondage and freedom. However, through being fettered by dualistic clinging, it appears to be real as the two identities of persons and phenomena. Due to taking what does not exist to be existent and then clinging to it, this situation resembles a circling firebrand. Phenomena are not established by nature as outer objects and are simply maturations of the latent tendencies of the inner mind. For this reason, in this realm of saṃsāra, the one and the same daytime is perceived by some such as humans as brightness, while for others such as owls it is darkness. Likewise, a single river appears for gods as if being nectar, for humans as if being water, and for hell beings as if being fire, thus creating all kinds of pleasure and suffering. Such mutually exclusive notions simply follow the diverse habitual patterns of our latent tendencies, while there is nothing definite about them from the perspective of objects. As the *Precious Treasury That Fulfills All Wishes* says:

> Mind causes formations and mind performs all actions.
> [Everything] appears to mind and mind labels it.
> Therefore, make efforts to tame this deluded mind.

For yet another presentation of the three kinds of unawareness, the four conditions of delusion, and the twelve links of dependent origination, see Longchen Rabjam 1989, 54–57.

513 I.55–57.

514 Tib. *bye brag rnam rtog* emended to *bye brag rnam dag*.

515 Klong chen rab 'byams pa dri med 'od zer 1999b?, 50–53. That is, each component of saṃsāric appearances has its pure counterpart that is its underlying ultimate reality, such as the all-ground's correlation with the dharmakāya, the correlations of the five elements with the five lights, and

the correlations of the five primary afflictions with the five wisdoms. This is followed by extensive quotations that list the many pure counterparts of the plethora of the impure aspects of saṃsāra. For example, all we say and do is actually the conduct of empty lucid awareness (that is, of essence, nature, and compassionate responsiveness), all good and bad thoughts are the great river stream of meditation, all wrong views and correct assertions are the unbiased view of meditation, and all clinging to hope and fear is the unobstructed fruition.

The second chapter of Longchenpa's text concludes with a very detailed discussion of how the physical body forms, including its associated nāḍīs, vāyus, and bindus.

516 Elsewhere, Longchenpa equates buddha nature with the ground, innately present buddhahood, and great fundamental wisdom (see Germano 1992n292).

517 "Pervade" indicates that buddha nature pervades all sentient beings as their fundamental reality, while the dynamic manifestation of this pervasion is expressed in a number of sets of five in terms of both pure and impure dimensions (such as the five kāyas as opposed to the five skandhas, and so on; for details, see section B of this appendix). Thus, what pervades is tathāgatagarbha, what is pervaded are sentient beings, and the qualities of pervasion refer to the characteristic features in which tathāgatagarbha expresses itself.

518 Anonymous 1973–77, 1:334 (omitting "exists inherently," Longchenpa condenses this into one sentence).

519 Following Anonymous 1973–77 (2:24), *dang bcas par snang* in the fourth line is emended to *dang rang chas su*.

520 Ibid., 1:110.

521 Ibid., 1:526.

522 II.1.12. This is followed by extensive quotes from the *Mahāparinirvāṇasūtra*, providing the example of a hidden treasure beneath the house of a poor woman that is revealed to her by a wise person. Likewise, tathāgatagarbha exists in sentient beings obscured by all-pervasive afflictions but is revealed by the buddhas. Furthermore, tathāgatagarbha in its obscured state in sentient beings is said to possess the ten powers, the four fearlessnesses, and all the major and minor marks of a buddha.

523 I.28.

524 II.4.69. As here, the Tibetan of the last two lines of this verse is often contracted into a single line.

525 Lines 321–22 (a.k.a. "People Doha").

526 This indicates a universe that includes three sets of world systems. The first set (a chiliocosm) consists of one thousand worlds as presented in ancient Indian cosmology, with each one containing Mount Meru, the four continents, and so on. The second set (a dichiliocosm) consists of the first set

plus one thousand worlds that each have the size of the first set, and the third set consists of the first two sets plus one thousand worlds that each have the size of the second set.

527 This refers to the *Prajñāpāramitāsūtra in Twenty-Five Thousand Lines* (Prajñāpāramitā is commonly referred to as "Mother" because she is taught as the mother of all four kinds of noble ones—śrāvaka arhats, pratyekabuddha arhats, bodhisattvas on the bhūmis, and buddhas).

528 That is, if the first cycle has already taught seeming reality or the expedient meaning, while the second one on emptiness has already taught ultimate reality or the definitive meaning, there would be no need for a third cycle that teaches buddha nature as the ultimate or definitive meaning.

529 This simile is of a breastfeeding mother whose infant has fallen ill. A physician instructs the mother to discontinue her breastfeeding for a while so that the prescribed medicine can be properly digested. Thus, she smears bile on her breasts to prevent the infant from drinking. Once the child has recovered, the mother removes the bile and welcomes her baby back to drinking her rich, nutritious milk.

530 D119, vol. nya, fol. 116a.2–6.

531 I could not locate this passage in either the *Mahāparinirvāṇasūtra* or any other text in the Kangyur.

532 This refers to the statement in the popular *Kaṭhopaniṣad* (I.12–13) that the true self or soul (*puruṣa* as an equivalent of ātman) has the size of a thumb, dwells in the body (that is, in the heart), and is a light without smoke. Other upaniṣads describe the *puruṣa* as a golden being (*hiranmaya puruṣa*) and give varying sizes of it (the size of a rice, barley, or millet seed). The *Śvetaśvataropaniṣad* (5.9) holds that the size of the ātman is a ten-thousandth part of the tip of a hair.

533 This refers to a rather convoluted story about a king's sword that did not look at all as a pauper and ministers had imagined without having seen it (though the pauper once caught a brief glimpse of it but could not describe it correctly later; for details, see Germano 1992nn313 and 314). As the following quote from the *Mahāparinirvāṇasūtra* makes clear, the point of the story is that the tathāgata heart (the actual sword of the king) is not like what the tīrthikas say about a true self (the ramblings of the pauper in his dream) and that those Buddhists such as śrāvakas and pratyekabuddhas who conflate the two are also utterly mistaken (the king's ministers who fantasized about the actual sword based on the ramblings of the pauper). Therefore, the Buddha taught that there is no such self (the king's declaration that he has no such sword as fantasized by the pauper and the ministers). However, just as the king's actual sword in all its majestic purity and brilliance did in fact exist and could be shown (though its features did not at all correspond to what the pauper and the ministers thought), the Buddha taught that the empty yet luminous tathāgata heart that exists in all sentient beings is the true "self."

534 Klong chen rab 'byams pa dri med 'od zer 1999b?, 80–88.

535 I reversed the order of the first two sets in this list of the impure elements so that they match the order of the corresponding first two pure sets.

536 In due order, these five wisdoms appear as the impure afflictions of hatred, pride, desire, envy, and ignorance. As mentioned before, Dzogchen texts usually distinguish between the primordial wisdom that is self-arising (Tib. *rang byung ye shes*) and the kinds of wisdoms that are not considered to be self-arising but expressions of the dynamic energy of primordial awareness. These include the five wisdoms that represent the fundamental change of the eight consciousnesses (or the five primary afflictions) and are thus impermanent and involve modulations through conditions and/or objects.

537 Elsewhere, Longchenpa says that "as if being" indicates these colors are not just the ones that we know as our visual sense data; rather, they represent the energetic resonances that these colors evoke in us in the form of certain emotions and associations, just as different musical notes evoke different mental states. In addition, the rainbow spectrum of these colors signifies the pure fivefold radiance of awareness as it unfolds "outwardly" and, if unrecognized, becomes solidified as the five material elements. In due order, these five lights appear as the impure elements of water, earth, fire, wind, and space (for details, see Germano 1992n332). Furthermore, when not recognized, these five lights also appear as the five main afflictions—ignorance, pride, desire, envy, and hatred, respectively.

538 The following quote from the *Guhyagarbhatantra* correlates earth, water, fire, wind, and space with the female buddhas Buddhalocanā, Māmakī, Pāṇḍaravāsinī, Samayatārā, and Dhātvīśvarī, respectively.

539 The following quote from the *Vajra Mirror* correlates the eyes, the ears, the nose, the tongue, and the body with the vajra, karma, padma, ratna, and buddha families, respectively.

540 Elsewhere, Longchenpa describes this wind as "prajñā's cutting off the life-force of saṃsāra and nirvāṇa" and says that it dwells within the heart inseparable from awareness, functioning to free saṃsāra within dharmatā. Thus, it has no mercy or compassion for saṃsāric clinging and transfers into the entirely new eon of buddhahood (as opposed to the standard three Dzogchen eons of the ground, the ground manifestations, and the appearances of delusion). For more details, see Germano1992n281 and n337.

541 That is, the following three sets of five qualities each of essence, nature, and compassionate responsiveness are encapsulated in the three wisdoms of essence, nature, and compassionate responsiveness that are correlated with the dharmakāya, sambhogakāya, and nirmāṇakāya, respectively.

542 That is, the above-listed five kāyas of Vairocana and so on, not in their manifest form but as pure potentials at the time of the ground.

543 That is, a being who is a proper recipient of the Dharma.

544 As Germano (1992n342) says, the most straightforward correlation between these five qualities of compassionate responsiveness and the five wisdoms that are mentioned in the previous sentence would be in the order they are presented here: that is, the five forms of compassion correspond to mirror-like wisdom, the wisdom of equality, discriminating wisdom, all-accomplishing wisdom, and dharmadhātu wisdom, respectively. Another instruction presents a correspondence in the order of dharmadhātu wisdom, mirror-like wisdom, discriminating wisdom, all-accomplishing wisdom, and the wisdom of equality. However, it is not clear whether Longchenpa here intends any specific one-to-one correlation, beyond their general correspondence in terms of representing the basic facets of the mental functionality of a buddha's fully awakened mind.

545 Following Anonymous 1973–77 (1:446), *rig pa rtog med gnas pa chos kyi sku* ("awareness's presence as nonconceptuality is the dharmakāya") is emended to *rig pa rtog med chos sku'i ngo bo yin*.

546 Anonymous 1973–77, 1:472. Here "the buddhas of the three times" does not refer to all the buddhas of the past, present, and future but this tantra specifically identifies them as the past buddha Dīpaṃkara (corresponding to the dharmakāya), the present buddha Śākyamuni (corresponding to the nirmāṇakāya), and the future buddha Maitreya (corresponding to the sambhogakāya). The tantra also correlates these three buddhas with our own luminous awareness: in its being luminous in our heart's maṇḍala, it is the buddha of the past; in its unimpeded appearance as the visions during the intermediate state, it is the buddha of the future; and in its appearance in the objective dimension of the four lamps on the path to awakening, it is the buddha of the present (ibid., 1:471).

547 Klong chen rab 'byams pa dri med 'od zer 1999b?, 89–98. On the innate purity of saṃsāric appearances and the presence of buddha nature in the body, Longchenpa's *Precious Treasury of Philosophical Systems* (Klong chen rab 'byams pa dri med 'od zer 1999b?, 365–66 and 369–70) says this:

> When thus being deluded as the six forms of existence, sentient beings are deluded in the form of [ordinary] body, speech, and mind. However, though the wisdom of awakened body, speech, and mind is not apparent [in them], it is not that it does not exist. The body supports channels, and those channels support winds and subtle elements. Their pure essence exists in the innermost middle of the four cakras, the mansion of self-arising wisdom. [In particular,] in the heart [cakra], the palace of Dharma, the essence of luminous self-arising wisdom exists in a steadfast manner together with its retinue—the host that consists of an ocean of wisdom ...

> In the center of the heart, the quintessence of that pure essence supports a luminous channel of light, from which a fine channel that looks as if it radiates light rays everywhere manifests. Therefore, [this channel] is called "the one pervaded by the sugata heart." Awareness, whose essence is empty, whose nature is present as the five lights, and whose compassionate responsiveness is pervasive as light rays, abides as the great source of [all] kāyas and wisdoms. However, the dimension of its essence—the empty dharmakāya, the pure vision of wisdom—is obscured by the all-ground and the eight collections [of consciousness]. Its nature, which is present as the five lights, is obscured by the material skandha of flesh and blood. Its compassionate responsiveness, which is present as what makes light rays and awareness arise, is obscured by karma and latent tendencies. Though [awareness] is present as having the character of being very difficult to observe, it is not that it is nonexistent. Rather, it exists in such a way that it pervades all sentient beings, with each of their individual bodies as its support ...
>
> Since this awareness—the sugata heart—is enmeshed in the web of an ordinary body, it is called a "body-possessor" [Tib. *lus can*; one of the terms for a sentient being]. Since it is enmeshed in the web of mind—the eight collections [of consciousness]—it is a "mind-possessor" [Tib. *sems can*, the most common term for a sentient being]. Since it is enmeshed in karma and latent tendencies, it is an "obscuration-possessor." Since it is obscured by the nature of unawareness, it is a "darkness-possessor." These and other such names express awareness at the time when it is present in [saṃsāric] existence. Topics that are hidden in lower levels of the secret mantra are taught here in an explicitly obvious manner. Therefore, the original expanse—self-arising wisdom, the sugata heart—is present in the body in its entirety in an all-pervasive manner right now.

548 As Germano (1992n395) points out, this example of the all-ground being just like a pond (with the latent tendencies in it resembling the pond's water) contrasts sharply with the following example of the dharmakāya or the ground being like an ocean. A pond is very small, shallow, often murky, and can dry up at any point due to changing conditions. By contrast, the ocean is very vast, deep, clear, and never dries up.

549 Longchenpa's *Precious Treasury of the Supreme Yāna* (Klong chen rab 'byams pa dri med 'od zer 1999d?, 5:1025–27) elaborates on this example as follows:

> The dharmakāya—the expanse of alpha-pure awareness in which stains never existed—resembles the clear ocean. It is the unimpeded spaciousness that is not established as anything whatsoever and yet arises as anything whatsoever. Since this primal ground is naturally pure and free from the conditions that consist of adventitious stains, to seize this expanse as a stronghold is its dimension of being endowed with twofold purity. On the other hand, the all-ground resembles a ship on the ocean that has been boarded by passengers. At the time when delusion [arises] from the primal expanse, the unawareness of the ground is present as the support, the pervader, and the essence of all [appearances of delusion, thus being] like a ship. It is filled with the many passengers who consist of the delusions of mind, mental factors, karmas, and latent tendencies ...
>
> Stainless awareness—the essence of the dharmakāya—is that from which one never needs to turn away; it exists as the ultimate ground of freedom. On the other hand, it is necessary to awaken from the sleep-like all-ground that serves as the support for the arising of all the dreams that consist of the appearances of delusion. Therefore, the difference between them is very big. Though it is necessary to turn away from the sleep and the dreams of the [all-ground], it is not necessary to turn away from self-awareness. Hence, the dharmakāya is the ground that is to be realized, its natural state represents what needs to be familiarized with, and the fruition is to identify it as the locus of freedom. [By contrast,] the all-ground and the phenomena that are supported by it are to be understood as the stains that are to be purified.

550 Klong chen rab 'byams pa dri med 'od zer 1999b?, 103–4.

551 As Germano (1992n416) points out, elsewhere, Longchenpa describes these four as follows: (a) The primordial ultimate all-ground refers to the initial ground-source of the entirety of saṃsāra, which is the initial stirring of cognitive processing (of the ground manifestations) in conjunction with unawareness. (b) The ultimate all-ground of linking indicates that if that all-ground is not self-aware, it links up with saṃsāra; if it is aware, it links up with nirvāṇa. (c) The all-ground of diverse latent tendencies is the sole foundation or source of all impure karmas and latent tendencies. (d) The all-ground of the bodies of latent tendencies means that the all-ground has the latent tendencies for embodiment in that it manifests as flesh and blood, light, or mental bodies. Thus, (a)–(d) are not four discrete phenomena but simply four aspects of the single all-ground.

552 As Germano (1992n422) says, elsewhere, Longchenpa lists the main function of each one of the four kinds of all-ground: (a) The primordial ultimate all-ground serves as the foundation of straying from awareness. (b) The ultimate all-ground of linking serves to connect our body and mind with all kinds of pleasures and sufferings in saṃsāra. (c) The all-ground of diverse latent tendencies serves to accumulate karmas and afflictions via their latent tendencies, and also acts as the condition that determines them. (d) The all-ground of the bodies of latent tendencies serves as the conditioning of distinct bodies and the constellations of their distinctive features.

553 Germano (1992n430) adds that the final fruition of awakening divested of all adventitious stains is thus based on the natural qualities of primordial awareness and not on the impure all-ground, even though the actions that effected this divesture were based or happened within the all-ground. For example, when clouds part to reveal the sun, which was obscured by them, the sun's own purity, radiance, illumination, and warmth that then manifest for us are based on the sun itself (and not created by the parting of the clouds), though the dissipation of the clouds was a necessary condition for us to experience the sun's qualities.

554 I.5.

555 Klong chen rab 'byams pa dri med 'od zer 1999b?, 105–9.

The *Tantra of the Wisdom Expanse of Samantabhadra* ('Jigs med gling pa mkhyen brtse 'od zer 1973, 3:81–82) explains the arising and the distinctive features of the eight consciousnesses within the context of the all-ground, as well as the difference between the all-ground and the all-ground consciousness, as follows:

> When the appearances of the all-ground's own dynamic energy stir from it and it thus begins to engage in objects, the all-ground consciousness rises. For example, [this is as if] the constituent that is the all-ground has just woken up from deep sleep [but is not really cognizant yet]. Apprehended objects (the five [sense] objects) do not actually arise yet but a very subtle apprehending cognizance rises. This [cognizance] rises as the intrinsic dependent origination of its apprehending the reflections of [its own false] imagination, similar to [seeing one's own reflection in] a mirror. Through the functions of the nāḍīs and vāyus of each of the five [sense] gates, that cognizance is led to its objects. Thus, the five constituents [that are the sense objects] of consciousness rise: form as the object of the eyes, sound as the object of the ears, smell as the object of the nose, taste as the object of the tongue, and contact as the object of the body. By virtue of the nature of the afflicted mind and the mental consciousness, that [cognizance] is

> apprehended as desire, anger, and oblivion, and thus the causes of saṃsāra—ignorance, karma, and latent tendencies—as well as all their results are formed. In brief, one speaks of the all-ground because it is like the container or ground of all this. From the point of view of this [all-ground's] providing space, it [appears as] the all-ground consciousness. From the point of view of its looking outward and waking up toward objects, it [appears as] the five [sense] gates. From the point of view of its appropriating afflictions [through moving away] from its own place, it [appears as] the afflicted mind. From the point of view of its distinguishing all kinds of phenomena, it appears as the mental consciousness. These are called "the eight collections of consciousness."

Based on a number of Longchenpa's works, Germano (1992n410) elaborates that the all-ground

> signifies our most fundamental substratum of distorted psychic energy (though itself derivative of the pure enlightened nucleus of radiant awareness within our heart), which is indeterminate in the sense that it is the basic dimmed awareness or non-recognition that operates as the transcendental condition of all the other emotional distortions, yet in itself is without any positive or negative ethical valuation—it is merely a deficiency in knowledge, evoking that initial moment in the Ground-presencing [*gzhi snang*] when its cognizance fails to recognize itself, a moment which inexorably leads into cyclic existence while as yet devoid of any of the active dualism, enframing, and emotional fury characteristic of alienated life ... This substratum then acts as the basis for all other modes of consciousness, and in that its radiance tends to diffuse outwards into these diverse modes of psychic activity, it is labeled "the consciousness of the universal ground" (the universal psychic ground in its tendency towards perceptual modes of consciousness, as yet undivided into "external" or "internal" orientation ...). This consciousness-substratum then becomes actualized into the five sensory modes of consciousness, the psychic or intellectual consciousness which organizes sense data and engages in conceptuality, and the emotionally distorted psychic consciousness which signifies our emotional life ... our universal ground is the luminous channel's radiation as present in the vitality channel under the condition of nonrecognition, showing that it is twice removed from our core gnostic energy—not only is it the core's "radiation"

> rather than the core itself, but also it is distorted and dimmed radiation at that. Its radiation being unceasingly lucent and clear is then labeled the "universal ground consciousness," which is also present in the vitality channel. Thus while the "universal ground" is our secondary psychic core (though in terms of functioning in our present neurotic state the primary one), the "universal ground consciousness" is its dynamics as it begins to spread out into manifest consciousness from the unconscious pool of energy, such that its radiation spreads out from the vitality channel to our five senses ... "the universal ground of diverse karmic propensities" is "like a mirror" and the "consciousness of the universal ground" is "like the mirror's clarity and brightness," while the five sensory modes of consciousness are "like the manifestation of reflections (in the mirror)." The initial manifestation of the thought "this" with respect to the percepts of the five senses, i.e. the initial discursive processing of the sensory data, is the "psychic consciousness," while its subsequent association with feelings of attachment, aversion, and indifference is the "emotionally distorted psychic consciousness."

Furthermore, the primordial ground and its ground manifestations per se represent the awakened sphere as opposed to the deluded sphere that consists of the all-ground (in particular, the primordial ultimate all-ground) and the all-ground consciousness (see also appendix 2). Thus, at least for Longchenpa and those who follow him, "the all-ground" (*kun gzhi*) is *not* "the ground" (*gzhi*). On this, see also the distinction between mind and wisdom (or mind and awareness) in appendix 5B. In brief, the all-ground refers to the dimension of unawareness that has simultaneously arisen within awareness since primordial time. Thus, this all-ground can serve as the basis of either pure or impure phenomena (nirvāṇa or saṃsāra), depending on whether its own true nature (the primordial ground or original awareness) is recognized or not. Strictly speaking, however, among the four forms of the all-ground, the three except for the second one—"the ultimate all-ground of linking"—represent the basis of saṃsāra alone. It is only "the ultimate all-ground of linking" that serves as the indeterminate basic support of linking with and propelling into either saṃsāra (through the nonrecognition of the ground and the ensuing individual afflictions and karmas) or nirvāṇa (through practicing the path and recognizing the ground). Therefore, as Longchenpa says, it is only in the following sense that the all-ground is tenable as the ground of both saṃsāra and nirvāṇa: the virtues conducive to liberation that link with nirvāṇa exist within the all-ground, functioning as the causes for dispelling the stains that obscure nirvāṇa. Though these virtues are labeled as the cause of nirvāṇa, they are not a producing cause, nor is nirvāṇa their produced result because the essence of nirvāṇa is unconditioned. This all-ground is further equated with the initial subtle cognizance that stirs as a part of the ground manifestations but that represents the mistaken subject that erroneously perceives them as external objects and thus fails to recognize them as the self-appearances of the primordial ground (for details, see the extensive explanation of how delusion arises from the primordial ground through not recognizing the ground manifestations for what they are in appendix 3A).

556 Anonymous 1973–77, 1:129.

557 Ibid., 1:129.

558 The glosses on these verses in Anonymous 1973–77 (1:432) say that the dharmakāya's conduct is unceasing appearance, without clinging to objects, and without attachment to mind. The meditation of the dharmakāya is lucid in its being nonconceptual, naked in its being undistracted, and without distraction in its being unmoving. The dharmakāya's view is our own awareness, which is unviewable in that it is perfect in itself, already viewed in that it is perfect within the ground, and the perfect view in that there is nothing to be done. The dharmakāya's fruition is not produced from anything other, did not arise (implying in the past), and is not arising at present. The dharmakāya's enlightened activity is unaccomplishable in that it is the freedom from extremes, is already accomplished in that it is associated with the dharmakāya itself, and is the perfect accomplishment in that it is naturally unmoving (*ngang gis la g.yos pa* emended to *ngang gis ma g.yos pa*).

As for the dharmakāya's qualities, "a single one arising" refers to awareness, "two arising" to the two lamps (that is, the lamp of the pure expanse and the lamp of empty spheres in the context of Direct Leap), and "all arising" to the wisdom of the four visions (in Direct Leap). Alternatively, "a single one" may refer to the dharmakāya's essence, "two" to the sambhogakāya and nirmāṇakāya, and "all" to all the displays of the kāyas and wisdoms that flow forth from awakening (for more details, see Germano 1992n441). Longchenpa's *Treasure Trove of Scriptures* (Klong chen rab 'byams pa dri med 'od zer 1999a?, 505 and 507) says the following about the relationship between primordial awareness and view, meditation, conduct, and fruition:

> The essence of awareness in its infinite evenness is beyond view, meditation, conduct, and fruition and yet is the very essence of view, meditation, conduct, and fruition and the great underlying basis that ties them all together ... These do not refer to anything like the common [Buddhist] system in which the view is taken as the ground, meditation is taken as the path, conduct is taken as an aid, and the fruition arises at the end [of all that] because awareness is beyond view,

meditation, conduct, and fruition. The *Great Garuda* says: "It is the actuality free from conduct and pure of meditation that cannot be viewed." Therefore, if awareness's own essence is divided in terms of [conceptual] isolates, it can be distinguished into four at one and the same time: the essence of awareness is the view, its nature is meditation, its compassionate responsiveness is conduct, and their inseparability is the innately present fruition.

559 Klong chen rab 'byams pa dri med 'od zer 1999b?, 109–10. In brief, despite their functional similarities and their ultimately common source in pristine awareness, the all-ground and the dharmakāya are phenomenologically very different in that they, as *The Aspiration Prayer* says, represent the two distinct outcomes of the two paths of delusion and freedom that arise from the single primordial ground. As Longchenpa's following general distinction between mind and wisdom in appendix 5B makes clear, the all-ground and the dharmakāya also differ greatly in their implications for the Dzogchen system as a whole. For a detailed treatment of the disctinction between all-ground and dharmakāya in Dzogchen, see Higgins 2013 (especially 18–30 and 140–82).

560 The distinction between mind and wisdom is a recurring theme in Dzogchen literature in general and Longchenpa's writing in particular. It is more often phrased as the distinction between mind and awareness, and sometimes, similar to Mahāmudrā texts, the one between mind (*sems*) and mind as such (*sems nyid*).

561 Here, the text mistakenly repeats the heading of this paragraph (*gnyis pa ma shes pa'i skyon ni*).

562 Anonymous 1973–77 (1:256) glosses the last line as "because wisdom has no latent tendencies."

563 See the above explanation of the all-ground in this appendix. In brief, as Germano (1992n399) rightly says:

> Such a rejection [of the identity of the all-ground and the dharmakāya] is in line with Longchenpa's overall hermeneutical approach, which is to maintain that our ordinary consciousness, physical existence, and material elements are mere nonoptimal derivative reflections of a primary reality that is empty, radiant, and intelligent, such that rather than being a question of the former being "transformed" into the latter by yogic techniques, the latter is primordially and uninterruptedly present as the former's ongoing source and reality—enlightenment is in the end an epistemological question of "recognition" not an ontological matter of "transformation" ... Additionally, he rejects more subtle interpretations that describe the "stainless" mind or "purified" universal ground

as the Reality Body, such that by contemplatively "polishing up" the former we can arrive at the latter (such descriptions appear to be found throughout Indian Buddhist literature). Longchenpa consistently rejects these interpretative trends as well, since they describe the primary reality in terms of its secondary derivatives, such as describing the "sun" as "unobscured clouds," since the clouds obscure the sun from our view, and their dissipation reveals its glorious, life-giving presence to us—the mind obscures our spontaneously present enlightened nucleus of pristine awareness from our consciousness, while when we contemplatively dispel its obscuring neuroses, that radiant light naturally expands outwards to permeate our being with its high-intensity energy (the "cloud-like" mind is *dispelled*, not transformed or "cleaned").

564 The glosses in Anonymous 1973–77 (2:516–17) explain that "mind gathers the afflictions and therefore arises as a gathered collection." "It is filled with stains" refers to "the actual afflictions," "and so on" refers to "what is established as the body through collecting," and "the enumeration of stains" consists of "afflictive obscurations and cognitive obscurations."

565 Following Anonymous 1973–77 (2:165), *sems su shes* ("cognizes as mind") in the third sentence is emended to *sems su 'du shes* ("entertains the notion of a [perceiving] mind").

566 Klong chen rab 'byams pa dri med 'od zer 1999b?, 110–18. The last quote is Anonymous 1973–77 (2:164–65); following this text, *rig pa nyid kyi ye shes la dbang bsgyur ba'o* ("gain mastery over the wisdom that is awareness itself") is emended to *rig pa nyid kyis ye shes la dbang bsgyur nus pa'o* ("are able to gain mastery over wisdom through awareness itself").

567 Klong chen rab 'byams pa dri med 'od zer 1999b?, 118–20.

568 This resembles the typical Yogācāra triad of mind (ālaya-consciousness), mentation (afflicted mind), and consciousness (the mental consciousness and the sense consciousnesses). Thus, "mentation" here appears to refer to both the afflicted mind (the omnipresent clinging to a self) and the mental consciousness (experiencing all generally and specifically characterized phenomena). Or, if "mentation" applies to the mental consciousness alone, this means that, different from the sense consciousnesses, the mental consciousness is able to experience all kinds of objects everywhere (all five sense objects as well as conceptual phenomena, which include phenomena in the past and the future).

569 In this context, mind is often described as being like a paralyzed person with good eyesight who rides on a blind horse (the winds).

570 Ibid., 120–22.

571 Following Anonymous 1973–77 (1:129), *da lta* ("now") is emended to *de ltar* ("just as it is").

572 Klong chen rab 'byams pa dri med 'od zer 1999b?, 122. For more details on these wisdoms, see appendix 6.

573 Elsewhere, Longchenpa describes the third and fourth together as follows: "Wisdom is based on the mustard seed-sized quintessence of the quintessence at the center of the four channel petals of radiant light, which are in the middle of the precious citta that resembles a pitched tent" (see Germano 1992n500). As mentioned before, "citta" refers to the seat of the mind at the heart cakra.

574 "The far-reaching lasso water lamp" is an expression for the eyes.

575 Klong chen rab 'byams pa dri med 'od zer 1999b?, 122–23. Compare Longchenpa's *Treasure Trove of Scriptures* (Klong chen rab 'byams pa dri med 'od zer 1999a?, 303 and 308) on the distinction between mind and wisdom:

> Wisdom refers to awareness's own essence that is [present] at all times—the awakened mind that is free from any objects. It is free from all thoughts, expressions, and reference points. Mind is the cognizance that apprehends objects. The root of mind comes down to wisdom and there is something like the radiance or dynamic energy of wisdom in the very midst [of mind]. Therefore, based on the [appropriate] timing, its own essence must be identified as wisdom. If it is not identified [as such], it is called "stains." Since there is this difference between the essence of awareness and its dynamic energy, mind and wisdom are to be distinguished ...
>
> What stirs from self-arising wisdom is the dynamic energy of compassionate responsiveness. The cognizance that dawns as [and apprehends] objects is explained as "the play that arises from the dynamic energy" but it is not self-arising wisdom. For this cognizance operates according to whether there are objects or not; if not embraced by [skillful] means, it functions as the karmas and afflictions that cause engagement in [saṃsāric] existence, and its nature of examination and analysis does not transcend saṃsāra's own essence.

As for the distinctions between awareness and unawareness as well as mind and awareness (the most common distinction in Dzogchen), *Self-Arising Awareness* (Anonymous 1973–77, 1:667) uses the following examples: "The examples for awareness and unawareness are the modes of being of water and a drawing [on water]: [unawareness] is dependent on conditions. The examples for awareness and mind are the modes of being of water and foam: [awareness] is not under the sway of mind." Jigmé Lingpa's *Differentiating the Three Essential Points of Dzogchen* ('Jigs med gling pa mkhyen brtse 'od zer 1973, 3:118) says:

> Mind and awareness are like wind and space, respectively.
> Mind involves the aspect of deceptive reference points,
> vividly swirling, pouring out, filling up,
> suddenly surging up, like gales of a tempest.
> It is the basic foundation that conditions all kinds of sensations.
> Awareness is without support and all-pervasive.
> It is empty and provides room, just like the expanse of space.
> It is lucid and nonconceptual, similar to a polished clear crystal.
> Hence, the Heart Essence's [second] essential point is to seize
> The expanse of awareness free from mind, the basic nature's stronghold.

For a very detailed treatment of the mind-wisdom disctinction in Dzogchen, see Higgins 2013 (especially 18–30, 57–139, and 222–54). Higgins (124–29) summarizes the fundamental problems when not distinguishing mind and wisdom properly as follows: "The failure to differentiate mind and primordial knowing lends itself to two basic kinds of erroneous premise that are identified and criticized by Klong chen: (1) that mind is unceasing and (2) that cessation of mind (*cittanirodha* : *sems 'gog pa*) is possible but results in a blank state utterly devoid of conception."

As for the former, according to Longchenpa, mind is what ceases, while primordial wisdom remains. Thus, "mind and mental factors" refer to what arises as the examination and analysis of objects, which is produced through the causes of apprehender and apprehended. By contrast, "wisdom" refers to the bare awareness of an object by virtue of the utter subsiding of apprehender and apprehended.

As for the latter, Higgins says that

> basing one's path on a sheer voidness devoid of anything whatsoever ... proves self-stultifying: instead of eliciting the inborn qualities (*yon tan*) inherent in one's natural condition, it leads to their suppression or negation ... To construe fulfillment in purely negative terms, as an absence of suffering, of emotionality and discursiveness, as absence *per se*, is clearly only part of the picture and may, if taken as an end in itself, lead to the negation of spiritual awakening. The question becomes whether the immediacy of prethematized experience is mute or meaningful. Klong chen pa's arguments for the primacy of primordial knowing go hand and hand with the recognition of a depth dimension of experience—as part of an integral approach that makes room for a sense of fullness as well as emptiness ... Another related position that Klong chen pa attributes to the lack of clear differentiation between *sems* and *ye shes* consists in the thesis that all knowledge (*jñāna* : *ye shes*) ceases to exist on the level of buddhahood ... As could

be expected, Klong chen pa and other classical rNying ma scholars rejected the position that a buddha has no jñāna on the grounds that it disregards a critical distinction between consciousness per se (the event of self-presencing itself) and the reifying superimpositions and elaborations that both prescind from it and objectify it. It is Klong chen pa's view that such an oversight leads adherents of this position to conclude, among other things, that primordial knowing and the specific forms of knowledge arising from it derive from ignorance, the source of reification, and are therefore abandoned when the reifications are abandoned. Without differentiating knowledge grounded in nondual primordial knowing—as exemplified by spontaneous altruism—from knowledge grounded in dualistic ignorance, one risks throwing out the proverbial baby with the bath water (emphasis by Higgins).

576 For another presentation of five kāyas, see Kangyur Rinpoche's comments on Jigmé Lingpa's *Treasury of Precious Qualities* in this appendix below.

577 The following is an abridged summary of Klong chen rab 'byams pa dri med 'od zer 1999b?, 454–77.

578 Following Anonymous 1973–77 (1:437), *pa'i sku* in each line is emended to *pas sku*. Note that this quote represents only a part of the hermeneutical etymology of the sambhogakāya in this tantra's chapter on the sambhogakāya.

579 Anonymous 1973–77, 2:396–97.

580 Ibid., 1:200.

581 Tib. *drug* should be *drug cu*.

582 Anonymous 1973–77 (1:197–99) omits "body" in the first line, has *spyod pa* ("conduct") instead of *dpyod pa* ("discernment") in line eight, an additional *byas pa med* ("unproduced") in line twelve, and *gang byung* ("that arise") instead of *gang 'dul* ("that guide") in line thirty-four. "The five excellences" refer to the excellent teacher, retinue, place, teaching, and time.

583 Tib. *brjed du med pa* ("unforgettable") emended to *brjod du med pa*, which is more likely in this context.

584 The point "samādhi" is omitted in all the permutations of the sambhogakāya and the nirmāṇakāya, which differs from the permutations of the dharmakāya.

585 This is the pure realm of Vajradhara.

586 Here, Longchenpa omits the point "teaching."

587 This is the highest god realm on the level of the first dhyāna in the form realm.

588 Skt. *gṛdhrakūṭa*, Tib. *bya rgod phung po'i ri* (usually translated as "vulture peak"). Though the Sanskrit *kūṭa* can mean both "peak" and "flock" (or "heap"), it is usually explained to mean the latter (which corresponds

to the Tibetan *phung po* instead of *rtse mo* or the like). According to the *Śatasāhasrikāvivaraṇa* (D3802, fols. 3b.7–4a.1), Praśāstrasena's commentary on the *Heart Sūtra* (P5220, 292.3.7–8), and other sources, the mountain received its name from the shape of its rock formations, which resemble a flock of vultures huddling together. Jñānamitra's commentary on the *Heart Sūtra* (P5217, 285.5.1–2) says that the name comes from flocks of vultures gathering on its top. Ngag dbang bstan dar lha ram pa's (1759–1831) commentary on the *Heart Sūtra* (trans. in Lopez 1988, 141) lists five ways of explaining this name by referring to Sde srid Sangs rgyas rgya mtsho's (1653–1705) *Bai durya g.ya' sel*—(1) the mountain is shaped like a vulture, (2) the mountain is shaped like a flock of vultures, (3) vultures protect the mountain, on which many such birds feed on corpses, (4) the mountain is a heap/flock due to the brilliance of the birds, which are beings that understand emptiness, and (5) the Buddha's robe was snatched by a demon in the form of a vulture and dropped on the mountain (which is shaped like a vulture's head), where it turned to stone in four layers, which are known as "the great vulture heap."

589 Longchenpa's *Treasure Trove of Scriptures* (Klong chen rab 'byams pa dri med 'od zer 1999a?, 595–98) explains the three kāyas in terms of the five excellences of teacher, teaching, place, retinue, and time. In the context of the dharmakāya, (1) the teacher is Samantabhadra, the teacher of perfect mastery; (2) the teaching consists of the natural Great Perfection that is truly effortless; (3) the place is the inconceivable dharmadhātu; (4) the retinue consists of the vast ocean of self-arising wisdom; (5) the time is the time of fourfold perfection without change or transition—"the indeterminate time." In the context of the sambhogakāya, (1) the teachers are the five regent teachers of the five buddha families; (2) the teaching is solely the Mahāyāna; (3) the place is Richly Adorned Akaniṣṭha—the Akaniṣṭha of pure self-lucidity; (4) the retinue consists of the buddhas, bodhisattvas, and so on who are the sambhogakāya's self-appearances and not other than it, as well as those whose fortunes equal that of bodhisattvas on the ten bhūmis, such as ḍākinīs and awareness holders; (5) the time is an incessant wheel. In the context of the nirmāṇakāya, (1) it is with regard to their guiding impure beings that the teachers are called "the teachers who are genuine guides"; (2) the teaching consists of all kinds of yānas in accordance with the faculties of sentient beings; (3) the places consist of all kinds of worlds of those to be guided, thus being multiple and not definite; (4) the retinues consist of countless beings to be guided, such as gods and humans; (5) the time is either the past, the present, or the future, and in particular, refers to "the present time" when the Dharma occurs by virtue of the coming together of the four preceding excellences—the nirmāṇakāya promotes the welfare of sentient beings for as long as saṃsāra lasts.

Since the three kāyas are of a single taste as the dharmakāya, they are beyond appearing and not appearing. However, from within that natural state, the play that arises from the dynamic energy of compassionate responsiveness dawns as the two rūpakāyas and is therefore labeled as "sambhogakāya" and "nirmāṇakāya." This is a case of labeling the result with the name of the cause, just as when saying "the sun shines inside" when the rays of the sun enter a house. The actual sambhogakāya is the dimension of the innately present lucid nature of awareness in the context of the dharmakāya and this dimension is present as the ground of arising. The actual nirmāṇakāya is the dimension of compassionate responsiveness that is present as wisdom. Therefore, the three kāyas are an inseparable unity.

The dharmakāya is the empty essence—unobstructed awareness. Its play is an ocean of nonconceptual wisdom. The sambhogakāya is the nature—the innate presence of lucidity. Its play consists of the five buddha families adorned by the major and minor marks. The nirmāṇakāya is compassionate responsiveness—the dimension that is the ground of the arising of all-pervasive wisdom. Its play consists of the teachers who appear as suitable guidance for whomever is to be guided. Thus, it is crucial to distinguish between the three kāyas and their plays. Otherwise, there would be the following flaws: Since the three kāyas are of a single essence, it would follow that just as the sambhogakāya and the nirmāṇakāya appear for those to be guided, the dharmakāya also appears in that way. Or it would follow that just as the dharmakāya does not appear, it is impossible for the two rūpakāyas to appear because all three are of a single essence.

Thus, since the three kāyas are present within the dharmakāya, it is tenable that the two plays of the sambhogakāya and the nirmāṇakāya shine forth as outer luminosity for those to be guided. This is similar to the following: by virtue of the potential to refract light in five colors that is present inside a crystal, once the crystal comes into contact with sunlight as a condition, five-colored light shines forth as outer luminosity.

590 Tib. *mngon par byang chub pa'i sku* ("the kāya of fully perfect awakening").

591 Note that the use of this term here is different from its usual meaning as the all-ground of delusion (see appendix 5A).

592 This is another name for tathāgatagarbha.

593 Klong chen ye shes rdo rje 1991, 534–38.

594 Yon tan rgya mtsho 1982–87 (738) explains the following in this context: "It should be understood that the discussions of the dimension of inner luminosity as the three kāyas (dharma[kāya], sambhoga[kāya], and nirmāṇa[kāya]), [the two wisdoms of knowing] suchness and variety, and [the five wisdoms] such as dharmadhātu [wisdom] and mirror-like [wisdom] represent [the kāyas and wisdoms that constitute] the essence or the actual ones, whereas the kāyas and wisdoms of the dimension of outer luminosity are [just] the play that arises from the dynamic energy [of inner

luminosity].” This highlights the distinction between the sambhogakāya and nirmāṇakāya of inner luminosity (corresponding to nature and compassionate responsiveness, respectively, in the triad of essence, nature, and compassionate responsiveness) from the sambhogakāya and nirmāṇakāya of outer luminosity, which represent the rūpakāyas in the classical sense.

595 This is the common Mahāyāna explanation of what the sambhogakāya enjoys. In the internally oriented explanation of the Vajrayāna and the Great Perfection, the sambhogakāya's enjoyment refers to awareness's enjoyment of its own dynamic energy.

596 The following detailed explanation (ibid., 541) says that this is the unconditioned time of Samantabhadra, which is beyond the three times of past, present, future, and so on, as these have expired in the ground that is unalterable dharmatā.

597 The dharmakāya is usually said to be permanent by nature because it is without any change, the sambhogakāya is permanent in terms of continuity because it is endowed with the five certainties, and the nirmāṇakāya is permanent in the sense of an uninterrupted series because the deeds of enlightened activity are uninterrupted until saṃsāra is empty. Though individual nirmāṇakāyas, such as Buddha Śākyamuni, appear and disappear from the perspective of those to be guided, at any given time, there are always some nirmāṇakāyas somewhere, and their enlightened activities as a whole are considered to be a single uninterrupted continuum.

598 This is followed by a detailed explanation of the natural nirmāṇakāyas in six points: (1) the places (the buddha realms Akaniṣṭha, Abhirati, Śrīmat, Padmakūṭa, and Karmaprasiddhi), (2) the corresponding teachers (Vairocana, Akṣobhya, Ratnasambhava, Amitābha, and Amoghasiddhi, who can appear in all kinds of peaceful and wrathful forms), (3) the corresponding five wisdoms, (4) the retinues (bodhisattvas on the ten bhūmis), (5) the time (until the end of saṃsāra), and (6) the obscurations to be purified by the bodhisattvas in the retinues. In the following, only the third section, on the five wisdoms, is translated. As the description of the “natural nirmāṇakāya” shows, it consists of buddha appearances for bodhisattvas on the bhūmis. These appearances that display in pure realms are half nirmāṇakāya and half sambhogakāya. Just as the sambhogakāya, these appearances seem to be more related to the luminous nature of awareness from among the triad of essence, nature, and compassionate responsiveness. Thus, to highlight this fact, “natural nirmāṇakāya” could also be rendered as “the nirmāṇakāya of the nature.”

599 In this combination, “attachment and obstruction” are equivalents of the afflictive and cognitive obscurations, respectively.

600 Ibid., 538, 550–55, and 566–77.

601 XI.17.

602 It is often held that the *Prāsaṅgika Madhyamaka view and the Dzogchen view are the same. However, though important Dzogchen masters accept that Dzogchen accords with the *Prāsaṅgika view, they clearly distinguish the two and always assert the superiority of Dzogchen, similar to Kangyur Rinpoche here. In the nine-yāna doxographical approach of the Nyingma School in general, the *Prāsaṅgika view is only considered to be the highest one within the three causal yānas (representing the pinnacle of the Bodhisattvayāna), which are said to be inferior to both the views and practices of the six fruitional yānas—the three outer and the three inner classes of tantra that culminate in the atiyoga of the Great Perfection.

More specifically, Longchenpa's *Treasure Trove of Scriptures* (Klong chen rab 'byams pa dri med 'od zer 1999a?, 360) distinguishes *Prāsaṅgika and the Great Perfection as follows: "The manner in which the freedom from extremes is assessed by the system of this natural Great Perfection is for the most part in accord with *Prāsaṅgika Madhyamaka. However, what Madhyamaka takes as its basis of evaluation is utter emptiness, which is like space. Here, by taking nothing but naked and bare alpha-pure awareness that has not [ever] been established [as anything] and yet is unceasing as our basis, we assess that awareness as well as the phenomena that arise within its natural state are free from extremes."

The Third Dodrupchen Jigmé Tenpé Nyima (as quoted in Longchen Rabjam 2001b, x–xi) elaborates:

> *Chöying Dzö* and other [Dzogpa Chenpo] sources praise the view of Prasangika-Madhyamaka. So [Dzogpa Chenpo] is in accord with Prasangika regarding the definition of the limits to the object-of-negation (*dgag bya'i mtshams 'dzin*). However, in Prasangika—having separated the aspects (*ldog ch'a*) of appearances and emptiness by distinguishing the particularities (*spu ris*) of each or by separating the emptiness aspect [from the apparent aspect]—one apprehends the aspect of emptiness that is a nonaffirming negation (*med dgag*). This is a method of maintaining [the view] using concepts. It also asserts that after conceptually distinguishing between them and gaining experiences [of it] in meditation, one attains what is called "the fruition of the blissful, clear, and nonconceptual intellect." Dzogpa Chenpo, on the other hand, solely maintains intrinsic awareness (*rig pa*) [the true nature of the mind], and uses it as the path. It does not employ concepts (*rtog pa*), since concepts [are the province of] mind (*sems*), and Dzogpa Chenpo involves meditation [on intrinsic awareness after] distinguishing mind from intrinsic awareness.

According to Gedsé Mahāpaṇḍita Gyurmé Tsewang Chogdrub (Tib. Dge rtse mahā paṇ ḍi ta 'gyur med tshe dbang mchog grub; 1761–1829), Dzogchen represents the essence of both the second and third turnings of the wheel of Dharma. In the second turning, the Buddha taught the inconceivable nature through the ways of not conceptualizing any characteristics of reference points but did not reveal the presence of buddha nature. In the third turning, he revealed buddha nature but not the definitive path of realizing it. Without contradicting either of these turnings, the Great Perfection embodies the ultimate view of both the great system founders of the Mahāyāna: the view of the second turning elucidated by Nāgārjuna in his collection of reasonings, the *Dharmadhātustava*, and so on, as well as the view of the third turning elucidated by Maitreya, Asaṅga, and Vasubandhu (see Longchen Rabjam 1989, 93).

Moreover, the descriptions of and emphasis on the presence of tathāgatagarbha and primordial wisdom or awareness in all sentient beings that are found in the writings of Longchenpa and other Dzogchen masters are a far cry from what *Prāsaṅgikas say on that subject (they regard the teachings on tathāgatagarbha as being of expedient meaning and consider even the wisdom of a buddha as being only a part of seeming reality). The same goes for the essential Dzogchen notion of the unity of alpha-purity, innate presence, and compassionate responsiveness (with the latter two including all the innate qualities of awareness and awakening) and the incorporation of significant Yogācāra elements, such as the eight consciousnesses, the three natures, the notion of fundamental change (*āśrayaparivṛtti*), and the buddhalogy of the three kāyas and four (or five) wisdoms. As Higgins (2013, 26) says, Longchenpa "define[d] the guiding ideas, ideals and practices of classical rDzogs chen while disclosing their continuity with antecedent Buddhist doctrines; specifically, *tathāgatagarbha* theories, certain Yogācāra-Cittamātra models of mind (viz. the ālayavijñāna and *trisvabhāva* doctrines), *Prāsaṅgika Madhyamaka views on the 'cessation of mind,' and Mantrayāna doctrines concerning the transformation of perceptual consciousness (*vijñāna*) into primordial knowing (*jñāna*)."

Higgins (ibid., 23) also points to a typical example in Longchenpa's commentary on his *Mind as Such Resting at Ease* (Tib. *Sems nyid ngal gso*) that summarizes the essence of the teachings and explicitly or implicitly contains several of the above elements, such as the imaginary nature, the unchanging perfect nature, the fundamental change, and tathāgatagarbha (mind as such, luminosity): "In brief, if one cultivates the path through penetrating mind as such—the true reality of unchanging luminosity—and realizing that all phenomena are empty in that they are merely imaginary, [all] impure appearances of delusion including the mind that imagines them undergo the fundamental change or become pure. Thus, the original natural state is reached and complete mastery over the pure realm of the inexhaustible adornment wheel of awakened body, speech, and mind is gained. This is the synopsis of the dharmas of the genuine teaching" (translated from the Tibetan as quoted in Higgins).

In brief, as Higgins (ibid., 117–18) summarizes: "The main point can be expressed in this way: when all that is added to life by way of superimpositions and elaborations is stripped away, what remains is not simply neutral or merely empty (*stong nyid rkyang ma*) but emphatically positive (*kun tu bzang po*). Primordial knowing is characterized as being *both* empty *and* luminous (*stong gsal dbyer med*). In later formulations, it is held to be originally pure (*ka dag*) in being devoid of any trace of substances and attributes yet spontaneously present (*lhun grub*) in being naturally replete with all positive qualities and capacities. It is further characterized as being compassionately responsive (*thugs rje*) in an all-pervasive (*kun khyab*) manner" (emphasis by Higgins).

603 Klong chen ye shes rdo rje 1991, 579–82.

604 For a brief explanation of these three, see *Lamp* (fol. 19a–b). For more details, see the Dalai Lama, *Dzogchen: Heart Essence of the Great Perfection* (Snow Lion Publications, 2004), 83–84 and 186–87; and Sogyal Rinpoche, *The Tibetan Book of Living and Dying* (HarperCollins, 2002), 167–70. In the context of explaining the Expanse Series, Longchenpa's *Precious Treasury of Philosophical Systems* says that all the teachings of this series are included in the three categories of (1) being free from what is produced or created (Tib. *byas grol*), (2) being free upon or within settling (Tib. *gzhag grol*), and (3) being nakedly free (Tib. *gcer grol*).

605 3:292. Compare also Bdud 'joms 'jigs bral ye shes rdo rje 1991, 334.

606 Krang dbyi sun et al. 1985, 415, 744, 1202, 2593, and 2643.

607 Anonymous 1973–77, 1:125. As mentioned in chapter 8, these lines in the tantra are preceded by four additional modes of freedom, of the mind that is present as being empty and self-lucid (ibid., 1:124–25):

> Since it is free through the essential point, it is unbiased.
> Since it is free of time, it lacks any basis to depend on.
> Since it is free without toil, there is no exerting or accomplishing.
> Since it is free through confidence, there is no effort.

608 Ibid., 1:179. Bracketing these four lines, the tantra (ibid., 1:178–79) here also repeats "being free through the essential point" and "being free of time" with different explanations and adds "being naturally free" and "being free from the extreme of [saṃsāric] existence":

> Since it is free through the essential point, any effort is exhausted.
> ...
> Since it is free of time, there is no need for becoming familiar with it.

> Since it is naturally free, it is uncontrived.
> "Being free" is nothing but a conventional expression:
> Whose attributes are realization and nonrealization?
> In whom is "being free in it" observed?
> For whom is engaging in the three realms possible?
> This is the dharmatā of being free from the extreme of [saṃsāric] existence.

609 Dzogchen Ponlop 2006, 108–10.

610 Mdo sngags chos kyi rgya mtsho 1996, 178. For another more detailed explanation of these four in accordance with Patrul Rinpoche's commentary on Garab Dorjé's *Three Words that Strike the Vital Point*, see Reynolds 1996, 114–16.

611 Anonymous 1973–77 (2:465–66) glosses these lines as follows:

> Apart from awareness that is unimpeded in an unobstructed manner internally as well as externally, there is primordially no delusion. Therefore, everything is free in itself and thus there are no thoughts. Since it is primordially free without being examined and analyzed by others, it is absolutely supreme. Since it is free in itself, object conditions are exhausted, as in the example of a knot in a snake. Since it is nakedly free as the seeing that is pure on its own, appearances are pure. Since it is primordially free from the extremes of permanence and extinction, the four possibilities of existence and nonexistence cease. Since it is free as the one in which [all] numbers are exhausted, it is empty of many.

Earlier, the same tantra (ibid., 2:452) says:

> It does not become free through effort—
> It primordially abides as being free.

The first line is glossed as "because the Great Perfection is beyond exertion and accomplishing."

612 Klong chen rab 'byams pa dri med 'od zer 1999d?, 6:1604–32.

613 Anonymous 1973–77 (2:452) glosses the first line as "because the Great Perfection is beyond exertion and accomplishing."

614 In accordance with Longchenpa and a gloss in the tantra, Tib. *med pa* ("nonexistence") is emended to *bsam pa* ("thinking").

615 Following the tantra, Tib. *byas pas byung sa med* is emended to *byas pa byung ba med*.

616 Following the tantra, Tib. *'gyur med* ("unchanging") is emended to *rgyu med* ("without a cause").

617 Longchenpa has "is the primordially and naturally complete buddhabhūmi" (Tib. *ye nes lhun rdzogs sangs rgyas sa*).

618 Anonymous 1973–77 (2:442–44) glosses these lines as follows:

Because unawareness abides primordially as awareness, it is self-arising and therefore the very cause of delusion is primordially awakened [or vanished] without any effort. Since the all-ground—one's own body—is self-arising as the dharmakāya, without assuming any birth of a mind stream later, it is free in itself, severed at its root. Since what is wish-fulfilling—ascertaining the mentation that roams everywhere, the determining mental consciousness—primordially abides as awakened mind, the factors that cause stirring are self-settled because they are beyond the mind that creates thinking. Since the breath—the body's wind that is primordially without any nature—has been primordially interrupted, there is no birth and death from the origin; since awareness is free in that it is unborn, there is no dying in its essence, which constitutes buddhahood. Since the sense objects—the qualities of form, sound, smell, taste, and touch—are primordially perfect, meditation itself is the end of clinging because it is understood that objects are devoid of the mind that entertains thoughts about a self. Since there is primordial arrival without having moved any limbs, this is called "the luminous wisdom that is pure as the abode without any arrival." Thus, the very path to travel has been traversed primordially—in accordance with this self-arisen abode, there is no path to travel. Since spoken words are inexpressible as primordially free sound-emptiness, objects of speech and thought are transcended primordially because ground awareness is beyond thinking and mind is exhausted. The proliferation and withdrawal of thinking is primordially empty—with mind being primordially without thinking, it abides as an abode that is not established. Therefore, it primordially abides as the great dhyāna, originally abiding as the natural dhyāna. Since the stains of the elements and deluded afflictions are self-pure, they abide as great unobstructed stainlessness—the dharmakāya that is not obscured by anything whatsoever. Since this is not found through any exertion and accomplishing, what is produced is without arising. Therefore, there is freedom of producer and produced right from the beginning—they are not found in the ground through any exertion or accomplishing. Since there are no phenomena other than the ground, they are [the ground] itself. Therefore, this is the sole originally self-arising state from the beginning—the awareness that is difficult to realize and profound is the single kāya. Since the numbers of one—the awareness that does not exist as two—and therefore two are exhausted, this is the nonferential sphere without any counterpart—awareness's freedom from reference points. Since darkness—saṃsāra—is buddhahood primordially, it is originally pure. Therefore, the manifestations of awareness that dwell within itself are the pervasive fivefold luminosity. Since saṃsāra without a cause has already ceased (having found the seat of awareness), it is the buddhabhūmi primordially—it is buddhahood in itself because there is the trust that it does not exist anywhere else. Since entities in the form of all appearances and the clinging to a self of the appearances of characteristics are purely empty, the mind of clinging to a self has been exhausted primordially—the wisdom of not abiding in objects is beyond mind and entities. Conditions are free in themselves through these conditions—having thoughts that a face in a mirror is to be freed by that mirror turn to their own place and thus have awakened. Therefore, dependent phenomena—all kinds of object conditions—are resting directly within themselves as themselves.

619 Anonymous 1973–77, 1:80.

620 Anonymous 1973–77 (2:442) glosses these lines as follows: "The five elements, which are primordially pure appearances, are limpid appearances of objects. Therefore, appearances are thus free as luminosity unobscured by any stains. Since the five sense faculties of the eyes, ears, nose, tongue, and body are nakedly settled by virtue of their objects' being settled in their own place, the five objects of clinging, such as sounds, are free in their own place as the character of the dharmakāya."

621 Anonymous 1973–77, 1:124–25.

622 Ibid., 2:465–66. For the glosses of these lines, see note 611.

623 The phrase "nothing to become free" (Tib. *grol rgyu med*) here and in (iii) right below could also be read as "no cause to become free."

624 "The principle of dharmatā" (Skt. *dharmatāyuktiḥ*, Tib. *chos nyid kyi rigs pa*) is the last one of "the four principles" (Skt. *yukti*, Tib. *rigs pa*), with the other three being the principles of dependence (Skt. *apekṣāyuktiḥ*, Tib. *ltos pa'i rigs pa*), performing activity (Skt. *kāryakāraṇayuktiḥ*, Tib. *bya ba byed pa'i rigs pa*), and demonstrating evidence (Skt. *upapattisādhanayuktiḥ*, Tib. *'thad pas grub pa'i rigs pa*). Though these four principles are often rendered as "the four reason(ing)s" (particularly in translations from Tibetan), as the discussions of these four in the Śrāvakabhūmi, the *Abhidharmasamuccaya*, the *Saṃdhinirmocanasūtra*, and the *Ratnagotravibhāgavyākhyā* clarify, *yukti* is equivalent to *yoga* and *upāya*, any of which can also mean "application," "means," and "expedient."

625 In the Great Perfection, the triad of "tantras, scriptures, and pith instructions" (Tib. *rgyud lung man ngag*) specifically refers to the teachings of Mahāyoga, Anuyoga, and Atiyoga, respectively.

626 Tib. *chos nyid mngon sum*. This is the first of the four visions of Direct Leap.

627 Given the context and a parallel sentence at the beginning of C2a above, the negative "not" was inserted, though the text has none.

628 This expression is interesting in this context for two reasons. First, as mentioned before, the term "freedom from extremes" also stands for the view of "the earlier Mādhyamikas" in Tibet (referring to the proponents of what was understood as the correct Madhyamaka view before Tsongkhapa). This Madhyamaka approach results in an unqualified negation of all four positions of the typical tetralemma without asserting anything instead—including any notion of "middle"—in order to completely overcome all conceptualizations and reference points. As such, it is certainly an accurate portray of the Indian *Prāsaṅgika Madhyamaka approach.

Second, some Tibetan masters, such as the Eighth Karmapa, interpret the syllable *ma* in the Tibetan term *dbu ma* for Madhyamaka as a negative (grammatically, it renders *dbu* an abstract noun) and thus say that it means "not even a middle" (let alone any extremes). In any case, "the later Mādhyamikas" in Tibet—the Gelugpa School—criticized this view by saying that "lack of real existence" is the correct Madhyamaka view and thus *not* to be negated. At the same time, there were attempts to discredit "the Madhyamaka of freedom from extremes," Mahāmudrā, and Dzogchen through associating them with the notorious stereotype of the Chinese Hvashang Mahāyāna. Given all this, it seems not at all coincidental that Longchenpa here uses this expression "the view of lacking extremes and not observing any middle."

629 Tib. *las ma rtogs pa* emended to *las ma gtogs pa*.

630 The end of Longchenpa's last line reads "because it is intrinsic" (*rang chas*). Anonymous 1973–77 (2:467–68) glosses these lines as follows:

> Therefore, in the awareness that is the own essense of what is present as the ground, appearances are perfect because they are self-dawning from awareness within saṃsāra's and nirvāṇa's simultaneity. The ground itself is perfect because it is self-arisen from the very beginning. Objects are perfect because all appearances are self-appearing. The ground of delusion is perfect because it is free in itself, that is, free from any phenomena that depend on something else. All paths are perfect because stains are self-pure from the very outset. Knowable objects are perfect because they are known to be self-awareness primordially. The fruition is perfect because it is self-pervasive, just as a sesame seed is pervaded by its oil. Causes and conditions are perfect because awareness, which does not

> go anywhere whatsoever, is their own place. Dharmatā is perfect because it is self-realizing without being contingent on any other conditions. Saṃsāra and nirvāṇa are perfect because they are self-reversing in that they are primordially free without any effort. Tantras and scriptures are perfect because they are self-abiding with all discursiveness of words at peace. The single time is perfect because it is self-perfect in that it is primordially without arising. The instructions are perfect because they are self-knowing, being self-awareness's realization uncontrived by anything else. Dhyāna is perfect because it is self-settled without any transition. The expanse is perfect because it is wisdom free of perishing and therefore self-abiding.

(Tib. *'jigs pa* ["fear"] emended to *'jig pa* ["perishing"], which seems to make more sense in conjunction with "self-abiding.")

631 Anonymous 1973–77 (2:468–69) glosses these lines as follows:

> The dharmakāya of great self-perfection is the exhaustion of stains because it is the alpha-purity whose essence is self-appearing wisdom beyond mind [Tib. *blos dngos* emended to *blo 'das*]. Since it arose before at the beginning, any continuum is exhausted. Since it lacks the counterpart that is unawareness, it is beyond calculation in terms of being or not being something. Devoid of any causes of suffering, it is the great bliss (for suffering creates the opposite pole of happiness). It is beyond speech and thought, lacking any causes of expression. It is the pure awareness that is primordially self-aware. It is not established as material form because contaminations are exhausted. It remains empty because entities are exhausted—phenomena with characteristics are primordially empty. It is the very essence itself alone without any proliferation—it is not split into the two of saṃsāra and nirvāṇa through duality. As the self-arising pith instruction, it is free from dharmas [this could be understood as either phenomena or the teachings] and therefore beyond extremes. Since cognizant awareness abides in its own seat, it is lucid and therefore movement has vanished. It is the perfection of the two accumulations of merit and wisdom because it is without both outer matter and inner awareness. It is the very letting be of appearances' own essence without any rival because awareness is pure in itself. Since this cannot be altered by words, it lacks any words of contrivance and is all-pervasive. In its being nonconceptual, it is without a thinking mind and in its being free in itself without clinging, it is free from any minding; it is sheer freshness—the very emptiness of not departing from the native state. Being the

> supreme uncontrivedness, it abides as the true naturalness free from manifesting any clearer or fading.

632 Yon tan rgya mtsho 1982–87, 607–16.

633 Anonymous 1973–77, 2:465–66. The first two lines of this quote as they appear in Yönten Gyatso's text read:

> In unimpeded awareness,
> There is no cause of delusion and thus no coming to its end.

634 Ibid., 2:452.

635 Klong chen ye shes rdo rje 1991, 510–12.

636 For *Lamp*'s explanation of the five modes of freedom as being primordially free, free in itself, nakedly free, completely free, and free from extremes, see the end of its section "2.2.1. The manner in which desire is free as discriminating wisdom" (fols. 19b–20b).

637 For a translation of this chapter, see Longchen Rabjam 2001b, 319–88. Compare also Patrul Rinpoche's two texts on the essential point of practice—all thoughts and afflictions being free in themselves—and on recognizing the five afflictions as the five wisdoms in appendices 9 and 10.

638 For some examples, see http://www.skydancerpress.com/gal/khorlo/.

639 Turpeinen (2016, 202–7) discusses freedom through wearing based on the ten pertinent texts in the cycle *Samantabhadra's Unobstructed Awakened Mind*, saying this (203):

> Human beings are already Buddhas, and all that is necessary to trigger the process of spontaneous liberation is the recognition of our awakened nature. The idea of our inherent Buddha nature that is readily accessible via methods as simple as recognition is reflected in the possibility of getting enlightened automatically just by wearing, seeing, reading or hearing the tantras and mantras that possess the liberating blessing power. However, the liberation through wearing, seeing and so forth is not instant, but the texts frequently present a disclaimer by stating that the liberation will only occur in the bardo or subsequent lives.
>
> In addition to the Dzokchen philosophical ideas of spontaneity and easy liberation, the amulets of liberation through wearing draw their power from the narratives of their divine origin in Samantabhadra's compassion and their primordial production in the beginning stages of cosmogonic creation. The easy liberation via the amulets is also connected to the social dimension of yogic communities. The yogis depended on the lay population for material support, and in return provided services in the form of periodic rituals, teachings, blessings, guidance, healing, death rites, divination and so forth.

> Easy liberation for laity is reflected especially in the possibility of being born in a pure land, retreats of consciousness transference (*'pho ba*) and the amulets of liberation through wearing. However, the amulets were not meant for open distribution, at least rhetorically, but the texts of the *Liberation Through Wearing* instruct that they should only be given to worthy vessels, or their power is ruined like the fruit of a rotten seed.

Turpeinen also further contextualizes this practice as follows (ibid., 78):

> This radical overriding of the karmic model is particularly evident in the cycle of the *Liberation Through Wearing*, because the gnostic energy of blessings saturating the amulet causes one to become enlightened automatically upon wearing it. The *Tantra of Becoming a Buddha by Merely Seeing, Hearing, Wearing, or Praying to this Great Tantra* states this in strong terms: one cannot help but to get enlightened (*sangs mi rgya ba'i dbang med*). This may seem extreme and one can justly wonder as to how wearing an amulet can enlighten a person. However, the situation is not quite that simple, because the teachings on the liberation through wearing are given in the framework of the entire anthology and occasionally contain instructions on the practices of direct transcendence [*thod rgal*], so we have to understand these radical claims in their context; the amulets are made and worn especially by practitioners, who are on the path and do not rely merely on the amulets to attain enlightenment. Moreover, the standard Buddhist reasoning explaining the efficacy of swift practices is also employed here, for it is stated that one has to have accumulated merit for a thousand eons (*kalpa*) to encounter the teachings of the Liberation Through Wearing—a notion that emphasizes the complex web of gnostic and karmic interrelations and acknowledges the value of the sūtric path as a foundation of the Great Perfection.

640 The commentary on this aspiration prayer by Gedsé Mahāpaṇḍita ('Gyur med tshe dbang mchog grub 2001, 51) explains that view, meditation, conduct, and fruition enter the womb of the fourfold letting be (the core of the practice of Cutting through Solidity): (1) mountain-like letting be is the gauge of the view, (2) ocean-like letting be is the gauge of meditation, (3) letting be in appearances is the gauge of conduct, and (4) letting be in awareness is the gauge of the fruition. (1) Through mountain-like letting be (the view), one rests without change or transition in the actual way of being—great self-lucid awareness free from all thinking—in a carefree manner without engaging in any mental clinging, effort, or remedies of

deliberate meditation. (2) Through ocean-like letting be (meditation), with the body in a cross-legged position and the eyes gazing straight ahead into space, without engaging in any examination and analysis in terms of clinging to the appearances of the eight consciousnesses, cognizance rests in a transparently clear and pure manner within its natural state that resembles an ocean not stirred by any waves. (3) Through letting be in the pith instructions (conduct), the three gates are relaxed in an immediate manner, while self-lucid wisdom stripped from the sheath of view and meditation is allowed to sustain itself through striking it and bringing it out nakedly. (4) Through letting be without any contrivance (the fruition), self-lucidity shines nakedly and vividly clear within the state of the five objects' being naturally settled.

641 Gedsé Mahāpaṇḍita (ibid., 57–58) explains that the outer luminosity of kāyas and wisdoms (the rūpakāyas) is reabsorbed into the sphere of the primordial ground through a gradual reversal of the eight gateways of innate presence, similar to light radiating from a crystal withdrawing back into it. In other words, the rūpakāyas find their nirvāṇa within the expanse of the dharmakāya. For example, the awareness that is separated from the basic expanse and thus locked within the body resembles the space inside a vase, which is still connected to the space outside through the opening of that vase. Once the vase is broken, all the space inside it, outside of it, and in between blends into one. Similarly, once the awareness in the body is linked with original alpha-purity through the four visions (of Direct Leap), the awareness that is free from both body and mind dwells in the great alpha-purity that is the inner expanse without any before, thereafter, or in between.

The six distinctive features of the sphere of the youthful vase body (or of Samantabhadra's freedom) consist of (1) its being superior to the ground, (2) its appearing as its very own face, (3) its being differentiated (or recognized for what it is), (4) its differentiation being freedom, (5) its not arising from anything other, and (6) its remaining in its very own domain (for more details on these six features, see appendix 2C; especially note 482).

642 This refers to the *Longchen Nyingtig*.

643 Tib. Kong smyon sbas pa'i rig 'dzin.

644 Tib. Nam mkha'i snying po. One of the twenty-five main disciples of Padmasambhava in Tibet.

645 This aspiration prayer is found in Jigmé Lingpa's *Longchen Nyingtig* ('Jigs med gling pa mkhyen brtse 'od zer 1973, 2:1–3).

646 This is a translation of Dpal sprul o rgyan 'jigs med chos kyi dbang po 2003a.

647 The following are verses 50–59 from Dpal sprul o rgyan 'jigs med chos kyi dbang po 2003b (*The Speech That Is Virtuous in the Beginning, the Middle,*

and the End). The title for this excerpt here was chosen according to the content.

648 This refers to the six-syllable mantra of Avalokiteśvara: OṂ MAṆI PADME HŪṂ.

649 Skt. Gaganarāja. This and the following names are epithets of Avalokiteśvara.

650 Skt. Amoghapāśa. "The meaningful lasso" is similar to a wish-fulfilling gem in that it fulfills all the wishes and needs of sentient beings.

651 Skt. Mahākāruṇika.

652 Skt. Jinasāgara. This is a tantric manifestation of Avalokiteśvara, red in color, depicted either alone with four arms or in union with his female counterpart and two arms.

653 Since Advavajra and Avadhūtipa are well-known epithets of Maitrīpa, this text and the two under Advayavajra are often attributed to him. However, his authorship is not certain since the names Advavajra and Avadhūtipa were also held by others.

654 BDRC's search function does not allow to establish the page numbers of a given text in this last collection. The Tibetan of *The Aspiration Prayer* is also found in Dzogchen Ponlop Rinpoche 2002 (150–57), Khenchen Palden Sherab Rinpoche and Khenpo Tsewang Dongyal Rinpoche 2010 (37ff.), and Gangteng Tulku Rinpoche 2003 (28–72).

English–Tibetan Glossary

actual reality	yang dag don
actuality	don
all-accomplishing wisdom	bya ba grub pa'i ye shes
all-encompassing equality	mnyam brdal
all-ground	kun gzhi
all-ground of diverse latent tendencies	bag chags sna tshogs kyi kun gzhi
all-ground of the bodies of latent tendencies	bag chags lus kyi kun gzhi
alpha-purity	ka dag
awakened mind	dgongs pa
awareness	rig pa
basic mode of being	gnas tshul
basic nature	gnas lugs
cognizance	shes pa
cognizant awareness	shes rig
compassionate responsiveness	thugs rje
completely free	yongs grol
connate unawareness	lhan cig skyes pa'i ma rig pa
Cutting through Solidity	khregs chod
depth-lucidity	gting gsal
dharmadhātu wisdom	chos dbyings ye shes
Direct Leap	thod rgal
discriminating wisdom	so sor rtog pa'i ye shes

dynamic energy	rtsal
ear-whispered lineage of persons	gang zag snyan brgyud
eight gateways of innate presence	lhun grub kyi 'char sgo brgyad
essence	ngo bo
expanse	dbyings
Expanse Series	klong sde
firmly decide on this one thing	thag gcig thog tu bcad pa
free; freedom	grol ba
free as one	gcig grol
free from extremes	mtha' grol
free in itself	rang grol
free in its own place	rang sar grol ba
free upon arising	shar grol
fundamental ground	gshis
gain confidence in being free	gdengs grol thog tu bca' ba
general ground	spyi gzhi
glow	mdangs
ground	gzhi
ground manifestations	gzhi snang
ground of all	kun gzhi
ground of arising	'char gzhi
ground of delusion	'khrul gzhi
ground of freedom	grol gzhi
imaginative unawareness	kun brtags pa'i ma rig pa
inner luminosity	nang gsal
introduce the true face (essence) on the basis of itself	ngo rang thog tu sprod pa
isolate	ldog pa

letting be	cog bzhag
liberation	thar pa
lineage of the awakened mind of the victors	rgyal ba dgongs brgyud
locus of freedom	grol sa
mentation	yid
mind as such	sems nyid
mindfulness	dran pa
minding	dran pa
mindlessness	dran med
mirror-like wisdom	me long lta bu'i ye shes
mode of delusion	'khrul lugs
mode of freedom	grol lugs
nakedly free	gcer grol
innate presence	lhun grub
nature	rang bzhin
nescience	gti mug
nonminding	dran med
outer luminosity	phyi gsal
own domain	rang mal
Pith Instructions Series	man ngag sde
play	rol pa
primordially free	ye grol
primordial ultimate all-ground/ primordial ultimate ground of all	ye don gyi kun gzhi
pure in its own place	rang sar dag pa
radiance	gdangs
relax in its own place	rang sar klod pa
resolve, being convinced, leap	la bzla ba

seize its own place	rang sa zin pa
self-appearance	rang snang
self-arising	rang byung
self-awareness	rang rig
spaciousness, expanse	klong
sphere of innate presence	lhun grub kyi sbubs
symbolic lineage of awareness holders	rig 'dzin brda'i brgyud
take its very own seat	rang so zin pa
treasure revealer	gter ston
treasure text	gter ma
true reality	de (kho na) nyid
ultimate all-ground of linking	sbyor ba don gyi kun gzhi
ultimate reality	don dam
unawareness	ma rig pa
unawareness that has the same identity as the cause	rgyu bdag nyid gcig pa'i ma rig pa
unawareness of same identity	bdag nyid gcig pa'i ma rig pa
unity	zung 'jug
unobstructed	zang thal
wisdom of awareness	rig pa'i ye shes
wisdom of equality	mnyam nyid kyi ye shes
wisdom of knowing suchness	ji lta ba mkhyen pa'i ye shes
wisdom of knowing variety	ji snyed pa mkhyen pa'i ye shes
youthful vase body	gzhon nu bum sku

Tibetan–English Glossary

ka dag	alpha-purity
kun brtags pa'i ma rig pa	imaginative unawareness
kun gzhi	ground of all; all-ground
klong	spaciousness, expanse
klong sde	Expanse Series
khregs chod	Cutting through Solidity
'khrul gzhi	ground of delusion
'khrul lugs	mode of delusion
gang zag snyan brgyud	the ear-whispered lineage of persons
grol ba	being free; freedom
grol gzhi	ground of freedom
grol lugs	mode of freedom
grol sa	locus of freedom
dgongs pa	awakened mind
rgyal ba dgongs brgyud	the lineage of the awakened mind of the victors
rgyu bdag nyid gcig pa'i ma rig pa	unawareness that has the same identity as the cause
ngo bo	essence
ngo rang thog tu sprod pa	introduce the true face (essence) on the basis of itself
cog bzhag	letting be
gcig grol	free as one

gcer grol	nakedly free
chos dbyings ye shes	dharmadhātu wisdom
'char gzhi	ground of arising
ji snyed pa mkhyen pa'i ye shes	the wisdom of knowing variety
ji lta ba mkhyen pa'i ye shes	the wisdom of knowing suchness
mnyam nyid kyi ye shes	wisdom of equality
mnyam brdal	all-encompassing equality
gti mug	nescience
gting gsal	depth-lucidity
gter ma	treasure text
gter ston	treasure revealer
thag gcig thog tu bcad pa	firmly decide on this one thing
thar pa	liberation
thugs rje	compassionate responsiveness
thod rgal	Direct Leap
mtha' grol	free from extremes
dran pa	mindfulness; minding
dran med	mindlessness; nonminding
gdangs	radiance
gdengs grol thog tu bca' ba	gain confidence in being free
bdag nyid gcig pa'i ma rig pa	unawareness of same identity
mdangs	glow
ldog pa	isolate
nang gsal	inner luminosity
gnas tshul	basic mode of being
gnas lugs	basic nature
spyi gzhi	general ground
phyi gsal	outer luminosity

bag chags sna tshogs kyi kun gzhi	all-ground of diverse latent tendencies
bag chags lus kyi kun gzhi	all-ground of the bodies of latent tendencies
bya ba grub pa'i ye shes	all-accomplishing wisdom
dbyings	expanse
sbyor ba don gyi kun gzhi	ultimate all-ground of linking
ma rig pa	unawareness
man ngag sde	Pith Instructions Series
me long lta bu'i ye shes	mirror-like wisdom
rtsal	dynamic energy
gzhi	ground
gzhi snang	ground manifestations
gzhon nu bum sku	the youthful vase body
zang thal	unobstructed
zung 'jug	unity
ye grol	primordially free
ye don gyi kun gzhi	primordial ultimate all-ground/ primordial ultimate ground of all
yongs grol	completely free
rang grol	free in itself
rang snang	self-appearance
rang byung	self-arising
rang mal	own domain
rang bzhin	nature
rang rig	self-awareness
rang sa zin pa	seize its own place
rang sar klod pa	relax in its own place
rang sar grol ba	free in its own place

rang sar dag pa	pure in its own place
rang so zin pa	take its very own seat
rig pa	awareness
rig pa'i ye shes	wisdom of awareness
rig 'dzin brda'i brgyud	the symbolic lineage of awareness holders
rol pa	play
la bzla ba	resolve, being convinced, leap
shar grol	free upon arising
shes pa	cognizance
shes rab	prajñā
shes rig	cognizant awareness
gshis	fundamental ground
sems nyid	mind as such
sems sde	Mind Series
so sor rtog pa'i ye shes	discriminating wisdom
lhan cig skyes pa'i ma rig pa	connate unawareness
lhun grub	innate presence
lhun grub kyi 'char sgo brgyad	the eight gateways of innate presence
lhun grub kyi sbubs	the sphere of innate presence

Bibliography

Classical Indic and Tibetan Works

Advayavajra. *Dohanidhikoṣaparipūrṇagītināmanijatattvaprakāśaṭīkā.* (*Mi zad pa'i gter mdzod yongs su gang ba'i glu zhes bya ba gnyug ma'i de nyid rab tu ston pa'i rgya cher 'grel pa*). P3102. D2257.

———. *Dohakoṣapañjikā.* (*Do ha mdzod kyi dka' 'grel*). P3101. D2256.

Anonymous. 1973–77. *Rnying ma'i rgyud bcu bdun.* 3 vols. New Delhi: Sanje Dorje.

———. 1982. *Rnying ma rgyud 'bum (Mtshams brag dgon pa'i bris ma).* 46 vols. Thimphu, Bhutan: National Library, Government of Bhutan.

Avadhūtipa. *Dohakoṣahṛdaya arthagītiṭīkā.* (*Do ha mdzod kyi snying po don gyi glu'i 'grel pa*). P3120. D2268.[653]

Bdud 'joms gling pa. 2004. *Rang bzhin rdzogs pa chen po'i rang zhal mngon du byed pa'i gdams pa ma bsgom sangs rgyas.* In *Sprul pa'i gter chen bdud 'joms gling pa'i zab gter gsang ba'i chos sde*, 16:291–358. Thimphu, Bhutan: Lama Kuenzang Wangdue.

Bdud 'joms 'jigs bral ye shes rdo rje. 1999. *Gsang sngags snga 'gyur rnying ma pa'i bstan pa'i rnam gzhag mdo tsam brjod pa legs bshad snang ba'i dga' ston.* In *Rnying ma bka' ma shin tu rgyas pa*, 115:153–616. Chengdu, China: Published by Kaḥ thog mkhan po 'Jam dbyangs.

Dpa' bo gtsug lag phreng ba. n.d. *Byang chub sems dpa'i spyod pa la 'jug pa'i rnam bshad theg chen chos kyi rgya mtsho zab rgyas mtha' yas pa'i snying po.* Rouffignac, France: Nehsang Samten Chöling.

Dpal sprul o rgyan 'jigs med chos kyi dbang po. 2003a. *Nyams len gnad 'gags.* In *Dpal sprul o rgyan 'jigs med chos kyi dbang po'i gsung 'bum*, vol. 3: 127–29. Chengdu, China: Si khron mi rigs dpe skrun khang.

———. 2003b. *Thog mtha' bar sum du dge ba'i gtam nyams len dam pa'i snying nor.* In *Dpal sprul o rgyan 'jigs med chos kyi dbang po'i gsung 'bum*, vol. 8: 127–73. Chengdu, China: Si khron mi rigs dpe skrun khang.

'Gyur med tshe dbang mchog grub (Dge rtse Mahāpaṇḍita). 2001. *Gzhi lam 'bras bu'i smon lam gyi don gsal bar byed pa kun tu bzang po'i zhal lung.* Chengdu, China: Dmangs khrod dpe dkon sdud sgrig khang.

'Jigs med gling pa mkhyen brtse 'od zer. 1970–75. *Kun bzang smon lam 'dren byed ṭika'i thur mas gsal ba*. In *Kun mkhyen 'jigs med gling pa'i gsung 'bum*, 5:591–96. Gangtok, Sikkim: Sonam T. Kazi. Also in *The Collected Works of 'Jigs med gliṅ pa rang byuṅ rdo rje mkhyen brtse 'od zer*, 5:581–86. Gangtok, Sikkim: Pema Thinley for Dodrupchen Rinpoche, 1985, and *'Jigs med gling pa'i bka 'bum*, 5:619–25. Chengdu, 1999?.

———. 1973. *Klong chen snying thig*. 3 vols. New Delhi: Ngawang Sopa.

'Ju mi pham rgya mtsho. 1984. *Dbus dang mtha' rnam par 'byed pa'i 'grel pa od zer 'phreng ba*. In *Collected Writings of 'Jam-mgon 'Ju Mi-pham-rgya-mtsho*, 4:660–784. Paro, Bhutan: Lama Ngodrup and Sherab Drimay.

Klong chen ye shes rdo rje (Bka' 'gyur rin po che). 1991. *Yon tan rin po che'i mdzod kyi mchan 'grel theg gsum bdud rtsi'i nying khu*. Delhi: Shechen Publications.

Klong chen rab 'byams pa dri med 'od zer. 1999a?. *Chos dbyings mdzod kyi 'grel pa lung gi gter mdzod*. In *Mdzod bdun (A 'dzom spar ma)*, 3:209–630. Dkar mdzes bod rigs rang skyong khul, Dpal yul rdzong, Tibet: A 'dzom chos sgar.

———. 1999b?. *Gsang ba bla na med pa 'od gsal rdo rje'i gnas gsum gsal bar byed pa tshig don rin po che'i mdzod*. In *Mdzod bdun (A 'dzom spar ma)*, 4:1–485. Dkar mdzes bod rigs rang skyong khul, Dpal yul rdzong, Tibet: A 'dzom chos sgar.

———. 1999c?. *Theg pa mtha' dag gi don gsal bar byed pa grub pa'i mtha'i rin poche'i mdzod*. In *Mdzod bdun (A 'dzom spar ma)*, 7:1–411. Dkar mdzes bod rigs rang skyong khul, Dpal yul rdzong, Tibet: A 'dzom chos sgar.

———. 1999d?. *Theg mchog rin po che'i mdzod*. In *Mdzod bdun*, 5:37–1185 and 6:1187–2179, based on the Oddiyana Institute edition published by Tarthang Rinpoche. Chengdu, China: Bum skyabs?.

Kong sprul blo gros mtha' yas. 1982. *Theg pa'i sgo kun las btus pa gsung rab rin po che'i mdzod bslab pa gsum legs par ston pa'i bstan bcos shes bya kun khyab*; includes its autocommentary, *Shes bya kun la khyab pa'i gzhung lugs nyung ngu'i tshig gis rnam par 'grol ba legs bshad yongs 'du shes bya mtha' yas pa'i rgya mtsho* (abbreviated as *Shes bya kun kyab mdzod*). 3 vols. Beijing: Mi rigs dpe skrun khang.

———. 2005. *Rnal 'byor bla na med pa'i rgyud sde rgya mtsho'i snying po bsdus pa zab mo nang don nyung ngu'i tshig gis rnam par 'grol ba zab don snang byed*. Seattle: Nitartha International Publications.

Mdo sngags chos kyi rgya mtsho. 1996. *Snyan dgon sprul sku gsung rab pa'i gsung rtsom gces bsgrigs*. Zi ling, China: Mtsho sngon mi rigs dpe skrun khang.

Mkha' khyab rdo rje (Karmapa XV). 1993–94. *Byang gter dgongs pa zang thal las byung ba'i kun bzang smon lam gyi don 'grel nyung ngu mchan bu'i tshul gyis gsal bar bkod pa rnam bshad ke ta ka*. In *Rgyal dbang mkha' khyab rdo rje'i bka' 'bum*, 9:487–515. Delhi: Konchhog Lhadrepa.

Rgod kyi ldem 'phru can dngos grub rgyal mtshan. 1973a. *Sems can la sangs rgyas kun tu bzang po'i dgongs pa zang thal du bstan pa'i rgyud*. In *Rdzogs pa chen po dgongs pa zang thal dang ka dag rang byung rang shar*, 3:409–23. Leh, Ladakh: S. W. Tashigangpa. Also in *Byang gter rdzogs pa chen po kun bzang dgongs pa zang thal dang thugs sgrub kyi chos skor*, 3:159–68 (Sumra, India: Orgyan Dorji, 1978); *Rdzogs pa chen po dgongs pa zang thal gyi chos skor*, 3:409–23 (Leh, Ladakh: S. W. Tashigangpa, 1979); *Rdzogs pa chen po dgongs pa zang thal gyi chos skor: A Cycle of Rdzogs chen Practice of the Rnying ma pa Atiyoga*, 3:409–23 (Simla, India: Thub bstan rdo rje brag e wam lcog sgar, 2000); and *Snga 'gyur byang gter chos skor phyogs bsgrigs*, 2:435–46 (n.p.: Byang gter dpe sgrig tshogs chung, 2015).

———. 1973b. *Rdzogs pa chen po kun tu bzang po'i dgongs pa zang thal gyi rgyud chen mthong ba dang thos pa dang btags pa dang smon lam btab pa tsam gyis sangs rgya ba'i rgyud*. In *Rdzogs pa chen po dgongs pa zang thal dang ka dag rang byung rang shar*, 4:81–181. Leh, Ladakh: S. W. Tashigangpa. Also in *Byang gter rdzogs pa chen po kun bzang dgongs pa zang thal dang thugs sgrub kyi chos skor*, 2:1–69 (Sumra, India: Orgyan Dorji, 1978); *Rdzogs pa chen po dgongs pa zang thal gyi chos skor*, 4:81–181 (Leh, Ladakh: S. W. Tashigangpa, 1979); *Rdzogs pa chen po dgongs pa zang thal gyi chos skor: A Cycle of Rdzogs chen Practice of the Rnying ma pa Atiyoga*, 4:81–181 (Simla, India: Thub bstan rdo rje brag e wam lcog sgar, 2000); and *Snga 'gyur byang gter chos skor phyogs bsgrigs*, 2:447–522 (n.p.: Byang gter dpe sgrig tshogs chung, 2015).

———. 199?. *Kun tu bzang po'i smon lam*. In *Rin chen gter mdzod chen mo*, i:735–41. Chengdu, China: Lho nub mi rigs dpar khang. Also in *Zab chos zhi khro dgongs pa rang grol*, 663–72 (Sde dge rdzong: Snga 'gyur mtho slob rdzogs chen shrī singha lung rtogs chos gling, 2001); *O rgyan rtsa gsum gling pa'i ring lugs zab gter*, 1:519–25 (Kathmandu: Bka' gter sri zhu e waṃ dpe skrun khang, 2002 [computer input]); *Gter chen rdo rje gling pa'i zab chos phyogs bsdebs*, ka:515–22 (Kathmandu: Khenpo Shedup Tendzin and Lama Thinley Namgyal, 2009 [computer input]); and *Ri dgon bkra shis chos gling gi phyag bzhes rgyun mkho'i chos spyod kyi rim pa phyogs gcig tu bkod pa rnam grol lam gyi shing rta* (Kathmandu: Karma Leksheyling, n.d. [www.tbrc.org/#!rid=W3JT13341; computer input]).[654]

Rog bandhe shes rab 'od. 1999. *Chos 'byung grub mtha' chen mo bstan pa'i sgron me*. In *Rnying ma bka' ma shin tu rgyas pa*, 114:105–315. Chengdu, China: Published by Kaḥ thog mkhan po 'Jam dbyangs.

Rong zom chos kyi bzang po. 1999. *Theg pa chen po'i tshul la 'jug pa zhes bya ba'i bstan bcos*. In *Rong zom chos bzang gi gsung 'bum*, 1:415–555. Chengdu, China: Si khron mi rigs dpe skrun khang. Also in *Rong zom bka' 'bum*, 41–335. Thimpu: Kunsang Topgay.

Tshul khrims bzang po. n.d. *Kun bzang smon lam gyi rnam bshad kun bzang nye lam 'od snang gsal ba'i sgron ma*. In *Sprul sku tshul khrims bzang po'i gsung 'bum*, 1: 391–444. n.p. Also in *Snga 'gyur byang gter chos skor phyogs bsgrigs*, 56:385–434. n.p.: Byang gter dpe sgrig tshogs chung, 2015.

Yon tan rgya mtsho. 1982–87. *Yon tan rin po che'i mdzod kyi 'grel pa zab don snang byed nyi ma'i 'od zer*. In *Rñiṅ ma bka' ma rgyas pa*, 40:5–855. Kalimpong, India: Dupjung Lama.

Modern Works

Anspal, Sten. 2005a. "The Space Section of the Great Perfection (rDzogs-chen klong-sde): a category of philosophical and meditative teachings in Tibetan Buddhism." MA thesis, University of Oslo.

———. 2005b. "Lost in Space: Tibetan formulations of the *rDzogs-chen klong sde*." *Acta Orientalia* 66: 117–93.

Bdud 'joms 'jigs bral ye shes rdo rje. 1991. *The Nyingma School of Tibetan Buddhism*. Translated by Gyurme Dorje and M. Kapstein. 2 vols. Boston: Wisdom Publications.

Bhakha, Tulku, and Steven Goodman, trans. 2006. "The Prayer of Kuntuzangpo." In Tulku Urgyen Rinpoche, trans. and compiled by Erik Pema Kunsang and Marcia Binder Schmidt, *Quintessential Dzogchen: Confusion Dawns as Wisdom*. Hong Kong: Rangjung Yeshe Publications, 79–84.

Boord, Martin J. 1993. *The Cult of the Deity Vajrakīla According to the Texts of the Northern Treasures Tradition of Tibet (byang gter phur ba)*. Tring, U.K.: The Institute of Buddhist Studies.

———. 2013. *Gathering the Elements: The Cult of the Wrathful Deity Vajrakīla According to the Texts of the Northern Treasures Tradition of Tibet*. Berlin: Wandel Verlag.

Brunnhölzl, Karl. 2007. *Straight From the Heart*. Ithaca, N.Y.: Snow Lion Publications.

———. 2010. *Gone Beyond: The Prajñāpāramitā Sūtras, "The Ornament of Clear Realization," and Its Commentaries in the Tibetan Kagyü Tradition*. Vol. 1. Ithaca, N.Y.: Snow Lion Publications.

———. 2014. *When the Clouds Part*. Boston and London: Shambhala Publications.

Cabezón, José I. 2013. *The Buddha's Doctrine and the Nine Vehicles. Rog Bande Sherab's* Lamp of the Teachings. Oxford and New York: Oxford University Press.

Chamgon Kenting Tai Situ Rinpoche. 2012. *The Aspiration Prayer of Kuntu Zangpo*. Auckland, New Zealand: Zhyisil Chokyi Ghatsal.

Dowman, Keith. 2003. *The Flight of the Garuda*. Boston: Wisdom Publications.

Dzogchen Ponlop Rinpoche. 2002. *Penetrating Wisdom. The Aspiration of Samantabhadra*. Vancouver, Canada: Siddhi Publications.

———. 2006. *Mind Beyond Death*. Ithaca, N.Y.: Snow Lion Publications.

Forman, Robert. 1989. "Paramārtha and Modern Constructivists." *Philosophy East and West* 39: 393–418.

Gangteng Tulku Rinpoche. 2003. Trans. by Susanne Schefczyk. *Das Samantabhadra-Dzogchen-Gebet*. Osterby, Germany: Khampa-Buchverlag.

Germano, David Francis. 1992. "Poetic Thought, the Intelligent Universe, and the Mystery of Self: The Tantric Synthesis of *rDzogs Chen* in Fourteenth-century Tibet." Ph.D. diss., University of Wisconsin-Madison.

Goodman, Steven D. 1992. "Rig-'dzin 'Jigs-med gling-pa and the Klong-Chen sNying-Thig." In *Tibetan Buddhism: Reason and Revelation*, edited by Ronald M. Davidson and Steven D. Goodman. New York: State University of New York Press, 133–207.

'Gos lo tsā ba gzhon nu dpal. 1996. *The Blue Annals*. Trans. G. N. Roerich. Delhi: Motilal Banarsidass.

Gyatso, Janet. 1998. *Apparitions of the Self: The Secret Autobiographies of a Tibetan Visonary*. Princeton, N.J.: Princeton University Press.

Herweg, Jürgen Wilhelm. 1994. *The Hagiography of Rig 'dzin Rgod kyi ldem 'phru can and Three Historical Questions Emerging from it*. MA thesis. University of Washington.

Higgins, David. 2013. *The Philosophical Foundations of Classical rDzogs Chen in Tibet. Investigating the Distinction Between Dualistic Mind (*sems*) and Primordial Knowing (*ye shes*)*. Wiener Studien zur Tibetologie und Buddhismuskunde. Heft 78. Vienna: Arbeitskreis für tibetische und buddhistische Studien Universität Wien.

Jigme Lingpa and Kangyur Rinpoche. 2013. *Treasury of Precious Qualities*. Book 2. Translated by the Padmakara Translation Group. Boston: Shambhala Publications.

Kapstein, Matthew. 1992. "The Amnesic Monarch and the Five Mnemic Men: 'Memory' in Great Perfection (Rdzogs-chen) Thought." In *In the Mirror of Memory*, edited by Janet Gyatso, 239–69. Albany: State University of New York Press.

———. 1995. "The Prayer of the Primordial Buddha." In *Buddhism in Practice*, edited by Donald S. Lopez Jr., 80–87. Princeton: Princeton University Press.

———. 2008. *The Sun of the Heart* and the *Bai-ro-rgyud-'bum*." *Revue d'Études Tibetaines* 15: 275–88.

Karmay, Samten G. 1988. *The Great Perfection (Rdzogs Chen). A Philosophical and Meditative Tradition in Tibetan Buddhism*. Leiden: Brill.

Khenchen Palden Sherab Rinpoche and Khenpo Tsewang Dongyal Rinpoche. 2010. *Discovering Infinite Freedom: The Prayer of Küntuzangpo*. Sidney Center, New York: Padma Samye Ling.

Kongtrul Lodrö Tayé, Jamgön. 1995. *The Treasury of Knowledge: Book One: Myriad Worlds*. Translated by the Kalu Rinpoché Translation Group. Ithaca, N.Y.: Snow Lion Publications.

———. 2005. *The Treasury of Knowledge: Book Six, Part Four: Systems of Buddhist Tantra*. Translated by the Kalu Rinpoché Translation Group (Elio Guarisco and Ingrid McLeod). Ithaca, N.Y.: Snow Lion Publications.

———. 2010. *The Treasury of Knowledge: Books Two, Three, and Four: Buddhism's Journey to Tibet*. Translated by the Kalu Rinpoché Translation Group (Ngawang Zangpo). Ithaca, N.Y.: Snow Lion Publications.

Krang dbyi sun et al. 1985. *Bod rgya tshig mdzod chen mo*. 2 vols. Beijing: Mi rigs dpe skrun khang.

Lama Kunsang, Lama Pemo, and Marie Aubèle. 2012. *History of the Karmapas. The Odyssey of the Tibetan Masters with the Black Crown*. Ithaca, N.Y.: Snow Lion Publications.

Longchen Rabjam. 1989. *The Practice of Dzogchen*. Introduced, translated and annotated by Tulku Thondup. Ithaca, N.Y.: Snow Lion Publications.

———. 2001a. Trans. by Richard Barron (Lama Chökyi Nyima). *The Precious Treasury of the Basic Space of Phenomena*. Junction City, Calif.: Padma Publishing.

———. 2001b. Trans. by Richard Barron (Lama Chökyi Nyima). *A Treasure Trove of Scriptural Transmission. A Commentary on* The Precious Treasury of the Basic Space of Phenomena. Junction City, Calif.: Padma Publishing.

———. 2007. Trans. by Richard Barron (Lama Chökyi Nyima). *The Precious Treasury of Philosophical Systems*. Junction City, Calif.: Padma Publishing.

———. 2015. Trans. by Lama Chönam and Sangye Khandro. *Precious Treasury of the Genuine Meaning*. Ashland, Ore.: Light of Berotsana.

Lopez, Donald S., Jr. 1988. *The Heart Sūtra Explained*. Albany: State University of New York Press.

Lopez, Manuel. 2018. "The 'Twenty or Eighteen' Texts of the Mind Series: Scripture, Transmission, and the Idea of Canon in the Early Great Perfection Literature." *Revue d'Études Tibétaines* 43: 50–94.

Martin, Dan. 1987. "Illusion Web—Locating the *Guhyagarbha Tantra* in Buddhist Intellectual History." In *Silver on Laps: Tibetan Literary Culture and History,* edited by C. I. Beckwith, 175–220. Bloomington, Ind.: The Tibet Society.

Namkhai Norbu, Chögyal. 1996. *Dzogchen. The Self-Perfected State*. Ithaca, N.Y.: Snow Lion Publications.

———. 2006. *Dzogchen Teachings*. Ithaca, N.Y.: Snow Lion Publications.

Nyoshul Khenpo. 2005. Trans. by Richard Barron (Chökyi Nyima). *A Marvelous Garland of Rare Gems*. Junction City, Calif.: Padma Publishing.

Pettit, J. W. 1999. *Mipham's Beacon of Certainty*. Boston: Wisdom Publications.

Reynolds, John Myrdhin. 1996. *The Golden Letters*. Ithaca, N.Y.: Snow Lion Publications.

Sardar-Afkhami, Abdol-Hamid. 2001. *The Buddha's Secret Gardens: End-Times and Hidden Lands in Tibetan Imagination*. Ph.D. diss., University of Michigan.

Smith, Malcolm, trans. 2016. *Buddhahood in This Life: The Great Commentary by Vimalamitra*. Boston: Wisdom Publications.

Thondup, Tulku. 1996. *Masters of Meditation and Miracles: Lives of the Great Buddhist Masters of India and Tibet*. Boston: Shambhala Publications.

Tsuda, Shinichi. 1970. "The Saṃvarodaya-tantra. Selected Chapters." Ph.D. diss., Autralian National University, Canberra.

Turpeinen, Katarina. 2016. *Vision of Samantabhadra—The Dzokchen Anthology of Rindzin Gödem*. Ph.D. diss., University of Virginia.

Valentine, Jay Holt. 2013. *Lords of the Northern Treasures: The Development of the Tibetan Institution of Rule by Successive Incarnations*. Ph.D. diss., University of Virginia.

———. 2015. "The Family and Legacy of the Early Northern Treasure Tradition." *Journal of Global Buddhism* 16: 126–43.

———. 2016. "Introduction to and Translation of *The Garland of Light: Lives of the Masters of the Northern Treasure Tradition*." *Revue d'Etudes Tibétaines* 39: 133–65.

Van Schaik, Sam. 2004a. "The Early Days of the Great Perfection." *Journal of the International Association for Buddhist Studies* 27 (1):165–206.

———. 2004b. *Approaching the Great Perfection. Simultaneous and Gradual Methods of Dzogchen Practice in the Longchen Nyingtig*. Boston: Wisdom Publications.

About the Author

Karl Brunnhölzl, MD, PhD, was originally trained as a physician. He received his systematic training in Tibetan language and Buddhist philosophy and practice at the Marpa Institute for Translators, founded by Khenpo Tsültrim Gyamtso Rinpoche, as well as the Nitartha Institute, founded by Dzogchen Ponlop Rinpoche. Since 1989 he has been a translator and interpreter from Tibetan and English. Karl Brunnhölzl is a senior teacher and translator in the Nalandabodhi community of Dzogchen Ponlop Rinpoche, as well as at Nitartha Institute. Living in Seattle, he is the author and translator of numerous texts. Currently, he is working on the Seventh Karmapa's compilation of Indian Mahāmudrā works.

What to Read Next from Wisdom Publications

The Nyingma School of Tibetan Buddhism
Its Fundamentals and History
Dudjom Rinpoche, Gyurme Dorje, Matthew Kapstein

"A landmark in the history of English-language studies of Tibetan Buddhism."
—***History of Religions***

The Self-Arisen Vidyā Tantra and **The Self-Liberated Vidyā Tantra**
The Seventeen Dzogchen Tantras, volumes 1 and 2
Translated by Ācārya Malcolm Smith

"Ācārya Malcolm Smith has certainly given the world a rare gift by presenting to English-reading Dzogchen practitioners this skilled translation of the first two volumes of the Seventeen Tantras."
—Sangye Khandro, translator and teacher, Light of Berotsana Translation Group

Düdjom Lingpa's Visions of the Great Perfection
Translated by B. Alan Wallace

This limited-edition set includes elegant clothbound editions of all three volumes, beautifully presented in a slipcase.

Open Mind
View and Meditation in the Lineage of Lerab Linga
Translated by B. Alan Wallace
Foreword by His Holiness the Dalai Lama

"Tertön Sogyal is celebrated as one of the greatest Tibetan Buddhist teachers in the twentieth century. This is a precious book that carries

his profound wisdom. Thanks to Alan Wallace for doing such a great job in translating it into English. *Open Mind* is a gift to those who have affinity with the way of Dzogchen."
—**Anam Thubten**, author of *The Magic of Awareness*

Stilling the Mind
Shamatha Teachings from Dudjom Lingpa's Vajra Essence
B. Alan Wallace

"A much needed, very welcome book."
—**Jetsun Khandro Rinpoche**

About Wisdom Publications

Wisdom Publications is the leading publisher of classic and contemporary Buddhist books and practical works on mindfulness. To learn more about us or to explore our other books, please visit our website at wisdompubs.org or contact us at the address below.

Wisdom Publications
199 Elm Street
Somerville, MA 02144 USA

We are a 501(c)(3) organization, and donations in support of our mission are tax deductible.

Wisdom Publications is affiliated with the Foundation for the Preservation of the Mahayana Tradition (FPMT).